About OKCIR

Omar Khayyam Center for Integrative Research in Utopia, Mysticism, and Science (Utopystics)

www.okcir.com

OKCIR (est. 2002) is an independent research, pedagogical, and publishing initiative dedicated to exploring, in a simultaneously world-historical and self-reflective framework, the human search for a just global society.

Since the world's utopian, mystical, and scientific movements have been the primary sources of inspiration, knowledge, and/or practice in this field, OKCIR aims to critically reexamine the shortcomings and contributions of these world-historical traditions—seeking to clearly understand why they have failed to bring about the good society, and what each can integratively contribute toward realizing that end.

The center aims to develop new conceptual (methodological, theoretical, historical), practical, pedagogical, inspirational and disseminative structures of knowledge whereby the individual can radically understand and determine how world-history and her/his selves constitute one another.

OKCIR promotes creative exercises in liberating sociology and alternative pluriversities of knowledge production and publication in the global cyberspace. As a virtual research center, its publications are available in part freely online in its open-stacks digital library, in part via subscription to its own or other academic database member-stacks, and others for purchase online via the Okcir Store and other online distributors. Selected publications are also available in print for online purchase by libraries, institutions, and interested print readers.

OKCIR pursues innovative editorial, digital, and print publishing practices reflecting its substantive goals, and is the publisher of *Human Architecture: Journal of the Sociology of Self-Knowledge* (ISSN: 1540-5699, est. 2002) which explores issues pertaining to the center's interests. *Human Architecture* is a hybrid scholarly journal whose edited and monographed issues are simultaneously published also as individual books in hardcover, softcover, and pdf and/or epub ebook formats (with separately assigned ISBNs).

Tayyebeh Series in East-West Research and Translation (2014-) and Ahead Publishing House (imprint: Okcir Press) (1991-) respectively honor Tayyebeh Tamjidi (1928-2020) and Mohammed (Ahad) Tamjidi (1930-2007) whose parental love and support made the life and works of Mohammad H. (Behrooz) Tamdgidi, the founder of OKCIR, possible.

Published to Date in the Series

Omar Khayyam's Secret: Hermeneutics of the Robaiyat in Quantum Sociological Imagination: ***Book 1****: New Khayyami Studies: Quantumizing the Newtonian Structures of C. Wright Mills's Sociological Imagination for A New Hermeneutic Method* (Okcir Press, 2021)

Omar Khayyam's Secret: Hermeneutics of the Robaiyat in Quantum Sociological Imagination: ***Book 2****: Khayyami Millennium: Reporting the Discovery and the Reconfirmation of the True Dates of Birth and Passing of Omar Khayyam (AD 1021-1123)* (Okcir Press, 2021)

Omar Khayyam's Secret: Hermeneutics of the Robaiyat in Quantum Sociological Imagination: ***Book 3****: Khayyami Astronomy: How Omar Khayyam's Newly Discovered True Birth Date Horoscope Reveals the Origins of His Pen Name and Independently Confirms His Authorship of the Robaiyat* (Okcir Press, 2021)

Omar Khayyam's Secret

Hermeneutics of the Robaiyat in Quantum Sociological Imagination

---

BOOK 2

Khayyami Millennium

Reporting the Discovery and the Reconfirmation of the True Dates of Birth and Passing of Omar Khayyam (AD 1021-1123)

About this Book

Omar Khayyam's Secret: Hermeneutics of the Robaiyat in Quantum Sociological Imagination is a twelve-book series of which this book is the second volume, subtitled *Khayyami Millennium: Reporting the Discovery and the Reconfirmation of the True Dates of Birth and Passing of Omar Khayyam (AD 1021-1123)*. Each book is independently readable, although it will be best understood as a part of the whole series.

In the overall series, the transdisciplinary sociologist Mohammad H. Tamdgidi shares the results of his decades-long research on Omar Khayyam, the enigmatic 11th/12th centuries Persian Muslim sage, philosopher, astronomer, mathematician, physician, writer, and poet from Neyshabour, Iran, whose life and works still remain behind a veil of deep mystery. Tamdgidi's purpose has been to find definitive answers to the many puzzles still surrounding Khayyam, especially regarding the existence, nature, and purpose of the Robaiyat in his life and works. To explore the questions posed, he advances a new hermeneutic method of textual analysis, informed by what he calls the quantum sociological imagination, to gather and study all the attributed philosophical, religious, scientific, and literary writings of Khayyam.

In this second book of the series, Tamdgidi lays down an essential foundation for the series by revisiting the unresolved questions surrounding the dates of birth and passing of Omar Khayyam. Critically reexamining the manner in which Omar Khayyam's birth horoscope as reported in Zahireddin Abolhassan Beyhaqi's *Tatemmat Sewan al-Hekmat* (*Supplement to the Chest of Wisdom*) was used by Swāmi Govinda Tīrtha in his *The Nectar of Grace: Omar Khayyam's Life and Works* (1941) to determine Khayyam's birth date, Tamdgidi uncovers a number of serious internal inconsistencies and factual inaccuracies that prevented Tīrtha (and, since then, other scholars more or less taking for granted his results) from arriving at a reliable date for Khayyam's birth, hurling Khayyami studies into decades of confusion regarding Khayyam's life and works. Tamdgidi then shares in the book the detailed account of his own discovery of Khayyam's true date of birth for the first time, a finding that eluded Khayyami studies for centuries and is bound to revolutionize the studies for decades to come.

Tamdgidi then turns his attention to the task of definitively establishing the true date of passing of Omar Khayyam. Conducting an in-depth, superposed analysis of Beyhaqi's *Tatemmat Sewan el-Hekmat (Supplement to the Chest of Wisdom)*, Abdorrahman Khazeni's *Mizan ol-Hekmat (Balance of Wisdom)*, Nezami Arouzi's *Chahar Maqaleh (Four Discourses)*, and Yar Ahmad Rashidi Tabrizi's *Tarabkhaneh (House of Joy)*, amid other relevant texts, he succeeds in firmly reconfirming and further discovering, in a textually reliable way, not only the year, the season, the month, and the day, but even the most likely time of day at which the poet mathematician, astronomer, and calender reformer died as a solar centenarian, completing his 102nd solar year age.

Strange is that these discoveries are made just in time as we approach the first solar millennium of Omar Khayyam's birth date on June 10, AD 1021, at sunrise of Neyshabour, Iran, and the ninth solar centennial of his passing on June 10, AD 1123, on the eve also of his birthday, closing the circle of his life's "coming and going."

Omar Khayyam's Secret

Hermeneutics of the Robaiyat in Quantum Sociological Imagination

BOOK 2

Khayyami Millennium

Reporting the Discovery and the Reconfirmation of the True Dates of Birth and Passing of Omar Khayyam (AD 1021-1123)

Mohammad H. Tamdgidi

Human Architecture: Journal of the Sociology of Self-Knowledge • XV • 2021

Monograph Series: Tayyebeh Series in East-West Research and Translation

Okcir Press

OMAR KHAYYAM'S SECRET

Hermeneutics of the Robaiyat in Quantum Sociological Imagination

Book 2: Khayyami Millennium: Reporting the Discovery and the Reconfirmation of the True Dates of Birth and Passing of Omar Khayyam (AD 1021-1123)

Author: Mohammad H. Tamdgidi

First Edition: June 1, 2021
Okcir Press • P. O. Box 393, Belmont, MA 02478, USA • www.okcir.com
For ordering or other inquiries contact: info[at]okcir.com

Okcir Press is an imprint of Ahead Publishing House, which is a division of OKCIR: Omar Khayyam Center for Integrative Research in Utopia, Mysticism, and Science (Utopystics)

Library of Congress Control Number: 2021906827

Publisher Cataloging in Publication Data

Omar Khayyam's Secret: Hermeneutics of the Robaiyat in Quantum Sociological Imagination
Book 2: Khayyami Millennium: Reporting the Discovery and the Reconfirmation of the True Dates of Birth and Passing of Omar Khayyam (AD 1021-1123) / Mohammad H. Tamdgidi, 1959- /
First Edition: June 1, 2021
Human Architecture: Journal of the Sociology of Self-Knowledge • Volume XV • 2021
Monograph Series: Tayyebeh Series in East-West Research and Translation

332 pages • 6x9 inches • Includes charts, tables, references, and index.
ISBN-13: 978-1-64098-006-8 • ISBN-10: 1-64098-006-7 (hardcover : alk. paper)
ISBN-13: 978-1-64098-007-5 • ISBN-10: 1-64098-007-5 (softcover : alk. paper)
ISBN-13: 978-1-64098-008-2 • ISBN-10: 1-64098-008-3 (EPub ebook)
ISBN-13: 978-1-64098-009-9 • ISBN-10: 1-64098-009-1 (PDF ebook)

1. Omar Khayyam—Biography. 2. Omar Khayyam—Criticisms and Interpretations—Biography. 3. Omar Khayyam—Manuscripts. 4. Omar Khayyam—Robaiyat (Rubaiyat). 5. Omar Khayyam—Robaiyat (Rubaiyat)—Translations into English. I. Omar Khayyam, AD 1021-1123 II. Title

First Edition: June 1, 2021
Front cover/spine: Statue of Omar Khayyam, by Abolhasan Seddiqi, Laleh Park, Tehran, Iran (author)
Jacket flap: Omar Khayyam Mausoleum/ Neyshabour, Iran (author)
Licensed cover images from Dreamstime:
Front cover: "Arabic Astrolabe" (24157038) | Back cover: "Mercury Transiting the Sun" (26145220)
Cover and Text Design: Ahead Publishing House, Belmont, MA, USA

The paper used in the print editions of this book is of archival quality and meets the minimum requirements of ANSI/NISO Z39.48-1992 (R1997) (Permanence of Paper). The production of this book on demand protects the environment by printing only the number of copies that are purchased.

for

Omar Khayyam (AD 1021-1123)

who
"Phoenix-like flew to the peak empyrean sphere"

In celebration of the imminent millennium of Omar Khayyam's birth and the soon forthcoming ninth centennial of his passing

"Omar Khayyam said: 'How strange! What service do I offer the king!? For a thousand years heavens and stars must toil to exhaustion in their orbits and motions down and up until, from this tiny mill, a seed like Omar Khayyam may spring and from these high-standing seven cities and low-lying seven villages a caravan-leader of science like me may arise. However, if you wish, from any village around Kashan I will produce hundreds of folks like you, sir, and replace you with them, since any of them can do your job.'"

— Khaqani Sharvani (d. AD 1199), "letters"

for my mother,
Tayyebeh Tamjidi
(March 20, 1928 - December 31, 2020)

About the Author

Other books beside this series by Mohammad H. Tamdgidi

Liberating Sociology: From Newtonian Toward Quantum Imaginations: Volume I: Unriddling the Quantum Enigma (Okcir Press, 2020)

Gurdjieff and Hypnosis: A Hermeneutic Study (Palgrave Macmillan, 2009)

Advancing Utopistics: The Three Component Parts and Errors of Marxism (Routledge/Paradigm, 2007)

Mohammad-Hossein (a.k.a. 'Behrooz') Tamdgidi (pronounced "tamjidi") is the founder and editor respectively of OKCIR: Omar Khayyam Center for Integrative Research in Utopia, Mysticism, and Science (Utopystics) and its publication, *Human Architecture: Journal of the Sociology of Self-Knowledge* (ISSN: 1540-5699) which have served since 2002 to frame his independent research, pedagogical, and publishing initiatives. Formerly an associate professor of sociology specializing in social theory at the University of Massachusetts (UMass) Boston, he has also previously taught sociology as full-time lecturer at SUNY-Oneonta, and also as adjunct lecturer at SUNY-Binghamton. He has published numerous books and edited more than thirty journal collections, in addition to other peer reviewed articles and chapters.

Tamdgidi's areas of scholarly and applied interest are the sociology of self-knowledge, human architecture, and utopystics—three fields of inquiry he invented in his doctoral studies and has since pursued as respectively intertwined theoretical, methodological and applied fields of inquiry altogether contributing to what he calls the quantum sociological imagination. His research, teaching, and publications have been framed by an interest in understanding how world-historical social structures and personal selves constitute one another. This line of inquiry has itself been a result of his longstanding interest in understanding the underlying causes of failures of the world's utopian, mystical, and scientific movements in bringing about a just global society.

It was during his undergraduate studies at U.C. Berkeley and in the course of his mentorship by the painter and design architect Jesse Reichek (1916-2005) that Tamdgidi's notion and project "human architecture" was born. During his graduate studies at SUNY-Binghamton, he was mentored in methods, theory, and world-systems studies by Terence K. Hopkins (1928-1997) and Immanuel Wallerstein (1930-2019), and further in dialectics by Dale Tomich and on space and society by Anthony D. King, amid a uniquely autonomous and flexible transdisciplinary Graduate Program in Sociology founded by T. K. Hopkins.

Tamdgidi holds a Ph.D. and M.A. in sociology in conjunction with a graduate certificate in Middle Eastern studies from Binghamton University (SUNY). He received his B.A. in architecture from U. C. Berkeley, following enrollment as an undergraduate student of civil engineering in the Technical College of the University of Tehran, Iran. In Dec. 2013 he retired early from his tenured and promoted position at UMass Boston in order to pursue his independent scholarship in quantum sociological imagination and its application in Khayyami studies through the conduit of his research center, OKCIR.

آنم که پدید گشتم از قدرت تو
صد ساله شدم بناز در نعمت تو
صد سال به امتحان گنه خواهم کرد
یا جرم منست بیش یا رحمت تو

عمر خیّام

I'm he who from Thy power to existence came,
And amid Thy kind bounties a hundred became.
For hundred more years test my sins to see what's more:
These misdeeds or Thy mercy forgiving the same.

— Omar Khayyam (Tamdgidi translation)

Contents

List of Figures

List of Tables

Notes on Transliteration

In the English edition of this book and its parent series, texts in languages using diacritics in their Latin alphabet are rendered as in the original.

When quoting Persian and Arabic texts transliterated by others, I will render them (including their diacritics) as found in the source, whatever transliteration system the source has used, which can vary from one source to another.

My own transliterations of Persian and Arabic texts will follow their pronunciation in Persian; that is, Arabic (or any other language) words internalized in Persian language will be transliterated according to their Persian pronunciation, except for the commonly transliterated words that have already been established in public discourse, as further explained below.

The main goal of the transliteration system newly designed for and applied in this series as explained in the appendix to each book is to make it possible to pronounce Persian words and those in Arabic (or in other languages) internalized in the Persian language the way a native Persian speaker would usually pronounce it (local dialects of Persian notwithstanding). Fulfilling this need is important, since otherwise we would lose the Persian pronunciations of Persian and its internalized (including Arabic) words over time. In reading Persian poetry, in particular, we need to produce Persian, and not Arabic, pronunciations of the words.

In Persian transliteration systems prevalent today, at times native and internalized words in Persian are transliterated in ways that result in Arabic pronunciation. The word "Rubaiyat" (used for رباعیات which is actually an Arabic word), for instance, does not readily produce the Persian pronunciation of the word, which is Robāʿiyāt; Khayyam should be pronounced as Khayyam (not Kayam), Isfahan as Éṣfahān, Ibn Sina as ébn-e Sinā, Iran not as "I ran" but as Earān (Ear+ān), Ramadan as Rameẓān, Islam as Éslām, and so on.

Some of the above word examples have been already transliterated in Western languages in common forms (such as Iran, Islam, Isfahan, etc.), so I will maintain the same spelling in the main text while providing their full Persian transliteration in a cumulative glossary following the transliteration system introduced in the appendix of each book of the series. In others, when needed or found substantively needed, I will render the word in a way that emphasizes the Persian pronunciation. In doing so, however, in the main text I will strip it of diacritics, while providing its full transliteration in the cumulative glossary placed in the appendix to each book. This is to avoid cumbersome experiences of reading and writing native and internalized Persian words; even in English, we do not use diacritics to distinguish how 'u' sounds differently in "bus," "busy," "cute," or "mouse."

The use of diacritics in the main text, following one or another transliteration system, poses its own challenges. The difficulties generated by a confusing and at times conflicting diversity of transliteration systems used today for Persian and Arabic do not in my view warrant making the reading and writing of the text itself cumbersome. In this age of the Internet, such diacritics also make online rendering of the texts, and digital searching for them, often challenging, if not impossible and unsuccessful. Moreover, at times, rare diacritics make the words in which they appear impossible to render online depending on browsers used, resulting in their being replaced by wrong or distorted words.

It is for the above reasons that in this series I will avoid using diacritics for the words transliterated in the main text, but will offer full diacritics for them in a glossary following the transliteration system explained in the appendix to each book. So, for instance, while in my proposed system رباعیّات is transliterated as Robāʿiyāt, in the main text I will simply render the same as Robaiyat. If خیام is fully transliterated as Khayyām, in the main text I simply render it as Khayyam. ʿOmar is simply rendered as Omar. All diacritics, including ʿein (ع) and hamzeh (ء) are omitted to simplify the renderings of the words (such as Arouzi, Ismaili, or Shafa), while the transliteration system as described in the appendix is used as a guide to make sure the Persian pronunciations of native and internalized words in Persian are rendered. As noted, for established words such as Isfahan, Iran, Islam, etc., I will just use the common form in the main text.

For substantive reasons, the word "Rubaiyat" will only be used when referring to the particular tradition arising from the FitzGeraldian and Western translation efforts, while I will use instead "Robaiyat" to distinguish the new tradition I hope to engender by advancing the new Khayyami studies as initiated in the present series.

Where it is needed in the main text, such as when sharing of transliterations of poetry, for the readers' convenience I will include them in full transliteration next to the original Persian and my English translations in the main text itself.

Acknowledgments

Without the contributions of countless scholars and writers, past and present, in Iran and abroad, who have explored the life and works of Omar Khayyam over the many centuries, the conduct and results of this study would have been impossible. The list of these individuals is long, and I hope my specific engagements with some of their works throughout this series may serve as expressions of my deep appreciation for their valuable contributions.

I thank my wife Anna Beckwith for her patience and encouragements during the many decades it took me to conduct this research on Khayyam. I also thank Ramón Grosfoguel for his kind interest in my work, including that on Khayyam, and for inviting me to offer a seminar presentation on Khayyam in March 2011 at U. C. Berkeley.

I further thank the staff of the Interlibrary Loan at UMass Boston's Healey Library for their professionalism and timely processing of my requests.

My sabbatical year (2010-11) after being granted tenure and promotion at UMass Boston allowed me to spend more focused time on earlier phases of this research. Ironically, the sabbatical gave me a sense of the enormity of the effort needed for this research, resulting in my decision to retire early, in Dec. 2013, from my academic position so as to devote full-time to this urgent study while also attending to the needs of my mother in Iran, who unfortunately passed away on the last day of the year 2020, from natural causes in old age.

What ultimately made this study possible have been the love, support, and sacrifices of my parents, Tayyebeh Tamjidi (1928-2020) and Mohammed (Ahad) Tamjidi (1930-2007). My only wish and hope is that this engagement with the immortal spirit of Omar Khayyam will keep the names and memories of both my parents, and my endless love for them, alive forever.

This series as a whole is dedicated, beside Omar Khayyam himself, to the memory of my mother and in celebration of the universe of love, search for justice, and spiritual curiosity she bequeathed to me. I have already shared, in an extended acknowledgement in my recent work *Liberating Sociology: From Newtonian Toward Quantum Imaginations: Volume 1: Unriddling the Quantum Enigma* (2020), her life's story in the context of the broader history of contemporary Iran, so I refer interested readers to consult that writing for further insights into the motivations behind this series. It may suffice here again to say that this series is entirely a work of her life as well, as superposed with mine, in search of understanding by way of Omar Khayyam the enigma of our common human existence.

Despite her progressing Alzheimer's in the last decade or so of her life, during which she became oddly a love poet reliving her younger years, Tayyebeh lived long enough to walk me through the last day of the calendar year 2020 into 2021. Her 94th birth day on March 20, 2021, would have fallen also on the last day of Iran's calendar year and nominal century 1399 (SH), just a day before the 1400 SH Nowrooz holidays began. So, I see this book and series as also a Nowrooz gift from and to her as well.

I wish to thank my mother's kind nurse and caretakers in Iran, Mrs. Sakineh and Mr. Qasem Rahimi, and also Mr. Ashtiani, for providing me with the peace of mind needed to carry out this research, during the recent years I frequently traveled to Iran to attend to my mother's needs.

As the studies being reported in this series demonstrate, the timing of the simultaneous publication of the first three books of this twelve-book series ahead of June 10, 2021, or Khordad 20, 1400 SH, at sunrise, Neyshabour's time, of the Iranian Islamic solar calendar (one that Khayyam himself and his team of astronomers reformed centuries ago) is uniquely significant as far as Omar Khayyam and new Khayyami studies are concerned.

As expressed in one of his quatrains, Khayyam wished to be reborn like a green after a hundred thousand years. Now we know exactly when those hundred thousand years began, and on what day and time exactly its first millennium falls. So, I dedicate this series to him toward that aim, hoping that it will serve to renew interest in ever resurrecting his legacy as a wonderful gift from Iran's rich culture for 99 more and counting millennia to come. Perhaps somebody then will remember me too!

The astrological charts used in this series were prepared by the author using the Swiss Ephemeris database using software Time Cycles Research (TCR) for which he holds license. The online resources and the Swiss Ephemeris database available also on the online resources of the site Astrodienst were also helpful in the research conducted for this book. I thank them both, and also the site Medieval Astrology Guide, for providing their online resources and services.

The images used for book covers (including any inside from Dreamstime) have also been licensed for use. Many sources on which this study has drawn are old, out of print, and freely available online. Other acknowledgments and credits are given in the text itself or in footnotes. I draw on others in the spirit of fair use for educational and research purposes.

Preface to Book 2: Recap From Prior Book of the Series

In each book of the *Omar Khayyam's Secret* series following the first book, I will include in its preface what I included by way of conclusion in prior book(s) of the series, sharing the summaries of all the prior books, drawing on the abstracts offered for each previously. This way the reader will find in the preface of each book an overall summary of the findings of all prior books. However, as stated previously, it is important to note that such abstracts and overall summaries cannot substitute for a careful reading of the main text of the book itself, since it is obviously impossible to convey the entirety of the findings of any book in the brief space of a conclusion or a preface.

Omar Khayyam's Secret: Hermeneutics of the Robaiyat in Quantum Sociological Imagination is a twelve-book series of which the book subtitled *New Khayyami Studies: Quantumizing the Newtonian Structures of C. Wright Mills's Sociological Imagination for A New Hermeneutic Method* was the first book. Each book is independently readable, although it will be best understood as a part of the whole series.

In the overall series, I share the results of my decades-long research on Omar Khayyam, the enigmatic 11th/12th centuries Persian Muslim sage, philosopher, astronomer, mathematician, physician, writer, and poet from Neyshabour, Iran, whose life and works still remain behind a veil of deep mystery. The purpose of my research has been to find definitive answers to the many puzzles still surrounding Khayyam, especially regarding the existence, nature, and purpose of the Robaiyat in his life and works. To explore the questions posed in the series, I advance a new hermeneutic method of textual analysis, informed by what I call the quantum sociological imagination, to gather and study all the attributed philosophical, religious, scientific, and literary writings of Khayyam.

In the first book, following a common preface and introduction to the series, I developed the quantum sociological imagination method framing my hermeneutic study in the series as a whole.

In its prefatory note I shared the origins of this series and how the study is itself a moment in the trajectory of a broader research project. In its introduction, I described how centuries of Khayyami studies, especially during the last two, have reached an impasse in shedding light on Omar Khayyam's enigmatic life and works, especially his attributed Robaiyat.

The four chapters of the first book were then dedicated to developing the quantum sociological imagination as a new hermeneutic method framing the Khayyami studies in the series. The method builds, in an applied way, on the results of my recent work in the sociology of scientific knowledge, *Liberating Sociology: From Newtonian Toward Quantum Imagination: Volume 1: Unriddling the Quantum Enigma* (2020), where I explored extensively, in greater depth, and in the context of understanding the so-called "quantum enigma," the Newtonian and quantum ways of imagining reality. In the first book, I shared the findings of that research in summary amid new applied insights developed in relation to Khayyami studies.

In the first chapter of the first book, I raised a set of eight questions about the structure of C. Wright Mills's sociological imagination (1959) as a potential framework for Khayyami studies. In its second chapter, I showed how the questions are symptomatic of Newtonian structures that still continue to frame Mills's sociological imagination. In its third chapter, I explored how the sociological imagination can be reinvented to be more in tune with the findings of quantum science. In its last chapter, the implications of the quantum sociological imagination for devising a hermeneutic method for new Khayyami studies were outlined. In its conclusion, the findings of the first book of the *Omar Khayyam's Secret* series were further summarized.

Below, I provide a further detailed summary of the first book findings.

In the first book, the "Preface to the Series: Origins of This Study" served to shed light on why I launched this series on Omar Khayyam and how it is itself a moment in the trajectory of a broader research project.

The origin of the series on Khayyam goes back to my graduate doctoral research in sociology resulting in a dissertation titled "Mysticism and Utopia: Towards the Sociology of Self-Knowledge and Human Architecture (A Study in Marx, Gurdjieff, and Mannheim)" (2002). Therein, the more I explored the explanatory value of the overall thesis during my doctoral research, the more I found its echoes in Omar Khayyam's life and works. If Marx, Gurdjieff, and Mannheim represented respectively the one-sided human efforts in utopian, mystical, and social scientific liberation, Khayyam increasingly represented to me an integrative effort at overcoming mutually alienating traditions of utopianism, mysticism, and science as described above. However, the exploration of such a three-fold representation required further research in the deep structures of Khayyam's attributed texts amid wider Khayyami studies, one which I decided to undertake more systematically following my doctoral studies, resulting in the establishment of a research center in Khayyam's name and its scholarly journal and publications.

Following the publication of three books on Karl Marx (2007), G. I. Gurdjieff (2009), and a transdisciplinary study on Karl Mannheim and in the sociology of scientific knowledge of the quantum enigma (2020), my continuing interests in reinventing C. Wright Mills in favor of a quantum sociological imagination are explored in this series on Khayyam's life and works, serving as both exploratory and applied contexts.

In the first book's "Introduction to the Series: The Enigmatic Omar Khayyam and the Impasse of Khayyami Studies," I argued that nearly a thousand years after his birth, the life and works of Omar Khayyam are still wrapped deeply in veil, major puzzles about him still abound, and modern Khayyami studies in Iran and abroad, after nearly two centuries of active research, have grounded nearly to a halt, reaching an impasse.

Overviewing a series of puzzles and questions left unresolved about Omar Khayyam's life and works, I invited readers to ask why they may not consider what *they themselves already know* about Khayyam to be based on one or another myth. Acknowledging that not only others', but also our own, knowledges of Khayyam are myths—that they are socially and historically constructed stories about him—can be a good beginning in the true Khayyamian spirit of the term founded on healthy skepticism. Doubting what we know about him in a radical way can be a helpful starting point about developing new understandings of his life, works, and legacy.

It may be that we end up constructing new myths about him, but at least we would be doing so based on more reliable studies, being aware of the social constructedness of our own knowledges or myths about him, and based on efforts that do not pretend to contrast the presumed truths on our parts with lesser-valued myths constructed by others. So, it is not proper for us to assume the existing knowledges about him to be uncontroversially authentic, factual, and official to start with. The very method we use to study him, let alone the substantive knowledges about him, are to be treated as variables, and not as givens, taken for granted.

Instead of simply starting with drawing on this or that scholar's portrayals of who Khayyam was and what he wrote, we must start from the scratch by revisiting and rethinking the methodological grounds and frameworks we use in our Khayyami studies. So, in the first book, I set myself this task in order to let the exploration itself guide how the rest of this investigation in that and future books of this series will be organized and conducted.

In the first chapter of the first book titled "The Promises and the Classical Limits of C. Wright Mills's Sociological Imagination," I suggested that the study of texts to understand their meanings in social context falls in the subdisciplinary field of the sociology of knowledge, broadly defined as a branch of social scientific inquiry concerned with understanding how knowledge and social reality relate to one another. Studying Khayyam's attributed works and those of others about him in order to understand his views and life in historical context, therefore, can be framed as a study in the sociology of knowledge, broadly speaking.

In that chapter, using Khayyami studies as an applied setting, I revisited the Millsian sociological imagination, raising eight issues that I believe express the limits imposed by the classical Newtonian way of thinking on Mills's imaginative framework. I explored the eight issues in terms of the following questions: 1. The problem of dualism: can personal troubles be also public issues, and vice versa? 2. The problem of atomism: which self's personal trouble is it? 3. The problem of separability: whose public issues are these? 4. The problem of objectivity: can we as observers separate ourselves from others' personal troubles and public issues? 5. The problem of determinism: is it always the case that society shapes the individual/self, and that public issues always shape personal troubles? 6. The problem of continuity: are we supposed to find causal relations amid easily locatable and traceable causal chains? 7. The problem of disciplinarity: are we always better off dividing and specializing our knowledges into fragmented disciplines? And 8. The problem of scientism: is science always Western, and still Newtonian?

I asked and explored whether Mills's comments on Newtonianism and the Newtonian "way of thinking" in his book were meant to acknowledge that he himself was gripped by and embraced Newtonianism in his proposed critical return to "classical" pursuit of the sociological imagination, or did he instead mean to question such fundamental structures of thinking, seeking ways to move beyond them in favor of newer scientific, cultural, and sociological imaginations?

In the second chapter of the first book titled, "The Newtonian Imagination of Reality, Society, Sociology, and Khayyami Studies," in order to offer a heuristic model of the Newtonian way of imagining reality, society, sociology and the sociological imagination and demonstrate (in a following chapter) how such a perspective is different from the quantum way of imagining them, I used in the chapter the "billiard balls game" metaphor that has been widely used (in my view wrongly) to characterize the Newtonian way of imagining the world.

I suggested that the Newtonian way of imagining, or thinking about, the universe may be broadly characterized as having eight notional attributes—namely, its notions of (1) dualism, (2) atomism, (3) separability, (4) (subjectless) objectivity, (5) determinism (including its associated notion of predictability), (6) continuity, (7) disciplinarity, and (8) scientism—which can be illustrated by using a (what I argue is an ideologically distorted) metaphorical "billiard balls game" way of imagining reality as commonly used for the purpose.

More specifically the attributes of Newtonian imagination I explored were in terms of the following questions: 1. Dualism: can an object be A and non-A at the same time? 2. Atomism: what is the micro unit of analysis of the object? 3. Separability: what is the macro unit of analysis of the object? 4. Objectivity: does the object being observed have an independent reality? 5. Determinism: are causes and consequences in objects certain and predictable? 6. Continuity: is influence exerted through chains of local-causations? 7. Disciplinarity: fragmenting our knowledge of reality? And 8. Scientism: presuming the superiority of Western, Newtonian way of thinking?

I used the above framework to show how such parameters also have shaped our Newtonian conceptions of society, sociology, and the sociological imagination, and may also continue to frame our Khayyami studies if we fail in bringing them to conscious awareness as a precondition for reframing our sociological and Khayyami studies in more fruitful, quantum ways.

I concluded the second chapter of the first book by offering a vision of "classical," "Newtonian sociology" that can clarify further the implications the broader Newtonian vision I outlined above has for shaping the "classical" sociological vision, and the sociological imagination as a framework for conducting Khayyami studies. Introducing a diagram for the Newtonian sociological imagination, I noted that what makes the sociological imagination Newtonian is not simply that it avoids studying linkages between its elements. What makes it Newtonian is its treating those elements in a "chunky" way, in presuming that the elements are separate billiard balls to begin with, that they do not overlap with one another, instead simply needing to be linked with another, to interact with one another from "without," in order to make the imagination work. It does not imagine those elements as already embedded in dialectical part-whole relations of identity in difference.

In the third chapter of the first book titled, "Quantum Sociological Imagination as A Framework for Khayyami Studies," I offered an overview of how classical Newtonianism as a product of an historical compromise between a receding religiosity and an emerging secularism in the West met its limits and fell into crisis when confronted with the new findings of quantum science.

Using the same eight-fold model I used to describe the attributes of the Newtonian way of thinking, I suggested that the quantum way of imagining reality can also be characterized as having eight sets of attributes: 1-Simultaneity (not "duality," nor "complementarity"); 2-Superpositionality; 3-Inseparability; 4-Relativity (subject-included objectivity); 5-Probability; 6-Transcontinuity (which is a term I prefer to call what is commonly referred to as "discontinuity"); 7-Transdisciplinarity; and (8) Transculturalism. In my view, we have to always distinguish between *three* kinds of Newtonianism: *classical*, *incompletely relativistic*, and *completely relativistic*. The classical Newtonianism universalizes the eight attributes as listed earlier. The incompletely relativistic Newtonianism is the kind prevalent today, confused, enigmatized, still not freed from the classical bounds but not yet fully embracing attributes that it could have independently discovered for itself, ones that it would have found to be "completely" resonating with the quantum science findings (itself stripped of elements contributive to the quantum enigma, such as the "wave-particle duality," "Complementarity Principle," and so on). For the completely relativistic Newtonianism I have coined (2020) the term *Quantum Newtonianism*. It is a Newtonianism that treats the reality from the standpoint of any observer's reference frame to be a local reference frame or fold of the broader quantum reality as a whole.

I suggested that quantumizing the Newtonian in favor of a quantum sociological imagination invites the following considerations regarding each of which I offered illustrations, and from each of which I drew inspiration, about how Khayyami studies can be framed: 1. Relating personal troubles and public issues: from dualism to simultaneity (not "duality," nor "complementarity"); 2. Relating personal troubles (or not) of many selves: from atomism to superpositionality; 3. Relating public issues world-historically: from separability to inseparability; 4. Relating the sociological imaginations of others to those of ourselves: from subjectless objectivity to relativity (subject-included objectivity); 5. Reimagining causal patterns creatively: from determinism to probability; 6. Reimagining causal chains also as causal leaps: from continuity to "transcontinuity" (also known as "discontinuity"); 7. Reimagining sociology: from disciplinarity to transdisciplinarity; and 8. Reimagining science: from eurocentrism to tansculturalism.

I illustrated in a figure how, by reimagining the elements of the sociological imagination in terms of overlapping and superposing circles, we can arrive at a non-dualistic, both/and, conception of elements that previously could only be imagined in terms of a formal, either/or logic. I argued that using the notion of "Khayyami" as a reference both to the person and to the tradition associated with him can offer a sociologically imaginative quantum device involving a language of simultaneity when referring to Omar Khayyam's life, works, and legacy—especially when it comes to the study of the attributed Robaiyat—one that can have significant methodological, substantive, and practical consequences for framing and conducting our Khayyami studies.

In the fourth and last chapter of the first book, titled, "Hermeneutics of the Khayyami Robaiyat in Quantum Sociological Imagination: Source Availability and Secrecy," I relaxed my prior assumptions and abstractions from matters of source availability and secrecy as maintained in the previous three chapters of the book, and tried in the chapter to elaborate in more detail on both of the above challenges confronting Khayyami studies.

In the first section, my purpose was to draw a preliminary, basic outline of the sources of information available (or not) for the research on Khayyam conducted for this series. My aim at that point was not to delve into the historical, bibliographic, or manuscript conditions or the extent of authenticity of these sources. Those details will be carefully introduced, examined, and evaluated during the substantive explorations of this series in conjunction with careful studies of their contents.

I offered a categorization of sources for Khayyami studies as follows:

1. Primary Sources: texts that are attributed, unanimously or not, to Omar Khayyam himself. In this category, I identified the following subcategories: A) As a first subcategory of primary sources, we should include works that Khayyam may have written, intended to be shared or not during his own lifetime, of which we do not yet have any knowledge or records whatever; B) As a second subcategory of primary sources, we have works specifically reported by Khayyam (as acknowledges also by others) to have been written by him on definite topics from which we do not (yet) have any complete or even partial manuscripts; C) A third subcategory of primary sources are surviving works bearing Khayyam's name that are universally accepted to have been authored by him, these include a variety of sources that I listed in the section; D) The Khayyami Robaiyat: A fourth subcategory of surviving primary sources are the Robaiyat (quatrains) written in Persian that have been attributed to Omar Khayyam in various manuscripts down the centuries; it was given a separate subcategory status given the disputed nature of their attribution.

2. Secondary Sources: old accounts and information about Khayyam's life and works from the pre-FitzGeraldian era, among which I identified also four subcategories as explained in the text.

3. Tertiary Sources: include all the modern and recent sources written about Khayyam's life and works in the post-FitzGeraldian era. I noted further that fourth (possible architecture related works) and fifth (burial related material) categories can also be considered as sources in Khayyami studies.

In my view, the most reliable strategy for conducting Khayyami studies must be one that lays the most emphasis on the primary material as the source of the most reliable information about Khayyam. However, we will have to avoid treating all the various categories and subcategories as chunky, separate billiard balls to be struck with one another from without, but will approach them in their overlapping and superposed nature, in such a way that despite their apparently fragmented state, they are imagined as being superposed expressions of a life in progress, works produced along a lifetime, and commentaries made by others on his life and works amid a wider world-history context they all share.

I then elaborated on my hermeneutic method to be used in the series, noting that I will be particularly interested and careful to seek, as far as possible, the symbolic meanings amid the language Khayyam *himself* uses from his own texts as part of the landscape of his own subjective universe, rather than assuming in an *a priori* fashion that simply because Khayyam admired Avicenna (or anyone else for that matter) he retained and applied the same meaning in the same way as Avicenna or others did in their work.

Finally, while offering the broad contours and a gist of my thesis advanced in the series, I encouraged my readers to consider and understand that my presentation method of revealing the "secret" of Khayyam in the series has to remain respectful of Khayyam's style of teaching and writing, since understanding of that process is itself an integral part of the "secret" Khayyam wished to impart through his works, particularly his Robaiyat.

The second book of the *Omar Khayyam's Secret* that follows is dedicated to exploring in depth the hitherto findings and controversies surrounding the dates of birth and passing of Omar Khayyam.

Abstract

This essay, titled "Book 2 Preface: Recap From Prior Books of the Series," is an opening to the second book of the twelve-book series *Omar Khayyam's Secret: Hermeneutics of the Robaiyat in Quantum Sociological Imagination,* authored by Mohammad H. Tamdgidi. The second book is subtitled *Khayyami Millennium: Reporting the Discovery and the Reconfirmation of the True Dates of Birth and Passing of Omar Khayyam (AD 1021-1123).* It offers a summary, based on the section and chapter abstracts, of the first book of the series. The purpose of the preface is to provide the readers of the second book of the series a brief background about the major findings of the prior book(s) of the series.

In the overall series the author shares the results of his decades-long research on Omar Khayyam, the enigmatic 11th/12th centuries Persian Muslim sage, philosopher, astronomer, mathematician, physician, writer, and poet from Neyshabour, Iran, whose life and works still remain behind a veil of deep mystery. The purpose of Tamdgidi's research has been to find definitive answers to the many puzzles still surrounding Khayyam, especially regarding the existence, nature, and purpose of the Robaiyat in his life and works. To explore the questions posed in the series, Tamdgidi advances a new hermeneutic method of textual analysis, informed by what he calls the quantum sociological imagination, to gather and study all the attributed philosophical, religious, scientific, and literary writings of Khayyam.

In the first book of the series, subtitled *New Khayyami Studies: Quantumizing the Newtonian Structures of C. Wright Mills's Sociological Imagination for A New Hermeneutic Method*, following a common preface and introduction to the series, Tamdgidi developed the quantum sociological imagination method framing his hermeneutic study in the series as a whole. In the prefatory note he shared the origins of this study and how the study is itself a moment in the trajectory of a broader research project. In his introduction, he described how centuries of Khayyami studies, especially during the last two, have reached an impasse in shedding light on his enigmatic life and works, especially his attributed Robaiyat.

The four chapters of the first book were then dedicated to developing the quantum sociological imagination as a new hermeneutic method framing the Khayyami studies in the series. The method builds, in an applied way, on the results of Tamdgidi's recent work in the sociology of scientific knowledge, *Liberating Sociology: From Newtonian Toward Quantum Imagination: Volume 1: Unriddling the Quantum Enigma* (2020), where he explored extensively, in greater depth, and in the context of understanding the so-called "quantum enigma," the Newtonian and quantum ways of imagining reality.

In the first book, he shared the findings of that research in summary amid new applied insights developed in relation to Khayyami studies. In the first chapter, Tamdgidi raised a set of eight questions about the structure of C. Wright Mills's sociological imagination as a potential framework for Khayyami studies. In the second chapter, he showed how the questions are symptomatic of Newtonian structures that still continue to frame Mills's sociological imagination. In the third chapter, the author explored how the sociological imagination can be reinvented to be more in tune with the findings of quantum science. In the last chapter, the implications of the quantum sociological imagination for devising a hermeneutic method for new Khayyami studies were outlined. In conclusion, the findings of the first book of the *Omar Khayyam's Secret* series were summarized.

The second book of the *Omar Khayyam's Secret* that follows is dedicated to exploring in depth the hitherto findings and controversies surrounding the dates of birth and passing of Omar Khayyam.

Introduction to Book 2: The Dilemma and Significance of Omar Khayyam's Dates of Birth and Passing

In recent decades, an uneasy consensus has emerged in Khayyami studies and public media regarding the dates of birth and passing of Omar Khayyam.

Nowadays, one can readily find various online, bibliographic, encyclopedic, academic, or other published sources stating that Khayyam was born on Thursday, May 18, AD 1048, and died on Friday, December 4th, AD 1131. Such dates are then celebrated or commemorated according to the solar Gregorian Christian calendar used today in the West.

The above dates (treated as if they are Gregorian calendar dates) correspond respectively to Thursday, 25th of Dhu al-Qadah, 439 LH (Lunar Hejri, hereafter LH), and Friday, 5th of Muharram, 526 LH, in the lunar Islamic calendar. According to the Solar Hejri (hereafter SH) calendar used in Iran, a calendar Khayyam and collaborating astronomers reportedly helped reform during his lifetime, the above dates of birth and passing would be (again, treated as if they are Gregorian calendar dates) respectively Thursday, 28th of Ordibehesht, 427, and Friday, 12th of Azar, 510 SH. In Iran, 28th of Ordibehesht (corresponding to May 18th) is now the official date of celebration of Khayyam's birth date.

The lunar and solar Islamic calendars commonly start on the year the prophet Muhammad and his followers migrated—"hejri," meaning "attributed to migration" in Arabic and Persian—from Mecca to Yathrib (or today's Medina) in the year AD 622 of the Christian calendar. Because the lunar Islamic calendar is based on the lunar cycle (consisting of 354, or 355 leap-year, days), which is shorter than the solar cycle (consisting of 365, or 366 leap-year, days), their associated year lengths are different, the solar year count always falling behind the lunar year count in time.

Friday, January 1, 2021, for instance, corresponds to Friday, Dey 12, 1399 SH (in Iranian Islamic *solar* calendar), and Friday, Jumada al-Awwal 17, 1442 LH (in Islamic *lunar* calendar). This means, say on January 1, 2021, 1399 solar hejri years have passed since the prophet's migration, compared to 1442 lunar years since then, a numerical difference of about 43 years for the same length of time, or a numerical difference of about 3 nominal years per *solar* century (that is, 43 divided by 14 solar centuries).

By implication in terms of age, if someone lived to a hundred *lunar* years, he would have lived to the *solar* age of about 97 actually, or, if she lived to a hundred *solar* years, her *lunar* age would be about 103. In Iran, even still today, while for religious anniversaries the lunar Islamic calendar is used, for considering the age of persons the solar calendar is usually implied. In the West such a qualification need not usually be made, since only one solar calendar is used. In nations using the lunar calendar officially, counting a person's age according to their lunar calendar would be higher than if they counted it according to the Western solar calendar. In Iran, since the official calendar is solar hejri, the distinction has been more immediately relevant and has to be always kept in mind. For shorter time spans, the solar-lunar time span differences may be somewhat negligible depending on the purpose for which they are considered, but for longer time spans the difference can be noteworthy and significant.

For the same reason, regular (such as Islamic religious) annual anniversaries marked on the lunar calendar year do not regularly correspond to the same annual dates in the solar calendar year; so, for instance, the month of Ramadan (Islam's month of fasting) falls on continually changing times of the Christian or Iranian solar calendars. Events falling on (today's Gregorian) Christian and Iranian Islamic calendars, however, generally follow the same cycle, since they are both solar.

According to the solar Gregorian Christian, lunar Islamic, and solar Islamic calendars, if we follow the above-mentioned consensus dates for Khayyam birth and passing, he would be considered to have lived respectively for about 83 (1048-1131 AD), 87 (439-526 LH), and 83 (427-510 SH) years.

As noted above, a higher age results in the lunar calendar calculation since the number of days per lunar year are fewer than those in the solar calendar years constituting both the Gregorian and Persian timeline.

Now, if you compare what I noted earlier above about the 3-year usual difference between lunar and solar century spans, and notice that the difference in Khayyam's supposed lunar age above is 4 (87 minus 83), the reason is as follows, which is another subtle, yet important, point we have to always keep in mind in this study, to which I will return.

Because lunar and solar years are different in length, and even across the two solar calendars of the West and in Iran, since the beginning and the ending days of the three calendars each year do not coincide, days in one calendar year can fall into two successive of other calendar years. So, say the year 2020 in Western calendar corresponded to the years 1398-1399 in Iranian calendar, or to 1441-1442 of the lunar calendar years. So, for the same lunar year in which someone is born, it may fall on a year less or more on the solar calendar, which explains the difference we noted above. Dhu al-Qadah is the 11th month of the lunar calendar while Muharram is the first, so they fall on different years of the solar calendars, accounting for the 4 nominal years, instead of the usual 3 year difference, I noted earlier. Even though the age range being considered above for Khayyam is within the range of 80s, it is close enough to 100 for the 3 to 4 year nominal year spans to be counted, given there are many months within a year in which the age would still count the same for those months.

Obviously, the determination of the exact dates for Omar Khayyam's birth and passing, which would then identify the exact historical period during which he lived (marked by rapidly changing events, rulers, and personalities), is vital for any adequate and realistic research on his life and works amid the broader context of his times.

Khayyam himself, in his reliably attributed scientific writings, complained about the nature of the troubled times during which he lived and the impact they had on the careers and personal lives of scientists such as himself and on their scientific pursuit in general. He seemingly contrasted better and worse periods or conditions as far as scientists' works were concerned—allowing for, or preventing, for instance, his completing one or another treatise. So, if we have reliable information about his birth and death dates, we could more realistically correspond various stages of his life-course with particular historical periods during which he lived, and with the same in the lives of others among his contemporaries.

Studying the interplay between personal troubles and broader public issues involving Khayyam's life in a quantum sociological imagination framework (as introduced in the preceding first book of this series) requires such a careful determination of the outer boundaries of the chronology of his life and works in relation to those of his contemporaries amid local, regional, and broader world-history contexts. An accurate determination of the dates of Khayyam's birth and passing can provide significant information about more exact intersections of various periods of his biography with those of others amid the tumultuous times during which one or another of his writings, including his poetry, if any, may have been composed.

However, the uneasy consensus on Khayyam's dates of birth and passing as noted above is not in any way a universally settled matter. Indicative, or perhaps more so symbolic, of the ambiguities surrounding the birth date and his age at the time of his passing is the inscription found presently on Khayyam's tombstone in his mausoleum in Neyshabour, Iran. There, his date of passing is still stated as the year 517 LH (not the previously noted consensus date, 526 LH), corresponding to the year AD 1123 (for now just assuming it did not fall in AD 1124) (not the previously noted consensus date, AD 1131) in the Gregorian Christian calendar, or the year 502 SH (not the previously noted consensus date, 510 SH) in the solar Islamic calendar used in Iran.

Moreover, although it is a common practice to offer the dates of both birth and passing for the deceased in Iran on their tombstones, and it is more so expected for a famed figure such as Khayyam, it is interesting to note that no birth date is inscribed on his present tombstone.[1] There is only a reference to his age, stating that he lived "seventy plus years," which could somewhat (but not exactly) support the prevalent consensus held today regarding his birth date—that is, counting backwards "seventy plus (presumably solar) years," we could arrive, with a few years more or less, at the birth date of 439 LH (corresponding to the Gregorian and solar Islamic years respectively of about AD 1048 or 427 SH). This would resolve to the age calculations of 77 or 75 (i.e., "seventy plus years") lunar and solar years respectively.

---

1. Omar Khayyam's present tombstone reads, following a verse from the Quran, meaning "All things die except for His Face" (كُلُّ شَيْءٍ هَالِكٌ إِلَّا وَجْهَهُ): "The resting place of the Sage Abu al-Fath Omar Ibn Ibrahim Khayyam Neyshabouri who joined God's Mercy in the year 517 Lunar Hejri after living seventy plus years" (see https://commons.wikimedia.org/wiki/File:Tombstone_of_Omar_Khayyam.JPG):

آرامگاه حکیم ابوالفتح عُمَر بن ابراهیم خیّام نیشابوری که پس از هفتاد و چند سال زندگانی در سال ۵۱۷ هجری قمری برحمت ایزدی پیوست.

In other words, even though the date of birth is not explicated on Khayyam's present tombstone, the inscription implies that his birth date was around AD 1048, as follows: Solar Gregorian: AD 1123 - 1048 = 75 years old; Lunar Islamic: LH 517 - 439 = 78 years old; Solar Islamic/Persian: SH 502 - 427 = 75 years old. If we contrast the above with the consensus dates we find nowadays online for Khayyam's dates of birth and passing, we find below: Solar Gregorian: AD 1131 - 1048 = 83 years old; Lunar Islamic: LH 526 - 439 = 87 years old; Solar Islamic/Persian: SH 510 - 427 = 83 years old, keeping in mind of course what I stated above about each calendar year falling on two different years in other calendars, which can slightly affect the number of years for the ages given.

The lack of an explicitly given birth date on Khayyam's tombstone may still be regarded as indicative of the lack of a universal consensus on when he was born, however. Note how the age given ("seventy plus years") on the inscription compares with the consensus age figures (83 or 87) implied for Khayyam's birth and death dates, depending on whether we use the solar or lunar calendars for our calculations respectively, and depending on what date of passing we attribute to Khayyam (AD 1123 or 1131).

One may regard the discrepancy between the consensus dates and the tombstone inscription to be a result of delays in updating the tombstone or its inscription (simply for architectural, archeological, budget, or perhaps even neglect, reasons) to reflect the "correct" consensus dates for Khayyam's birth, passing, and age on the tombstone inscription. That may be the case, but it may also be indicative, or at least symbolic, of the still unresolved doubts about the exact dates of Khayyam's birth and death.

Why should Iran change the tombstone/inscription if no one is still sure when Khayyam was born or died? If it is the case that a death date 517 LH (AD 1123) has been handed down through traditional sources, would it be wise to change it in light of a claim made by a still uneasy consensus in recent times?

A quick review of the history of Khayyam's tombstones in light of the foregoing may also be helpful here.

The present mausoleum of Omar Khayyam in Neyshabour was inaugurated on April 1st, AD 1963 (hereafter "AD" not expressed when implied for modern times), corresponding to the Persian solar calendar date of Farvardin 12th, 1342 SH. Its construction was completed on Shahrivar 6th, 1341 SH, or August 28th, 1962. It was designed and built by the late

Iranian architect, Houshang Seyhoon (1920-2014), in the shape of a tall tent resembling an observatory, with stars visible through openings in its frame, and selected Robaiyat written using Persian calligraphy on its turquoise-colored, flower-ornamented, tilework. Its tent-like, twisting, structure follows in design a complex mathematical formula that converges to form a ten-pointed star on top around which one can see from below Neyshabour's blue sky in daytime and its stars at night.

The frame is based on ten legs symbolizing the first 2-digit number which is the basis of the decimal number system (that is, "10"). It is positioned amid an area around which in the back are several smaller, triangular, tent-like structures with narrow water pathways and tilework originally intended to be symbolizing the seven cosmic spheres as conceived in Islamic philosophy.

The structure was originally set such that the surrounding apricot trees, planned to be elevated at a certain height, could shed blossoms over the tombstone in springtime, as Khayyam had reportedly spoke of his future tomb a few years before passing away. Overall, intended or not, the structure also looks like an inverted (tall) cup.

The mausoleum as a whole was built on the eastern side of a large garden that separately includes the tomb of Imamzadeh Mahrouq (literally meaning "the burnt one who was born to an Imam," burned to death in the area centuries before Khayyam, for whose martyrdom the early structures of the present shrine were originally built).

A great grandson of Imam Hussein (who was a martyred son of Imam Ali who was himself the martyred fourth caliph of Islam and a cousin of the prophet of Islam), Muhammad Mahrouq was a Shia who was burnt to death on 200 LH (AD 816), per whose martyrdom the tomb or shrine was built in Neyshabour, serving today also as a mosque. The construction is traced to the Timurid (AD 1370-1506/773-912 LH) and its later renovations to Safavid (AD 1501-1722/907-1135 LH) periods. So, at least in their earlier forms, the garden and the shrine's construction was pre-existing when Khayyam died in the twelfth century AD, or the sixth century LH, and it may have served as a focal point for the choice of the original tomb of Khayyam.

Khayyam's original tomb was reported by his contemporary Nezami Arouzi (who respected Khayyam as his teacher), to have been located in a cemetery named Heireh in the old Neyshabour, beside a garden wall, which Nezami Arouzi reported (according to some manuscript copies or interpretations thereof) to have visited in AD 1135-1136/530 LH ("some," "four," or "fourteen" years before which—depending on the manuscript used and interpretations made of the text—Khayyam had died) in person, finding it, as Khayyam had told him in Balkh in AD 1112-1113 (506 LH) a few years before his passing, covered with blossoms of pear and apricot trees.

In fact, the source of the present uneasy consensus on Khayyam's date of passing in AD 1131/526 LH is this same Nezami Arouzi account, or at least an interpretation of it. Those who wish to read the word for the number of years before 530 LH (when he visited Khayyam's grave) as "four" (when Khayyam had according to him had died), conclude that his date of passing must have been AD 1131/526 LH. This also provides such observers with an opportunity to add more years to Khayyam's age. I will return later to the above and also to how the month and date of the consensus date has been also guessed.

Given the invasions, earthquakes, social upheavals, and calamities befallen Neyshabour after Khayyam's death, it is not known whether the original grave of Khayyam was exactly the same that survived into the modern times. But it has been reported and even portrayed in paintings in the Western traveler chronicles that a nameless, simple raised grave in a semi-enclosed terrace adjacent to the Mahrouq shrine belonged to Omar Khayyam.

In late nineteenth century and early twentieth centuries, mainly as a result of Khayyam's increasing fame due to the publication of the free translations of his "Rubaiyat" into English by Edward FitzGerald, interest grew among Western travelers to Iran in visiting his grave. Having encountered the simplicity, relative obscurity, and namelessness of the tomb of a poet so increasingly revered in the West, diplomatic pressures grew on the then current Qajar administration ruling Iran to renovate the tomb.

Having responded to the pressures, reluctantly at first, the Iranian Qajar government at the time finally decided to renovate Khayyam's tomb, which resulted in building a monument (a tall column with inscriptions of a poem of its dedication to Khayyam, written by Malek ol-Shoara-ye Bahar, a famed poet of that time) adjacent to the same place Khayyam's unmarked raised grave used to be, with an inscription that identified Omar Khayyam by name and offered the year 516 LH as the date of his passing.

The columnar monument was later moved (during the final renovation of Khayyam's tomb that resulted in the opening of his present mausoleum in 1963/1342 SH) to an urban square in Neyshabour bearing Khayyam's name, which is still standing. During formal ceremonies involving religious rites performed, the little that was assumed to be from Khayyam's body was relocated to its present mausoleum; accounts of the transfer do not indicate there were any doubts the remains where that of Khayyam, some folks later on even speculating about the skeleton's tall stature (given the length of leg bones, perhaps) and larger than normal size of the skull, the accuracy of such accounts not being verifiable, of course; some Khayyami quatrains speak of its composer's having had a tall stature, like a cypress tree. The final resting place of Khayyam as it stands today and previously described was established on the eastern flank of the garden, one whose tombstone reports the lunar Islamic year 517 LH as his date of passing, as I described earlier.

The discrepancy between 516 LH and 517 LH for the death year given across the last two tombstone inscriptions for Khayyam may have been most likely a result of the simple fact that (as I noted earlier) lunar and solar calendar years do not always begin and end at the same time (apart from cycling differently from one another). So, translating, say, the Christian solar year AD 1123 (Jan. 1 to Dec. 31) into the lunar calendar, we arrive at the period from 23rd of Shawwal, 516 LH to 4th of Dhu al-Qadah, 517 LH. So, if someone was trying to follow a Christian calendar instruction of offering AD 1123 for Khayyam's year of passing without knowing the exact month of his passing (which has indeed been the case), he or she would not be technically incorrect to say it took place in the year 516 LH or 517 LH. However, note that the converse may also happen. For instance, if the original date 516 LH was to be regarded as a basis, it can be translated into either AD 1122 or 1123, since, again, the 516 LH year as a whole corresponds to the period March 19, 1122 to March 7, 1123. Of course, the same can be stated for the year 517 LH falling in both years AD 1123 and 1124.

As a rule of thumb, the reader can consider that by adding 621 or 622 years (depending on the months considered) to Iran's solar Islamic calendar, one can arrive roughly at the equivalent year in the Gregorian Christian calendar, which is also solar. In the Iranian solar Islamic calendar, if the month is before March 21/Farvardin 1, 622 years must be added to the local calendar to determine the Gregorian Christian calendar. If it is after March 21/Farvardin 1, which marks the beginning of the Iranian new year, 621 years must be added for the purpose. However, these calculations do not work for translating lunar calendar dates to solar calendar dates, given their differing numbers of days per year (as noted before).[2]

It is also worth noting here that the currently used Christian calendar is

2. See, for example, Iran Chamber Society's helpful calendar converter tool at http://www.iranchamber.com/calendar/converter/iranian_calendar_converter.php.

Gregorian (G) or "Western," introduced in AD 1582 by Pope Gregory XIII which took about 300 years to be commonly used across the world. So, its contrast with the earlier Julian (J) calendar should always be kept in mind. Apart from slight, but important differences in the length of year (Gregorian's being 365.2425 days versus Julian's 365.25), and in order to initially offset the accumulated drift of uncalculated time in the old calendar, the old calendar date October 4, 1582 was followed the next day by October 15, 1582 (that is the numerical difference of the *same day* between the two calendars for that century was 10; so after October 4th in that year, instead of October 5th, they counted October 15th). However, depending on various considerations, including leap years, local variations, etc., the standard difference between the calendar dates from our standpoint today has to be varied in time. For Oct. 4, 1982, the variation would be 13 days, for 1882 it would be 12 days, for 1782 it would be 11, for 1682 it would be 10, for 1582 it would still be 10, for 1482 it would be 9, for 1382 it would be 8, for 1282 it would be 7, for 1182 it would still be 7 days, for 1082 it would be 6 days, and so on.[3]

Note that the two calendar's difference is important when it comes to designating the Julian/Gregorian equivalents of Khayyam's dates of birth and passing since they fall across two centuries of the calendar. For the date of passing, of course, the 7 days of difference may not come into play if we do not have sufficient data to trace the day of the demise, which in principle could make a difference in the month the death would fall if the day is within a 7 day range going across two months. But for the birth date, if we can narrow down the time to the day, then it would hypothetically make a difference not only regarding the day, but also the month, if the day falls within the range of 6 days difference between the Julian and Gregorian calendars.

So, moving backward from that date, the calendar month days do not correspond with one another. This means that if, for instance, we say Khayyam passed away on Muharram 5th, 526 LH, this would fall on the Gregorian date December 4th, AD 1131, but differently on the Julian date of November 27, AD 1131 (seven days difference).[4] This is important, especially

3. See the helpful calendar converter by Stephen P. Morse, https://stevemorse.org/jcal/julian.html.

4. These dates are just used here as examples. As I will explain it fully later on, and also briefly in this introduction, errors have been made in translating some proposed dates of passing for Khayyam, confusing Gregorian and Julian calendar dates. It may suffice here to say that Dec. 4, AD 1131 is actually a Julian date which must be corrected to Dec. 11, AD 1131 in the Gregorian calendar. So, to convert the Dec. 4, AD 1131 to the lunar calendar, we must actually be converting Dec. 11 (Greg.), which would correspond to Muharram 12, 526 LH.

in historiography, since a birth or a death date, or a war declaration or peace treaty event date, that happened in such a distant past according to the Julian calendar, must be determined to fall on the exact same day according to our today's Gregorian calendar to correspond to the same exact time, especially in relation to other events that must have preceded or followed it.

In fact, I think this provides some clue and explanation for why the month and day of Dec. 4th has come about for Khayyam's date of passing. Originally, Swāmī Govinda Tīrtha (to whom I shall return) had proposed (in 1941) the date of Thursday, Muharram 12, 516 LH, as the date of passing of Khayyam. This would have corresponded to March 30th, AD 1122. However, those scholars who disagreed with his proposed year (516 LH), preferring instead the year 526 LH, decided nevertheless to hold on to the proposed month and day of lunar year as proposed by Tīrtha, since it happened to fall on a Friday, for the year 526 LH, corresponding to December 11, AD 1131.

However, in their calculations, instead of using the Gregorian calendar, they must have used the Julian calendar, instead coming up with and deciding on the Dec. 4th as the day of the month for the alleged date AD 1131 for Khayyam's passing. In fact, this may raise a question as to whether in his calculation of Khayyam's date of birth, Tīrtha at all considered the difference between the Julian and Gregorian Christian calendars—one which can be clearly demonstrated from his text that he inadvertently simply ignored.

I will return to these important issues later, but the above may offer a brief introductory glimpse into both the intricacies as well as the confused state of the efforts made to date to determine Khayyam's dates of birth and passing.

My purpose in sharing the above, aside from calendar calculation protocols which will be needed later in our explorations and to which I shall return in the course of this second book of the series, is simply to offer a glimpse at the background of the uneasy consensus held today surrounding the dates of birth and especially of death of Omar Khayyam and how it compares to the most visible of locations where one would expect to find the definitive dates of his birth and death, i.e., his tombstone inscriptions. For now, it suffices to consider in general that his prior tombstones have historically been either unmarked, or given no definitive dates for his birth, or been varied in offering dates of 516 or 517 LH for his date of passing, one that is different from his consensus date of demise as uneasily held today (526 LH, corresponding to AD 1131).

Of course, it is not surprising to find such biographical information previously lacking about a famed scholar or thinker who lived more than nine hundred years ago. However, the move away from dates previously conjectured for Khayyam's birth and passing—which allowed for the possibility of certain historical possibilities or events that are now considered to be in doubt—is noteworthy.

The uneasy consensus held today regarding Khayyam's birth date, if not exactly his date of passing, is rooted in a specific piece of biographical information passed on from his contemporaries to the present: his birth horoscope, or natal chart. In this regard, the study by the Indian scholar Swāmī Govinda Tīrtha is of singular importance.

Amid his major study of Omar Khayyam's life and writings in his *The Nectar of Grace: Omar Khayyām's Life and Works* (1941), one that included studies and translations of several excerpts of the philosophical (not scientific) writings and (his own) free verse translations of quatrains attributed to Khayyam, Tīrtha proposed a way of calculating Khayyam's birth date based on the horoscope of his birth handed down in a manuscript of biographical entries by the scholar of medieval Islamic period and Khayyam contemporary (as a young child) Zahireddin Abolhasan Beyhaqi, titled *Tatemmat Sewan el-Hekmat (Supplement to the Chest of Wisdom).*

It was through the specific study of that horoscope as given in the specific copy of the Beyhaqi manuscript he consulted that the year AD 1048 was claimed and reported by Swāmī Govinda Tīrtha to have been allegedly discovered, one that became gradually established and reportedly "confirmed" by others including a few Soviet Russian scholars and experts in astronomy, and accepted as a consensus date of birth among the scholars of Omar Khayyam.

The overall consensus that Khayyam's birth year was AD 1048, however, soon led to many questions and confusions about several aspects of Khayyam's biography or writings.

For instance, in his own writings, Khayyam refers to Avicenna (Ibn Sina) as his teacher with whom he reports having had actual personal conversations, several other specific events of his life being also indicative of a significant association Khayyam must have had with the great thinker of medieval Islam and world. However, given the reliably known date for Avicenna's death falling in the year AD 1038, it would be simply impossible for such a personal, live, discipleship or conversation to have taken place, if we regard Khayyam's birth year to be AD 1048. So, scholars, scratching their heads, so to speak, gradually became accustomed, again amid an uneasy consensus, to treating such a seemingly definitive commentary by Khayyam regarding his relationship to Avicenna (made amid one of his undoubtedly attributed writings) as signifying an intellectual discipleship only—that is, in spirit, rather than in person.

As another instance, the famous story of Khayyam having been childhood friends with Nezam ol-Molk (the famous chief minister of Soltan Malekshah, the Seljuk king) and Hasan Sabbah (an Ismaili Shia nemesis of the latter both), would seem impossibly plausible, if we accept today's consensus date of birth and passing for Khayyam. The reason is as follows.

Hasan Sabbah's birth date is not known and his conjectured death around AD 1124 would fit the story of a childhood friendship with Khayyam, no matter what birth date we presume for them. However, Nezam ol-Molk's reliable date of birth falling in the year AD 1018 would lead to the implication that a Khayyam born around then and dying at the now uneasy consensus date of AD 1131, must have lived to a nearly impossible age of about 113 *solar* years—even 3-4 more, if we count in lunar years. This would be a rare possibility that could not have easily escaped the attention of biographical or historical chroniclers. Even the story narrated by Beyhaqi about Khayyam's last day (to which I shall return in due course in this book) tells of someone still sound in mind, which is not usually expected for someone dying at 113-117 (if not even more) years of age. I will of course also explore the above implied issues as part of my critical revisitation of Tīrtha's study.

We owe to Swāmī Govinda Tīrtha the wonderful idea of determining the date of birth of Khayyam through a study of his birth horoscope, and his efforts at and sources used for determining Khayyam's date of passing also offer material that can shed helpful lights toward solving that question as well. However, we should keep in mind that the *soundness* of the way he went about determining those dates *based on the way he interpreted and analyzed the horoscope* and other sources using the specific manuscript copies he had at hand is a completely *different* matter, worthy of critical revisitation.

My purpose in this second book of the *Omar Khayyam's Secret* series is (1) to carefully and critically revisit Swāmī Govinda Tīrtha's study of Khayyam's horoscope which lies at the very source of the prevailing uneasy consensus today regarding the dates of birth and death of Omar Khayyam, and, if Tīrtha's findings are verifiably proven to be wrong, (2) to search for an alternative solution to the determination of the true dates of birth (and by implication and further investigation, passing) of Omar Khayyam by way of careful reexaminations of that horoscope.

The literature written on Omar Khayyam, scientific or not, is enormous and we can hardly exhaust exploring everything at once. We need a careful investigative strategy that limits the scope of each stage of the effort at hand to a specific focus, and purposely abstracts from other details in the hope of exploring them at a later stage of research.

For this reason, in the rest of this second book of the series, I will purposely focus solely on the question of determining Omar Khayyam's dates of birth and passing, and explore other aspects of Khayyam's life or works only if they pertain to that question. I will engage with other matters only if any new findings on that question themselves offer hints at initiating and exploring new insights about other aspects of his life and writings, to be explored in the later books of the series.

In the English edition of this second book, since readers may not be familiar with Arabic or Persian alphabet or writing (which are relevant to the purpose of this study as far as the horoscope, its associated manuscripts, and ways of interpreting them are concerned), or with lunar or solar Islamic calendars, I will try to explain things as if writing for broad audiences not specializing in Khayyami studies. However, I will explain in sufficient detail to satisfy the needs of specialists as well.

What follows in this book, despite its technical details, should be accessible to all readers, specialist or not. Understanding what follows requires some knowledge of Arabic or Persian alphabets and their abjad[5] numerology, as well as specific knowledge about the Zodiac months, or the nature of the astrolabe as an astronomical measurement instrument (as shown on the book cover) whose use was prevalent in medieval times and certainly during Khayyam's time. However, I am certain that with explanations offered, careful and patient readers will appreciate and understand the intricacies of the new findings reported in this volume and their historically unprecedented significance.

5. The name "abjad" is based on the first four letters (a, b, j, d) of a specific ordering of the Arabic (and Persian) alphabet, which also actually correspond roughly with the four letters of the Latin alphabet, A, B, C, D. The letters are assigned numerical values (alef=1, b=2, j=3, d=4 and so on). In the abjad alphabet, the letter "j" is used for "c" following "b." Abjad numerology was not necessarily an esoteric subject (though some have used it for that purpose, and it also has a long and rich tradition) when employed in common use; for instance, in Khayyam's treatise on algebra abjad letters are used, as are today A, B, C, D, for notating geometric figures, such as triangles, squares, and cubes. In astrolabes also numbers are rendered in abjad letters, rather than in straightforward Arabic numbers. So, readers should not fear that using abjad alphabet necessarily takes us into esoteric subjects here. They are in this book mainly discussed in terms of an alternative way of giving numbers to things.

I am not a specialist in astronomy, nor in the Zodiac system and astrology, nor in the use of astrolabe, even though for the purpose of this research I had to familiarize myself with sufficient details in these fields in order to make sense of Swāmī Govinda Tīrtha's study and to critically reevaluate his claimed discovery of Khayyam's dates of birth and passing based on his sources by way of the interpretation and calculations of Khayyam's reported horoscope.

Transdisciplinary sensitivity and curiosity is essential when conducting research of this kind, especially when dealing with a subject matter such as Khayyam whose spirit engaged all fields of knowledge in a unitary way. For the conduct and application of quantum sociological imagination, transdisciplinary research in the borderlands of disciplinary knowledge and cultural traditions is inescapable and an indispensable requirement.

Therefore, I encourage readers to be patient withe details and open to encountering and grasping seemingly unfamiliar pieces of information about separate fields of knowledge that are required for the exploration that follows. It is only through integrating separate and "chunky" topics or fragments of knowledge that we can hope for arriving at new answers that have eluded researchers for almost a millennia about Khayyam's life and works.

If you, the reader, find yourself at times confused while we walk through the maze, so to speak, know that it will not be always your fault, since the confusion can also be a result of errors historically committed by others in the subject matter being explored. Patience will eventually bear fruit, I am sure, resulting in quite interesting findings and clarifications.

In order to invite and encourage readers' careful attention to and evaluation of what they are about to read as an unprecedented discovery about Omar Khayyam's dates of birth and passing to be reported in this book, I wish to note here that I am aware that this finding will set the groundwork for new Khayyami studies and by their implication for a radical reassessment of the existence, nature, and purpose of the Khayyami Robaiyat in his life and works. So, careful attention to what follows in this book, especially for those interested in Khayyam's life and works, is necessary.

For the more attentive readers in sociology, the findings as reported in this volume also offer opportunities in an applied setting to understand how our sociologies and sociological imaginations as they have hitherto been approached and applied in Newtonian ways to social problems can be transformed in favor of more fruitful quantum ways.

For those readers even more attentive, I wish to note that the quantum sociological imagination as previously outlined in the first book and applied in this book and its broader series to solve major questions in Khayyami studies by example and illustration, offers a glimpse into how I have gone about solving, in applied ways, the quantum enigma itself, as reported in my recent work *Liberating Sociology: From Newtonian Toward Quantum Imaginations: Volume 1: Unriddling the Quantum Enigma* (2020). In other words, this study will hopefully demonstrate in practice what difference quantumizing the Newtonian structures of our sociological imaginations can actually make in providing us with a radically new and different way of solving questions and problems, including the enigmas that have surrounded Khayyam's life and works for nearly a millennia.

In the exploration that follows in this book, I present in Chapter I the basic effort Swāmī Govinda Tīrtha made in his 1941 study to determine the dates of birth and passing of Omar Khayyam. I will then, in the same chapter, evaluate that effort in more detail on the basis of its own internal logic, analysis, promise, grounding in data, and results. Then, in Chapter II, I will report on my own alternative effort at determining the true date of birth of Khayyam. This will then be followed by another effort, across the three Chapters III, IV, and V, at determining Omar Khayyam's true date of passing. This second book of the series then concludes with a summary of its findings.

Abstract

This essay, titled "Introduction to Book 2: The Dilemma and Significance of Omar Khayyam's Dates of Birth and Passing," is an introduction to the second book of the twelve-book series *Omar Khayyam's Secret: Hermeneutics of the Robaiyat in Quantum Sociological Imagination,* authored by Mohammad H. Tamdgidi. The second book is subtitled *Khayyami Millennium: Reporting the Discovery and the Reconfirmation of the True Dates of Birth and Passing of Omar Khayyam (AD 1021-1123).*

In recent decades, an uneasy consensus has generally emerged in Khayyami studies and public media regarding the dates of birth and passing of Omar Khayyam. Nowadays, one can readily find various online, bibliographic, encyclopedic, academic, or other published sources stating that Khayyam was born on Thursday, May 18, AD 1048, and died on Friday, December 4th, AD 1131. Such dates are then celebrated or commemorated according to the solar Gregorian Christian calendar used today in the West.

Obviously, the determination of the exact dates for Omar Khayyam's birth and passing, which would then identify the exact historical period during which he lived (marked by rapidly changing events, rulers, and personalities), is vital for any adequate and realistic research on his life and works amid the broader context of his times.

Studying the interplay between personal troubles and broader public issues involving

Khayyam's life in a quantum sociological imagination framework (as introduced in the preceding, first book of this series) requires such a careful determination of the outer boundaries of the chronology of his life and works in relation to those of his contemporaries amid local, regional, and broader world-history contexts. An accurate determination of the dates of Khayyam's birth and passing can provide significant information about more exact intersections of various periods of his biography with those of others amid the tumultuous times during which one or another of his writings, including his poetry, if any, may have been composed.

However, the uneasy consensus on Khayyam's dates of birth and passing as noted above is not a universally settled matter. The uneasy consensus today regarding Khayyam's birth date, if not exactly his date of passing, is rooted in a specific piece of biographical information passed on from his contemporaries to the present: his birth horoscope, or natal chart. In this regard, the study by the Indian scholar Swāmī Govinda Tīrtha is of singular importance.

Amid his major study of Omar Khayyam's life and writings in his *The Nectar of Grace: Omar Khayyām's Life and Works* (1941), one that included studies and translations of several excerpts of the philosophical (not scientific) writings and (his own) free verse translations of quatrains attributed to Khayyam, Tīrtha proposed a way of calculating Khayyam's birth date based on the horoscope of his birth handed down in a manuscript of biographical entries by the scholar of medieval Islamic period and Khayyam contemporary (as a young child) Zahireddin Abolhasan Beyhaqi, titled *Tatemmat Sewan el-Hekmat (Supplement to the Chest of Wisdom)*.

We owe to Swāmī Govinda Tīrtha the wonderful idea of determining the date of birth of Khayyam through a study of his birth horoscope, and his efforts at determining Khayyam's date of passing also offer ideas that can shed helpful lights toward solving that question as well. However, we should keep in mind that the *soundness* of the way he went about determining those dates *based on the way he interpreted and analyzed the horoscope* and other sources using the specific manuscript copies he had at hand is a completely *different* matter, worthy of critical revisitation.

In the introduction, some preliminary information about the nature of the Islamic lunar and Iranian Islamic solar calendars as well as Gregorian and Julian Western calendars are provided, while an overview of Khayyam's tombstones and their inscriptions are also shared. Tamdgidi then states his purpose in this second book of the *Omar Khayyam's Secret* series to be as follows: (1) to carefully and critically revisit Swāmī Govinda Tīrtha's study of Khayyam's horoscope which lies at the very source of the prevailing uneasy consensus today regarding the dates of birth and death of Omar Khayyam; and, if Tīrtha's findings are verifiably proven to be wrong, (2) to offer an alternative solution to the determination of the true dates of birth (and by implication and further investigation, passing) of Omar Khayyam by way of careful reexamination of that horoscope.

CHAPTER I—Contributions, Inconsistencies, and Inaccuracies of Swāmī Govinda Tīrtha's Findings Regarding Omar Khayyam's Dates of Birth and Passing

In 1941, in his published book *The Nectar of Grace: Omar Khayyām's Life and Works,* the Indian scholar Swāmī Govinda Tīrtha offered solutions to longstanding doubts about Omar Khayyam's dates of birth and passing, his approach and findings subsequently contributing significantly to the uneasy world consensus held today regarding those dates.

In the first section of this chapter I will offer an overview of how Tīrtha went about determining Omar Khayyam's dates of birth and passing, my purpose not being yet to critique Tīrtha's efforts. I will then offer in the second section of this chapter further details, explanations, and clarifications in the course of my critique of Tīrtha's contribution.

1. Tīrtha's Solutions to the Problems of Determining Omar Khayyam's Dates of Birth and Passing

In his work, Tīrtha basically proposed that the solution to the problem of determining the date of birth of Omar Khayyam can be found from the clues given in a horoscope for Khayyam's birth that had been reported long ago in

Zahireddin Abolhasan Beyhaqi's[1] *Tatemmat Sewan el-Hekmat (Supplement to the Chest of Wisdom)*, a passage of which Tīrtha said several scholars before him had taken notice but had not realized its significance for the purpose at hand (Tīrtha, p. XXXII). In his biographical entry on Khayyam, Beyhaqi (AD 1106-1170/499-565 LH) reported having accompanied his father as a seven year old on a visit with Omar Khayyam in 507 LH (AD 1113/1114), offering other biographical information about Khayyam as well. Beyhaqi's *Supplement to the Chest of Wisdom* was intended as a compilation of more or less brief biographies about important intellectual figures of Persia and Islam around his time.

More relevant to our focus here, Beyhaqi shared in his entry the birth horoscope for Khayyam in Arabic, one that Tīrtha translated as follows:

> His ascendant was the Gemini. The Sun and the Mercury were on the degree of the ascendant in the third degree of the Gemini. The Mercury was "Ṣamīmī," and the Jupiter was aspecting (Nāẓar) both from triangulation (Tathlīth). (Tīrtha, p. XXXII; the transliterations are Tīrtha's in his text)

Note that the passage quoted above is *the way Tīrtha read* and translated the handwritten original in Arabic *in the copy that was accessible* to him for his study, an image of which Tīrtha himself shared in his book, one that I again reproduce as such in Figure I.1. Tīrtha's images are in the negative, white on black background. The two manuscript columns that I reproduce from his book in Figure I.1 are parts of the longer 5-page (as such) entry by Beyhaqi on Khayyam, the rest of which I am not reproducing here, as they are not the focus of our investigation at this point.

Arabic (and Persian) is written from right to left, in lines and in pages. The statement on Khayyam's horoscope begins on the one before last line of the right column in Figure I.1, written from right to left, and continues to the end of the first top line of the left column (again reading from right to left).

As it can be seen from Figure I.1, the passage referring to Khayyam's birth horoscope was of quite a poor quality in the image Tīrtha shared in his book, such that important parts of the passage especially when giving the degree of Gemini (on the bottom line of the right column) is quite illegible. Tīrtha did not himself refer in his text to the poor quality of his original

1. Beyhaqi is transliterated as Beihaqi by Swāmī Govinda Tīrtha. Note that in this book and series, I will relay Tīrtha's transliteration style when I am quoting him, rendering the transliterations as it is found in Tīrtha's own book. In my own writing, however, I will follow the system introduced in the front matter of this book and further explained in the appendix.

image, so we may assume that he had access to a better image which was not clearly printed in his book, or at least in the copy available to us of his book today.

I have obtained a better quality image of exactly the same passage and copy from another source (Shafi 1932[2]), which I share in Figure I.2. Considering both Beyhaqi pages, the horoscope passage in Arabic is typed as follows:

و طالعه الجوزا و الشمس و عطارد على درجة الطالع فى ح من الجوزا و عطارد صميمى و المشترى من التثليث ناظر اليهما

In the above, I have rendered the Arabic passage as how others have usually done it, in particular regarding the words/letters appearing between الطالع (meaning "horoscope" or "birth chart") and من الجوزا (meaning "of the Gemini"), offering the degree of ascendant in the Gemini in Khayyam's birth horoscope.

The first thing we should note is that Tīrtha must have interpreted the letter given in the horoscope for the degree of Gemini as the letter جـ or ج (with a dot underneath, or inside for the large version of the letter, not a حـ) corresponding to number 3 in the abjad numerical system. This is despite the fact that the letter as given in the original is clearly the letter حـ (with no dots) in the Arabic alphabet, a large version of which is the letter ح. The abjad numerical system, in Arabic and in its Persian version, is basically a system of assigning numbers to the letters of a specific ordering of Arabic alphabet, "abjad" itself relaying the first four letters (الف ب ج د reading from right to left) of that alphabet corresponding to numbers 1 through 4 respectively. I will return to this system further below.

Tīrtha did not specifically spell out what the Arabic letter is that he translated into number 3, and his copy of the handwritten manuscript page was not legible for us to decipher for ourselves whether the letter in question was read by him as a حـ (a small version of the letter ح in Arabic or Persian, pronounced like the "h" in "hat," usually transliterated as ḥ) or a جـ (a small version of the letter ج in Arabic/Persian, pronounced like the "j" in "job"), both of which appear in the Arabic/Persian and the abjad alphabet and carry different numerical values following the standard abjad numerical system.

2. Al-Imam Zahireddin Abolhasan Ali Ibn al-Qasem al-Beyhaqi. 1351 LH (1932) (565 LH). *Tatemmat Sewan el-Hekmat*. Edited by Mohammad Shafi. Includes the Arabic and old Persian translations with extensive footnote commentaries. India: Lahore. Available at: https://archive.org/details/Islaam_20161228_1447/page/n197.

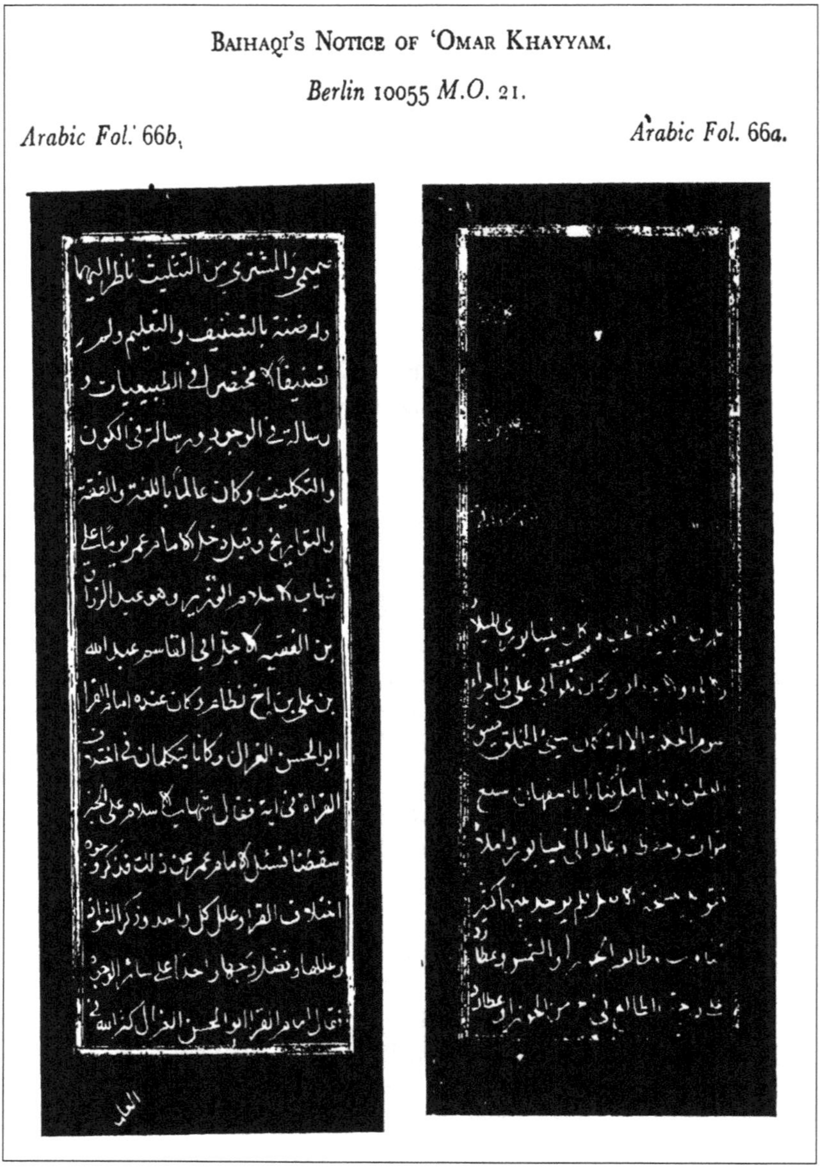

Figure I.1

Tīrtha's Scan of the First Two Pages of Beyhaqi's Biography of Omar Khayyam

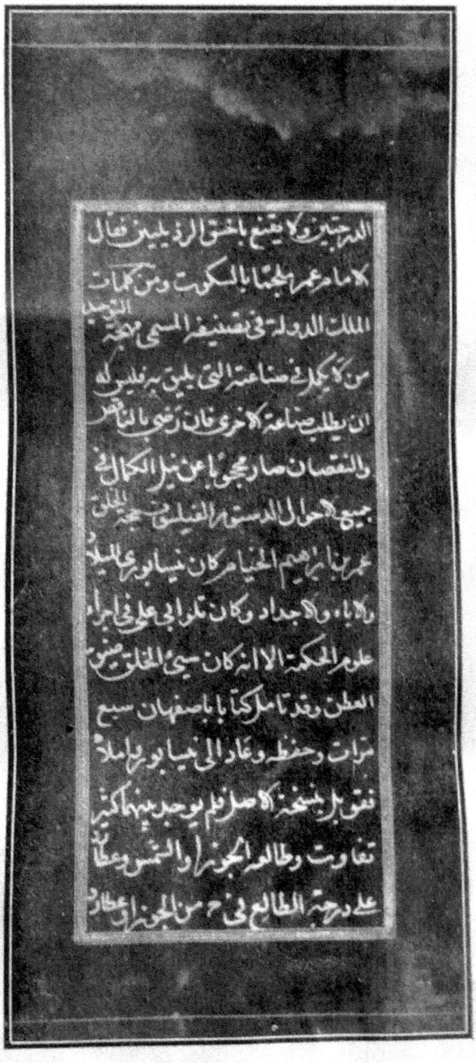
الدرجتين ولا يقنع بالمشتق الرذيلتين فقال
الامام عمر الخيام بالسكوت ومن كلمات
الملك الدولة في تصنيفه المسمى محجة التوحيد
من لا يكمل في صناعته التي يلي بها فليس له
ان يطلب صناعة اخرى فان رغب بالناقص
والنقصان صار محجوبا عن نيل الكمال في
جميع الاحوال الدستور الفيلسوف حجة الحق
عمر بن ابراهيم الخيام كان نيسابوري الميلاد
والآباء والاجداد وكان تلو ابي علي في اجزاء
علوم الحكمة الا انه كان سيء الخلق ضيق
العطن وقد تامل كتابا باصفهان سبع
مرات وحفظه وعاد الى نيسابور فاملاه
فقوبل بنسخة الاصل فلم يوجد بينهما كثير
تفاوت وطالعه الجوزا والشمس وعطارد
على درجة الطالع في ح من الجوزا وعطارد

Berlin Pm. 737, f. 66a.
(=p. 111 of this Edition).

Figure I.2

A Clearer Scan of the First Page of Beyhaqi's Biography of Omar Khayyam

In the abjad system, nine single digit (1-9), nine double digits (10-20-...-90), and 10 triple digits (100-200-...-900) and one four-digit (1000) are assigned to the alphabet letters. In scientific, religious, and other measurement practices, at times the letter, and not the digits, were used, still signifying their numerical values. In such a system, for example, the letter ج or جـ is assigned the numerical value 3 (where it is also the third letter of the abjad alphabet), and the letter ح or حـ is assigned the numerical value 8 (where it is the eighth letter of the abjad alphabet).

Importantly, note that given the poor quality of the handwritten manuscript page copied in *The Nectar of Grace*, one should assume that Tīrtha must have had read the letter as جـ to be giving it a numerical value of 3. Or, somehow, he read it as حـ, but for an unexplained reason gave it a value of 3. He does not offer any reason or explanation for why he simply took for granted that the degree of Gemini reported in the image he was reading and copying in his book was interpreted to have the numerical value of 3.

There is only a "dot" difference between these two letters in Arabic/Persian alphabet, as you can see by comparing the two letters. But the distinction is important. Either Tīrtha simply misread the faded original manuscript in Arabic, thinking that it must be a جـ corresponding to number 3, or he may have had access to another manuscript to have made such an assumption (which, as we shall see, also exists). But he does not offer references to any such manuscript, so we should assume that he simply chose, advertently or not, to interpret the letter as جـ to give it the numerical value of 3, or, he read it as حـ but still gave it the value of 3. If the letter had been determined to be the letter حـ it would have needed to be given a different numerical value according to the abjad system. Accordingly, the degree of Gemini would have had to be translated a 8, and not 3.

From the clearer copy I have separately obtained and is shared in Figure I.2, it is evident that the letter noted in the above is a حـ and not a جـ. Others who have published, commented on, and typed the same specific manuscript passage used by Tīrtha, have also interpreted it to be a حـ having a numerical value of 8. In other words, the degree of Gemini given in Khayyam's horoscope would have had to be determined, as far as that specific letter in that specific manuscript copy is concerned, to be 8.[3]

3. In Iran, one can find scholars, such as the late Kazem Bargnaysi, who in their writings (حکیم عمر خیام و رباعیات or *Hakim Umar Khayyam and Robaiyat,* 2007, p. 34) point to a copying tradition in the past whereby for the letter ج the small variation حـ is used in notations. So, instead of writing a small جـ for ج they would write a small حـ instead. This may explain why some scholars (including Tīrtha in India, as well, perhaps) have taken for granted that even a

For now (when we are trying to reconstruct his effort), let us not fault Tīrtha for why and how he arrived at the number 3 for the degree of Gemini in Khayyam's reported horoscope, and whether he is correct or not in doing so. In the above, I am simply drawing the readers' attention to how that specific original manuscript in Arabic used by Tīrtha was interpreted and translated by him, establishing the basic grounds for his further considerations for determining Khayyam's birth date.

In order to follow up on the lead provided by the above horoscope as translated by him, Tīrtha then proceeded to define the terms used in its passage as follows, using definitions traditionally used by astronomers or astrologers for the purpose.

A planet being "Ṣamīm" (or, Samimi) means that "the difference in its longitude from that of the Sun is less than 16 minutes, so that this much distance may pass before its centre reaches the centre of the Sun ... [Istilahāt-i Funūn, p. 856]"—quoted Tīrtha from his reference book of terms for astronomy/astrology (Tīrtha 1941:XXXII). This term has been Latinized in Western astrological language as "Cazimi," to which I will return in later chapters.

Regarding "Tathlīth" (Taslees), what is today called 'Trine' in astrology, Tīrtha quoted another source to note that Taslees or triangulation happens when "one planet is in the fifth sign of another planet ... because the distance between them is one third of an arc [SI Faṣl, ch. 12]" (Tīrtha 1941:XXXII).

---

small حـ could represent the letter ج leading them to assign an abjad numerical value of 3 to a letter that should be assigned the value 8 instead.

This practice is also evident in Rahim Rezazadeh Malek's renderings, in his *Khayyami Encyclopedia* (1998), of notations of figures for Khayyam's treatises in algebra or on Euclid. It is in fact possible that Malek did the latter following what he assumed to be the reason why the obviously rendered letter حـ in Beyhaqi was interpreted by Tīrtha to be a ج having an abjad numerical value of 3.

However, there is no evidence for such a confusing use of the letter حـ to represent ج in the old manuscript copies of Khayyam himself, where clearly a small letter جـ is used to represent ج in contrast to a large ح to represent itself. Even Gholam-Hossein Mosaheb, the noted mathematician, mathematics educator, and original translator of Khayyam's treatises in algebra into Persian (1960, 2000), used the letter جـ to represent ج in the graph notations of the manuscript, since even in the old manuscripts he was reading the letter جـ is used to represent ج.

I will explore more the issue of the Gemini degree in a following chapter; however it is important to note that in this chapter, this issue does not have any relevance for the presentation being made, since in this chapter we are taking for granted Tīrtha's argument which relies on interpreting the Gemini letter as having the abjad numerical value of 3, seeking to show that it is internally flawed and factually inaccurate on its own.

Since "third of an arc" can often be considered within a range and not involve an exact addition or subtraction of 120 degrees (a third of 360 degrees for a whole circle) from the position of the planet under consideration, Tīrtha quoted from the same source a passage indicating that the range of determination for whether a planet is in Taslees (Trine, or triangulation) of another is 9 degrees behind or in front of the exact 120 degrees distance, adding that "The limit for the aspect of an outer planet is between 9 degrees from behind to 9 degrees in front of it" (ibid.).

Note here that Tīrtha was offering a commentary on what is called in astrology the "orb" of aspectation here, which is about the allowable range in which a particular aspectation is said to be holding. If the distance is 120 plus or minus 9 degrees, in other words, Trine holds. If the distance is less or more than that, Trine is not considered to hold. Orbs vary in astrology for different planets, and for the "outer planet" Jupiter it is considered to be 9 degrees.

Note again that here Tīrtha's comment is not in reference to the last element of Khayyam's reported horoscope (Jupiter "aspecting" or being "Nāẓar," or Nazer, on both the Sun and Mercury), but in reference to a proximity range for determining the "triangulation" (Trine or "Tathlīth"/Taslees requirement). "Nazer" in Arabic and Persian also means "observer," or "observing."

In his text, Tīrtha did not provide any separate working or specific definition for "Nazer" as included in Khayyam's horoscope, nor did he elaborate on or draw on such a concept in his calculations or determination of Khayyam's birth date in his book.

Based on the horoscope, as interpreted by him, and the technical definitions offered above, Tīrtha then proceeded to establish the following basic parameters for Khayyam's birth date, which I quote from his text:

> (a) He was born at Sunrise.
>
> (b) The Geocentric Longitude of the Sun and Mercury was 63° (measured by the Persians from the point of Vernal Equinox 0° Aries).
>
> (c) The Geocentric Longitude of Jupiter was 63°±120°, i.e., 183° or 303° within 9 degrees of this position.
>
> (d) Mercury was tending to be Ṣamīm, i.e., approaching towards the Sun so as to come within 16 minutes of an arc. (Tīrtha 1941:XXXIII)

For later considerations, note Tīrtha's subtle wording on the line (d).

Here he seemed to be referring to the Samimi requirement not in the more strict sense of Mercury *falling within* the 16 minute range (what he himself quoted as "its longitude from that of the Sun is less than 16 minutes"), but a more approximate language of "tending to be" or "approaching" to do so.

Basically, his list meant that, according to the reported horoscope *as translated and interpreted by Tīrtha*, when Khayyam was born, if you were facing the eastern horizon in Neyshabour (where Khayyam was reportedly born[4]) you could see that the Zodiac constellation Gemini (which begins on the 60th degree from Vernal Equinox 0° Aries on the first day of the Spring of the year) was rising in the horizon. The Sun being *ascendant* at the moment of Khayyam's birth on the third degree of Gemini (hence 63° from Vernal Equinox 0° Aries, that is 30 degrees for Aries, plus 30 degrees for Taurus, plus 3 degrees into Gemini) means that Khayyam was born very early morning at sunrise, when, in addition, Mercury was very close to the Sun, within 16 minutes of it, both being on the third degree of the Gemini.

Moreover, at that very same time, Jupiter was "aspecting" (or in the literal meaning of the word used in the horoscope, "observing") them from five constellations away, that is, from within a distance whose location was somewhere around ±120 degrees from the Sun and Mercury both (since they are reported to have been very close to, within 16 or less minutes of, each other on the longitude 63°). This location could be on either side of the constellation Gemini, which means that Jupiter was on the longitude 63°±120°, that is, 183° (=63°+120°) or (63°-120°=) -57° (that is, 360°-57°=303°) from the point of Vernal Equinox 0° Aries in the opposite direction. Note that according to Tīrtha and his sources regarding technical definitions, the Jupiter could have been located 9° before or after of either of those two longitudinal possibilities.

To reiterate, the determination of Khayyam's day and time of birth was based on *Tīrtha's interpretation* of Khayyam's reported horoscope suggesting that his ascendant was Gemini with the Sun *ascendant* on the *third degree* of Gemini with Mercury being about 16 minutes or less nearby, while Jupiter was "aspecting" ("observing") them both from a distance of a roughly equilateral triangle's side's length from them, minus or plus 9 degrees.

Given the above interpretation of Khayyam's horoscope, Tīrtha then proceeded to first determine the day of month and the time of day when

4. Tīrtha, when acknowledging the assistance provided by Mr. S. R. Subrahmania Shastry in performing his astronomical calculations, reiterates that the coordinates used by him for Neyshabour (or, as he puts it, Nishapur) were Lat. 36° 13′ N. Long. 58° 45′. East Greenwich (Tīrtha, 1941:XXXVII).

Khayyam was born. To do this, he needed to determine on what day the Vernal Equinox of 0° fell around the time Khayyam was born.

To find that out, he reminded his readers that Khayyam and several other astronomers had reportedly been invited by the Seljuk king, Soltan Jalaleddin Malekshah, and his chief minister Nezam ol-Molk, to construct an observatory, undertaken in 467 LH (for which Tīrtha gives the AD 1074 Christian calendar year date). As a result of the team's work, a new Malekshahi or Jalali solar calendar was commenced from (dates below are in Lunar Hejri, any brackets or emphasis are in the original):

> ... Friday 10th Ramaḍān 471 H.[5] (15 March 1079) on which date the Sun entered Vernal Equinox [Si Fasl, ch. 6, Zīch Īlkhānī, ch. 5, Istilahāt-i-Funūn, p. 59]. The Sun takes 63 days to complete the first 62 degrees [Indian Ephemeris, Vo. I], and was in the third degree of Gemini 63 days after 15th of March, i.e., on 18th May. We thus know that 'Omar was born *at Sunrise on 18th May.* (Tīrtha 1941:XXXIII)

Let us not enter into evaluating one or another element of the above passage by Tīrtha at this point. He is basically saying that if the first day of the Persian year falling on the first day of Spring is March 15 (which presumably would be the first day in Aries), sixty three days from then falls on May 18 (30 days for Aries, 30 days for Taurus, and 3 days into Gemini, altogether adding up to the equivalent of 63 degrees from the Vernal Equinox 0°).

Tīrtha thus claimed to have discovered at least the month, day, and time, of Khayyam's birth to be at Sunrise on May 18th.

Now, to find the *year* of Khayyam's birth, Tīrtha proceeded as follows.

To expedite such a search, Tīrtha wished to establish a broad range of years within which Khayyam's birth date could fall. He reminded us that at the end of one of Khayyam's treatises, on Euclid, the date of its completion was given as follows:

> Finished copying this compilation in the Dārul Kutub of ( )[6] on the last day of Jamādi al awwal of the year 470 H. (Tīrtha 1941:XXXIII)

For Tīrtha this meant that Khayyam completed that treatise on 30th of Jumadi ul-Awwal 470 LH, coinciding, according to Tīrtha, with 20th of November 1077, that is, three years after the Malekshahi observatory was founded in 1074, and two years before the new Jalali calendar was commenced

5. Tīrtha uses the designation "H." in general in the lunar sense of the term, unless otherwise specified.

6. This was left blank in the original due to its illegibility.

in 1079 (Ibid.).

Here Tīrtha speculated that to be invited by a king to establish a new observatory (in 1074, earliest of the above dates), then compile his treatise on Euclid (in 1077), and then establish a new calendar (1079) in collaboration with current expert astronomers, Khayyam must have been at least 20 years of age at the time of the earliest of the above dates (that is, 1074). For some reason (not explicated by him) Tīrtha assumed that Khayyam also could not have been older than 55 years of age at that time. So, he concluded that the possible range of Khayyam's birth date could not be outside the range of years 1019 (=1074 minus 55, if 55 years old) and 1054 (=1074 minus 20, if 20 years old).

Having presumably discovered the month and the day of Khayyam's birth date to be May 18th, Tīrtha then proceeded to find out on which year during that range of years (AD 1019-1054) the Jupiter could have been on the coordinate given on Khayyam's reported horoscope, that is, when its longitude fell "either on 183° or 303° or within nine degrees of both these positions" (Tīrtha 1941:XXXIV). This means that the permissible ranges would have to be between the ranges (183°±9=) 174°-192° or (303°±9=) 294°-312°.

Having consulted the Indian Ephemeris data, Tīrtha found (and reported in a chart on p. XXXIV of his work) that only in years 1021, 1024, 1036, and 1048 did the Jupiter fall on longitudes that met that criteria, namely and respectively for the above years, longitudes 189.9°, 295.9°, 301.0°, and 306.3°. So, Tīrtha had narrowed down the choices of Khayyam's birth year to the above four possible dates.

Now, Tīrtha embarked upon finding a way to further narrow down the possibilities by eliminating some of the four choices per some criteria.

To do so, he went back to the criterion of the position of Mercury being "in the 63rd degree on 18th May" (ibid.). By consulting again the Indian Ephemeris data, he found that on the four possible years given above, Mercury's longitude respectively fell on the following degrees: 82.2°, 59.1°, 48.2°, 62.7°. Evidently, for Tīrtha, this showed that the only date in which Mercury fell on the longitude of, or close to (or as he had said, "approaching"), 63° is that of AD 1048; in other words, only for the Mercury on 62.7° choice the Jupiter on 306.3° fell within the range 294°-312°.

So, Tīrtha triumphantly announced: "Thus the problem is solved, and we find that Omar Khayyam was born *at Sunrise on 18th May* 1048" (Tīrtha 1941:XXXIV).

To verify the accuracy of his determination of the exact birth date of Omar Khayyam, Tīrtha continued, by another route, to what he called a "direct calculation from Zīch-Ilkhāni" (ibid.:XXXV), or the Ilkhani ephemeris data.

"I felt it necessary," Tīrtha wrote,

> ... to verify the solution by direct calculation of the positions of the Sun, Mercury and Jupiter according to their motions known to the Persians in those times. The Zīch-i Malik Shāhī by Omar Khayyam and Zīch-i Sanjarī by `Abdul Rahmān Khāzin being known in name only, the next in time comes Zīch-i Īlkhānī by Naṣīr ud Dīn Tūsī (d. 1259). The MS. of this [SML. Hyderabad] contains tables for computing the positions of planets for a hundred years commencing from first noon of the Yezdijardī year 601. (Ibid.:XXXV)

Starting from the beginning first noon of the Yazdgerdi year 601 and calculating backwards, Tīrtha found that for the time of "sunrise [4 h. 48m. a.m.] of 18th May 1048" (ibid.), corresponding to "183 Yazdijardi [Yazdgerdi] years 290 days and 7 hours before the epoch of the Zīch Īlkhānī" (ibid.),

> ... the positions of the Sun, Mercury and Jupiter are respectively 62° 23′, 62° 46′, and 303° respectively, and the Mercury is in retrograde motion hence Ṣamīmī and Jupiter in exact triangulation as stated by Baihaqī. (Ibid.)

At this point, in this first section of this chapter, my purpose is not to go into the details of this other method Swāmī Govinda Tīrtha uses to verify his claimed discovery of Khayyam's birth date. I will go back to such details later in the second section of this chapter when I conduct a critique of his efforts. For our purpose of gaining a synoptic sense of what Tīrtha was trying to do, it suffices here to consider the above quoted passage, where he states the second method also confirms his original discovery.

Note that Tīrtha's effort in verifying the discovered birth date for Omar Khayyam by another method was done basically to confirm the positions of the Sun, Mercury, and Jupiter for the date May 18th, 1048 specifically. It was *not done, starting from the scratch*, to use another method to explore all possible dates that could have fulfilled the requirements of Khayyam's horoscope.

In other words, his second method was just to check to see the date he had discovered by his first method also confirmed that May 18th, 1048, 4h. 48m. a.m. fulfills the Sun, Mercury, and Jupiter position requirements of the horoscope. Whether the numbers he reports fulfill the horoscope conditions itself is a different matter and is something we need to consider in our critique. But we should keep in mind that his second method does not necessarily rule out the possibility that the three positions could have been available for other dates in such a way that could still satisfy the horoscope conditions of Omar Khayyam's birth even as translated/interpreted by Tīrtha—not even considering whether the latter translation/interpretation on his part was correct in the first place.

This basically concluded the manner in which Tīrtha claimed to have solved the puzzle of Omar Khayyam's birth date. Following these calculations, Tīrtha proceeded in his book to offer astrological reflections on what Omar Khayyam's personality and biography would have been like, based on his horoscope and date as discovered. The information he reported based on his consultations with Mr. S. R. Subrahmania Shastry whom he credited for supplying the readings led him to conclude that "the readings remarkably coincide with the life and character of Omar Khayyam" (ibid., p:XXXVII).

For my specific purpose *in this section* and reevaluation of Tīrtha's solution to the problem at hand, such further astrological interpretations are not yet relevant or necessary, so I will skip that section for now.

It is important to note that in his *The Nectar of Grace* (1941) Tīrtha also offered his view on Omar Khayyam's date of passing as well.

His consideration, like most others speculating on the matter, was based on a few passages left from Khayyam's near-contemporaries reflecting on him and on the approximate time of his passing.

At this point in my investigation, in this section, my purpose is not to delve too deeply into a textual analysis of these literary sources in order to evaluate how Tīrtha treated them. Rather, I am just offering a brief synopsis of his approach and his conclusion so that a framework or a map, so to speak, may be drawn for further analysis and evaluation of his effort, particularly in relation to the manner in which he went about determining Khayyam's dates of birth and death.

The most important texts on which Tīrtha's attention was, like other Khayyami scholars, cast in order to determine the date of passing of Omar Khayyam were (1) the same text by Beyhaqi from which his horoscope was derived to determine his birth date, and (2) another text from *Chahar Maqaleh (Four Discourses)* (or, as Tīrtha transliterates it, "*Chahār Maqāla*'," meaning 'four essays') by Nezami Arouzi (or, "'Urūḍi," as Tīrtha transliterates his name), who regarded Khayyam his teacher as reported in the text itself, one that he wrote after Khayyam's death reflecting on an earlier meeting he had with Khayyam when later on he visited his grave.

The parts of the passage by Beyhaqi which offer some indications of around what date Khayyam was still alive and what happened on the day Khayyam died, are as follows (Tīrtha inserted Western calendar equivalents and offers his notes in his own parentheses):

> I visited the Imām with my father—May God have mercy on him!—in the year 507 H. (1113). He asked me the meaning of the following verse in Hamāsah' (Baihaqī gives the verse and how he explained). After this 'Omar asked me to enumerate different kinds of arcs. I replied there are four. The circle, the semi-circle, arc less than a semi-circle, and the arc greater than a semi-circle. Then he said to my father, "Like father like son."
>
> His *Khutan* (son-in-law or brother-in-law) Imām Muḥammad Baghdādī told me as follows:—"'Omar Khayyam was picking his teeth with a golden toothpick and reading *Ash Shafā* (Avicenna's book). When he came to the chapter dealing with "The One and the Many," he placed the toothpick between the leaves and said: 'Invite pious persons so that I may bequeath.' He bequeathed, got up and said his prayers. He took neither food nor water. After his last prayers at night, with his head bent on ground he said: 'O God! Thou knowest I perceive Thee to the utmost of my capacity. Forgive me, because my acquaintance with Thee is my Mediator to Thee,' and he expired. (Beyhaqi as quoted in Tīrtha, 1941:LI-LII)

As for the passage from Nezami Arouzi, Tīrtha offers E. Brown's translation of this text by Nezami as follows:

> "In the year five hundred and six Khwājā' Omar Khayyam and Khwājā' Imām Muẓaffar Isfazārī had sojourned at the palace of Amīr bin Sa'd in the street of Slave Traders in Balkh. I was present there. In the course of the entertainment I heard Ḥujjat ul Ḥaq 'Omar say "My grave will be in a place where every spring the northern winds will shower blossoms." I was wonder-struck, but knew that he will not utter false. When in the "thirty" I reached Nishāpūr it was four [or some or fourteen] years since that great man had concealed his face under the veil of dust, and left the world an orphan. He was my teacher. On Friday I started to visit his grave. I took a person to show me the place. He took me out to the graveyard of Ḥaira'. I turned to the right and found him buried near the basement of a garden-wall, guava and peach trees protruded from the garden and showered blossoms so profusely on the grave that it was hidden thereunder. I then remembered what he had said in Balkh and began to weep. Nowhere in all the world I had found the like of him." (Nezami Arouzi as quoted in Tīrtha, 1941:LIV-LV)

Again, let us not yet question here how Tīrtha goes about translating the original(s), our aim being simply to offer a synoptic sense of his findings.

Tīrtha was not convinced of the accuracy of the readings of the original text of Arouzi as far as one of the dates mentioned is concerned.

The first date given, 506 LH (around AD 1112/1113), when Nezami Arouzi stated he was at a meeting including Khayyam, was clear enough for Tīrtha, indicating that Khayyam was alive at that time. However, when Nezami Arouzi later in his passage stated that in the year 530 LH (AD 1135/1136) he arranged to go and visit the grave of Khayyam who had died "four," "fourteen," or "some" years before (depending on which manuscript copy is consulted, or how it is interpreted, for the word used), this did not definitively establish when Khayyam actually had died.

According to Tīrtha, it was unlikely that a man of high circles by then, that is Nezami Arouzi, could have remained ignorant for even four, let alone fourteen, years of the passing of a man of such fame as Khayyam, so dear to him (ibid, p. LV). While Tīrtha acknowledged that others have arrived, based on the above text, at the conclusion that Khayyam's death must have occurred around the year 526 LH (AD 1131/1132), he himself elsewhere in his book, when surveying what others had wrote about Khayyam, offered a different approximation for the date of passing of Khayyam.

Regarding the above, the following statements from Tīrtha are noteworthy:

> Death news flies quick. Omar Khayyām was a famous person, and Niẓāmi 'Urūdī was moving in high circles. One cannot conceive how Niẓāmi 'Urūdī remained ignorant of the demise of his famous master for "four or fourteen or some" years! or forgot him for twenty-four years "506" to "thirty"! The indecisive readings show that even the Stambul[7] MS. may have not been properly copied. (Tīrtha, 1941:LV)

> Evidently Mr. E. Browne's copyist could not decipher the Stambul MS. and wrote *Chand* (*chand'an*)[8]—on the basis of this Maulanā Qazwīnī fixes the date of Omar Khayyām 526 or a few years before 530 H. Sayyid Sulaiman Nadwī prefers to take 526 H. as the date of Omar Khayyām's demise (Omar Khayyām, p. 56). (Tīrtha, 1941:LV)

Tīrtha, elsewhere in his book, drew on another copy of the manuscript of Nezami Arouzi as found and quoted by another chronicler of Khayyam, "Yār Aḥmad Hussain Tabrīzī" (or, Yar Ahmad Rashidi Tabrizi) centuries later (AD 1462/867 LH), who offers a different account of the meeting between Nezami Arouzi and Khayyam.

In that manuscript, Nezami Arouzi was quoted as saying that he met

7. This is how Istanbul, in Turkey, was pronounced or spelled by some in the past.

8. These words "Chand" or "Chandan" in Persian mean "some" or "many."

Khayyam in the year 512 LH (not 506 LH), seeking to receive his blessings for his own planned trip to Mecca for pilgrimage.

In that meeting, Khayyam told him that when Arouzi returns (to see him next, presumably), he would find him (Khayyam) passed away and buried in a grave covered with spring blossoms. Nezami Arouzi wrote there that it happened that he returned to Neyshabour about three years later, finding his teacher passed away. He visited the grave, finding the spring blossoms covering his grave.

Comparing the Tabrizi's report to be in his view a more accurate version of Nezami Arouzi account with that commonly used still today, Tīrtha wrote:

> The readings of the MSS. of Chahār Maqāla' [sic] are evidently incorrect. We know from the MS. of Omar Khayyām's Algebra ... that in 527 H. when the MS. was copied the numerals were written in contracted Arabic words. It is quite possible that Niẓāmi Urūḍi wrote 512 in this peculiar notation which was misread by later scribes.
>
> On the whole, the version given by Tabrīzī from the MS. he actually saw may be accepted as correct. Niẓāmi Urūḍi [sic] met Omar Khayyām in the later part of 512 H., and returned after more than three years, i.e., in the early 516 H. to find that his master had demised recently. We may reasonably accept Thursday 12 Moharram 516 H. as the date of 'Omar's demise which Tabrīzī meant to give. The date inscribed on 'Omar's tomb in Nīshāpūr is 516 H. (Tīrtha 1941:LXXI)

Tīrtha finds this (Tabrizi's) copy rendition of Nezami Arouzi's account to be more plausible and an indication that Khayyam must have passed away around the year 516 LH. He believes that the dates in the original Nezami Arouzi text was written in what he calls "Arabic contract letters" customarily used in the trades (also known as Siaq script, to which I shall return in this book), but unfamiliar to later scribes, so they simply guessed, misread and miswrote the dates in future manuscripts.

In Tabrizi's account, we also find Tabrizi offering a date of Muharram 12th with a year deciphered by him as 555 LH which Tīrtha interprets to be somehow (in his view mistakenly) attributed to Khayyam's death (not birth), so ceases upon this opportunity to use at least the month and the day parts of it for his efforts in designating a day and month date for Khayyam's passing, even though he himself agreed that the specific day, Muharram 12th, 555 LH, would not fall on a Thursday (as noted by Tabrizi to fall)—aside from the fact that the year 555 LH would be a date completely in error, as Tīrtha agrees (as would all scholars), since it could be neither a date of Khayyam birth nor of his death.

So, even though the date Tīrtha finally claimed in his *The Nectar of Grace* to have discovered to be Khayyam's date of passing, that is, 516 LH, is not the one which later emerged and was established as the uneasy consensus today (525 LH, or AD 1131), he somehow contributed to the idea that Khayyam's passing may have taken place in the month of Muharram, on one or another of its days. Tīrtha thus concluded—offering a photo image of Khayyam's tombstone column as existing at that time (not the one existing in his mausoleum today)—that Khayyam's date of passing was in 516 LH.

Based on Tīrtha's calculations and considerations, therefore, Omar Khayyam's dates of birth and death were "discovered" by him to be as follows: Birth date: 4:48 a.m., Wednesday, May 18, AD 1048. Date of demise: Thursday, Muharram 12th, 516 LH (in the year AD 1122/1123).

According to these considerations by Swāmi Govinda Tīrtha, Khayyam lived about 74 solar years.

2. The Internal Inconsistencies and Factual Inaccuracies of Tīrtha's Findings

In this section, I will explore both the internal consistencies as well as the factual accuracies of Swāmī Govinda Tīrtha's solutions to the problems of determining Omar Khayyam's dates of birth and passing.

It is one thing to invalidate a claim based on external facts, and another to show that it is internally flawed, that is, it does not even fulfill the conditions it has *itself* set for its claim. Below, I will show that Swāmī Govinda Tīrtha's findings have been both internally inconsistent as well as factually inaccurate.

I will assume in this chapter that Tīrtha's reading of Beyhaqi's reported horoscope for Omar Khayyam in *Tatemmat Sewan el-Hekmat (Supplement to the Chest of Wisdom)* is correct. In other words, I will intentionally take for granted that Tīrtha's reading that at the time of Khayyam's birth the Sun and Mercury were on the Ascendant on the *third* degree of the Gemini for Neyshabour's eastern horizon was correct. I will then evaluate whether Tīrtha followed *his own* definitional requirements and procedural guidelines when using Khayyam's reported horoscope for the purpose of determining Khayyam's dates of birth and passing, and whether the data *he himself provides* support his conclusions.

Then I will also evaluate his findings in terms of their external accuracy. By external accuracy I mean to evaluate whether what Tīrtha claimed to be the astronomical data or calendrical uses supporting his findings were actually correct. I will use several sources for tracing the astronomical ephemeris data and calendrical designations needed for the evaluation.

In the following chapter, however, I will relax the assumption of correctness of Tīrtha's reading of the *third* degree of the Gemini in Khayyam's reported horoscope, and further evaluate Tīrtha's solutions for Khayyam's dates of birth and passing accordingly. But for now in this chapter, let us set aside that consideration.

Nowadays, many resources and tools are available online and readers can use them on their own for evaluating Tīrtha's efforts, and for evaluating also my own critique of his findings and the alternative solutions I will offer to the problems at hand in this book.

The resources that I have used and are readily accessible online are as follows:

1) For astronomical ephemeris data (that is, exact and detailed historical data about the sky locations of the Sun and the planets of our solar system from the vantage point of any given time and place on Earth), I have used as the main point of reference the resources offered on the site Astrodienst (https://www.astro.com), which is a widely respected astrological site online.

Even though Astrodienst is mainly an astrological website, and the astrological dimension of its purpose may not appeal or be of interest to those not inclined toward astrology, the site nevertheless uses scientifically accurate, international, and historically long-term Swiss Ephemeris database as the basis for researching horoscopes, including detailed data on longitudinal and latitudinal coordinates of any place, including Neyshabour, Iran. Free login registration is necessary for using its basic tools effectively, though for more involved tools and uses, payments may be needed. Aside from running the data engine, so to speak, of their astrological software made available online, Astrodienst's Swiss Ephemeris data from 5000 BCE to 3999 CE are also separately accessible as pdf documents on its website and can be found at this address: https://www.astro.com/swisseph/swepha_e.htm.

The basic data needed for this study were available freely at the above site. However, it is not the only site using the Swiss Ephemeris database for its purposes. Nowadays, most astrological sites and software use the same database for their calculations and chart productions, since it offers accurate historical data for the motions of the Sun and the planets.

For the purpose of chart renderings used in this book, I will use the Time Cycles Research (TCR) software whose calculations are also based on the Swiss Ephemeris historical data.

2) Iran Chamber Society's Calendar Converter can be used online to convert the present Jalali solar Islamic calendar (used in Iran), the present lunar Islamic calendar, and the Gregorian Christian calendar, to one another. This calendar is available at the following address: http://www.iranchamber.com/calendar/converter/iranian_calendar_converter.php. Any other similar and reliable online calendar can also be used.

3) Stephen P. Morse's Julian and Gregorian calendar converter, available at the address https://stevemorse.org/jcal/julian.html is also a helpful tool for translating Julian and Gregorian calendar dates to one another. It is important to note for those unfamiliar with the conversion that the number of days' differences between the two calendars conventionally varies depending on the centuries considered, as I briefly explained in this book's introduction.

Now, let us begin exploring the internal consistency and the factual accuracy of Tīrtha's findings on *his own terms*, that is, assuming that the degree of Gemini given in Khayyam's reported horoscope, as he has read its statement, is 3.

1. Julian or Gregorian?

All other findings of Swāmī Govinda Tīrtha being assumed correct, the first glaring problem we encounter when evaluating Tīrtha's claimed solution to Khayyam's birth date on Wednesday, May 18, AD 1048, 4:48 a.m., is that he seems to have completely ignored the important fact that the date he reported was based on the *Julian* Christian calendar, and *not the Gregorian* which is the calendar used today in the West. In fact, the terms Julian or Gregorian does not appear even once in his entire book, let alone the sections devoted to discovering Khayyam's dates of birth and passing.[9]

Consequently, this problem was manifested in other places as well where he specifically wished to translate specific days in other calendars into those of the Christian calendar, such as when he tried to find the day when the first day of the Persian new year in the solar calendar reformed by Khayyam and colleagues was noted.

Tīrtha offered March 15 as the first day of the Persian calendar. As anyone from Iran or the region knows, the first day of the Spring falls usually on March 21 in the Gregorian calendar, unless leap years are involved. This indicates that the sources Tīrtha was using must have been based on the

9. Swāmī Govinda Tīrtha's book, *The Nectar of Grace: Omar Khayyām's Life and Works* (1941), is freely accessible and downloadable/searchable online as a pdf document at this address: https://archive.org/details/nectarofgrace031160mbp/page/n10

Julian Christian calendar, and that he failed to account for the conversions needed between the Julian and the Gregorian calendars, when needed. Most old ephemeris data are based on Julian calendar dates, so in order to compare with the Gregorian calendar used today, the Julian dates need to be converted.

For general purposes where translation of years across the two calendars are concerned, the differences may be negligible, such as when the specific days fall in the middle of a month (so the month remains the same across the Julian or Gregorian versions, even though the day will definitely change). But if a day falls in the very beginning or end of month, and more so of a year, a few days difference (the number would vary depending on the century involved, where it would be six days for the 11th century, for example) may lead to inaccurate designations of the month or even the year.

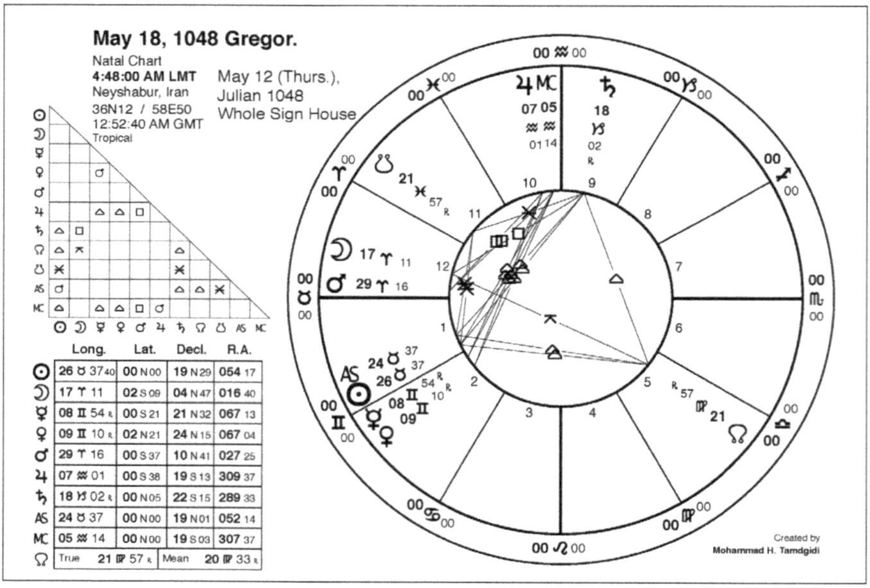

Figure I.3

Horoscope Chart for May 18, AD 1048, 4:48:00 a.m., Gregorian Calendar (May 12, AD 1048 Julian Calendar), Neyshabour, Iran

We should not ignore the implication Tīrtha's negligence in this regard had for his claiming of a specific day, Wednesday, May 18th, AD 1048, for Khayyam's date of birth. Were we to celebrate May 18 in our present,

Gregorian calendar—which nowadays we do—we are in fact celebrating a day that used to be May 12th in AD 1048, which would be a Thursday. That day will not correspond to a time that would satisfy the conditions of Khayyam's horoscope even based on the assumptions and calculations made by Swāmī Govinda Tīrtha. Conversely, if we wish to celebrate the anniversary of Khayyam's birth as reported by Tīrtha (May 18th, AD 1048 Julian), we should be celebrating it on May 24th in our present Gregorian calendar.

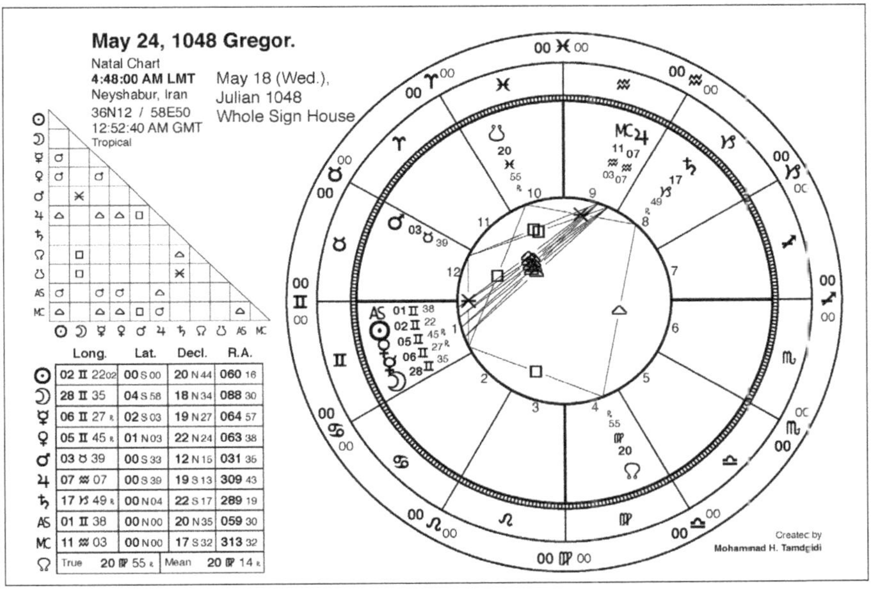

Figure I.4

Horoscope Chart for May 24, AD 1048, 4:48:00 a.m., Gregorian Calendar (May 18, 1048 Julian Calendar), Neyshabour, Iran

Above I present two natal charts, one for May 18, AD 1048, in the Gregorian calendar in Figure I.3, and one for May 18, AD 1048, in the Julian calendar in Figure I.4. As it is evident from the first chart based on the Gregorian calendar date May 18, AD 1048—the date we celebrate Khayyam's birthday today—the chart *does not actually yield a Gemini* but a Taurus Ascendant (since it falls on May 12, AD 1048 Julian). The Sun is not on that date and time in Gemini, but on the degree 26° 37′ of *Taurus*, while Mercury is a good distance away on the degree 8° 54′ of Gemini, about 12 *degrees* away from each other. This is far more than the maximum 16 *minutes* (not degrees) distance needed to fulfill their requirements of being Samimi (Cazimi) with each other according to Khayyam's reported horoscope.

By comparison, in Figure I.4, the same date and time based on the Julian Christian calendar of Wednesday May 18th, AD 1048, yields in the Gregorian calendar both the ascendance in Gemini, and the Sun being on the degree 2° 27′ (not in the third degree, by the way, let us keep in mind) of the Gemini requirements of Khayyam's horoscope. However, it is important to note that Mercury on that Julian calendar date is on the degree 6° 27′ of Gemini, about 4 *degrees* away from the Sun, which is certainly still much more than the maximum 16 *minutes* needed to fulfill the Samimi (Cazimi) requirement of Khayyam's reported horoscope. In fact, in this natal chart, Mars (on 5° 45′) is closer to the Sun than Mercury (which is in retrograde motion). To these issues I will return.

So, all things assumed correct, Tīrtha should have declared *May 24*, not May 18, to be the *Gregorian* calendar month and day anniversary for Khayyam's alleged date of birth. Some may regard this as a matter of convention and say that for old calendar dates the Julian date has usually been used for old events and anniversaries, so we should do the same for Khayyam. But, to be technically accurate, we should at least keep in mind the error in Tīrtha's account (and his total lack of consideration for the difference between the Julian and Gregorian calendars) and correct for it, since May 18th of Gregorian calendar today converts to May 12 of the Julian calendar, a date that does *not* fulfill *any* of the conditions of Khayyam's reported birth horoscope.

Omar Khayyam was a major astronomer, mathematician, and reportedly led the efforts to establish a most accurate and new Persian Islamic solar calendar in Iran. It is even more accurate than the prevalent Western solar calendar used today. So, does it not make good sense to celebrate his birth date, if and when truly known, on an astronomically and calendrically correct anniversary?

In his analysis, Tīrtha started from the Julian date of March 15 for the 0° Vernal Equinox in the Persian and Christian solar calendar, adding 63 days to arrive at his proposed May 18th Julian birth date for Khayyam. The reason he started with that date was that it itself also was being given in the Julian calendar. Had he started from March 21 (considering six days difference between the Julian and Gregorian calendars for the 11th century), which is the Gregorian calendar day starting the Persian new year at 0° Vernal

Equinox, adding 63 days (for Aries/Farvardin, and Taurus/Ordibehesht, plus three days in Gemini/Khordad, these being Persian month calendar-name equivalents of those Zodiac month names) would have yielded May 24th in the Gregorian calendar for his proposed birth date for Khayyam.

As a side note, in Figures I.3 and I.4, the reader may note that I have omitted the planets Neptune, Pluto, and Uranus, and their visual aspectations, from the natal charts. Obviously, these planets were not known to exist during Khayyam's time. Since my purpose is not to explore the present-day astrological interpretations of Khayyam's natal chart given our hermeneutic method, it is necessary that we visualize the elements of the chart as how it would have been known to Khayyam in his own time.

2. Does the Sun-Mercury Samimi (Cazimi) and the Ascendant Fall on the Same Third Degree of the Gemini?

In his efforts to solve the puzzle of Khayyam's birth date by way of his reported horoscope, Tīrtha made three attempts.

In the first attempt, he started by giving the reader the impression that he had assumed that the Sun was in degree 3° of Gemini, and used the Vernal Equinox degree of 63° to convey that impression. For example, he wrote:

> The Sun takes 63 days to complete the first 62 degrees [Indian Ephemeris, Vol. I], and was in the third degree of Gemini 63 days after 15th March, i.e., on 18th May. We thus know that 'Omar was born at Sunrise on 18th May. (p. XXXIII)

Or, elsewhere, when calculating the 120 degrees (with ±9 degrees orb allowance) needed for Sun/Mercury being in "triangulation" (Trine) with the Jupiter, he wrote:

> (c) The Geocentric Longitude of Jupiter was 63°±120°, i.e., 183° or 303° or within 9 degrees of this position. (Ibid.)

So, when it came to his further offering the position of Mercury for the four candidate years 1021, 1024, 1036, and 1048, where he found only the year 1048 resulting in a degree 62.7° for Mercury, he was assuming that the latter (1048) fulfills the Samimi (Cazimi) requirement of Khayyam's reported horoscope. He stated:

> The only year when Mercury was in the 3rd degree of Gemini on 18th May is 1048. Thus the problem is solved, and we find that 'Omar Khayyam was born at Sunrise on 18th May 1048. (p. XXXIV)

There are several significant problems with the assumptions and conclusions Tīrtha made in his first attempt at solving the puzzle.

First, he had not given an exact degree and minute location for the Sun. Being on the third degree could range from 1-60 minutes. So, by just noting that the Sun was on the third degree did not necessarily lead to the conclusion that its minute's position allowed for the Samimi (Cazimi) condition of the horoscope to be met, a conjunction that is determined by a rather strict criteria, 16 *minutes*, for its condition to be fulfilled. Technically, the Sun and Mercury could be even on the same degree, but not close enough in *minutes* to fulfill the Samimi ("being in the heart of the Sun") requirement, because a degree is comprised of sixty minutes.

Second, Tīrtha himself reported the Mercury's position to be 62.7°. This was given in decimal units. That location would be the equivalent of 62° and (0.7 x 60=) 42 minutes.[10] 42 minutes is still *18* minutes away from the next degree (3rd). So, even *if we assume* the Sun was exactly on the first minute of the third degree, the 18 minute difference could *not* fulfill the maximum 16 or even 17 minutes Samimi requirement of Khayyam's horoscope. If the Sun was in later minutes of the third degree, the difference would be *even more*. We have no indication or evidence reported by Tīrtha that the Sun was indeed on the first minute of the third degree of Gemini; as we shall see, he in fact reported later in his text in two occasions that the Sun was not even on the third degree of Gemini but somewhere in the second degree, and even then its corresponding distance from Mercury as modified in those occasions was more than 18 minutes in distance. To this I shall return later.

Third, in any case, as evident in the quoted passages above, even Tīrtha was not reporting Mercury to be on the third degree of Gemini, so he cannot declare that it fulfills the third degree of Gemini requirement of the horoscope. Given the missing details, there is absolutely no basis here for confidently claiming the problem solved, since the requirement of the horoscope involving a Samimi (Cazimi) configuration in the third degree of the Gemini had not been met, according to Tīrtha's *own* reported (or not) information in the first effort he made to solve the puzzle.

I think it is for this reason that Tīrtha used the words "tending" and "approaching" when referring to Mercury's retrograde motion elsewhere in

10. From the table of Jupiter positions Tīrtha offers on page XXXIV, it is evident that he is using a decimal system for offering the positions. So, we can safely assume that he means 0.7 of degree here, and not 7 minutes. The latter would in fact not help him in his argument, since it would take the Mercury even further away from the third degree needed to fulfill the reported horoscope requirements, whether or not it is moving straight or in retrograde.

his account, trying to persuade his readers to assume that Samimi (Cazimi) conditions were not really there but they would be "approached." He wrote:

> (d) Mercury was tending to be Ṣamīm, i.e., approaching towards the Sun so as to come within 16 minutes of an arc. (p. XXXIII)

In other words, the above passage is a rather clear indication that even for Tīrtha it was no yet evident that we already had a Samimi conjunction at hand, but that it was being "approached." Tīrtha had realized that the numbers he found did not exactly fulfill the horoscope requirement of Mercury falling close enough to the Sun to fulfill the Samimi (Cazimi) requirement, so he used the language of "approaching" to sidestep the condition.

Therefore, it is not *at all* evident that Tīrtha succeeded in his first attempt to solve the puzzle of Khayyam's birth date. The details he provided *himself* did *not* meet the requirements of the reported horoscope.

Apparently not fully satisfied himself, Tīrtha made a second attempt to calculate the results using the Ilkhani ephemeris (which he transliterated as Zīch Īlkhānī). We do not need to go into the details of how he performed that calculation (some of which I found to be themselves in error, in fact), since whatever the procedure, his reported findings themselves should support the claim he made for having discovered Khayyam's birth date.

Important is to carefully consider the now more specific numbers and details he actually reported for the location of the Sun and the Mercury according to his second attempt.

In his tables offered for his second attempt, Tīrtha reported the location 62° 27′ for the Sun (p. XXXV), and then the location 62° 46′ for Mercury (p. XXXVI). These numbers are important to consider. Note that these numbers reflect distances from the Vernal Equinox 0°. If we ignore the 60 degrees of each for the Aries and Taurus Zodiac signs, we basically have the locations 2° 27′ for the Sun (p. XXXV), and then 2° 46′ for Mercury (p. XXXVI) at hand.

First, now it becomes evident that even the Sun was not on the third degree of Gemini, according to Tīrtha's own second attempt efforts. So, here, in his second try, Tīrtha had *himself* basically undermined *his own* claim in his first attempt that the Sun was on the third degree of Gemini.

Second, Mercury was also found to be still *not* on the third degree of the Gemini, but somewhere in the second degree of the Gemini.

Third, these thankfully more specific numbers for the locations of the Sun and Mercury now clearly reveal that their difference of (46-23=) 23 minutes does *not* fulfill the Samimi (Cazimi) requirement of Khayyam's reported horoscope. The difference was clearly beyond the maximum 16 minutes needed for the Samimi conjunction to happen.

Remarkably, when we consider Tīrtha's third chance or attempt to set things straight, we find the following.

If you recall, in Figure I.4, I reported that according to the Swiss Ephemeris data, Mercury's location at the time proposed by Tīrtha at sunrise May 18, AD 1048 (Julian), was 6° 27′ of Gemini. In his first two efforts, Tīrtha gave consistently the location numbers around the 2° 27′ to 2° 46′ (or, decimally, 62.7°) spots.

—		True Geocentric				Right ascension		Declination		Geocentric daily motion in minutes	Heliocentric Longitude	
		Longitude		Latitude								
		°	′	°	′	Hrs.	Mins.	°	′		°	′
Sun	..	62	20	..	..	4	0.8	20	44	57	..	..
Moon	..	88	27	—5	3	5	53.2	18	30	733	..	..
Mercury	..	66	25	—2	3	4	20.1	19	29	—32	237	29
Venus	..	65	39	1	4	4	14.2	22	25	—37	241	1
Mars	..	33	37	—0	34	2	6.1	12	15	44	13	45
Jupiter	..	307	1	—0	39	20	38.4	—19	15	0	296	36
Saturn	..	288	27	0	3	19	20.0	—22	14	—2	284	16
Uranus	..	182	55	0	42	12	11.8	—0	31	—1	185	39
Neptune	..	13	23	—1	43	0	51.9	3	44	2	11	54
Pluto	..	313	50	—9	53	21	21.0	—25	58	0	312	23
Node	..	170	15	..	..	..	..	..	..	—3	..	..

Figure I.5

Swāmī Govinda Tīrtha's Listing of Planetary Locations Used to Offer His Astrological Reading (on page XXXVII) of Khayyam's Natal Chart

When starting his report on the astrological significance of the findings for understanding Khayyam's life, Swāmī Govinda Tīrtha shared another chart on page XXXVII of his book, *The Nectar of Grace* (1941), this time for the more specific location of Neyshabour. In doing so he gave, it seems inadvertently, the more accurate degree figures for the Sun and Mercury that even more clearly invalidated his earlier two attempts. I have included an image of his chart in Figure I.5.[11]

11. Note that in his table as shared in Figure I.5, the coordinates for Uranus, Neptune, and Pluto were given because Tīrtha was trying in that section of his text, based on the opinions of his expert sources, to draw astrological interpretive conclusions from the discovery he had reported about Khayyam's date of birth. Tīrtha's intention was not hermeneutic, but

In the chart, one can see that Tīrtha offered (again starting from the Vernal Equinox 0°) the positions 62° 20′ for the Sun, 66° 25′ for Mercury, and 307° 1′ for Jupiter. If you recall, he had previously given the two degree locations 62.7° for Mercury, and assumed the degree of 3° for the Sun, later sharing the location of 2° 27′ for Mercury in his second attempt.

Compare these with the Swiss Ephemeris chart numbers 2° 22′ for the Sun, 6° 27′ for Mercury, and 7° 7′ for Jupiter (the latter would be from the point of Vernal Equinox 0° Aries in the opposite direction about 360-60=300+7, about 307° to compare with Tīrtha's figures[12]). So, it happens that Tīrtha finally provided a chart of figures that nearly corresponds to the data *for Neyshabour* as reported in the Swiss Ephemeris, ones that altogether invalidates all of Tīrtha *own attempts* to argue that his proposed date and time meet the third degree of Gemini and Samimi requirements of Khayyam's reported horoscope.

Just consider again the significance of the numbers in this chart (Figure I.5). The figures given by Tīrtha (very close to the Swiss Ephemeris figures I have offered for that day and time as reported in Figure I.4) show that (1) neither the Sun nor Mercury were in the third degree of the Gemini, and (2) that their distance was about 4 degrees apart, which is *way* beyond the maximum 16 *minutes* requirement of Samimi (Cazimi) conjunction.

These numbers, reported by Tīrtha himself, do not support at all a natal chart in which the Sun and the Mercury are supposed to be in Samimi (Cazimi) conjunction with the degree of the Ascendant on the third degree of Gemini.

So, we have been able to demonstrate that Tīrtha's solution, on its own, is internally inconsistent. I have not even used external facts to prove this point. I have simply demonstrated that even Tīrtha's own numbers as reported in specific terms *by him* do *not* result in the definitive solution he claimed to offer for Khayyam's birth date puzzle. Neither the Sun, nor Mercury, fell on

---

to simply make astrological interpretation of the chart from the standpoint of his own time around 1941, not of Khayyam's time. So, we may ignore the numbers of the three planet given here.

12. Regarding the position of Jupiter, it is noteworthy that while my Figure I.4 displays a position of 7° 7′ for it, which results in a distance of 115° from the position of the Sun at 2° 22′, the distance reported in Tīrtha's second effort calculations between 62° 23′ for the Sun and 303° for Jupiter is 230° 37′ or, to deduct from 360°, equal to 129° 23′. Both these distances fulfill the Taslees or triangulation (Trine) requirement, though their difference (between Tīrtha's own calculation and that based on our Swiss Ephemeris data as displayed in Figure I.4) is noteworthy.

the third degree of the Gemini, and their distance did not fulfill the Samimi (Cazimi) requirement of the horoscope.

We do not even have to investigate the position of the Jupiter for now to see that Tīrtha basically failed in finding a birth date that fulfills Khayyam's reported horoscope convincingly.

When considering the Swiss Ephemeris horoscopes for May 18 (Julian, as proposed by Tīrtha) I have offered, which falls on May 24 on the Gregorian calendar, we are also confirmed in our evaluation of Tīrtha's inconsistent attempts at solving the puzzle at hand. So, let us know briefly turn to evaluate his findings based on external accuracy and facts as found in the Swiss Ephemeris data.

In Figure I.4, first, we find that the Sun is not in the degree 3° of Gemini (but about two thirds of a degree away from it, on 2° and 22′). In a sense, the external facts based on our own Swiss Ephemeris also has confirmed that on the date Tīrtha proposed as a solution, the Sun was not even on the third degree of the Gemini, but on 2° and 22′.

Second, again considering Figure I.4, we also find that Mercury on this date did not fall on degree 3° or even 2° of Gemini. It fell on its location 6° 27′.

Therefore, third, Mercury was not within a 16 *minutes* distance from the Sun, but about 4 *degrees* away from it; so, it was not Samimi (Cazimi) with the Sun at all, let alone "approaching" it closely enough any ways, according to the conventional definitions Tīrtha himself reported and used in interpreting the requirements of Khayyam's reported horoscope.

Fourth, Khayyam's reported horoscope requires that the Sun and the Mercury, being Samimi with one another (16 minutes difference in distance), should also conjunct with, or fall on, the degree of the Ascendant. However, as is evident from Figure I.4, at the time (4:48:00 a.m.), the Ascendant was on the location 1° and 38′ of Gemini. Based on the Swiss Ephemeris data, it was only at 4:50:33 a.m. that the Sun met the Ascendant at about 2° and 22′, both still away from the position of Mercury at 6° 27′, making it altogether impossible that the Sun, the Mercury, and the Ascendant could be at once within the same (third) degree near one another that morning.

These four serious flaws certainly point to the fact that Tīrtha's solution did not fulfill the requirements of Khayyam's reported horoscope, as read by Tīrtha. Again, note here that in this section, we are simply taking for granted and assuming Tīrtha's reading of Khayyam's horoscope regarding the requirement of the Sun and Mercury being Samimi (Cazimi) on the *third* degree of Gemini is correct. The requirement of being Samimi, according to Tīrtha's own cited definitions, is that a distance of *at most* 16 *minutes* must be observed between the two celestial bodies.

The fact is, therefore, that based on Tīrtha's *own* reported calculations (by two methods) in his *The Nectar of Grace* (1941) it is impossible to claim an unequivocal "solution" to the problem of Khayyam's birth date. A combination of unreported and reported details in Tīrtha's solution provides insufficient grounds for confirming the accuracy of his calculations for Khayyam's birth date to fall on May 18, AD 1048 (which we now know to be according to the Julian calendar). He even ignored the difference between the Julian and Gregorian calendars for the purpose.

We should realize that Tīrtha's calculations for the distance of Jupiter, and presumably of Mercury, from the Sun, as reported in his range of years for 1019-1054 on page XXXIV of *The Nectar of Grace* were based, as he himself acknowledges, on "tropical Longitudes" of these celestial bodies, and not necessarily those observed from the exact birth location in Neyshabour. This again indicates a lack of sufficient attention to details needed for arriving at an indubitable date for the birth of Omar Khayyam, and may explain why in his first two attempts he reported wrong numbers for the position of Mercury. His astrological table (see Figure I.5), however, clearly took the location of Neyshabour into account and offered more accurate location data for the planets. Of course, we have much easier access to data today than Tīrtha had in his time.

Of course, we should always offer due credit to Tīrtha for the basic idea that Khayyam's birth date can be discovered by way of examining his reported horoscope. Tīrtha's efforts in doing so is duly noted and appreciated as well. However, this does not mean that we can ignore the internal inconsistencies, nor the factual inaccuracies, of the attempts he made to solve the puzzle. Khayyami studies ever since his time have been significantly affected by his reported findings that are now found to be fundamentally in error. We need to rectify his errors as best as we can.

3. How About the Location of Jupiter?

Let us now turn our attention briefly to Jupiter at that time and consider other aspects of Tīrtha's solution that were supposed to fulfill Khayyam's reported horoscope, as Tīrtha read it.

Recall that Tīrtha's method as reported in his book was to determine the position of Jupiter being in triangulation (Trine) with the Sun in the years between AD 1019 and 1054. Based on his Indian ephemeris data sources and calculations, Tīrtha found only four of those years—AD 1021, 1024, 1036, and 1048—to have been years when on May 18th (presumably now, based on what we demonstrated above, of the Julian calendar) the distance between the Sun (presumed to be on degree 3°) and Jupiter were in Trine, that is, when Jupiter was in a (what is today called) orb's difference of plus or minus 9 degrees from a location 120 degrees distant from the Sun. He then argued that only in one of them (on AD 1048), the Mercury position satisfied the horoscope requirements (which now we know it does not).

From the Figure I.4, which offers the location of Jupiter to be 7° 7′ of Aquarius we can determine that the distance of Jupiter on that date from the Sun is about 115° (three full constellations of Pisces, Aries, and Taurus, being 30 degrees each, plus about 23 degrees in Aquarius, plus about 2 degrees in Gemini), which is within a distance range of 120° from the Sun plus or minus 9 degrees. So, this does fulfill Tīrtha's Jupiter location requirement, also (at 115+4=119 degrees distance) fulfilling the Trine requirement for Mercury, despite Mercury's not being clearly in a Samimi position relative to the Sun. Tīrtha's own numbers also more or less support the Trine distance requirement of Khayyam's reported horoscope.

However, there is another aspect of Tīrtha's investigation of Khayyam's horoscope that is absent in his effort. If you recall, Khayyam's horoscope ends with a reference to Jupiter "observing" ("Nazer") or "aspecting" both the Sun and the Mercury from triangulation (Trine). Although I will elaborate on this issue more in the following chapter, I wish to draw the reader's attention to that omission, which in my assessment points to Tīrtha's not realizing what significance that qualification had in the horoscope of Khayyam.

Suffice it to say here that we should keep in mind the position of Jupiter on this date. According to Tīrtha's findings, at the time of Khayyam's birth Jupiter was in the visible part of the sky. In astrology, planets' aspectation or observation of one another can be of the left-handed (counter-clockwise) and the right-handed (clockwise) kind, considering the chart's circle. If we consider the apparent motion of planets in the chart moving clockwise, in the May 18, AD 1048 chart, whether as Tīrtha has found or we did independently, Jupiter is in the visible part of the sky in the (emerging) day time, and as far as the shorter arc of the distance of observation is concerned moving clockwise, it is the Sun and Mercury that are "observing" the Jupiter in a right-handed way.

However, significantly, amid the precious few words of our master astronomer Khayyam's reported horoscope, we are specifically told that in his chart, it was Jupiter that was "observing" (presumably over the shorter arc[13] of the distance clockwise) the Sun and the Mercury, and not the other way around. So, in other words, we have a "right-handed" observation clockwise of the Sun and the Mercury Cazimi by Jupiter "from behind," so to speak, and not a longer arc around the circle, left-handed observation of the same by Jupiter. For this condition to be met, Jupiter must be in the invisible part of the sky, below the Earth, so to speak, in the night sky. In the May 18, AD 1048 date, however, we have the opposite configuration going on; the Jupiter is day-time emergent in the visible part of the sky, and its right-handed observation, clockwise, of the Sun-Mercury Samimi (Cazimi) can only happen over the longer distance arc of the natal chart.

I will return to this matter later in this volume. What is important to note here, as far as our critique of Tīrtha's effort is concerned, is that we find absolutely nothing in his efforts commenting on the significance of the references made in Khayyam's reported horoscope to the nature of the direction of the "observation" going on between the Jupiter on one hand, and the Sun-Mercury Cazimi, on the other. Had he paid closer attention to the subtlety of the aspectation and observation (Nazer) being reported in Khayyam's reported horoscope, one that in my view is itself indicative of the mind of a highly skilled astronomer at work expressing a precise horoscope statement, Tīrtha would have perhaps found another reason to doubt the accuracy of his own claimed discovery.

4. Tīrtha's Solution to Determining Khayyam's Date of Passing

Before concluding this chapter, it is necessary that I share a few words about Tīrtha's determination of the date of passing of Omar Khayyam.

As reported earlier, in his *The Nectar of Grace* (1941) Tīrtha tended to disregard the conclusions reached by most scholars for determining the date of passing of Khayyam based on the ambiguously scripted or deciphered conventional text from Nezami Arouzi in his *Chahar Maqaleh (Four*

13. When considering the significance of shorter or longer arcs of aspectation in reading astrological charts, we may recall the interesting question the old Khayyam asks the child Beyhaqi in 507 LH referring to types of arcs. This does not mean necessarily that Khayyam had his own natal chart in mind when asking that question. It just means that technical matters such as the shorter or longer arcs round natal charts can have significant interpretative value in how such charts are read and understood. In other words, we may consider that Khayyam's question from the child Beyhaqi was possibly related to astrological considerations lengths and kinds of arcs may evoke.

Discourses) regarding Khayyam.

As noted early on in this chapter, the young child Beyhaqi, future author of *Tatemmat Sewan el-Hekmat (Supplement to the Chest of Wisdom)*, met Khayyam during the year 507 LH, and this leaves little doubt for scholars that Khayyam was alive then. So, whether or not Nezami Arouzi's meeting him in 506 LH is accurate, we do not need any of the two accounts of his meeting Khayyam (on 506 LH or 512 LH) to corroborate his being alive around then.

In the same standard account, Nezami Arouzi reported coming back to Neyshabour in the year 530 LH to visit Khayyam's grave several ("four, fourteen, or some") years after Khayyam's passing and recalled the latter's comments years earlier (in 506 LH) about his then future grave to be always showered by blossoms. Others have used that ambiguous account to suggest that Khayyam must have died "four" years before 530 LH, that is, in 526 LH, which has resulted in the present, uneasy consensus year of AD 1131 for Khayyam's passing.

Tīrtha was not convinced, leaning more on the "fourteen" years reading of the word, which supported the notion of Khayyam's having passed away around 516 LH. However, Tīrtha still asked how it is possible that Nezami Arouzi, claiming to be so devoted to Khayyam, could have ignored Khayyam's death for fourteen years, if it was the case that Khayyam had died in 516 LH (as etched on his tomb, the one standing today, one that preceded it at the time Tīrtha conducted his study).

So, mistrusting those particular copies of Nezami Arouzi's manuscript containing such an ambiguity about "four, fourteen, or some," Tīrtha shifted his attention to a different copy of the manuscript as reported by Yar Ahmad Rashidi Tabrizi in his *Tarabkhaneh (House of Joy)*, one that the latter reports (written in AD 1462/867 LH) having had access to and read, offering a different account of Nezami Arouzi's meeting with Khayyam.

I have already relayed this account briefly, according to which Nezami Arouzi reported having met Khayyam in 512 LH before heading to Mecca for pilgrimage. In that meeting Khayyam told Arouzi that upon return he would find Khayyam dead and buried in a grave covered with blossoms. Nezami Arouzi was surprised at this prediction, but knew a man of Khayyam's stature would not speak lightly of such things. So, when he returned three years later, he found Khayyam having passed away recently. Tīrtha concludes that this corroborates his inclination that Khayyam, as also noted on his gravestone at the time of his writing, died in the year 516 LH (AD 1122/1123).

It happens that Rashidi Tabrizi in his account in *Tarabkhaneh (House of Joy)* offered a specific date for Khayyam, for which a numerical notation was used that has baffled scholars, one that Tīrtha says was an abbreviation script for numbers used by accountants in the trades (which is a script known as Siaq, an elaborate system of short-hand used especially by merchants and accountants in traditional bazaars). Since my purpose at this point in this chapter is not yet to launch my own search for Khayyam's date of passing, what I wish to point out here regarding Tīrtha's effort is that another error was also committed here, one that strangely, if not in an amusing way, explains why Khayyam's date of passing has been determined to fall in December of whatever year is attributed to his death.

In the Tabrizi passage, the date given for Khayyam was Thursday, Muharram 12th of the year --- (in Tabrizi copy, there are three symbols of the same digit, which let us for now consider to be illegible). Tīrtha, thinking that the year is 555 LH, attributed that date to Khayyam's year of death, what he himself then also regarded to be wrong, since on that year, he wrote, Muharram 12th did not fall on a Thursday. (In any case, no one believes that Khayyam could have died in the year 555 LH.) So, dismissing the year part of the date given by Tabrizi, once Tīrtha decided that 516 LH is the more likely date of Khayyam's passing, he basically must have told himself something like, "well, why not use the month and day of that inaccurate date as the month and day of Khayyam's passing." More fittingly so, since it happens that in 516 LH, Muharram 12th did fall on a Thursday.

Now, it happens that in the year 526 LH, which is a preferred passing date for Khayyam by some nowadays, Muharram 12th also fell on a Thursday. So, all these coincidences have led to the Muharram 12th to "stick" on the date of Khayyam's death, so to speak, being reported everywhere now for Khayyam's demise.

The only complication that explains why Dec. 4th is chosen in the Christian calendar, rather than Dec. 11th (according to the Gregorian calendar), is what I noted before regarding the use of Julian calendar for offering December 4th as a date. It seems Tīrtha's penchant for the Julian calendar (or just simply not taking the difference of Christian calendars into consideration inadvertently) led others to use the Julian calendar not only for Khayyam's date of birth (May 18, AD 1048), but also for his passing on Dec. 4, AD 1131. It may well be the case that those sticking with a Julian birth date believe it to be more consistent to use also the Julian date of demise for Khayyam. I doubt this is the reasoning behind Dec. 4th, rather than Dec.

11th, as a choice, but it is worth taking into account. For the 12th century, the difference of days between the Gregorian and Julian calendars increases to seven days (in contrast to its being six days in the 11th century); so, the equivalent of Dec. 4th (Julian) will be Dec. 11th (Gregorian).

What I wish to point out here is that the whole idea of using Muharram and December for Khayyam's date of passing—months which, by the way, do not necessarily always coincide as explained before regarding the difference between lunar and solar calendars—can be traced to a seeming error (or misunderstanding) on the part of Tīrtha that the peculiar date given in Tabrizi was in reference to Khayyam's date of passing, rather than to his date of birth or some other event.

Despite Tabrizi's obvious offering of a *birth location* alongside that *birth date*, indicating that he must have actually meant the (disputed) date being given in the text to be that of Khayyam's birth rather than one for his death, Tīrtha's misreading of the odd digits of the year led him to think that the date was for Khayyam's *death*, which has led to our inheriting his error in the form of being stuck with a Muharram (for 516 LH) and December (for 526 LH) date for Khayyam's passing.

As a last, seemingly unimportant, but perhaps not so, point to conclude this chapter, I should note that Tīrtha makes another translation error regarding the kinds of blossoms covering Khayyam's grave, as reported by Nezami Arouzi. Arouzi clearly notes the blossoms to be from the trees of apricot (zardalu) and pear (amroud). However, for some reason, perhaps due to his own taste or the kind of fruits available more readily in India, Tīrtha preferred to attribute them to "guava and peach trees." As we shall see, even this seemingly minute detail and error may prove helpful in determining Khayyam's true month of passing.

Just to speculate, it may suffice here to consider that if Tīrtha's Muharram 12th of LH 516 was the date of Khayyam's passing, it would fall on an early spring (March 30) time, when fruit blossoms were still blooming, not yet falling on the grave (if we follow Nezami Arouzi's account, in Yar Ahmad Rashidi Tabrizi's version, that Arouzi arrives just at the time Khayyam had passed away). And if we consider Muharram 12 to be in the year AD 526, which is a consensus date held today, it would fall on Dec. 4 or 11th (depending on considering Julian or Gregorian versions of the calendar), a time when ground is most likely covered with snow, or at least when it is past the season when Khayyam's grave would be covered with fruit blossoms, if, again, it was a time when Arouzi was visiting a recently deceased Khayyam.

From the foregoing in this chapter, it should be clear by now that there is absolutely no defensible grounds for considering Wednesday, May 18, AD 1048 to be Omar Khayyam's birth date.

For all practical purposes, Iran and the world are now celebrating Khayyam's date of birth on the *wrong* date. Tīrtha's otherwise worthwhile effort passes neither the test of internal consistency nor that of external, factual accuracy of his *own* premises and procedures.

Nor can we be sure that the exact year, let alone the month and day, of Khayyam's passing as proposed by Tīrtha or as prevalently accepted today are accurate.

Having deconstructed Tīrtha's solution to Omar Khayyam's birth date in this chapter and established its errors and failure in definitively determining that important date, I will turn in the next chapter to exploring further why and where Swāmī Govinda Tīrtha went wrong in his worthwhile efforts and how we may still find a way of finding a definitive solution to the problem at hand.

Abstract

This essay, titled "Contributions, Inconsistencies, and Inaccuracies of Swāmī Govinda Tīrtha's Findings Regarding Omar Khayyam's Dates of Birth and Passing," is the first chapter of the second book of the twelve-book series *Omar Khayyam's Secret: Hermeneutics of the Robaiyat in Quantum Sociological Imagination,* authored by Mohammad H. Tamdgidi. The second book is subtitled *Khayyami Millennium: Reporting the Discovery and the Reconfirmation of the True Dates of Birth and Passing of Omar Khayyam (AD 1021-1123).*

As a part of his book *The Nectar of Grace: Omar Khayyām's Life and Works,* published in 1941, the Indian scholar Swāmī Govinda Tīrtha tried to resolve longstanding doubts about Omar Khayyam's dates of birth and passing, his approach and findings subsequently contributing in a significant way to the uneasy consensus held today in the world regarding those dates.

In his work, Tīrtha basically proposed that the solution to the problem of determining the date of birth of Omar Khayyam can be found in following up on the clues given in a horoscope for Khayyam's birth that had been reported long ago in Zahireddin Abolhasan Beyhaqi's *Tatemmat Sewan el-Hekmat (Supplement to the Chest of Wisdom)*, a passage of which Tīrtha noted several scholars before him had taken notice but had not realized its significance for the purpose at hand (Tīrtha, p. XXXII). Based on Tīrtha's calculations and considerations, Omar Khayyam's dates of birth and death were "discovered" by him to be as follows: Birth date: 4:48 a.m., Wednesday, May 18, AD 1048. Date of demise: Thursday, Muharram 12th, 516 LH (in the years AD 1122/1123).

In the first section of this chapter, Tamdgidi offers an overview of how Tīrtha went about determining Omar Khayyam's dates of birth and passing. His purpose therein is not yet to critique Tīrtha's efforts. In the second section, however, the author explores both the internal consistencies and the factual accuracies of Swāmī Govinda Tīrtha's solutions to the problems of determining Omar Khayyam's dates of birth and passing. It is one thing to invalidate a claim based on external facts, and another to show that it is internally flawed, that is, it does not even fulfill the conditions it has itself set for its claim.

In offering his critique in this chapter, Tamdgidi assumes that Tīrtha's reading of Beyhaqi's reported horoscope is correct. In other words, he specifically takes for granted that Tīrtha's reading that at the time of Khayyam's birth the Sun and Mercury were on the Ascendant on the *third* degree of the Gemini for Neyshabour's eastern horizon was correct. He then evaluates whether Tīrtha followed his own definitional requirements and procedural guidelines when using Khayyam's reported horoscope for the purpose of determining Khayyam's dates of birth and passing, and whether the data he himself provides support his conclusions. Tamdgidi also evaluates Tīrtha's findings in terms of their external accuracy. By external accuracy he means to evaluate whether what Tīrtha claimed to be the astronomical data or calendrical uses supporting his findings were actually correct. He shows in the chapter that Swāmī Govinda Tīrtha's findings have been for the most part both internally inconsistent as well as factually inaccurate.

Tamdgidi demonstrates in the chapter that there is absolutely no defensible grounds for considering Wednesday, May 18, AD 1048 to be Omar Khayyam's birth date. For all practical purposes, Iran and the world are celebrating Khayyam's date of birth on the *wrong* date. Tīrtha's otherwise worthwhile effort passes neither the test of internal consistency nor that of external, factual accuracy of his *own* premises and procedures. Nor can we be sure that the exact year, let alone the month and day, of Khayyam's passing as proposed by Tīrtha as prevalently accepted today are accurate.

In a following chapter, Tamdgidi relaxes the assumption of correctness of Tīrtha's reading of the *third* degree of the Gemini in Khayyam's reported horoscope, and further evaluate Tīrtha's solutions for Khayyam's dates of birth and passing.

CHAPTER II—In Search of the Correct Gemini Degree: The Story of How Omar Khayyam's True Date of Birth Was Discovered Shortly Before Its Imminent Millennium

1. Chapter Introduction

In the previous chapter I showed how internal inconsistencies and factual inaccuracies in the efforts made by Swāmī Govinda Tīrtha (1941) to determine Omar Khayyam's birth date prevented him from offering a reliable and true solution to the problem, resulting in the erroneous consensus date (May 18, AD 1048) held today for Omar Khayyam's birth.

The same can also be said regarding Tīrtha's solution for Khayyam's date of passing, at least as far as the day and the month (12th of Muharram) of the uneasy consensus date of death held today are concerned. Although the year of Khayyam's death is still reported variously, often differently from what Tīrtha himself suggested it to be, one can argue that Tīrtha's AD 1048 birth date "solution" (a date I have now conclusively proven to be incorrect) has made the relatively later year AD 1131 more plausible as an uneasy consensus date for Khayyam's passing, making it more "preferable" to Tīrtha's own proposed year 516 LH—which (on Muharram 12th) fell in the year AD 1122—because it allows for a higher age of 83 for Khayyam.

What this means, in other words, is that the world still does not truly know when Khayyam was born, nor when he died.

I devote this chapter to a search for Khayyam's true date of birth, and the following chapter to that of determining anew his date of passing. In the process, I will enter into other aspects of Khayyam's life or works only to the extent they become necessary and/or possible as a result of any new information we may need or discover in the course of the specific inquiries at hand in this book regarding Khayyam's dates of birth and passing.

As noted before, Swāmī Govinda Tīrtha deserves credit for bringing scholarly attention to Omar Khayyam's horoscope as reported in Zahireddin Abolhasan Beyhaqi's *Tatemmat Sewan el-Hekmat (Supplement to the Chest of Wisdom)* as a pathway toward solving the problem of Khayyam's birth date, even though he himself erred in the effort, causing more confusion. Aspects of what Tīrtha contributed toward that question, and also toward solving the puzzle of Khayyam's date of passing, may still be helpful, however, even in the sense of allowing us to reject one or another false lead toward solving the puzzles, or in terms of exploring the manuscripts in alternative ways to achieve our aim. Still, as I have shown in the previous chapter, something in the way Tīrtha handled the information of Khayyam's reported horoscope prevented him from truly solving his birth date puzzle.

So, what did go wrong in Tīrtha's efforts?

To answer this question, in this chapter I will adopt the procedure of step by step peeling away one or another false lead toward a core solution, without revealing from the outset what my solution to the puzzles is. The reason for this procedure is to eliminate any other possibilities that may, one way or another, exist and thus cast doubt on the definitive solution we hope to reach for the puzzle at hand. After all, if there is more than one solution that may plausibly compete with, let alone nullify, the solution I offer, we cannot claim for sure that a definitive solution has been found.

Given the above procedure, therefore, I encourage the reader to consider the step by step efforts I will make in this chapter to rule out other possible alternatives as necessary contributive elements of the solution I will offer at the end of each of my explorations in this chapter and the next for the dates of birth and passing of Khayyam respectively. In other words, if I take up a question to explore, the reader should not assume that that specific step offers *the* solution to the problem, but that it offers a step *toward* the solution by eliminating a seemingly plausible "solution" that can be shown to be a false lead. Yet, once I reveal the solution, I will also make an effort to show why the earlier pathways in the maze were misleading and how they themselves can in fact be explained on the basis of the solution discovered.

Although aspects of what I will try to do to solve the puzzle may be easier than others to follow, I assure readers that despite some lingering confusions that may arise the definitiveness of the solutions I will offer for the two dates in this and the following chapter will be clearly understandable, regardless of the extent of readers' prior familiarity with matters astronomical, calendrical, astrological, cultural, or linguistic. Ultimately, the error preventing our determination of Khayyam's date of birth (and by implication, of his passing) will be shown to be so obvious in hindsight that, having discovered it, we may all wonder how we missed it. But even such wondering is an important topic that should not be left unaddressed and taken for granted, since it is itself of significant substantive and methodological value for our hermeneutic study of Khayyam in this series.

For now, needed for reexperiencing the wonderful, unprecedented discovery made is your careful attention while I share the story of how I solved a puzzle of birth date that have baffled generations of commentators and scholars, going back nearly a millennia. I say "nearly a millennia," since the solution will lead us to ask whether, how, or why Omar Khayyam himself seemed to pursue a secretive, or perhaps one may call it socratic, style of setting challenging puzzles for us to solve on our own even regarding the date on which he was born and how his passing could be remembered and perhaps enigmatically discovered a thousand years later.

2. Why Did Tīrtha Read the Gemini Degree As '3' Not '8'?

An image of the specific Beyhaqi manuscript copy of the text of the horoscope for Omar Khayyam that was used by Tīrtha was fortunately included in his *The Nectar of Grace* (1941).[1] I say "fortunately," because it offers us further information about which specific manuscript copy he used, how legible it possibly was, and how he read and translated it.

I have already copied, in the previous chapter in Figure I.1, the first two pages of the manuscript copy Tīrtha used, rendered in negative image (white on black). As I noted before, the copy of the first page (folio 6a) of the biography as reproduced in *The Nectar of Grace* was not legible, judging from

1. See the folios 66a through 68b following the page XXXII of Swāmī Govinda Tīrtha's book, *The Nectar of Grace: Omar Khayyām's Life and Works* (1941), whose pdf is accessible and downloadable/searchable online at this address: https://archive.org/details/nectarofgrace031160mbp/page/n10.

Tīrtha's included image of it, especially on the specific lines in which the important Gemini degree for Khayyam's horoscope was conveyed by Beyhaqi.

Either the quality of the original was poor in the copy Tīrtha himself used for his study, or the illegibility had resulted from the poor image processing quality of printing technologies available to his publisher in India around 1941, or both. However, it is also possible that there was nothing wrong with the original Tīrtha used for the purpose, given an edition of *Tatemmat Sewan el-Hekmat (Supplement to the Chest of Wisdom)* edited by Mohammad Shafi had just been published in 1932[2] and was cited by Tīrtha.[3]

In any case, since Tīrtha himself did not offer any indication in his book that the poor quality of his original may have caused him difficulty in accurately reading the text of Khayyam's horoscope, we should assume that either (1) he had access to at least what he regarded to be a clear copy from which he drew such a definitive conclusion regarding the degree of Gemini in Khayyam's reported horoscope, or (2) he tried other possible readings, such as considering that the abjad letter was a ح and not a ج and thus equivalent to being the eighth (not the third) degree of Gemini, finding that 8 would not produce the expected results fulfilling other conditions of Khayyam's reported horoscope, so he simply ignored it and focused instead on what seemed to be a more fruitful pursuit via the 3rd degree in Gemini. He may have even simply decided that there was an error in the copy he used such that the letter must be a ج, meaning that it is equivalent to 3 and not 8.

---

2. Al-Imam Zahireddin Abolhasan Ali Ibn al-Qasem al-Beyhaqi. 1351 LH (1932) (565 LH). *Tatemmat Sewan el-Hekmat.* Edited by Muhammad Shafi. Includes the Arabic and old Persian translations with extensive footnote commentaries. India: Lahore.

3. It is possible to consider that Tīrtha may have seen a copy of Shafi's book (already published in 1351 LH, or 1932), because he cites it (p. XXXII); however, we cannot be certain that he did. Shafi's edition contains the image of the first page of the Beyhaqi manuscript containing Khayyam's horoscope. Tīrtha produces *all* the pages of Beyhaqi's Khayyam biography, marking it as the Berlin 10055 M.O. 21 manuscript, folios 66a through 68b, while Mohammad Shafi shares only the first page of the same Khayyam biography manuscript, marked as a Berlin Pm. 737, f. 66a. This indicates that Tīrtha obtained his copy of Beyhaqi's biographical entry on Khayyam, as reproduced in his book in all its pages, from another source.

Still, given that Shafi's image of folio 6a (the first page of the biography containing the horoscope degree of Gemini) is legible, this indicates that Tīrtha may have had access also to a clear image of that first page of the biography, one way or another. A lack of any comments by Tīrtha on the quality of the images of the sources used by him indicates that the matter of illegibility was not a complicating issue for him. He may have then been aware that the abjad letter indicating the Gemini degree in Khayyam's reported horoscope was a ح and not a ج and, still, oddly, attributed a numerical value of 3 to it, and not an 8.

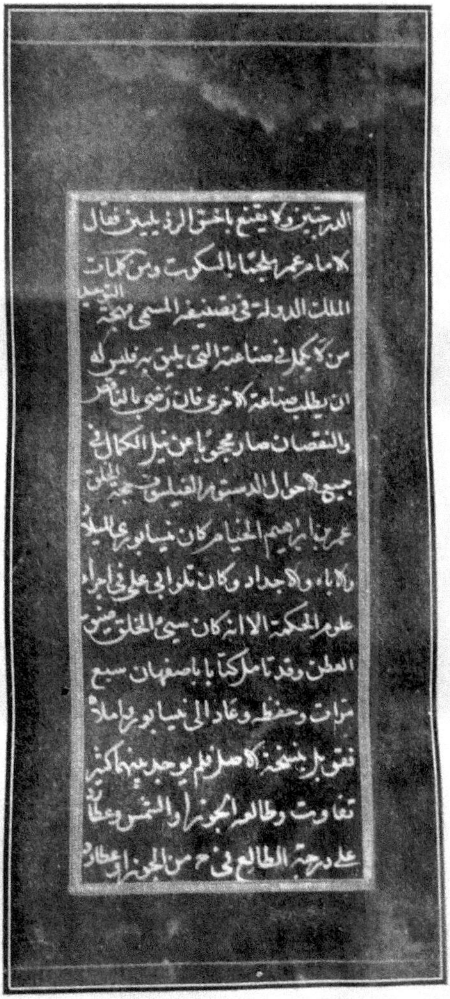

الدرجتين ولا يقنع بالحق الذي يليق فقال
الامام عمر الحجبا بالسكوت ومن كلمات
الملك الدولة في تصنيفه المسمى بهجة التوحيد
من لا يكمل في صناعته التي يليق به فليس له
ان يطلب صناعة الاخرى فان رضي بالناقص
والنقصان صار محجوبا عن نيل الكمال في
جميع الاحوال الدستور الفيلسوف حجة الحق
عمر بن ابراهيم الخيام كان نيسابوري الميلاد
والاباء والاجداد وكان تلو ابي علي في اجزاء
علوم الحكمة الا انه كان سيء الخلق ضيق
العطن وقد تامل كتابا باصفهان سبع
مرات وحفظه وعاد الى نيسابور واملاه
فقوبل بنسخة الاصل فلم يوجد بينهما كثير
تفاوت وطالعه الجوزا والشمس وعطارد
على درجة الطالع في ج من الجوزا وعطارد

Berlin Pm. 737, f. 66a.
(=p. 111 of this Edition).

Figure II.1

A Legible Scan of the First Page of Beyhaqi's Biography of Omar Khayyam in One of the Various Manuscript Copies of *Tatemmat Sewan el-Hekmat (Supplement to the Chest of Wisdom)*

In Figure II.1, for ease of reference, I again provide (as in the last chapter) the clearer and more legible copy of the same page Tīrtha used, one that was readily available in Mohammad Shafi edition of Beyhaqi's work. It is obvious from this manuscript copy—where the smallest of dots associated with the Arabic alphabet are clearly visible for the texts shown—that the letter used by the scribe in the copy of Beyhaqi's horoscope for Khayyam was indeed a ﺣ (that is, a small version of the letter ح in Arabic/Persian alphabet) and not a ﺟ (which is a small version of the letter ج in Arabic/Persian alphabet).

If Tīrtha's copy was clear, he should have recognized that the numerical value of the letter ﺣ in the abjad system is 8, and not 3. In his book, he did not say anything in support of one numerical value or another to be assigned to the letter. He never even raised a question, or doubt, about whether the letter to be considered is ﺣ or ﺟ . He simply assumed that the value of the abjad letter given for the Gemini degree is 3.

If his original was not clear, as evident in the quality of the image he copied in his book, then, at the very least he should have conveyed a certain sense of ambiguity as to how such an important degree of Gemini in Khayyam's reported horoscope should have been read/translated—and thus be less confident in announcing his results. At the very least, he should have, one would expect, explored both tracks of the degree being either 3 or 8, and offered convincing arguments and calculations to disqualify the option of reading the letter as a ﺣ , corresponding to the number 8. However, there are no such elaborations present, no doubts evident, in Tīrtha's study of Khayyam's reported horoscope in his book. It appears as if he could see that the letter was ﺣ , yet, contrary to the conventional abjad system, assigned a numerical value 3 to it, as if the abjad letter given for the degree was a ﺟ .

It is important to consider that other, more contemporary, studies of Beyhaqi's work citing the same copy of Beyhaqi's manuscript have generally read the Arabic letter in the original as a ﺣ thus routinely rendering its numerical value as 8.[4]

---

4. As we shall see, Mohammad Shafi, the editor/compiler of the source from which the image of the legible first page of Khayyam's biographical entry is shared in Figure II.1, *also* read the letter to be a ح representing the numerical value of 8 in Khayyam's horoscope. For other examples, see for instance, Jean Lambert and Alfred-Louis De, "Un récit nommé khayyām: La rivalité Gazāli-Khayyam selon al-Bayhaqi et la première notice biographique concernant le Maître de Nīshāpūr, *Arabica*, T. 34, Fasc. 2 (Jul., 1987), pp. 197-220, page [5] or 201. Also, a digital version of Beyhaqi's book in the Arabic can be downloaded from here http://www.al-mostafa.info/data/arabic/depot/gap.php?file=001509-www.al-mostafa.com.pdf, page 43, where the letter in question is also rendered as a ح implying the number 8.

I will show later in this chapter that the reading of the letter indicating the degree of Gemini in Khayyam's reported horoscope is far from being commonly rendered as in the improved image of Tīrtha's source shared in Figure II.1. The copy used by many scholars, including Tīrtha, is only one among different copies of Beyhaqi's manuscript available. It just happens that Tīrtha read his own copy as indicating the number 3, when he should have considered it as a letter offering the number 8 for the degree of Gemini in Khayyam's horoscope.

To make the matter even more interesting, and confusing, there is, as we shall see, another version of the manuscript that indeed offers the letter ﺟ (which is a small version of the letter ج in Arabic and Persian alphabets), resulting in a reading of 3 for the number of the degree, one which we have already established in the previous chapter to be one that does not lead to an accurate determination of Khayyam's birth date. The image of that copy is in fact also shared in Mohammad Shafi's book, as the "Mulla Murad" copy, on page 10. So, may we conclude that Tīrtha was aware of this copy, leading him to choose 3 for the degree in Gemini? Why not reproduce that one in his book in defense of his third degree of Gemini choice? His not including it is another reason that leads me to consider it as being possible that he had not directly consulted Mohammad Shafi's edition of Beyhaqi's book.

3. Do Either Degrees 3 Or 8 of Gemini Solve the Puzzle on Any Date During the Period?

Before I further address the issue of diversity of copies available for Beyhaqi's manuscript, let us first consider the possibility that the intended letter was indeed a ﺣ (that is, a small version of the letter ح in Arabic/Persian alphabet), from which one may conclude that the degree of Gemini in which the Sun and Mercury were in the Samimi (Cazimi) configuration was 8.

In consideration of this possibility, we no longer need to give priority to the year AD 1048 for exploring our options, since we need to explore not only that year, but also all the years in which Khayyam's birth day could have possibly fallen. So, in order to discover whether during Tīrtha's proposed period AD 1019-1054 there was *any* specific date(s) for which the conditions

Another study and translation of Beyhaqi's manuscript, in *Ali Ibn Zaid Al-Baikaqi Tatimma Siwan al-Hikma: Texts and Studies* (collected and reprinted by Fuat Sezgin in Collaboration with Carl Ehrig-Eggert, Eckhard Neuybauer, 2005) of Khayyam's biography and specifically of his horoscope offers the value of 8 (p. 54), and not 3, for the letter ح in the Arabic original (and Persian translation) included in the same book (p. 349).

as required by Khayyam's reported horoscope could be fulfilled based on an alternate reading of the 8th degree in the Gemini, we need to find a date which fulfilled the following combined four requirements:

1. The Ascendant must have been the Gemini;

2. The Sun must have been on the degree 8 of Gemini, with Mercury being in the Samimi (Cazimi) proximity of no more than 16 *minutes* in its distance from the Sun;

3. The Sun-Mercury Cazimi must have fallen on the degree of the Ascendant (sunrise);

4. Jupiter must have been on such a distance that its location was within 120 degrees, plus or minus 9 orb degrees, from the Sun (or Mercury, given they are so close to each other), forming a "Taslees"/"Triangulation," or Trine aspectation with them.

In order to leave no doubts regarding the possibility of the degree 3 of Gemini as offering *any year* solution during the range of years for fulfilling the requirements of Khayyam's horoscope, I will again also offer in another table the data for degree 3 for all the years during the period.

In the two tables below, the dates in which the Sun is ascendant in Gemini and is located on degree 8 (Table II.1) or degree 3 (Table II.2) of Gemini are listed for years AD 1018-1055. Note that I have widened the period Tīrtha suggested, by adding a year before and one after the period, to make it even more inclusive.

The Julian Christian calendar is used for the purpose of compilation of the two tables, since the data is itself available in Julian dates.[5]

---

5. For the purpose at hand at the scale of a year's interval, the difference with the Gregorian calendar will not be relevant here, and in any case it could be easily converted to its Gregorian equivalent if necessary. It does not matter which calendar we use here since the calendars only label differently the exact same days we wish to explore, times that would be picked up in our data collection in any case.

For those interested, as I briefly noted in the introduction to this book, the Julian days can be readily translated into the Gregorian days for the 11th century (which is of relevance here as far as Khayyam's birth date is concerned) by adding 6 days to the Julian day. The day of week remains the same, since the alternate labels are referring to the same day.

For the 12th century (when Khayyam's death occurred), the difference between the Julian and Gregorian days are 7 days, which means we have to add 7 days to the Julian day to arrive at the Gregorian day (as can be calculated at https://stevemorse.org/jcal/julian.html). Also note that in all these conversions, if the addition takes us to the next month, that should also be noted. For instance, if we have a Julian day of 26th of May, AD 1122, its Gregorian equivalent would be June 2nd of the same year. If this was in 11th century, the same Julian day would fall on June 1st of Gregorian calendar.

My data source is the comprehensive ephemeris data available for 9000 years at the Astrodienst website www.astro.com (specifically at http://www.astro.com/swisseph/swepha_e.htm) created from Swiss Ephemeris data. By clicking on "50 year files, 5000 BCE to 3999 CE" on the above linked page, one can readily access further clicks for the pdf files for 1000 CE and 1050 CE, which contain the data for years AD 1000-1049 and 1050-1099 respectively.

In the two tables below, following the Sun's location, the location for Mercury is also given. I include the Jupiter location data only when the 16 minutes or less Samimi (Cazimi) requirement for the Sun-Mercury distance is fulfilled, since otherwise the day would not fulfill all the requirements of Khayyam's reported horoscope, so there would be no point in exploring whether the location of Jupiter meets the horoscope requirements or not.

The Sun and Mercury location data are provided only if they fall in the Gemini. If no specific location numbers are given under the Mercury column, this means Mercury for that day did not fall in the Gemini; so I just note the constellation in which Mercury falls.

Days are marked by the day of week abbreviation followed by day of the month. Since the dates are based on the Julian calendar, to determine their Gregorian equivalent, you can simply add 6 days to the day for these dates since they belong to the eleventh century. Again, the day of the week would remain the same, since the two calendars are basically referring to the same actual days of the week.

The location for which the data are collected is Neyshabour, Iran, whose coordinates are 58e50 and 36n12.

In the tables, for the sake of simplicity, I have not included the condition of the Sun-Mercury Samimi (Cazimi) falling on the degree of the Ascendant (sunrise), since without the former (Cazimi) condition being met, meeting the latter condition would not produce any acceptable result in any case.

Note also that the Sun was positioned on the degree 8 (for the year AD 1044) and 3 (for year AD 1045) twice in consecutive days, so I have provided data for both options.

Also, for the year AD 1048, given it is Tīrtha's (now conclusively rejected) proposed birth year for Khayyam, I have provided locations data for three consecutive days (one before and one after May 18th) for comparison purposes, simply to further demonstrate that neither option fulfills the Samimi (Cazimi) distance requirement of less than 16 minutes between the Sun and Mercury.

Table II.1

Sun and Mercury (And Jupiter, When Needed) Locations for Years AD 1018-1055 for Sun Locations Falling in Degree 8 of the Gemini

Year (AD)	Month	Day (Julian)	Sun (S) Gemini	Mercury Gemini	Jupiter (J)	J-S Distance
1018	May	Su 25	8° 18′	5° 51′ Not Samimi		
1019	May	M 25	8° 4′	23° 26′ Not Samimi		
1020	May	W 25	8° 47′	3° 16′ Not Samimi		
1021	May	Th 25	8° 33′	22° 45′ Not Samimi		
1022	May	F 25	8° 20′	Taurus (Not Gemini)		
1023	May	Sa 25	8° 6′	Taurus (Not Gemini)		
1024	May	M 25	8° 50′	Taurus (Not Gemini)		
1025	May	Tu 25	8° 35′	14° 39′ Not Samimi		
1026	May	W 25	8° 22′	29° 15′ Not Samimi		
1027	May	Th 25	8° 8′	Cancer (Not Gemini)		
1028	May	Sa 25	8° 51′	10° 47′ Not Samimi		
1029	May	Su 25	8° 37′	Taurus (Not Gemini)		
1030	May	M 25	8° 23′	Taurus (Not Gemini)		
1031	May	Tu 25	8° 9′	2° 25′ Not Samimi		
1032	May	Th 25	8° 53′	22° 35′ Not Samimi		
1033	May	F 25	8° 38′	Cancer (Not Gemini)		
1034	May	Sa 25	8° 25′	26° 9′ Not Samimi		

Year (AD)	Month	Day (Julian)	Sun (S) Gemini	Mercury Gemini	Jupiter (J)	J-S Distance
1035	May	Su 25	8° 11′	Taurus (Not Gemini)		
1036	May	Tu 25	8° 55′	Taurus (Not Gemini)		
1037	May	W 25	8° 41′	Taurus (Not Gemini)		
1038	May	Th 25	8° 27′	11° 14′ Not Samimi		
1039	May	F 25	8° 14′	27° 12′ Not Samimi		
1040	May	Sa 24	8° 0′	Cancer (Not Gemini)		
1040	May	Su 25	8° 57′	Cancer (Not Gemini)		
1041	May	M 25	8° 43′	15° 41′ Not Samimi		
1042	May	Tu 25	8° 29′	Taurus (Not Gemini)		
1043	May	W 25	8° 15′	Taurus (Not Gemini)		
1044	May	Th 24	8° 1′	Taurus (Not Gemini)		
1044	May	F 25	8° 59′	1° 13′ Not Samimi		
1045	May	Sa 25	8° 45′	19° 38′ Not Samimi		
1046	May	Su 25	8° 31′	Cancer (Not Gemini)		
1047	May	M 25	8° 17′	28° 46′ Not Samimi		
1048	May	Tu 24	8° 3′	3° 12′ (Tirtha's proposed year would not also satisfy the Samimi (Cazimi) requirement for degree 8 of Gemini)		

Year (AD)	Month	Day (Julian)	Sun (S) Gemini	Mercury Gemini	Jupiter (J)	J-S Distance
1049	May	Th 25	8° 46′	Taurus (Not Gemini)		
1050	May	F 25	8° 33′	Taurus (Not Gemini)		
1051	May	Sa 25	8° 19′	7° 44′ (Not on 8° and more than 16 m. away from the Sun). Samimi (Cazimi) requirement not met.	11° 24′ Taurus	Jupiter's house is just one house away from Gemini (should be five houses away). Taslees (Trine) requirement not met.
1052	May	Su 24	8° 5′	24° 49′ Not Samimi		
1053	May	Tu 25	8° 48′	Cancer (Not Gemini)		
1054	May	W 25	8° 34′	20° 11′ Not Samimi		
1055	May	Th 25	8° 21′	Taurus (Not Gemini)		

Table II.2

Sun and Mercury (And Jupiter, When Needed) Locations for Years AD 1018-1055 for Sun Locations Falling in Degree 3 of the Gemini

Year (AD)	Month	Day (Julian)	Sun (S) Gemini	Mercury Gemini	Jupiter (J)	J-S Distance
1018	May	Tu 20	3° 31′	Aries (Not Gemini)		
1019	May	W 20	3° 17′	13° 32′ Not Samimi		
1020	May	Th 19	3° 3′	25° 45′ Not Samimi		
1021	May	Sa 20	3° 47′	22° 46′ Not Samimi		
1022	May	Su 20	3° 33′	Taurus (Not Gemini)		
1023	May	M 20	3° 20′	Taurus (Not Gemini)		

Year (AD)	Month	Day (Julian)	Sun (S) Gemini	Mercury Gemini	Jupiter (J)	J-S Distance
1024	May	Tu 19	3° 6′	Taurus (Not Gemini)		
1025	May	Th 20	3° 49′	3° 45′ Samimi (Cazimi) requirement of less than 16 minutes distance from the Sun is met.	1° 30′ Pisces	Jupiter is about 92° and its house only 4 houses away from Gemini (should be within 111-129 degrees distance and 5 houses away). Taslees (Trine) requirement not met.
1026	May	F 20	3° 36′	20° 42′ Not Samimi		
1027	May	Sa 20	3° 22′	27° 20′ Not Samimi		
1028	May	Su 19	3° 7′	13° 39′ Not Samimi		
1029	May	Tu 20	3° 51′	Taurus (Not Gemini)		
1030	May	W 20	3° 37′	Taurus (Not Gemini)		
1031	May	Th 20	3° 23′	Taurus (Not Gemini)		
1032	May	F 19	3° 9′	10° 18′ Not Samimi		
1033	May	Su 20	3° 52′	25° 47′ Not Samimi		
1034	May	M 20	3° 39′	24° 56′ Not Samimi		
1035	May	Tu 20	3° 25′	0° 56′ Not Samimi		
1036	May	W 19	3° 11′	Taurus (Not Gemini)		
1037	May	F 20	3° 54′	Taurus (Not Gemini)		

Year (AD)	Month	Day (Julian)	Sun (S) Gemini	Mercury Gemini	Jupiter (J)	J-S Distance
1038	May	Sa 20	3° 41′	0° 15′ Not Samimi		
1039	May	Su 20	3° 27′	18° 5′ Not Samimi		
1040	May	M 19	3° 13′	27° 4′ Not Samimi		
1041	May	W 20	3° 56′	17° 28′ Not Samimi		
1042	May	Th 20	3° 43′	Taurus (Not Gemini)		
1043	May	F 20	3° 29′	Taurus (Not Gemini)		
1044	May	Sa 19	3° 15′	Taurus (Not Gemini)		
1045	May	Su 19	3° 1′	6° 55′ Not Samimi		
1045	May	M 20	3° 58′	9° 5′ Not Samimi		
1046	May	Tu 20	3° 45′	24° 4′ Not Samimi		
1047	May	W 20	3° 31′	26° 21′ Not Samimi		
1048	May	W 18	2° 19′ (This is Tīrtha's proposed date, which also according to his own data does not fall on degree 3 of Gemini.)	6° 29′ More than 16 minutes from the Sun required for Samimi condition. It does not fulfill the Samimi requirement.		
1048	May	Th 19	3° 17′	5° 57′ The same comment as directly above applies here.		

Year (AD)	Month	Day (Julian)	Sun (S) Gemini	Mercury Gemini	Jupiter (J)	J-S Distance
1048	May	F 20	4° 14′ Not on 3rd degree.	5° 24′ The same comment as directly above applies here.		
1049	May	F 19	3° 3′	Taurus (Not Gemini)		
1050	May	Su 20	3° 46′	Taurus (Not Gemini)		
1051	May	M 20	3° 32′	Taurus (Not Gemini)		
1052	May	Tu 19	3° 18′	15° 11′ Not Samimi		
1053	May	W 19	3° 4′	26° 18′ Not Samimi		
1054	May	F 20	3° 48′	20° R55′ Not Samimi		
1055	May	Sa 20	3° 34′	Taurus (Not Gemini)		

As can be seen, there were no dates during the AD 1018-1055 period when the conditions of Khayyam's reported horoscope could be fully met for either degree positions 3 or 8 of the Sun in the Gemini. I have commented in the table cells on the rare dates that come somewhat close but not to the point of fulfilling the requirements.

Regarding the date AD 1025 in Table II.2 (for the Sun being in the 3rd degree of the Gemini), Mercury is found to have been close enough to the Sun to fulfill the Samimi (Cazimi) requirement, but Jupiter was in a position of 1° 30′ in Pisces. This means the Jupiter was in a distance of about 92 degrees from the Sun/Mercury. The permissible distance would have to be between 111-129 degrees (i.e., 120±9 degrees) to fulfill Khayyam's horoscope requirement of Taslees (Triangulation, or Trine); as can be observed, the Jupiter's position is out of that range of distances from the Sun/Mercury. In other words, Jupiter is not in Trine aspectation with the Sun-Mercury Cazimi on that date. To fulfill the Trine requirement, the Sun/Mercury and Jupiter must also be five Zodiac houses apart (including their own houses), but they are only four houses apart.

Since AD 1025 is the only date in which at least a partial condition of the reported horoscope is met for the degree 3 of Gemini option, I include its chart in Figure II.2 so it can be visually observed how this date cannot fulfill all of the requirements of Khayyam's reported horoscope.

Using this chart, the distance of about 92 degrees between the Sun/Mercury and Jupiter can be visually calculated by adding about 3 house differences between them (each house has 30 degrees). Jupiter being in the Pisces degree of about 1, and Sun/Mercury on the Gemini degree of about 3, means they are about 92 degrees apart. Also one can see how the Sun/Mercury and Jupiter positions are separated by only four houses (including the houses in which each appear). To fulfill the Trine requirement, they must be five houses apart. Another matter to consider is that Jupiter is in the visible part of the sky, so clockwise the Jupiter must make a longer arc of aspectation round the circle to "observe" the Sun-Mercury Cazimi.

The graphic program uses the symbol of triangles on aspectation lines to indicate whether a Trine relation is present between planets. Not only it is absent, a square aspectation governs instead Sun/Mercury and Jupiter.

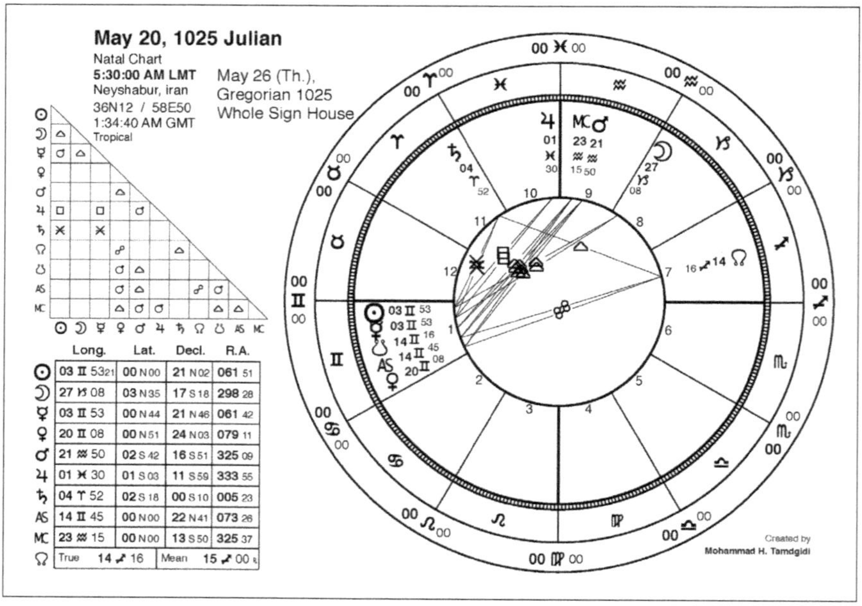

Figure II.2

The Constellations Chart for May 20 (Julian), or May 26 (Gregorian), AD 1025

4. How Have Other Copies Rendered the Gemini Degree?

So, we find ourselves in the paradoxical situation that the Sun's position on neither of the two degree locations 3 or 8 in the Gemini could provide a definitive date at which all of Khayyam's horoscope requirements could be fulfilled between the years AD 1018 and 1055.

Given that most likely the horoscope information as phrased was provided by Khayyam himself as a master astronomer to whomever Beyhaqi drew upon in his biographical entry in his *Tatemmat Sewan el-Hekmat (Supplement to the Chest of Wisdom)*, and given Khayyam's expected expertise and precision in astronomical matters (having established, for instance, a solar calendar that is reportedly more precise in 5000 years than even the Christian calendar used today), it is logical to conclude that there must be something still missing in how the horoscope was transmitted across various manuscripts, and received by us at the present.

Indeed, there is a variety of renderings of the horoscope statement across the extant manuscript copies. Even though I noted earlier that Tīrtha's copy of Beyhaqi's text whose image was copied in his book was illegible and what he may have read as a letter جـ or ج denoting the number 3 in the abjad alphabet was in fact a letter حـ or ح to which the number 8 must be associated in abjad numerology, we find that indeed there exists another manuscript copy in which the letter is clearly rendered as a جـ or ج denoting the number 3 in the abjad alphabet.

For example, I share in Figure II.3 another manuscript copy of Beyhaqi's account of Khayyam's biography included in Mohammad Shafi's edition, where the small letter جـ is evidently offered for the degree of Gemini in which the Sun and Mercury fall per Khayyam's horoscope.

Reading from right to left, at the beginning of the fifth line from the top, after another word (to which I shall return), the letter جـ is clearly visible. Should we then conclude that Tīrtha was correct all along in reading the letter as one that gives us the degree 3 of the Gemini?

We know now that the 3rd degree of the Gemini does not lead us to a solution. Even in this second copy version, although the letter has a dot, if we look carefully, we find words in which the same letter is used, but for which no dots are given. For instance, in just two words after (visually to the left of) the letter جـ on the same line, where "the Gemini" (الجوزا) is written, it is rendered *without* the dot for "جـ". So, to be skeptical, should we not also assume that the letter جـ for the degree is not faithfully rendered, as the scribe seems not to be consistent with rendering the dots for the alphabet in his or her writing? I am myself inclined to think that the scribe must have written the letter ﺟ deliberately, but doing so not being sure whether what he was reading in his original was a ﺟ or a ﺣ . He may have even mistook the dot over what he thought was a ﻓﻰ in his original, and placed its dot below the ﺣ . After all, if you look at the middle of the second line from the top, you find that the word ﻓﻰ (before اجزا) is rendered *with* a dot in the same style.

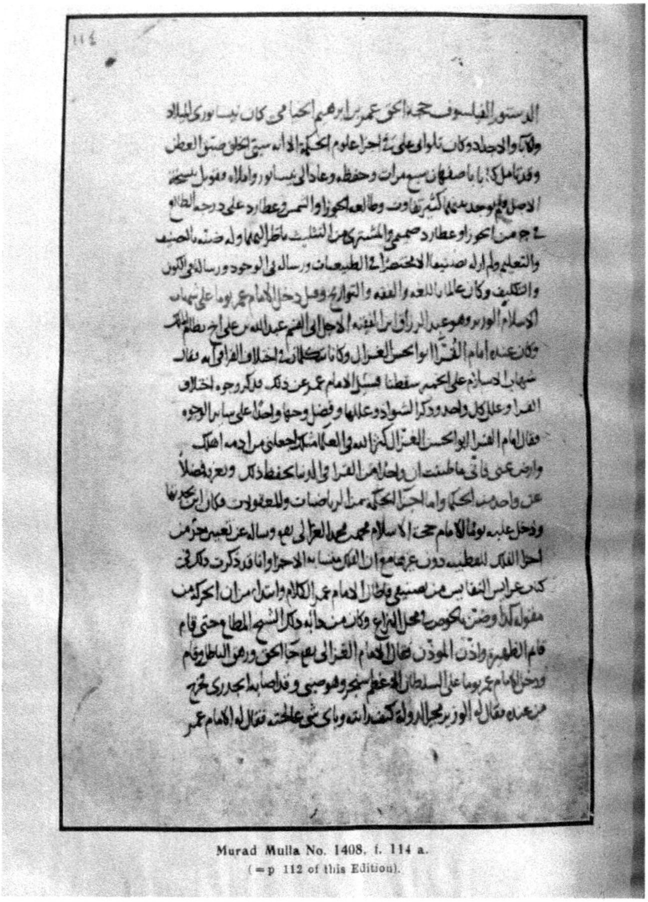

Figure II.3

Scan of the Page of Beyhaqi Biography of Omar Khayyam from a Different Manuscript (page 10)

So, here we have two copies of the same text by Beyhaqi, made by different scribes, giving two different version of the degree of Gemini for Khayyam's horoscope, two versions (3 and 8), neither of which leads us to any specific date that fulfills all the requirements of Khayyam's reported horoscope.

Does knowing their date of copying, that is, knowing which is older than the other, provide us with any measure for determining which should be counted as the "correct" one of our inquiry?

Does "being older" necessarily imply being more correct?

May they both be failing to lead us toward a solution to our problem?

5. Does An Older Copy Necessarily Mean It Is More Authentic?

This brings us to an issue that is important to consider not only for this book of the series but also for the series as a whole, an issue that I briefly noted in the methodological first book of the series when offering an overview of the sources available for our Khayyami studies.

It has to do with the extent to which we can take for granted the accuracy of the "older" manuscripts we find and use as sources for our hermeneutic study, in this case of Khayyam's life and works.

While it may appear that a handwritten manuscript from long past is a reliable evidence to base an exploration on, we should always keep in mind that unless we have a clean copy of the *very original, author-drafted*, manuscript available, we may be confronting a copy that may or may not be a faithful replica of the original author's copy, no matter how old it is.

In earlier times when modern printing technologies did not exist to produce identical copies of a given document, the original manuscripts were copied by scribes at one time or another. It was possible, therefore, that depending on the quality of the "original" a given scribe used for his copying, and the accuracy of his or her own effort at copying itself, separate chains of different versions of the original author-produced manuscript could spread in time in diverse handwritten copies to become later, in more recent times, mass duplicated in print and further digital forms.

Imagine that an author wrote a manuscript X of his own, say, seven centuries ago. Inadvertent errors therein aside (which are hypothetically possible even for an author himself), then it was recopied by other scribes down the line with (during the author's lifetime) or without (after his passing) the supervision of the original author. Each copy had to be done one at a time.

So, let us say three scribes A-1, B-1, and C-1, first used the very original author-written manuscript to do their initial copying. Scribe A-1 copied perfectly well, and a next scribe A-2 copied perfectly from his copy, and so on, until the last scribe A-n left the last and only surviving copying from the A chain just *a century ago*. Scribe B-1 also did a perfect copying, but the one after him, B-2, could not read one word or another, because of unfamiliarity with the subject or the damage to the "B-1 copy" he was using, so interpreted a word in error, and every B series scribe after him repeated the same error quite faithfully in "clean copy" until *two centuries ago*, when the last copy of chain B-n was made. Scribe C-1 copied in a sloppy way, from the beginning committing errors, but the next scribe C-2 copied *from him* very diligently, thinking he was doing a magnificent job, and so on, down the line, all the rest of C series thinking they did an excellent job at it. The last of scribes in this chain, C-n, did his copying *four centuries ago*.

Now, let us say we find ourselves fortunate enough to have all the *last* versions of each chain A, B, and C, series at our disposal. C is the oldest, next is B, and the latest is A. We may tend to think that the oldest manuscript we have is the most reliable. But, from the above hypothetical scenario, we would be led astray in assuming such a thing. Just because a copy is more recent does not mean it is less accurate or authentic. Nor is the oldest written copy the most accurate. This does not mean that we should assume, not knowing the quality of copying of various scribes, that any of the copies we possess is more accurate than the other. In some cases the oldest may be most accurate; in others, not. What this means is that we have to make our judgment on other, especially substantive, grounds to sift the more from the less accurate, and not, simply, because a manuscript is older or more recent.

The above example should lead us to not take for granted that (1) any "old" manuscript (unless it is the exact, clean copy produced by the author him/herself) is accurate simply because it is an old manuscript, and that (2) an older manuscript is necessarily any more accurate than a later copy.

The copies made by scribes in the chains A, B, and C, are made across generational times and geocultural areas. They are made by scribes not necessarily sharing the same specialties in the subject, or the cultural or linguistic background of the original author (say, an Arabic manuscript is copied by someone whose primary language is Persian, Hindi, Urdu, Turkish, Greek, and so on).

In offering the above, I do not mean to suggest that one or another aspect of the scenarios I just drew up applies to our specific problem at hand in studying Khayyam's reported horoscope. We shall have to see whether it applies or not. It may, or not. My point is that if we find one of the manuscripts I have shared is older than the other, we should not readily assume it must be more accurate. My purpose is to encourage readers to consider what may be involved in the decisions contemporary scholars have to make regarding the reliability of one or another copy of the same manuscript.

Some of these issues will certainly come up when we arrive at the point of exploring the various copies and manuscripts of the Khayyami Robaiyat or other writing. But we are not there yet, and we have a very specific question to explore presently regarding the puzzles involving Khayyam's dates of birth and passing, for which some of the manuscript and textual analysis complications and considerations that we will need to deal with at a later time in the series are already beginning to present themselves.

The example before us regarding the two copies of the Beyhaqi manuscript simply offers a good illustration of the hypothetical scenario I drew up above, i.e., how the same manuscript may end up being copied differently across difference copying chains. My point here is that in this case also, it does not really matter whether one copy is made earlier than the other, since their age (how long ago they were drafted relative to one another) may not offer any reliable indication *in and of itself* regarding whether one copy is more accurate than the other. In this case, in fact, both manuscripts offering a solution of two different abjad letters as such resolving to the degrees 3 or 8 of Gemini seem to offer false leads.

6. A Survey of Various Manuscript Copy Renderings of the Gemini Degree in Khayyam's Birth Horoscope

To make it easier for understanding how many such extant versions or copies of Khayyam's reported horoscope may be around, and to add further insight and in fact even more confusion and complexity (as far as adding to the number of extant variations of our manuscript is concerned) on the matter of conflicting manuscript renderings of Khayyam's reported horoscope in Beyhaqi's account, consider the following statement by the late Rahim Rezazadeh Malek (1940-2010) who compiled his *Daneshnameh-ye Khayyami* (*The Khayyami Encyclopedia*) as a collection of extant Arabic and Persian manuscripts and translations of works (or excerpts thereof) attributed to Omar Khayyam, gathered in a volume published in Iran in 1998 (1377 SH).

Since the passage offers a broad survey by a Khayyami scholar in Iran who was familiar with the extant manuscripts on Khayyam on the questions of the dates of Khayyam's birth and passing, I will translate a long passage from him below. The texts in brackets are from Rezazadeh Malek, adding his own additional notes to the sources he cites or quotes from. The translation is mine, and any comments I wish to add are offered in footnotes:

> In *Tarabkhaneh*[6] written by Yar Ahmad Ibn-e Hossein al-Rashidi al-Moshtaher bel-Tabrizi, it has been stated:
>
> > "The birth date of the honorable authority of philosophy [: Khayyami] was Thursday 12th of the month of Muharram of the year 455[7] in a village in the suburbs of Firouzghand of the blocks of Astarabad ...".
>
> And in another copy of the same manuscript, the same point has been expressed as follows:
>
> > "His birth date [: Khayyami] was Thursday, twelfth of the Muharram of the year five hundred fifty five of lunar calendar in a village of Dehestan suburbs of Astarabad ...[8], his ascendant was in Taurus, whose ruler, Venus, is in Sharaf[9] location ..."
>
> It is evident that the date of birth given, that is the year 455 Lunar Hejri, is not correct. On the year 470 Lunar Hejri, or before, Khayyami authored the treatise "Explanation of Problems of Postulates in Euclid's Book" and on the year 472 Lunar Hejri, translated Ibn Sina's "Splendid Sermon" into Persian, and on the year 473 Lunar Hejri wrote the treatise "On Universe and Obligation" for the Judge Imam Abi Nasr Mohammad Ibn Abdol-Rahim al-Nasavi. If Khayyami had been born on the year 455 Lunar Hejri, then he must have written such difficult and mature treatises when aged 17-18 years old, and this does not seem realistic given the content of those treatises and the ancient ways of education.

---

6. "House of Joy (or Happiness)." This is a name Yar Ahmad Rashidi Tabrizi gave to his collection of Khayyami Robaiyat and commentaries on his life in the book.

7. Note here that in this manuscript of *Tarabkhaneh* Rezazadeh was reading, the date was rendered not as 555 (to which I referred in the last chapter) but as 455, which is another variation found for that manuscript. To these matters I will return in the following chapter. He actually offers the other variation in his following paragraph (for the date 555 LH).

8. "که حالا داخل باز است". The meaning of this statement is not clear to me. It literally means, "which is now inside open." Its meaning has no bearing on my study here, so can be ignored.

9. "Sharaf" in astrological terms is the point of "exaltation," the house/degree in/on which a particular planet is exalted. Venus is exalted on the degree 27 of Pisces, but rules and thus is exalted in both Pisces and Taurus, according to medieval astrology. Tabrizi is offering a horoscope for Khayyam that we know is incorrect in terms of its Taurus ascendant (since his ascendant is Gemini). But, the reference to Venus being exalted in his horoscope is noteworthy, more so since it is in reference to Venus's exaltation in its Taurus location.

As we have seen in the commentaries about Khayyami, Zahireddin Abolhasan Beyhaqi, in *Tatemmat Sewan el-Hekmat*, has shared the birth horoscope of Khayyami. This birth horoscope, in the Arabic copies of *Tatemmat Sewan el-Hekmat*, is as follows:

> "His Ascendant was the Gemini and the Sun and Mercury were on the degree of the Ascendant (- -) of the Gemini, the Mercury being Samimi, and the Jupiter observing both from Taslees."[10]

The same piece is rendered as follows in the Persian translation of *Tatemmat Sewan el-Hekmat*:

> "His Ascendant was the Gemini, and the Sun and the Mercury were on the degree of the Ascendant (- - -) of the Gemini and [Mercury was Samimi] and the Jupiter observing [both] from Taslees."[11]

What we enclosed in parentheses with the dash line, in one of the copies of the Arabic manuscript is rendered as (حـ) and in other copies as (ح) and (يو)[12]. And in Persian translation as (ک و ر).[13]

Swāmī Govinda Tīrtha, in his book *The Nectar of Grace (Omar Khayyām's Life and Works)*, assuming that the noted letter (حـ) in Khayyāmi's horoscope stands for 3, has found Khayyami's birth to have taken place on the year 427 Solar Hejri, corresponding to the year 439 Lunar Hejri.[14]

As Khayyami's birth date is not determined (at least definitively), we also do not know definitively his date of demise.

---

10. In Rezazadeh's book, the Arabic texts in the original is as follows:

«طالعه الجوزا و لشمس و عطارد على درجه الطالع (- -) من الجوزا و عطارد صميمى و المشترى من التثليث ناظر اليهما».

11. In Rezazadeh's book, the Persian texts in the original is as follows, the brackets are given in Rezazadeh's original:

«طالعش جوزا بوذ و آفتاب و عطارد بر درجهٔ طالع (- - -) الجوزا و [عطارد صميمى] و مشترى از تثليث ناظر [بر آن دو]».

12. This corresponds to the letter ى . Basically, it is like saying "Ef" for the letter F, or "Gee" for G.

13. As shared by Rezazadeh, this last part ک و ر would mean either as a combination of letters K, V, and R, or as a statement meaning "K and R," since the letter و stands for "and" in Persian. You may notice two things in his renderings of Khayyam's horoscope above, which I have tried to convey in my translated version. He includes two dashes in the Arabic version and three dashes in the Persian version inside his parenthesis. I have done the same in translating him. I think his doing so is deliberate, since he continues to point out that in the Arabic version the alternate renderings are in two letters, and in the Persian version, the alternate rendering are in two or three letters, perhaps depending on whether the letter standing for "and" is counted as such or as one of the degree connoting letters.

14. These dates in Islamic lunar or solar Hejri correspond to the year AD 1048.

In the book *Mizan ol-Hekmat*[15], in the section where it is recalling Khayyami's Qestas al-Mostaqeem,[16] it is written "On the straight balance of Master Leader[17] Abi-Hafs Omar Ibn-e Ibrahim al-Khayyami, may God have Mercy on him."

Since Abdorrahman Khazeni authored the book *Mizan ol-Hekmat* on the year 515 Lunar Hejri, does mentioning "may God have Mercy on him" after the name of Khayyami mean that Khayyami had died on (or before) the year 515 Lunar Hejri? Was "may God have Mercy on him" added by scribes of *Mizan ol-Hekmat*?

In one of the copies of *Tarabkhaneh* by Yar Ahmad Ibn Hussain Rashidi Tabrizi, it is noted:

> "His [: Khayyami's] date of demise was five hundred fifteen, and he is buried in the old city of Neyshabour."

In *Mojmal-e Faseehi* and also in *Majma ol-Fosaha*, the date of demise of Khayyam has been noted as 517 Lunar Hejri. Thomas Hyde in his book on the history of the Parthian Iranians and Ancient Medes (Veterum Persarum et Parthorum et Medorum Religionis Historia) published in Oxford on AD 1700, has quoted Khayyami's date of passing from a Persian source (which he has not identified) as follows:

> "... the demise of the Prince of the Wise[18], King of the Scientists[19], and Role Model of the Virtuous[20], Scholar Master Omar Khayyam was on the date five hundred seventeen in Neyshabour."

As we saw in the *Chahar Maqaleh*[21] by Nezami Arouzi, Nezami on the year 530 Lunar Hejri, visited the grave of Khayyami in Neyshabour, and on that date (on the basis of one of the manuscript copies of *Chahar Maqaleh*) has written: "It was four years that such a great man had been veiled by the dust." On this basis, Khayyami must have died on the year 526 of Lunar Hejri, but the word "four" in this piece has been rendered as "some"[22] in other manuscript copies of the *Chahar Maqaleh*.

(Rezazadeh Malek 1998: 33-36; my English translation)

---

15. "Balance of Wisdom." A book written/compiled by Abdorrahman Khazeni.
16. "Straight (or Upright) Balance."
17. "lel-Sheikh ol-Imam."
18. "Malek ol-Hokama."
19. "Soltan ol-Olama."
20. "Qodvat ol-Fozala."
21. "Four Essays" or "Four Discourses."
22. "Chand."

As is evident from the above, Rezazadeh Malek encountered a variety of renderings of the Gemini degree in Khayyam's reported horoscope across many manuscript copies in Arabic and (in one case) old Persian translations. We can add to his list also the one missing there, of course, based on what I have offered in Figure II.3, which is the ﺟ version as evident in the manuscript page I copied in that figure.

Rezazadeh Malek notes how Tīrtha assigned the number 3 to the Gemini's degree, implying that Tīrtha simply interpreted the letter ﺣ that way (which would be a fair assumption since, as we can see from the clean copy of the same manuscript Tīrtha used, that the letter was indeed a ﺣ). So, for Rezazadeh Malek, in compiling his collection of Khayyam's original texts in Persian or Arabic (or excerpts thereof, often with their Persian translations), it seems that he simply did not have access to, or missed considering, the version with the letter ﺟ that I have copied in Figure II.3.

What is also interesting to note in Rezazadeh Malek's reporting of various renderings of the horoscope in Arabic or Persian translation is that he has omitted the word "فی" (meaning "in") from the Arabic sentence, a word that just precedes the Gemini designation and is rendered as such in the Tīrtha copy version (and clearly visible in the more legible copy I also supplied for that copy), presumably including it as part of what he represents as dashes inside the brackets. The same word, however, seems to appear, without a dot on top, in the second version of the manuscript I copied in Figure II.3.

What I wish to convey from sharing Rezazadeh Malek's observations on the diverse ways in which the Gemini degree has been rendered across extant Arabic (and old translated Persian) manuscripts surviving from the past (to which I have added one of my own as noted in the previous paragraph, one that is actually available, together with the other copy cited by Tīrtha, as photos in the previously cited book of Arabic and its Persian translations of Beyhaqi's text edited by Mohammad Shafi), is that it appears at first there is no unanimity regarding what exactly the Gemini degree fulfilling the reported horoscope for Khayyam is. Is it possible that some or all of these sources could be telling of the same Gemini degree, one that fulfills all the requirements of Khayyam's reported horoscope?

Before moving to my direct examination of ephemeris data, I include below a figure (see Figure II.4) which compares the two manuscript copies previously shown, by focusing on the word "فی" which I mentioned above.

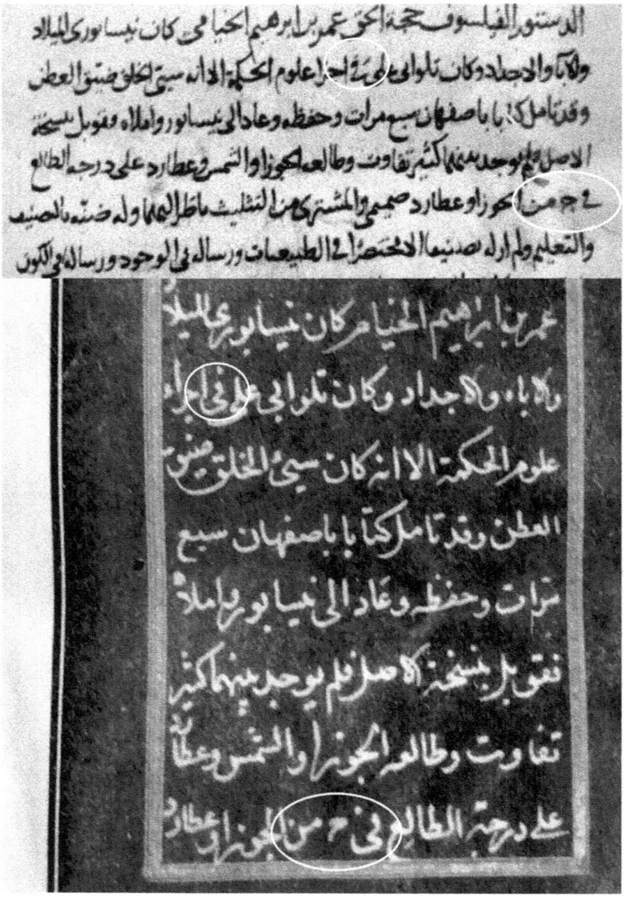

Figure II.4

In Mohammad Shafi's Book, Comparing the Two Different Renderings of the Arabic Letters ح or ج and ق Across Two Different Beyhaqi Manuscripts to Represent the Ascendant's Degree in Gemini

Since in each text there is another place where the same word is used, I have circled it in each copy, so the reader could visually notice how in one copy the word has a dot on top in both places (for the letter ف) whereas in the other copy, the dot appears only in one place and not in the other. To this issues I will return later.

7. If Neither 3 Nor 8 for the Gemini Degree Solves the Puzzle, What Degree Does?

Having already found Khayyam's birth date considerations on the basis of either the 3rd or the 8th degree for the Gemini incompatible with the requirements of Khayyam's reported horoscope, and encountering the manuscript source variations as reported above, I decided to take an alternative route and *directly* consult and report the ephemeris data for the entire years during AD 1018-1055.

I did so under the following conditions that one can still undisputably infer from Khayyam's reported horoscope across its many manuscript reporting, while still adhering to the technical definitions for Samimi (Cazimi) and Taslees (Triangulation, or Trine) as shared from his technical definitional sources by Tīrtha:

1. We know that Khayyam's ascendant sign at birth was the Gemini;

2. We know that the Sun and the Mercury were in a Samimi (Cazimi) conjunction in Gemini at the time, meaning that a distance of maximum 16 minutes separated them.

3. We know that the Sun-Mercury Samimi (Cazimi) fell on the degree of the Ascendant (exact sunrise) as well. We do not know exactly on what Gemini degree the Ascendant (and thus the Sun-Mercury Cazimi) fell, but we know now that it could not have been either of the degrees 3 or 8.

3. We know that the Jupiter was in Taslees or Triangulation (Trine) with both the Sun and the Mercury (we say both, given they were so close to each other) being "observed" by Jupiter from the distance of about 120 degrees plus or minus 9 orb degrees of that for approximation (meaning, the Sun-Mercury Cazimi distance should fall within a range of 111-129 degrees distance from or to Jupiter).

Given we do not know exactly the Sun/Mercury degree location in the Gemini in Khayyam's reported horoscope, we should be sifting the ephemeris data during the entire AD 1018-1055 range of years more broadly than the failed degrees 3 or 8 of the Gemini have confined us in the past.

The online horoscope or software search engines do not allow (as far as the site or software I have used are concerned) a "reverse" search based on the above noted conditions combined. So, I had to manually sift through all the noted years, confining my search to the Gemini ascendant days of the year.

I had to find a date in which the Ascendant was the Gemini, the Sun and the Mercury were close enough to be Samimi (Cazimi) within a distance of at most 16 *minutes*—note, this is *very* close, just above a quarter of a single degree—from one another in the Gemini, while, moreover, their Cazimi distance from the Jupiter were, relative to them, somewhere between 111 and 129 degrees, from or to it. Note that I could not from the outset determine a 360° position for the Jupiter, since, in the absence of a position for the Sun/Mercury, the distance of the Jupiter from them could only be found relative to their (still unknown, and yet to be known) position.

In order to simplify the search and the table to be shared below, I did not trace the degree of the Ascendant separately for all the dates. My assumption was that knowing the degree of the Ascendant (sunrise) would not help if any of the other conditions of the reported horoscope was not met. Conversely, if indeed we do find a date (or more) that fulfills all the Ascendant, Cazimi, and Trine requirements of the horoscope, then we have to also check to see if it also satisfies the degree of the Ascendant coinciding with the Sun-Mercury Cazimi as well. If it does, we have discovered our date(s), though the correct date must also fulfill the Jupiter position requirement. If not, then we cannot confidently say that such a date fulfills Khayyam's reported horoscope conditions entirely.

Also, it follows from our strategy as stated above that we are not particularly looking for 3, 8, or any specific Gemini degree in this ephemeris search. The various manuscripts being unclear and misleading, and themselves contradictory, they cannot be relied on regarding the specific degree of the Gemini we should be looking for. We are basically trying to find out whether indeed we can find *any* degree in the Gemini during the entire AD 1018-1055 period where its coordinates fulfill *all* other requirements of Khayyam's reported horoscope.

It must be obvious to readers as well that the criteria to be met are *very* strict, and it may well be very difficult to find such a date during the specific period when Khayyam would not be too young or too old to have been able to write maturely and perform activities during his lifetime for which we have definitive information and dates.

In Table II.3, I have listed all the dates on which the Ascendant was in the Gemini and the Sun and the Mercury were Samimi with (that is, within a distance of at most 16 minutes from) each other in the Gemini, also offering (if the above is fulfilled) the position of Jupiter, followed by the distance of Jupiter from the Sun/Mercury calculated for each case.

Note again that the dates are in the Julian calendar; so, to determine the Gregorian date in the eleventh century, we would need to add six days to the Julian date given. But this conversion is not generally needed for our purpose at hand, unless we find one (or more) exact date(s) that fulfill(s) all the requirements for Khayyam's reported horoscope. In that case, in order to know exactly when on our present calendar the solution date(s) would fall, we will definitely have to convert the Julian date to the Gregorian version.

In Table II.3, in brackets, I have included dates on which conditions were partly or closely met, while still not fulfilling the requirements one way or another, as noted. All the calculations were made from Neyshabour's longitudinal and latitudinal coordinates using the search engines of the Astrodienst website where the location can be specified on the basis of Swiss Ephemeris data. As noted before, the Swiss Ephemeris data separately consulted in previous Tables II.1 and II.2 do not offer the exact data for Neyshabour's location. For the purpose of rejecting dates that do not even come close to the conditions required by Khayyam's reported horoscope, that table suffices, and only the very close cases (that did not exist) had to be checked against the data for the more exact location of Neyshabour. I did so, for example, for the date AD 1025. In the following Table II.3, however, I used the search engine directly to explore compatible dates for Neyshabour's location, but did so only if the dates came close, where precise measurement of given data was needed.

In considering the Gemini position and the Cazimi and Trine requirements of Khayyam's reported horoscope, we should keep in mind that the conditions can be met not just for a single moment, but for a short while.

For example, the distance between the Sun and the Mercury can within a short time period remain less than 16 minutes, or Jupiter's distance from the Sun/Mercury may fulfill the condition of being within the 111-129 degrees for an interval of time, and not just for a single moment.

For this reason, it was important to use the search engine to fulfill not only the Neyshabour location requirement but also to be aware of the possibility of subtle measurements that in one moment may not fulfill a given requirement but in a second later it may. However, if the data for a given date is such that given the positions and distances the date can be ruled out, I offer just a single date listing to indicate such a lack of fulfillment for that date. The Swiss Ephemeris data available in the pdf files I referenced earlier do not allow for such subtle measurements, so I wish to alert the reader that I have taken the above considerations in mind in order to compile the data reported in Table II.3 below.

I have listed in Table II.3 all the moments I could find from the years during AD 1018-1055 at which the Sun and the Mercury actually shared the same or nearly the same degree in Gemini (for these cases, hour/minutes are given). I have included these even though they do not fulfill other requirements of Khayyam's reported horoscope; in some cases, nearby moments also are listed when the fulfillment of conditions improves with passage of time, but not to the extent that would entirely satisfy the horoscope conditions.

Since the data given in Table II.3 is inclusive of all the possibilities that come close to fulfilling the requirements of Khayyam's reported horoscope, it necessarily includes closely approaching cases for the degrees of 3 or 8 of the Gemini that I have already reported in Tables II.1 and II.2. The Table II.3, then, serves also to reconfirm (once again) with more subtle and Neyshabour-location measurements, the survey I reported in the previous two tables.

My procedure for compiling the data in Table II.3 was as follows. I first consulted the Swiss Ephemeris data that is not Neyshabour location specific, and the dates are given for day intervals only and not for the variations during the day. If the data came close to fulfilling the Gemini ascendance and Samimi (Cazimi) requirements, I reported it, cross-checking with the search engine for the more exact Neyshabour location and time variations, to the extent that it is necessary to rule out a date or regarding all the requirements of the horoscope, including the Taslees (Trine) requirement. I annotate each date sufficiently to explain why that date can be ruled out, or that it fulfills a given requirement.

Table II.3

Sun and Mercury (And Jupiter, When Needed) Locations for Years AD 1018-1055 Julian for Sun Locations Falling in Any Degree of Gemini While the Gemini is Ascendant (Except for Those in Brackets, Which Do Not Meet One or Both Above Conditions)—From the Vantage Point of Neyshabour, Iran, 36n12, 58e50

Year (AD)	Month	Day (Julian)	Sun (S) Gemini	Mercury Gemini	Jupiter (J)	J-S Distance
1018	May	Tu 27 Neyshabour	10° 13′ Gemini — Gemini ascendant fulfilled at 4:15 am	10° 16′ Gemini — Samimi (Cazimi) requirement fulfilled	19° 11′ Cancer	About 39° 1 house away (should be within 111-129 degrees distance and 5 houses away). Taslees (Trine) requirement not met

Year (AD)	Month	Day (Julian)	Sun (S) Gemini	Mercury Gemini	Jupiter (J)	J-S Distance
1019	May-June	Any Day Neyshabour	Any degree of Gemini	No degree of Gemini fulfills the Samimi (Cazimi) requirement		
1020	May-June	Any Day Neyshabour	Any degree of Gemini	No degree of Gemini fulfills the Samimi (Cazimi) requirement		
***1021** **Perfect and only match during the entire years range AD 1018-1055** — **Khayyam's exact date and time of birth discovered (reported in 2021) by Mohammad-Hossein (Behrooz) Tamdgidi, of Iranian descent, son of Tayyebeh and Mohammed (Ahad) Tamjidi, (both of Azeri ethnicity) for the first time in nearly a thousand years**	**June**	**Sunday 4 (Julian)** **or** **Sunday 10 (Gregorian)** **Neyshabour Iran**	**On 18° 7′ in Gemini on the Degree of Ascendant 18° 00′ to 18° 59′ all horoscope requirements met during the Sunrise Interval From 4:43:56 a.m to 4:47:55 a.m., Neyshabour 36n12, 58e50** ——— [Venus 2° 36′ Taurus, Moon 7° 03-05′ Pisces, Saturn 16° 41′ Aquarius Trining Sun-Mercury Cazimi and Jupiter, Mars 20° 17′ Libra Trining Saturn and Sun/Mercury Cazimi]	**On 18° 15′ in Gemini** **Mercury (in retrograde motion) requirement met (should be within 16 minutes of distance from the Sun)** **Samimi (Cazimi) requirement is met**	**On 11° 4′ in Libra (five houses away from the Sun / Mercury)** — **Important:** Jupiter is right-handed "aspecting" (observing) the Sun / Mercury from behind/ below, that is, it is in the other side of the Earth, not visible in the sky, night's sky, observing Sun / Mercury Cazimi from behind/ below from a shorter arc distance from them clockwise	**About 113° (11 in Libra + 30 in Virgo + 30 in Leo + 30 in Cancer + 12 in Gemini = 113 degrees) (should be within 111-129 degrees distance and 5 houses away).** **So, Taslees (Trine) requirement is met.**

Year (AD)	Month	Day (Julian)	Sun (S) Gemini	Mercury Gemini	Jupiter (J)	J-S Distance
1022	May-June	Any Day Neyshabour	Any degree of Gemini	No degree of Gemini fulfills the Samimi (Cazimi) requirement		
1023	May-June	Any Day Neyshabour	Any degree of Gemini	No degree of Gemini fulfills the Samimi (Cazimi) requirement		
1024	June	Th 4 5:48 p.m. Neyshabour	18° 54′ Gemini —— The date is Sagittarius ascendant, not fulfilling the Gemini ascendance requirement	18° 54′ Gemini Samimi (Cazimi) requirement is met	26° 0′ Capricorn	1 house away (should be 5 houses away). Taslees (Trine) requirement not met
1025	May	Th 20 Neyshabour	3° 53′ — Gemini ascendance requirement fulfilled at and around 5:30 a.m.	3° 53′ Samimi (Cazimi) requirement of less than 16 minutes distance from the Sun is met	1° 30′ Pisces —— Important: also Jupiter is in the visible sky, not "aspecting" or "observing" the Sun/Mercury from behind (it is in invisible sky)	About 92° and only 4 houses away from Gemini (should be within 111-129 degrees distance and 5 houses away). Taslees (Trine) requirement not met
1026	May-June	Any Day Neyshabour	Any degree of Gemini	No degree of Gemini fulfills the Samimi (Cazimi) requirement		

Year (AD)	Month	Day (Julian)	Sun (S) Gemini	Mercury Gemini	Jupiter (J)	J-S Distance
1027	June	F 16 Neyshabour	29° 17′ Leo ascendant — Does not fulfill the Gemini ascendance requirement	29° 17′ Samimi (Cazimi) requirement is met around 8:36 a.m.	7° 51′ Taurus	1 house away (should be 5 houses away). Taslees (Trine) requirement not met
1028	May	Su 26 Neyshabour	10° 3′ Leo ascendant — Does not fulfill the Gemini ascendance requirement	10° 4′ G Samimi (Cazimi) requirement is met at and around 10:18 a.m.	1° 10′ Gemini	Same house in Gemini (should be 5 houses away). Taslees (Trine) requirement not met
1029	May-June	Any Day Neyshabour	Any degree of Gemini	No degree of Gemini fulfills the Samimi (Cazimi) requirement		
1030	June	Su 14 Neyshabour	27° 39′ Leo ascendant — Does not fulfill the Gemini ascendance requirement	27° 39′ Samimi (Cazimi) requirement is met at and around 8:53 a.m.	26° 25′ Cancer	1 house away (should be 5 houses away). Taslees (Trine) requirement not met
1031	May	Sa 29 Neyshabour	12° 37′ Leo ascendant — Does not fulfill the Gemini ascendance requirement	12° 37′ Samimi (Cazimi) requirement is met around 7:39 p.m.	19° 0′ Leo	2 houses away (should be 5 houses away). Taslees (Trine) requirement not met

Year (AD)	Month	Day (Julian)	Sun (S) Gemini	Mercury Gemini	Jupiter (J)	J-S Distance
1032	May-June	Any Day Neyshabour	Any degree of Gemini	No degree of Gemini fulfills the Samimi (Cazimi) requirement		
1033	May-June	Any Day Neyshabour	Any degree of Gemini	No degree of Gemini fulfills the Samimi (Cazimi) requirement		
1034	June	F 7 Neyshabour	21° 16′ Scorpio ascendant — Does not fulfill the Gemini ascendance requirement	21° 16′ Samimi (Cazimi) requirement is met at and around 3:29 p.m.	17° 22′ Scorpio	About 146° 6 houses away (should be within 111-129 degrees distance and 5 houses away). Taslees (Trine) requirement not met
1035	May	Su 18 Neyshabour	1° 50′ Virgo ascendant — Does not fulfill the Gemini ascendance requirement	1° 50′ Samimi (Cazimi) requirement is met at and around 12:19 p.m.	25° 45′ Sagittarius	About 156° 7 houses away (should be within 111-129 degrees distance and 5 houses away). Taslees (Trine) requirement not met
1036	May-June	Any Day Neyshabour	Any degree of Gemini	No degree of Gemini fulfills the Samimi (Cazimi) requirement		

Year (AD)	Month	Day (Julian)	Sun (S) Gemini	Mercury Gemini	Jupiter (J)	J-S Distance
1037	June	Tu 7 Neyshabour	21° 21′ Virgo ascendant — Does not fulfill the Gemini ascendance requirement	21° 20′ Samimi (Cazimi) requirement is met at and around 10:44 a.m.	7° 37′ Pisces	About 104° 4 houses away (should be within 111-129 degrees distance and 5 houses away). Taslees (Trine) requirement not met
1038	May	M 22 Neyshabour	6° 19′ Capricorn ascendant — Does not fulfill the Gemini ascendance requirement	6° 19′ Samimi (Cazimi) requirement is met at and around 10:18 p.m.	8° 3′ Aries	About 58° 2 houses away (should be within 111-129 degrees distance and 5 houses away). Taslees (Trine) requirement not met
1039	May-June	Any Day Neyshabour	Any degree of Gemini	No degree of Gemini fulfills the Samimi (Cazimi) requirement		
1040	May-June	Any Day Neyshabour	Any degree of Gemini	No degree of Gemini fulfills the Samimi (Cazimi) requirement		
1041	May	F 29 Neyshabour	13° 9′ G Sagittarius ascendant — Does not fulfill the Gemini ascendance requirement	13° 9′ G Samimi (Cazimi) requirement is met at and around 7:37 p.m.	1° 39′ Cancer Date is Sag. Ascendant}	About 18° 1 house away (should be within 111-129 degrees distance and 5 houses away). Taşleeş (Trine) requirement not met

Year (AD)	Month	Day (Julian)	Sun (S) Gemini	Mercury Gemini	Jupiter (J)	J-S Distance
1042	May-June	Any Day Neyshabour	Any degree of Gemini	No degree of Gemini fulfills the Samimi (Cazimi) requirement		
1043	May-June	Any Day Neyshabour	Any degree of Gemini	No degree of Gemini fulfills the Samimi (Cazimi) requirement		
1044	May	Th 31 Neyshabour	15° 3′ Virgo ascendant — Does not fulfill the Gemini ascendance requirement	15° 3′ Samimi (Cazimi) requirement is met at and around 12:50 p.m.	20° 9′ Virgo	About 95° 4 houses away (should be within 111-129 degrees distance and 5 houses away). Taslees (Trine) requirement not met
1044	May	Th 31 Neyshabour	14° 51′ Cancer ascendant — Does not fulfill the Gemini ascendance requirement	14° 35′ Samimi (Cazimi) requirement is close to being met at 16+ minutes (but not quite, since it should be less than 16 minutes to become Samimi) at and around 7:39 a.m.	20° 8′ Virgo	About 94° 4 houses away (should be within 111-129 degrees distance and 5 houses away). Taslees (Trine) requirement not met

Year (AD)	Month	Day (Julian)	Sun (S) Gemini	Mercury Gemini	Jupiter (J)	J-S Distance
1045	May	Th 16 Neyshabour	0° 1′ Aquarius ascendant — Does not fulfill the Gemini ascendance requirement	0° 1′ Samimi (Cazimi) requirement is met at and around 0:36 a.m.	20° 37′ Libra	About 140° 5 houses away (should be within 111-129 degrees distance even though 5 houses away). Taslees (Trine) requirement not met
1046	May-June	Any Day Neyshabour	Any degree of Gemini	No degree of Gemini fulfills the Samimi (Cazimi) requirement		
1047	June	W 10 Neyshabour	24° 20′ Pisces ascendant — Does not fulfill the Gemini ascendance requirement	24° 20′ Samimi (Cazimi) requirement is met at and around 11:48 p.m.	28° 21′ Sagittarius	About 176° 7 houses away (should be within 111-129 degrees distance and 5 houses away). Taslees (Trine) requirement not met
1048	May	F 20 Neyshabour	4° 58′ Capricorn ascendant — Does not fulfill the Gemini ascendance requirement	4° 58′ Samimi (Cazimi) requirement is met at and around 10:07 p.m.	7° 8′ Aquarius	About 118° 5 houses away (should be within 111-129 degrees distance even though 5 houses away). Taslees requirement is met

Year (AD)	Month	Day (Julian)	Sun (S) Gemini	Mercury Gemini	Jupiter (J)	J-S Distance
1048	May	Sa 21 Neyshabour	5° 2′ Aquarius ascendant — Does not fulfill the Gemini ascendance requirement	4° 52′ Samimi (Cazimi) requirement is met at and around 0:10 a.m.	7° 8′ Aquarius	About 117° 5 houses away (should be within 111-129 degrees distance even though 5 houses away). Taslees requirement is met
1049	May-June	Any Day Neyshabour	Any degree of Gemini	No degree of Gemini fulfills the Samimi (Cazimi) requirement		
1050	June	Su 10 Neyshabour	23° 48′ Gemini ascendant — Fulfills the Gemini ascendance requirement	23° 49′ Samimi (Cazimi) requirement is met at and around 4:00 a.m.	15° 27′ Aries	About 52° 2 houses away (should be within 111-129 degrees distance and 5 houses away). Taslees (Trine) requirement not met
1051	May	Sa 25 Neyshabour	8° 34′ Leo ascendant — Does not fulfill the Gemini ascendance requirement	8° 20′ Samimi (Cazimi) requirement is met at and around 10:30 a.m.	11° 28′ Taurus	About 27° just 1 house away (should be within 111-129 degrees distance and 5 houses away). Taslees (Trine) requirement not met

Year (AD)	Month	Day (Julian)	Sun (S) Gemini	Mercury Gemini	Jupiter (J)	J-S Distance
1051	May	Su 26 Neyshabour	9° 16′ Leo ascendant — Does not fulfill the Gemini ascendance requirement	9° 56′ Samimi (Cazimi) requirement is met at and around 10:30 a.m.	11° 28′ Taurus	About 26° just 1 house away (should be within 111-129 degrees distance and 5 houses away). Taslees (Trine) requirement not met
1052	May-June	Any Day Neyshabour	Any degree of Gemini	No degree of Gemini fulfills the Samimi (Cazimi) requirement		
1053	May-June	Any Day Neyshabour	Any degree of Gemini	No degree of Gemini fulfills the Samimi (Cazimi) requirement		
1054	June	Th 2	16° 14′ Gemini ascendant — Fulfills the Gemini ascendance requirement	16° 14′ Samimi (Cazimi) requirement is met at and around 5:00 a.m.	1° 13′ Leo	About 45° 3 houses away (should be within 111-129 degrees distance and 5 houses away) Taslees (Trine) requirement not met
1055	May-June	Any Day Neyshabour	Any degree of Gemini	No degree of Gemini fulfills the Samimi (Cazimi) requirement		

Table II.3 shows that in Tīrtha's proposed AD 1048 birth date for Khayyam, there was only two times in consecutive *nights*, on Friday and Saturday, May 20 and 21 (based on the Julian calendar), that fulfilled the Samimi and Taslees (Triangulation or Trine) requirements, but they were also either Capricorn or Aquarius (*not Gemini*) ascendant respectively. In one of these (on Saturday) the Sun and the Mercury were Samimi (Cazimi) on degrees 5 and 4 of Gemini (*not on the same Gemini degree*, as also required by Khayyam's horoscope). The hour for these were, *at night*, around 10:07 p.m. or 0:10 a.m. respectively, *not at sunrise*. Therefore, AD 1048 can (once again) be *definitively ruled out* as a possible year for Khayyam's birth date.

Except for the year AD 1021 to which I will turn next, *no other date* fulfills the requirement of the reported horoscope for Khayyam during the AD 1018-1055 period, *no matter what degree* of Gemini is considered. In other words, there *is one, and only one, date* during the period which *perfectly* matches *all* the requirements of the reported horoscope, even fulfilling another aspect of the horoscope that escaped Tīrtha's attention and those of anyone else until the present. To this I shall return later.

To reiterate, I have searched for horoscope-requirements-fulfilling dates from the specific vantage point of Neyshabour, Iran, between AD 1018-1055 *regardless of the specific degree of Gemini* in which the Sun and the Mercury were supposed to fall. I have searched *all* Gemini degrees over the thirty-seven year period for a possible match that could fulfill all the requirements of Khayyam's reported horoscope except for the Gemini degree condition which I have relaxed due to the ambiguous and apparently inconsistent nature of manuscript information handed down the centuries.

As is evident from the above, there *is one, and only one, date* (marked by asterisk sign) between years AD 1018 and 1055 that *definitively* fulfills *all* the requirements of Khayyam's reported horoscope, including the degree of the Ascendant, when considering a degree of the Gemini in which the horoscope's Cazimi/Ascendant conjunction must fall.

This date is, in the Julian calendar, June 4, or in present commonly used Gregorian calendar June 10, AD 1021, at sunrise, Neyshabour's time. It is nearly a four-minute period from 4:43:56 to 4:47:55 a.m. During this short interval of time, the Gemini was Ascendant, the Sun and the Mercury were Cazimi on the same degree of the Ascendant 18° of Gemini (being in the Samimi distance of 8 minutes from each other), and Jupiter was positioned on the 11th degree of Libra, within a Taslees/Triangulation/Trine-fulfilling distance of about 113 degrees from both the Sun and Mercury.

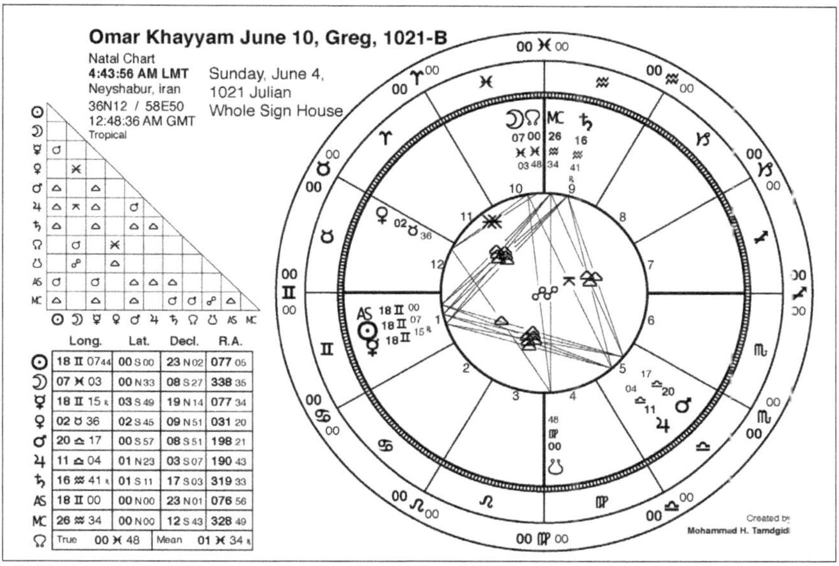

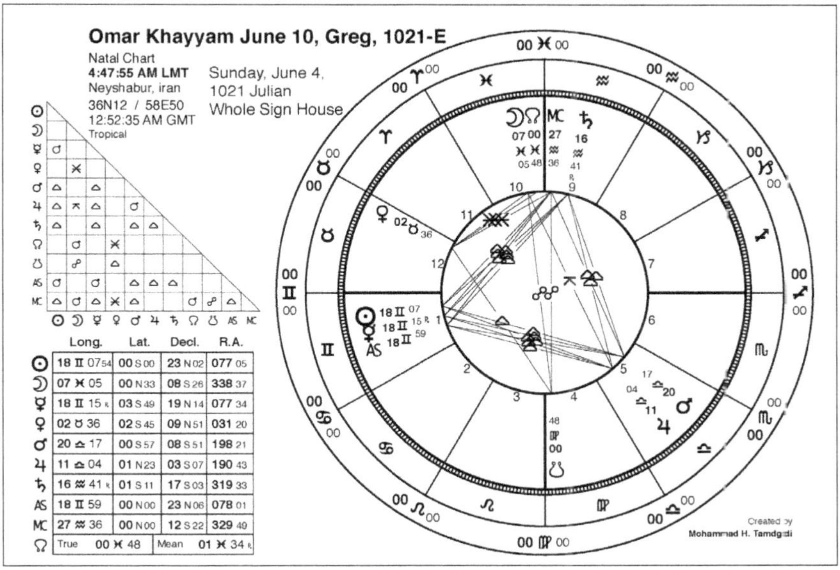

Figure II.5

The 11th Century Known-Planets Natal Charts of the Beginning and the Ending Seconds of the Nearly Four Minutes During which Omar Khayyam's Birth Took Place in AD 1021

In Figure II.5, I provide two natal charts for the beginning and the ending seconds of the nearly four minutes on June 10 (Gregorian), AD 1021, during which Omar Khayyam was born according to his reported horoscope. Again, note that I had, for the reason of ambiguities surrounding the degree of Gemini in Khayyam's horoscope reported in various extant manuscripts of Beyhaqi's *Tatemmat Sewan el-Hekmat (Supplement to the Chest of Wisdom)*, set aside the issue of that degree, and found by *direct and detailed* study of the ephemeris data adjusted to the *specific* location of Neyshabour, Iran, for the thirty-seven years during AD 1018-1055, that on *one and only one* date on the degree 18 of the Gemini, and on no other degrees of the Gemini, the requirements of Khayyam's horoscope are fulfilled.

In this historically unprecedented finding, there is an important note to be made regarding an aspect of Khayyam's horoscope that completely escaped Tīrtha's attention (since it also did not support his finding); it has also been entirely ignored by others when interpreting Khayyam's reported horoscope when searching for his date of birth.

If you recall, the reported horoscope ends with a statement referring to the condition whereby the Jupiter is said to be "observing" the Sun/Mercury Samimi (Cazimi), not the other way around. The term in the Arabic and Persian original is "Nāżer" which literally means observer/observing. Now, the question is, why is that expression included in the horoscope? Tīrtha translates the word as "aspecting," without further going into its explanation. The term "aspecting" is used in astrology and the terminology of astrolabe, the medieval instrument with which astronomical measurements were made.

Without going into the nature and ways of using the astrolabe, the instrument takes into account for its measurement a point on the other side of visible sky from whose vantage point the measurements are calculated. The point here is that the Jupiter could be in either side of the Zodiac wheel or circle when considering its distance from the Sun/Mercury Cazimi for our intended horoscope measurement.

In Tīrtha's original "solution" (now shown to be incorrect), as visualized in the charts Figures I.3 and I.4 in Chapter I, you may note that the Jupiter is in the visible, emerging daytime, sky at sunrise and given the motion of the sky (at that time the Earth was considered stationary and the sky/spheres moving) as depicted in the chart from left to right, Jupiter is *after* the Sun/Mercury, so the Jupiter is not observing them, but is *being observed by them.*

If Tīrtha had considered this other important data included in Khayyam's incredibly precise horoscope statement, he would and should have ruled out the solution at which he had arrived. In fact, among all the four possible dates he had chosen before arriving at his AD 1048 solution (1021, 1024, 1036, and 1048), it was only the date in AD 1021 (even for his erroneous reading of the third degree of the Gemini) that Jupiter was "observing" right-handedly (over a shorter arc), clockwise, the Sun-Mercury Cazimi.

In the year AD 1021 as noted in Khayyam's birth chart(s) in Figure II.5, Jupiter is not in the visible sky, but positioned below the Earth (so to speak), "observing" or "aspecting" the rising Sun/Mercury from behind in the invisible sky amid the apparent motion of the sky. At Khayyam's birth, Jupiter is watching the sunrise "from hiding," so to speak, where the Sun and the Mercury are Samimi/Cazimi exactly on the degree of the Ascendant.

So, the last remaining, previously ignored, piece of the puzzle of Khayyam's reported horoscope is now also finally solved in my discovery for the first time of the true and exact date of birth of Omar Khayyam.

8. Can the Gemini Degree 18 Shed Light on What the Extant Manuscript Copies of Beyhaqi's Reported Horoscope for Khayyam Were Trying to Tell Us?

Now that we have established the definitive date of birth of Omar Khayyam at sunrise, Neyshabour's time, on Sunday, June 10 (Gregorian), AD 1021, as the only time during the long range of 37 years from AD 1018-1055 that could fulfill all the requirements of his horoscope, we need to understand whether the Gemini degree on which this date and time fell provides any clues about how the various extant manuscript copies of Khayyam's reported horoscope can be reconciled with one another.

We can also use the definitive birth date information to provide more realistic assessments as to when his possible date of Khayyam's passing could have been. But I will postpone that inquiry regarding his date of passing to a following chapter. In the rest of this chapter, my focus will be on trying to understand whether there is any way the finding of the definitive birth date of Khayyam can shed light on how his horoscope has been reported and/or interpreted in the past.

First, regarding various copies of Beyhaqi's manuscript reporting the horoscope of Omar Khayyam, let me add a bit more to the confusion, or perhaps clarify (depending on how we interpret the matter), another version of Omar Khayyam's horoscope giving the degree of Gemini. This version was reported in a detailed study of the said manuscript, titled "The Author of the

Oldest Biographical Notice of Umar Khayyam and the Notice in Question" by Mohammad Shafi, which was published in the October 1932, Vol. VI, issue 4, of the journal *Islamic Culture*, pp. 586-623, in English with extensive Arabic and Persian text scattered throughout.

Shafi in fact published in the same year his in-depth compilations of both the English and an old Persian edition of Beyhaqi's *Tatemmat Sewan el-Hekmat (Supplement to the Chest of Wisdom)* in 1932, in Lahore. I have already introduced this book, and the article cited above is basically a report on one of the most important passages of Beyhaqi's book, the one dealing with Khayyam's biography.

In that book, both the Arabic and an old Persian translation of Beyhaqi's manuscript are compiled in detail with commentaries by Shafi and, interesting for us, as I noted before, a photocopy of the relevant handwritten passages/pages where Khayyam's horoscope is given are copied directly at the beginning of the Arabic and Persian sections, respectively. In fact, for the Arabic version, both of the horoscope pages across the extant manuscripts copies of Beyhaqi are given on pages 10 and 11 of the pdf; these are the same two versions I have previously included in this chapter in Figures II.1, II.3, and then in combined clips in Figure II.4.

Since I have not yet provided a copy of the old Persian version as given in Shafi's book (which can be found on the page 193 of that pdf), I do so now in Figure II.6. I have enclosed the horoscope statement inside the broken lines, and the place where the Gemini degree is given inside a circle.

In the article cited above, comparing the two, one Arabic and another Persian translation, of the manuscript text on Khayyam's biography available to him, and acknowledging earlier in the text that he could render the horoscope—"Here follows Khayyam's horoscope, which I am unable to render" (p. 608)—Shafi proceeds to offer a parallel copy of the Arabic and Persian passages of the horoscope. Similarly, in his book edition, on page 235 of the pdf or page 83 of the Persian section, Shafi has commented in a footnote on what he could not clearly follow in the old Persian translation of the book.[23]

---

23. The author of the old Persian translation was not known to Shafi at the time. However, in a recent new edition of the Persian translation of Beyhaqi's book published in Iran, edited and compiled by Ali Owjabi, titled *Dorrat ul-Akhbar va Lomʿat ul-Anvar: Bargardan-e Farsi-e Tatemmat Sewan el-Hekmat* (درّة الاخبار و لمعة الانوار: برگردان فارسی تتمه صوان الحکمة *meaning Pearls of Reports and Glitter of Lights: Persian Translation of Supplement to the Chest of Wisdom*), published by Hekmat press in Tehran, Iran, in (1388 SH) 2009, it is revealed that the translator of the old Persian translation was ناصرالدّین عمدة الملك منتجب الدّین منشی یزدی or Nasereddin

I think this Persian translation version of Khayyam's horoscope as reported by Mohammad Shafi is the source of what, as I have shared earlier in this chapter, the late Rezazadeh Malek (1998) reported on when overviewing the diverse extant versions of the horoscope in his primary source complications of works on and by Omar Khayyam.

What Shafi says he could not "render" in the horoscope, for which he cannot be blamed as it is indeed unclear given the—even to a Persian, let alone Arabic, speaking person—unfamiliar way he has tried to type the Gemini degree based on the handwritten original he must have had in his possession, could be very roughly rendered as the same ک و ر that Rezazadeh Malek reports in his compendium, the letter و serving as an "and" in the sentence. It is obvious from the original image, there is no و in between ک ر .

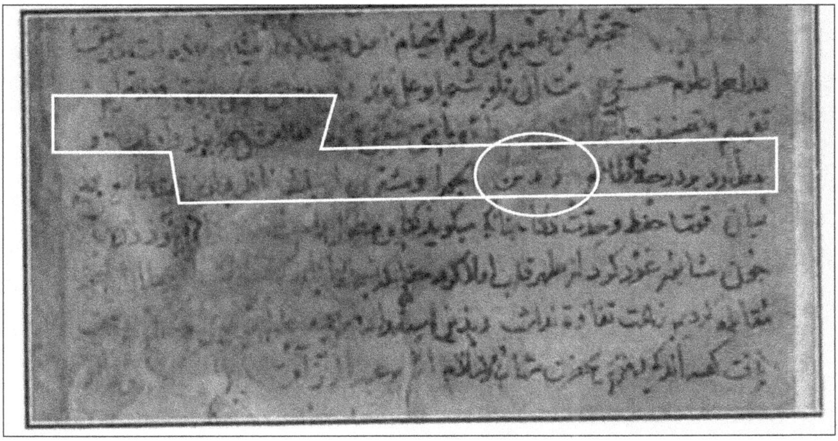

Figure II.6

Mohammad Shafi's Copy of the Persian Translation of the Beyhaqi Manuscript Where Omar Khayyam's Horoscope Appears (Inside Straight Lines), And Specifically Where the Gemini Degree Is Given (Inside Circle)

In his footnote in the book edition, Shafi writes (see Figure II.7, first footnote, written in Persian; I have added punctuation in bracket to distinguish what he is quoting from his comment on it, and added an X where the ambiguous expression is given):

ʿOmdat ol-Molk Montajebeddin Monshi Yazdi.

(۱) تتمه: و عطارد درجة الطالع فى ح من الجوزا، پس تصحيف "فى ح من" است.

> [My translation of the above:] (1) Tatemmat: ["...] and Mercury on the degree of the Ascendant in ح of the Gemini ["], so X is a misreading of "in ح of".

Shafi is basically commenting on his realization that the ambiguous degree expression X given in the old Persian translation is what in the Arabic original is given as "in ح of" "فى ح من". So, if we relate this to what Rezazadeh Malek had reported, what in the old Persian translation looks like ک و ر is a misreading of "فى ح من", again keeping in mind that و is an "and" Malek has added.

Note that in the image shared in Figure II.7, we are seeing not the original handwritten manuscript rendering which Shafi could not decipher, but only his own attempt at "typing in," so to speak, the undecipherable letters for the purpose of publication. The original handwritten image is the one I shared in Figure II.6 above.

At this point, we have to note an error on the part of Shafi in making a comparison between the Arabic and the old Persian manuscripts. In Figure II.6, it is clear that the ambiguous degree expression X does not include من whereas in his effort in correcting the "misreading" in his footnote, Shafi is including the word من in the Arabic original to substitute for.

So, to be accurate, Shafi cannot claim X is a misreading of "فى ح من" because in the handwritten original the word من is given separately from X. It is perhaps due to realizing this that in his article cited above, Shafi confesses to being unable to decipher the part where the degree of Gemini is given in the old Persian version of Beyhaqi's book. But he clearly indicates that in the Arabic version, the degree given is ح as given in the expression "فى ح من".

So, Shafi has ended up with an expression that for him does not make sense. It is the same ambiguous passage that Rezazadeh Malek tried to report on and convey, by suggesting that (reading from right to left), the first looks like a ک (a letter sounding like K) the second is just a و ("and") he has added and the third more like a ر (a letter sounding like R).

The reason I am reporting the above is to demonstrate, first, the further extent to which the extant manuscripts of Beyhaqi giving Khayyam's horoscope have been ambiguous and not equivocal in offering a definitive rendering of the Gemini degree in Khayyam's reported horoscope. Second, I wanted to provide further evidence for the source of the version/interpretation that Rezazadeh Malek reports in his Khayyam compendium, and where his interpretation could have come from. If you, the reader, find the above confusing, it is not your fault. But, I assure you things will become clearer.

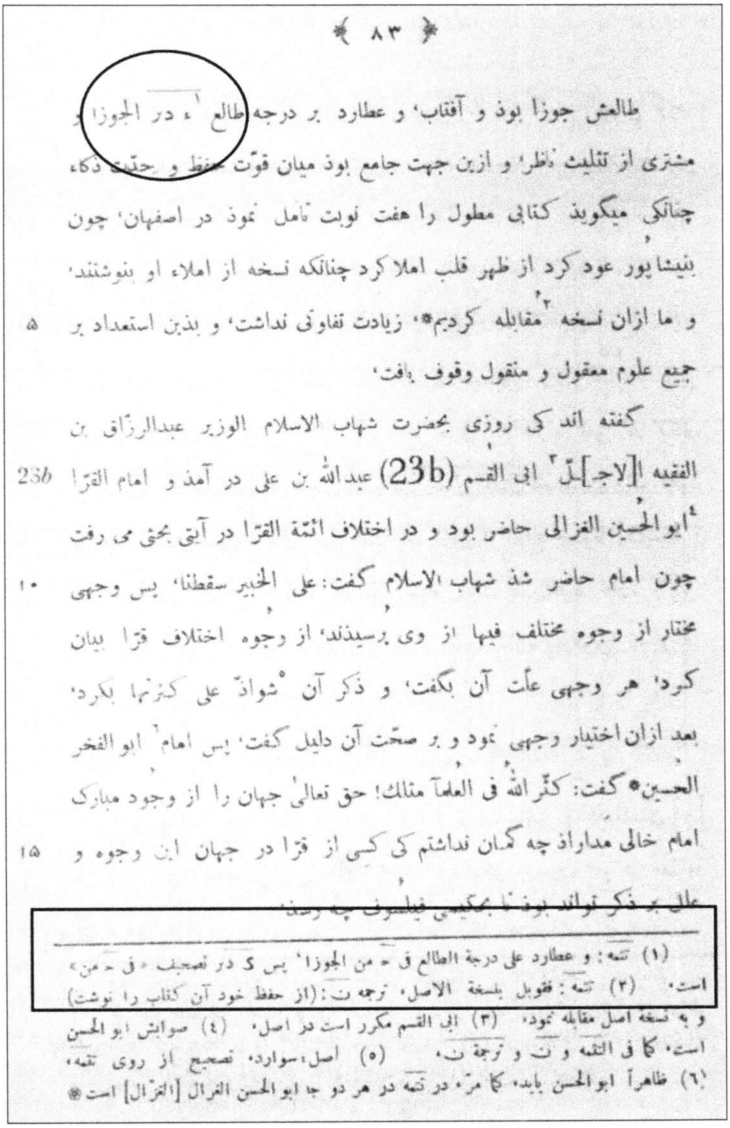

﴿ ٨٣ ﴾

طالعش جوزا بوذ و آفتاب، و عطارد بر درجه طالع [1] در الجوزا و مشتری از تثلیث ناظر، و ازین جهت جامع بوذ میان قوّت حفظ و حدّت ذکاء چنانکی میگویذ کتابی مطول را هفت نوبت تامل نموذ در اصفهان، چون بنیشاپور عود کرد از ظهر قلب املا کرد چنانکه نسخه از املاء او بنوشتند، و ما ازان نسخه [2] مقابله کردیم* زیادت تفاوتی نداشت، و بذین استعداد بر جمیع علوم معقول و منقول وقوف یافت،

کفته اند کی روزی بحضرت شهاب الاسلام الوزیر عبدالرزّاق بن الفقیه [الاجـ]ـلّ [3] ابی القسم (23b) عبدالله بن علی در آمذ و امام القرّا 23b [4] ابو الحسین الغزالی حاضر بود و در اختلاف ائمّة القرّا در آیتی بحثی می رفت چون امام حاضر شذ شهاب الاسلام کفت: علی الخبیر سقطنا، پس وجهی مختار از وجوه مختلف فیها از وی پرسیذند، از وجوه اختلاف قرّا بیان کرد، هر وجهی علت آن بکفت، و ذکر آن [5] شواذّ علی کثرتها بکرد، بعد ازان اختیار وجهی نمود و بر صحّت آن دلیل کفت، پس امام [6] ابو الفخر الحسین* کفت: کثّر الله فی العلمآ مثالك! حق تعالی جهان را از وجود مبارک امام خالی مداراذ چه کمان نداشتم کی کسی از قرّا در جهان این وجوه و عالی بر ذکر تواند بوذ تا بحکیمی فیلسوف چه رسذ

(١) تتمه: و عطارد علی درجة الطالع ق ـه من الجوزا، پس ک در تصحیف «ق ـه من» است، (٢) تتمه: فقوبل بنسخة الاصل، ترجه ت: (از حفظ خود آن کتاب را نوشت) و به نسخه اصل مقابله نمود، (٣) ابی القسم مکرر است در اصل، (٤) صوابش ابو الحسن است، کما فی التتمه و ت و ترجة ت، (٥) اصل: سوارد، تصحیح از روی تتمه، (٦) ظاهراً ابو الحسن باید، کما مرّ، در تتمه در هر دو جا ابو الحسن الغزال [الغزّال] است*

Figure II.7

Mohammad Shafi's Book Page Where the Arabic and Persian Translated Versions of Omar Khayyam's Horoscope Are Compared

The variation ک (و) ر comes from the old Persian translation of Beyhaqi's book, where the translator apparently has tried to also "translate" (perhaps) the degree of the Gemini given in the Arabic into an expression prevalent among his intended Persian speaking readers *at that time.*

Value	Letter		Value	Letter		Value	Letter
1	ا		10	ی		100	ق
2	ب		20	ک		200	ر
3	ج		30	ل		300	ش
4	د		40	م		400	ت
5	ه		50	ن		500	ث
6	و		60	س		600	خ
7	ز		70	ع		700	ذ
8	ح		80	ف		800	ض
9	ط		90	ص		900	ظ
						1000	غ

Figure II.8

The Kabir List of Arabic Abjad Numerical Values

Another point I wish to draw the reader's attention is how Mohammad Shafi has typed the Arabic version of the same manuscript passage, specifically where the degree of Gemini is given. Following the customary way scholars have rendered the degree, Shafi also has inserted في ح in the place between the words الطالع and الجوزا in the passage. In Arabic, the word في means "in" and the other letter ح is the eighth letter in the abjad alphabet which, as I noted previously, has the numerical value of 8 in the abjad system (Figure II.8).

I earlier noted how and why it is important for us to understand what the definitive date and the Gemini degree of 18 could tell us about the diversely ambiguous ways in which Khayyam's reported horoscope have been rendered across the handwritten manuscript copies surviving from the past. However, before I embark on answering that question, let me remind the reader that Beyhaqi's text is one of the most well-known, read, cited, and widely copied scholarly texts in Islamic studies, since it offers a succinct synopsis of biographies of many scholars, philosophers, and intellectuals of Islam and Iran during especially the fifth and the sixth centuries of the Lunar Hejri (or eleventh and twelfth centuries Christian) calendar. Therefore, understandably, it has gone through extensive copying and recopying by various scribes throughout many cultures across the centuries when the modern printing industries had not yet been invented and used. All copying were done by scribes who had more or less knowledge of the content they were copying. So, copies were made of copies of copies of copies, and so on, in the process of which some text could be corrupted.

In the case of regular texts, words, or sentences, one would expect less chances of corruption, since some basic understanding of what was being copied prevented gross corruption of the words. However, with abjad letters of the degrees in the Gemini, it is possible that a first miscopying by a scribe could lead to further miscopyings without the later scribes being at fault for not being able to decipher what they could not immediately figure out, since any corrections or questions in this regard required extensive knowledge of historical ephemeris data and of the astrolabe. So, each guessed the letter he or she was copying, and thus we ended up with numerous competing versions of the Gemini degree in Khayyam's reported horoscope.

However, I will demonstrate below that even despite such corruptions in the copies made, the information received from various manuscript copies can be successfully reconciled with one another to provide an indisputable and convincing support for our definitively discovered birth date of Omar Khayyam and the degree 18 of the Gemini in his horoscope.

9. The First Way to Account for the Various Extant Manuscript Copies With One Another

The most common way in which the Arabic version of the horoscope has been rendered in handwriting and more recent typed sources, is one in which the word فی (in Arabic, meaning "in" or "at" or "on") is included in the sentence as we find in the following:

«طالعه الجوزا و الشمس و عطارد على درجه الطالع فی ح من الجوزا و عطارد صميمى و المشترى من التثليث ناظر اليهما».

Also consider that the letter من in Arabic means "of" or "from." The word

على in Arabic also means "in" or "at." I have previously noted the interesting fact that in Rezazadeh Malek's overview of horoscope variations, he has omitted the word فى as if he intended to include it as part of the dashed lines giving the degree of Gemini, and not as part of the main sentence.

If we were to translate literally, word for word, the Arabic sentence above into English, we would have something like this (notice what I have emphasized in bold):

> His ascendant was the Gemini and the Sun and the Mercury were **on** the degree of the ascendent **in** 8 of Gemini and the Mercury was Samimi and the Jupiter from Taslees observed them both.

By comparison, per another example, Tīrtha translated the text as follows:

> His ascendant was the Gemini. The Sun and the Mercury were on the degree of the ascendant in the third degree of the Gemini. The Mercury was "Ṣamimi," and the Jupiter was aspecting (Nazar) both from triangulation (Tathlith). (Tīrtha, p. XXXII)

Now, also consider the general variation of the Arabic which Rezazadeh Malek conveyed in his Khayyam compendium, one where he omitted the word فى from the common part of the text, representing one of the dashes inside his parenthesis as copied again in below:

> «طالعه الجوزا و الشمس و عطارد على درجه الطالع (- -) من الجوزا و عطارد صميمى و المشترى من التثليث ناظر اليهما».

Notice in the last version that, in proceeding to offer the various renderings of the degree across the manuscripts, Malek was in effect suggesting that the word فى is not needed as part of the main sentence. And he would be correct, if that is what he intended to do.

What I wish to point the readers' attention to here is that it is most likely that through the process of successive recopying by various scribes, the letter ى became gradually corrupted, the letter being misread as the word فى such that later scribes assumed that the word was not a part of a degree given in abjad for ى but the word فى in the normal part of the sentence.

If we read the horoscope text again, we in fact can realize the word فى is not really needed as such for the sentence, and it is redundant, a repeated word.

When translated it would be redundant to say the word "on" or "in" twice—such as "... and the Sun and the Mercury were on the degree of the ascendant in ...." Just one "on" represented clearly by the word من suffices.

The sentence could thus be easily read and translated as follows without the فی or its translation :

«طالعه الجوزا و الشمس و عطارد على درجه الطالع ى ح من الجوزا و عطارد صميمى و المشترى من التثليث ناظر اليهما».

> His ascendant was the Gemini and the Sun and the Mercury were on the degree of the ascendent ى ح of the Gemini and the Mercury was Samimi and the Jupiter from Taslees observed them both.

Now, if we include instead of فی the letter ی , assuming the latter was the original expression and the former as the corrupted variation scribes thought was part of the sentence, then we have, based on abjad values of the letters the following since the letter ی in abjad system has a value of 10:

> His ascendant was the Gemini and the Sun and the Mercury were on the degree of the ascendent 10 [+] 8 of the Gemini and the Mercury was Samimi and the Jupiter from Taslees observed them both.

As it is practiced in abjad system, the use of both letters together implies addition of their numerical value, which is 18, confirming the correct Gemini degree we have ourselves discovered for Khayyam's horoscope.

10. The Second Way to Account for the Various Extant Manuscript Copies With One Another

Let us now consider the horoscope version in which the letter used is not ح or ح but ج , the large version of which in Arabic (or Persian) alphabet is ج .

I copied this manuscript in Figure II.3, and its magnified version in Figure II.4.

The first thing to consider is that there are letters in this writing that should have the usual "dots" for the alphabets they use, but they do not. For instance, as I had noted before, the word الجوزا appears once with the dot on the line above the ج and once without the dot after it (right after the place where the degree is given, indeed, on the fifth line, reading from right).

There are other places (such as in the word الطبيعيات in the last line of the image depicted in Figure II.4 on top) where, again, the expected dots are missing for the small versions of the letter ب and the second ی in الطبيعيات. It is common in handwriting, even at that time, to omit such dots when the context is obvious, and their inclusion depended on each scribe's style.

What I think is worth considering is the possibility of similar errors and omissions being responsible for the lack, or in the case of the degree given, for the appearance of dots.

Even what is supposed to be the word فى preceding where the degree is given lacks the expected dot for its first letter (ف), if it is mean to be a ق . In this case, I have raised the possibility earlier that the word may not be فى after all but a ى , but in this copy, it may be (or not) intended as such, as in other manuscripts that have used a corrupted interpretation of the Gemini degree in Khayyam's horoscope.

Important to note is that whether we read the letter as a ج or a ح, no matter whether we attribute the letters 3 or 8 to either respectively, there is no way we could arrive at a date during the period AD 1018-1055 when all the requirements of Khayyam's reported horoscope could be fully satisfied with those degrees each.

In other words, we did not find *any* dates where the horoscope conditions could be fulfilled on the degrees 3, 8, or 13 (if we were to consider ج to have been the intended second number, adding 10 for ى plus 3 for ج).

I think that this manuscript version is also, like others, one in which the correct Gemini degree of Khayyam's horoscope could not be adequately read or transcribed by the scribe in question, and the correct rendering of the abjad letters for the only Gemini degree that could fulfill Khayyam's reported horoscope is one combining the letters ح and ى adding up to the numerical value of the degree 18.

Again, note that were we to assume that a combination of letters ج and ى whose abjad numerical values would add up to 13 could have possibly been the intended letters offering the degree of Gemini on which the Sun was positioned in a Samimi configuration with the Mercury, from our ephemeris date given in Table II.3 earlier for all the years during AD 1018-1055, no dates and times in which the Sun was positioned on the 13th degree of the Gemini could fulfill the requirements for Khayyam's reported horoscope.

So, in no combination could the letter ج alone or with another letter solve the Gemini degree puzzle in Khayyam's reported horoscope. In any case, in most extant copies of the manuscript, the abjad letter used for the degree in Gemini has been ح and not ج.

It is then possible that we have another case of copying error here, where a dot for فى is misplaced to make ح a ج .

In any case, a rendering of ج for the Gemini degree (third) would not result in a horoscope-requirements-fulfilling solution.

11. The Third Way to Account for the Various Extant Manuscript Copies With One Another

Let us now turn to the other version Rezazadeh Malek reported on in his Khayyam compendium, namely his having seen Arabic manuscripts in which the degree of the Gemini in Khayyam's reported horoscope was rendered as ح and یو . To be more faithful to his statement, he uses the expression as ح و یو in his sentence. Malek's statement is as follows in Persian in the original (for which I offer my translation below):

آنچه که میان ابروان جای آن را خطّ تیره گذاشتیم، در یکی از نُسخ متن عربی (ح) و در نسخه های دیگر (ح) و (یو) آمده است. و در ترجمهٔ فارسی (ک و ر) است.

[My translation of the above:] What we included in parentheses as a dark dash, has been rendered in one of the Arabic manuscripts as (ح) and in two other manuscripts as (ح) و (یو) and in the Persian translation it is (ک و ر).

Malek's statement is somewhat unclear and could be read in two different ways.

He either means that in a given Arabic source, he has found both letters ح and یو listed together, or that in one source it is rendered as یو while in another sources it is rendered as ح . If both were listed together, he would have included the letters inside the same parenthesis, as he does so with the variation ک و ر , which we have already analyzed already; although in the latter و seems not to be in the original. However, he puts ح and یو in different parentheses, giving the impression that the second variation as I noted above could be what was intended. This may mean that he has seen an Arabic source in which the only letter used to denote the degree of Gemini was یو .

I have not come across any studies of Beyhaqi's manuscript where in the horoscope of Khayyam a letter such as یو was used alone. If it had been, meaning that the intended degree of the Gemini for Khayyam's birth chart was 10, we know now, having surveyed closely the years AD 1018-1055, that there was no date in which the Sun and the Mercury were Samimi on the degree of 10 of the Gemini. So, we can safely rule out the possibility of the letter یو having appeared alone, indicating the numerical value 10, to offer a degree for Khayyam's horoscope that fulfills its requirement.

The expression یو can be read as a way of pronouncing in Arabic (such as saying "ef" for F, or "ti" for T). So one way of reading یو is that of ی . But one can argue for the option of a combination of the letters ی and و which together combine to the value of 10+6=16. However, we know, again, that there is no degree 16 of Gemini when the requirements of Khayyam's horoscope can be fulfilled for the years considered. So, we can also safely rule out the possibility of یو as a compound abjad number signifying an acceptable degree for Gemini.

A small letter ح or large letter ح have almost universally been reported to have been used for the Gemini degree in Arabic manuscripts. Often, what has happened is that in the handwritten original the small letter is used, but when it has been typed in the published version, it has been rendered as the large version of that letter.

My reading of Rezazadeh Malek's text leads me to conclude that he actually meant to contrast two types of Arabic sources from one another, one in which only the letter ح was used versus another in which both ح and یو were used together. The reason he did not include both in the same parenthesis is that he did not intend to say that a letter و which means "and" was present in the original as such. He meant to say, in other words, that he saw an Arabic version in which he found ح and یو beside each other as in یو ح .

If this was the case, it is possible to consider that the scribe may have meant to write یـ و ح . In Arabic (or Persian) the letter ی when used at the beginning of a word is rendered as a یـ . It is possible that as some sources used the small letter ح to denote ح also this scribe used the small letter یـ to denote ی , separating them with a letter و (standing for "and"). The combination of these in that manuscript, or by those copying them later, may have then ended up with the variation یو ح . In other words, we would have a manuscript in which Khayyam's horoscope would be rendered as (in Arabic) یو ح . So, according to the standard abjad system we have a degree comprised of یـ and ح adding 10 and 8, equalling 18, which is our discovered degree of the Gemini for Khayyam's horoscope.

Now consider the following.

Note that, as I had said earlier when introducing Rezazadeh Malek's compendium for the first time, for some reason he did not include the word فی in his overview of horoscope expressions in Arabic, and only used two dashes in parenthesis to designate a general expression of the degree of Gemini found.

«طالعه الجوزا و الشمس و عطارد على درجه الطالع (- -) من الجوزا و عطارد صمیمی و المشتری من التثلیث ناظر الیهما».

Here, then, if we insert the rendering option یو ح in the sentence, we would have the following:

«طالعه الجوزا و الشمس و عطارد على درجه الطالع يو ح من الجوزا و عطارد صميمى و المشترى من التثليث ناظر اليهما».

This would be equivalent of the following reading:

«طالعه الجوزا و الشمس و عطارد على درجه الطالع يـ و ح من الجوزا و عطارد صميمى و المشترى من التثليث ناظر اليهما».

Even if we consider the variation ح يو or يو ح , it is possible to consider that the expression is a way of rendering the letter يو phonetically, as we would say "zed" for "z," we say ya or yo for ی . In any case, based on abjad numerical system the combination of abjad letters ی and ح together yield the total numerical value of 10+8=18, which is the exact degree of the Gemini we found for the definitive birth date horoscope of Omar Khayyam.

A final possibility regarding the above is considering that three letters يـ و ح were meant to be given for the Gemini degree, which would add numerically to 10+6+8=24. However, we know, again, that no degree of Gemini 24 during the considered period fulfills the requirements of Khayyam's reported horoscope. In any case, 24 can be rendered in abjad with two letters (20 and 4), so clearly the three-letter possibility of giving the number can be ruled out even for that reason.

12. The Fourth Way to Account for the Various Extant Manuscript Copies With One Another

Let us now consider the version as represented in Figure II.6 and appearing in typed form in Figure II.7.

First, we should consider the important point that the abjad letter used to indicate the degree of the Gemini in Khayyam's original/correct horoscope did not have to be a single digit number.

Zodiac signs have 30 degrees, and it is impossible to denote every degree number between 1 to 30 by a single abjad letter. The table of standard abjad letters and their numerical values as copied in Figure II.8 demonstrates that only 9 letters corresponding to single digits 1-9, plus the additional letters corresponding to letters 10, 20, and 30, could be represented by a single alphabetical letter. The rest of the degrees from 11 to 19 and 21 to 29 could only be represented by two letters. The customary way of doing that has been by combining two abjad letters. As noted, three letters are not needed for the purpose (so we can safely rule out the possibility of and need for 3 abjad letters to denote any of the degrees in, say the Gemini, Zodiac signs).

According to Rezazadeh Malek (who may have, or not, had access to the actual handwritten "Persian translation" source which Shafi had seen and reported on), the letters being reported could have been ک و ر .

The translator who had been trying to offer a Persian translation of Beyhaqi's book, may have been trying to "translate" even the degrees (given in abjad letters) of the Gemini he was reading in the Arabic original.

First, we should safely consider that the second letter being used, that is (the letter و) only stands for "and" and nothing else. As I noted above, three letters are not needed to denote the numerical values from 1-30 in any Zodiac sign. In Figure II.6, in fact, the letter و does not appear, which points to the possibility that it was Rezazadeh Malek who had added, in typing, the letter in order to simply say "and." The handwritten manuscript in Figure II.6 is comprised of two symbols, not three.

The trouble is that if we follow the numerical values of the standard abjad alphabets as used in Arabic (and Persian), as listed in Figure II.8, the letter ر (the equivalent of R in English language) would give us a value of 200 in the standard (Kabir) abjad system (Figure II.8). This could not be possible as a letter denoting a supposed Zodiac sign degree, since any Zodiac sign is divided into 30 degrees, so a value of 200 for a degree cannot be correct.

Besides, the first letter that is undecipherable by Shafi, and interpreted by Rezazadeh Malek as a ک most likely was not the letter usually rendered in Arabic as a ك (which is the equivalent of the letter K in English alphabet). The hamzeh sign ء which is usually accompanied in the Arabic (and not in the Persian alphabet, as visible in the two letters given above) for this letter would have to be present in the Arabic original for a Persian translator to translate the letter to a ک in Persian.

We know of no extant Arabic manuscript for Beyhaqi's book where a Gemini degree of ك has been given (in standard abjad system it has a value of 20). We can safely assume, then, that the "Persian translator" who was trying to translate the Arabic abjad letters he was witnessing in the Arabic original before him was intending to offer equivalents of the Arabic letters in an abjad system that was familiar to him and his intended *Persian* audience.

This intention to offer a "Persian translation" is obvious from the letter R used as noted above (if indeed it is an R) since, given its numerical value of 200, it could not have connotated the use of the standard abjad letters as usually used. So, it can plausibly be concluded that the intended Persian translator was trying to provide a Persian translation of the abjad letters he was reading in his Arabic original.

I think the letter Shafi finds undecipherable, and Rezazadeh Malek interprets as a ک is indeed the letter ى which also looks like a large hamzeh (hamzeh is in fact technically a very small ى). The similarity of the two letters ک and ى is obvious. Even in the typed version found in Shafi (see Figure II.7 footnote), one can see that the original handwritten letter that Shafi renders as a letter, one that is not readily present in any Arabic or Persian alphabet, is rendered in a letter similar to ى . In other words, the Persian translation that Shafi could not decipher and Rezazadeh Malek interpreted as a کر was in fact the letters ىر — so we are being given the abjad letters "ra and ya."

Value	Letter		Value	Letter		Value	Letter
1	ا		10	ى		4	ق
2	ب		8	ك		8	ر
3	ج		6	ل		ساقط	ش
4	د		4	م		4	ت
5	ه		2	ن		8	ث
6	و		ساقط	س		ساقط	خ
7	ز		10	ع		4	ذ
8	ح		8	ف		8	ض
9	ط		6	ص		ساقط	ظ
						4	غ

Figure II.9

The Saghir List of Arabic Abjad Numerical Values

It is here that we should consider the distinction often made in Islamic and especially Persian Islamic studies, especially within Sufi and astrological circles, between the Kabir (large) and Saghir (small)[24] abjad numerical systems. In Figure II.9 I provide a table of the Saghir abjad list.

24. For example, see the online tables of Kabir and Saghir Abjad Numerical Systems here: https://namnak.com/تفسیر-حروف-ابجد-کبیر-و-صغیر.p38073

As it is evident from the above, the letter ر or R or 'ra,' which has a numerical value of 200 in the standard Kabir abjad system (Figure II.8), has a value of 8 in the Saghir abjad system (Figure II.9). Moreover, in the same Saghir abjad system, the letter ی or 'ya' has the same value of '10.'

This yields the total value of 8+10=18 which is, again, the same degree of Gemini we have found to fulfill all the requirements of Omar Khayyam's birth chart.

13. The Fifth Way to Account for the Various Extant Manuscript Copies With One Another

Another possibility to consider would be that based on Rezazadeh Malek's reported Persian translation the letters were ک and ر , where we have already established that the abjad system used could not be the Kabir system. In the latter, ر would have a value of 200, and this would rule out its having been correct as valued, since Zodiac months have a maximum 30 degrees length.

Thus, if we use the Saghir abjad system as copied in Figure II.9 for determining the value of ک and ر , we arrive at the total 8+8=16, since the value of both these letters in the Saghir abjad system is 8. The question may even arise here as to why the translator would need to use different letters to denote the same value 8 in the above situation in the first place?

Besides, Table II.3 compiled previously shows that at no time during the thirty seven years during AD 1018-1055 did the Sun and the Mercury appear near the 16th degree of Gemini in Samimi (Cazimi) configuration with one another. So, the possibility that ک and ر , that is K and R, was the intended abjad letters giving the proper Gemini degree in Khayyam's reported horoscope is ruled out.

14. The Sixth Way to Account for the Various Extant Manuscript Copies With One Another

Another remote possibility—remote, since three letters are not needed to express a digit between 1-30 in a Zodiac cycle—is to consider ک و ر to be a three digit combination for which, again, we use the Saghir abjad system to arrive at a total of 8+6+8=22 as the supposed Gemini degree in Khayyam's horoscope.

Table II.3 again does not demonstrate that the Sun and the Mercury could have been anywhere close in a Samimi configurations on the degree 22 of Gemini during the AD 1018-1055 period.

15. The Use of Kufi Script in Arabic Astrolabes for Rendering Abjad Numbers

Now, finally, let me introduce the copy of an astrolabe in Figure II.10, where the degrees around the Meter of the astrolabe are rendered in Arabic, particularly using the Kufi script style which was common for the purpose in the past, as also evident in the image copied of another Arabic astrolabe in the cover of this book.

Figure II.10

Comparing the Letter ی Having the Numerical Value of 10 in Kufi Calligraphy in Astrolabes With the the Letter in One of Beyhaqi's Manuscript Copies (Source: Dreamstime 99397538).

In Figure II.10, it can be observed that in the abjad lettering system used to indicate the degree numbers around the circle, starting from the top (where the astrolabe handle is located), clockwise, we have the degrees in tens, divided in five degree intervals. The abjad letters for tens plus five (such 15, 25, more not shown as not needed), are expressed by adding the letter

ه to the abjad letter, as below. So, using the abjad letters for each quadrant (repeated four times for 360 degrees around the circle) the numbers are:

5 — ه (letter 'ha' in Arabic/Persian, number ٥)
10 — ي (letter 'ya' in Arabic/Persian, number ١٠) <<<<<<<<<<<<
15 — يه (letter 'ha' and 'ya' in Arabic/Persian, number ١٥)
20 — ک (letter 'kaf' in Arabic/Persian, number ٢٠)
25 — که (letter 'ha' and 'kaf' in Arabic/Persian, number ٢٥)
30 — ل (letter 'lam' in Arabic/Persian, number ٣٠)
35 — له (letter 'ha' and 'lam' in Arabic/Persian, number ٣٥)
40 — م (letter 'mim' in Arabic/Persian, number ٤٠)
45 — مه (letter 'ha' and 'mim' in Arabic/Persian, number ٤٥)
50 — ن (letter 'noon' in Arabic/Persian, number ٥٠)
55 — نه (letter 'ha' and 'noon' in Arabic/Persian, number ٥٥)
60 — س (letter 'sin' in Arabic/Persian, number ٦٠)
65 — سه (letter 'ha' and 'sin' in Arabic/Persian, number ٦٥)
70 — ع (letter "eyn' in Arabic/Persian, number ٧٠)
75 — عه (letter 'ha' and "eyn' in Arabic/Persian, number ٧٥)
80 — ف (letter 'fa' in Arabic/Persian, number ٨٠)
85 — فه (letter 'ha' and 'fa' in Arabic/Persian, number ٨٥)
90 — ص (letter 'sut' in Arabic/Persian, number ٩٠)

From the abjad table, it is evident that the letter denoting the "5" degrees is a ه in Arabic. After the first ه the reader can see the letter ى as rendered in the Kufi script ے (the letter is sometimes, as in the example of image shown, accompanied by two dots underneath as in ي but it is not essential[25]). After that, we have the letter ى which has the numerical value of "10." In other words the shape of the letter preceding what was regarded as the only letter indicating the degree of the Gemini (that is ح), is associated not with فى but with the letter ى whose numerical value is 10 as written in the manuscript in the commonly practiced Kufi script, ے (today identified as Unicode U+06D2, UTF-8, DB 92).

This now should leave us no doubt that what in the manuscript copy was rendered before ح is indeed the letter ى in Kufi script, conveying the numerical value "10."

This can mean only one thing: the horoscope of Khayyam had intended

25. The abjad number ے can be seen clearly in the following link being used without the two bottom dots https://en.wikipedia.org/wiki/Astrolabe#/media/File:Iranian_Astrolabe_14.jpg. In the example here https://lifeasahuman.com/2019/arts-culture/art/historical-marvels-the-journey-of-the-astrolabe/ the number "10" actually accompanies the abjad number ے.

to provide the number "18" as the degree of the Gemini on which his birth chart fell in the Gemini, and it was through inadvertent copying corruptions and misreadings that it became wrongly assumed that the degree was only a single digit number. Because in Kufi script the letter ی looks like a فی scribes mistook the letter ی to be a rendering of فی , thereby only the letter ح was left to be counted for the degree of the Gemini.

16. How and Where Russian Scholars and Astronomers Went Wrong In Evaluating and Confirming Swāmi Govinda Tīrtha's Mistaken Date of Birth for Omar Khayyam

An important factors that served to "officially" establish Swāmi Govinda Tīrtha's mistaken "discovery" of Khayyam's date of birth and (to an important extent, indirectly) his date of passing (to whose topic I shall turn in the next chapter), was the confirmation it received from the Soviet Russian scholars and astronomers later on, obviously all done with good intentions.

In their important contribution published in 1962 compiling and commenting on most of the various extant manuscripts of Omar Khayyam,[26] the Russian scholars Boris A. Rozenfeld and Adolf P. Iushkevich reported in their introduction on an effort they made in evaluating Tīrtha's findings, in part by consulting their Russian astronomer colleagues for the purpose.

In doing so, they ended up confirming Tīrtha's proposed date for Khayyam's birth date, while differing with the *year* Tīrtha had proposed in 1941 for Khayyam's date of passing while using Tīrtha's proposed month and day (12th of Muharram) to offer their own preferred date for Khayyam's passing on Dec. 4th, AD 1131. In a way, we can safely argue that the current uneasy world consensus dates for Khayyam's birth and passing (May 19, AD 1048, and December 4, AD 1131), building on Tīrtha's work, are owed to Soviet Russian scholars and astronomers who gave their official stamp of approval to them.

However, in light of my findings in this chapter, it is now rather quite easy to understand how the Russian scholars and astronomers went astray in their mistaken confirmation of an erroneous birth date (and I will also argue and demonstrate in the following chapter, date of death) for Omar Khayyam. This can be verified by directly accessing the introduction to the

26. Rozenfeld, Boris Abramovich, and Adolf Pavlovich Iushkevich. 1962. *Traktaty [Tracts or Treatises] of Omar Khayyam* [Treatises of Omar Khayyam - In Russian with reproductions of original sources on Khayyām]. Moscow: Izd. Vostochnoi Litery.

Moscow edition, its pages 16-21, where Rozenfeld and Iushkevich explain their effort as part of their introduction to their collection. Recently, a Persian translation[27] of this introduction was published in Iran, translated and edited by Baqer Mozaffarzadeh, whose translation efforts are well made in the short book comprising the Russian scholar's introduction (only). But even the Russian original text can also nowadays be read by non-Russian speakers using online translation tools.

The explanation for the errors Russian scholars and astronomers made in their evaluation can be briefly offered as follows.

First, all their efforts at evaluating Tīrtha's findings were based on the mistaken assumption Tīrtha made in reading the degree of Gemini in Khayyam's reported horoscope as a "3." They simply took for granted, uncritically, what Tīrtha had wrongly determined to be the Gemini degree. So, any efforts the Russian scholars and their astronomer consultants made to evaluate in order to confirm (or not) Tīrtha's findings were actually focused on reading the Gemini degree in the horoscope as 3. The Russian scholars and astronomers were not exploring any other possible Gemini degree and its associated date(s). I have already explained in detail in this chapter why neither 3 nor 8 degrees would result in finding a date of birth for Khayyam on which all the (other) requirements of Khayyam's horoscope could be met.

Second, however, there is another important error, "lost in translation," so to speak, that explains why the Russian scholars and astronomers failed in noticing otherwise glaring inconsistencies and inaccuracies in Tīrtha's efforts and catching his mistakes. Or, perhaps they did notice, but let it go, as I will further explain below. Actually, it is an odd error they made, but nevertheless quite interesting to note.

Even though in Tīrtha, there is clearly an effort made by him to notice and consider the Samimi (Cazimi) requirement in Khayyam's horoscope, where he even consults dictionaries to define what Samimi (Cazimi) requirement entails, that is the distance (in this case between the Sun and Mercury) should not exceed 16 *minutes*, in the Russian introduction (by Rozenfeld and Iushkevich), the word was translated, even in the supposed statement of the horoscope, as simply "conjunction" (in Russian, the word is соединении, one which Mozaffarzadeh, in this case correctly, since he was just translating from Russian, translated into مقارنه or "moqāreneh" in Persian astrological terms, which has the same meaning as "conjunction"). Unfortunately, the

27. مظفرزاده، باقر (مترجم). عمر خیام: زندگی و آثار. نویسندگان: باریس آبراموویچ روزنفلد و آدولف پاولوویچ یوشکیویچ. تهران: شرکت انتشارات علمی و فرهنگی. ۱۳۸۳، چاپ دوم ۱۳۹۱.

Persian translator did not notice and comment (in a footnote perhaps) this discrepancy with Beyhaqi's originally reported horoscope for Khayyam, but for this error, the translator was not too much at fault.

"Conjunction" considerably loosens the requirement of the Sun-Mercury distance to such an extent that even one or a few degrees may suffice for the horoscope condition to be met, but the Samimi (Cazimi) requirement is much more strict, precise and a much narrower requirement to meet. It is about 16 *minutes*, which is just a bit more than a quarter of a degree.

Actually, even though Tīrtha *nominally* acknowledges Samimi (Cazimi) as a requirement in Khayyam's horoscope, he never offers any facts that convincingly supports the notion that his findings meet that strict requirement, because on the degree 3 (or even 8) of the Gemini such a requirement is not met for his date, or even any other date in consideration of other requirements of the horoscope within the range of years he conducts his study (AD 1019-1054).

So, for this reason there is *absolutely* no discussion of a Samimi (Cazimi) requirement in the Russian scholars' introduction report. And this is quite odd, since they could readily read (in Tīrtha's plain English, if not in Arabic, which the scholars also were versed in) the Samimi (Cazimi) requirement in Khayyam's horoscope.

My own sense is that Russian astronomers must have actually noticed that Tīrtha's proposed date does not fulfill the Samimi (Cazimi) requirement, and opted to re-translate the term more broadly into a mere "conjunction" to by-pass the discrepancy, perhaps thinking that in old times, given the lack of precise astronomical instruments, it must have been difficult to judge a Sun-Mercury distance in terms of such precise minutes, rather than degrees, so made a decision to let it go, so speak, and consider the condition in terms of a general conjunction, than a Samimi (Cazimi).

The trouble, however, was that they underestimated the fact that it was the famous Omar Khayyam they were dealing with here, and the horoscope statement must have been one formulated by the masterful astronomer who helped establish the most precise solar calendar in the world, one that stands so to this day. So, when Khayyam said "Samimi" (Cazimi), he meant "Samimi" (Cazimi), not a mere "conjunction." It is actually an example of a master-stroke by a genius astronomer and scientist who passed on his knowledge in the most synoptic way possible, as is evident in his treatises and also in the Robaiyat attributed to him. He must have meant something very important when he formulated his horoscope statement precisely as it reached us by way of Zahireddin Abolhasan Beyhaqi in *Tatemmat Sewan el-Hekmat (Supplement to the Chest of Wisdom).*

So, the above must be the reason why the Soviet Russian scholars could not catch and correct Tīrtha's own errors and failures in proving, on the basis of a Gemini 3 degree, that the Sun and Mercury were Samimi for that date, since, of course, they were not. With such a loosened-up requirement broadening the condition to a "conjunction," it is then not also surprising to see that the otherwise able Russian astronomers to let Tīrtha's findings pass, so to speak, ending up confirming his mistakes, since "conjunction" is a much wider distance to be confirmed, or not, for the horoscope.

The Russian scholars and astronomers were also unaware (as was Tīrtha) of the significance of the last part of Khayyam's incredibly precise horoscope for his birth date, namely that it was Jupiter that was at the time observing from Trine aspectation the Sun-Mercury Samimi, *and not the other way around.* Had they noticed it, they would have found another reason to reject Tīrtha's finding, as I have already explained in detail in this chapter.

In any case, the errors in evaluation and confirmation by the Russian scholars and astronomers then set the ground for the way they went about evaluating Tīrtha's findings regarding Khayyam's date of passing (12th of Muharram, 516 LH, which for that day and month fell on the year AD 1122). I will explore the issues surrounding Khayyam's date of passing in detail in the next chapter, but it suffices here to say (as I have already done so already as well), that the legitimization of a mistaken late date of birth AD 1048 (relative to the correct AD 1021 birth date), allowed for the possibility of a late date of passing in AD 1131 to become and seem plausible. However, Rozenfeld and Iushkevich felt they could nevertheless find some use for that "12th of Muharram" by attaching it to their preferred year of demise AD 1131, which resulted in the Dec. 4, AD 1131 date held as an uneasy consensus date for Khayyam's passing today.

Although clearly paved with good intentions, the combined errors committed by Swāmi Govinda Tīrtha and the Russian scholars and astronomers in erroneously establishing wrong dates of birth and passing for Omar Khayyam cannot be underestimated. They, along with other Western scholars, have simply wrecked havoc in biographical and historical accounts of Khayyam's life and times in modern times, not to mention what Edward FitzGerald also did, as well, in parts with good intentions, to twist the meanings of the Khayyami Robaiyat, errors from which Khayyami studies must now recover in addition to other obstacles and difficulties historically inherited from and about the life and times of Omar Khayyam.

Still, we should not forget that it was Tīrtha's idea of discovering Khayyam's date of birth through his reported horoscope that eventually led us to discover it despite the errors in his efforts. So, as with other Khayyami studies to date, even that of Edward FitzGerald in "translating" Khayyam, we should always remember that, as the saying goes, any stick has two ends.

17. Chapter Conclusion: Omar Khayyam's True Date of Birth Discovered Shortly Before Its Millennium

Based on the foregoing in this chapter, the correct rendering of Khayyam's reported horoscope in Beyhaqi's biographical insert in his *Tatemmat Sewan el-Hekmat (Supplement to the Chest of Wisdom)* should be corrected as follows:

> «طالعه الجوزا و الشمس و عطارد على درجه الطالع ى ح من الجوزا و عطارد صميمى و المشترى من التثليث ناظر اليهما».
>
> His ascendant was the Gemini, and the Sun and the Mercury were on the degree of the ascendent 10 [+] 8 [=18] of Gemini, and the Mercury was Samimi [Cazimi, "in the heart of the Sun"], and the Jupiter from Taslees [Trine aspectation] observing them both.

Through gradual corruptions of the Beyhaqi manuscript across successive copying down the historical timeline, the letter ى was mistakenly read as the word فى which, as such, would not in and of itself be needed and is even grammatically redundant in the expression of Khayyam's horoscope.

I now have arrived at the point that I can claim that I have definitively discovered Omar Khayyam's definitive date of birth at last, reported for the first time in this second book of my series *Omar Khayyam's Secret*.

I have not only established this date to be the only date during the period AD 1018-1055 to perfectly fulfill all the requirements of Khayyam's birth horoscope as shared by Zahireddin Abolhasan Beyhaqi in his *Tatemmat Sewan el-Hekmat (Supplement to the Chest of Wisdom)*. I have also explained how the diverse extant copies of the manuscript providing seemingly conflicting and different versions of the degree of the Gemini given in the horoscope can be reconciled and cohered with one another based on a track of possible corruptions and misinterpretations over past centuries across successive copying chains.

There is one and only one solution to the puzzle of the reported horoscope for Omar Khayyam, and it has been discovered strangely as we approach the first millennial anniversary of Khayyam's birth date on June 10, 2021, of our Gregorian solar calendar, or in the Spring of the year 1400 of the Iranian Solar Hejri Calendar. The lunar millennium of his birth has already passed according to the Islamic Lunar calendar (given it would have fallen in 1412 LH; the Islamic Lunar calendar today has entered its 1440s).

To reiterate and further add, based on the above discovery, the renderings of the horoscope of Omar Khayyam as reported by Beyhaqi in his *Tatemmat Sewan el-Hekmat (Supplement to the Chest of Wisdom)* should be corrected to the following in its Arabic, Persian, and English expressions:

> «طالعه الجوزا و الشمس و عطارد علی درجه الطالع ی ح من الجوزا و عطارد صمیمی و المشتری من التثلیث ناظر الیهما».

> «طالعش جوزا بود و آفتاب و عطارد بر درجهٔ طالع ی ح از جوزا و عطارد صمیمی و مشتری از تثلیث ناظر بر آن دو».

> "His ascendant was the Gemini, and the Sun and the Mercury were on the degree of the ascendent 18 of Gemini, and the Mercury was Samimi [Cazimi], and the Jupiter from Taslees [Trine aspectation] observing them both."

For the years considered, the degree of the Gemini noted in Khayyam's horoscope was neither 3, nor 8, nor any other number from 1-30 except for 18.

Omar Khayyam's birth took place at the following time during a nearly four-minute interval that perfectly fulfilled all the requirements of Khayyam's horoscope. Below, first I offer the basic details in Persian:

تاریخ و زمان ولادت حکیم عمر خیام نیشابوری:
یکشنبه ۲۰ خرداد سال ٤۰۰ هجری شمسی (سال کبیسه در تقویم جلالی)
هنگام طلوع آفتابِ نیشابور
حین چهار دقیقه بین ٤:٤۳:٥٦ و ٤:٤۷:٥٥ صبح، سحرگاهان
طالع: جوزا
خورشید: در درجه ی ۱۸ و دقیقه ی ۷ جوزا
عطارد: در درجه ی ۱۸ و دقیقه ی ۱٥ جوزا
خورشید و عطارد صمیمی (فاصله ۸ دقیقه) واقع بر درجه طالع ۱۸ هنگام طلوع آفتاب
مشتری در درجه ی ۱۱ و دقیقه ی ٤ میزان، با فاصله ۱۱۳ درجه از عطاردِ صمیمی با خورشید، در تثلیث ناظر بر هر دو

Sunday, June 10th (Greg.), AD 1021, or
Yekshanbeh (Sunday), Khordad 20th, year 400 of Solar Hejri, a Leap Year for the Persian calendar (not for the other two calendars), or
Yawm al-Ahad (Sunday), Safar 19th, year 412 of Lunar Hejri

Early morning:

Between (differences of the two beginning and ending seconds in bold)

Neyshabour, Iran, Time: **4:43:56** a.m.
Universal Time: **12:48:36** GMT
Neyshabour Coordinates: 36n12, 58e50
When required horoscope conditions where as follows:
Gemini Ascendant
Ascendant on the degree **18° 00″**
Sun at 18° 7′ **44″** of Gemini
Mercury at 18° 15′ of Gemini (in retrograde motion)
Sun-Mercury Distance was exactly 8 minutes (within 16 minutes range, fulfilling the Samimi or Cazimi requirement of the horoscope)
Sun-Mercury Cazimi is on the degree of the Ascendant 18° (at sunrise)
Jupiter at 11° 4′ of Libra
Jupiter-Sun/Mercury Distance about 113 degrees and five houses away (within 111-129 range, fulfilling the Taslees/Trine requirement of the horoscope)
Jupiter is not in the visible sky, but behind/below the Earth, "observing" or aspecting along the shorter arc, right-handedly (clockwise), the motions of the Sun-Mercury Cazimi from behind. This also fulfills the Nazer [observation] requirement of the horoscope.

and

Neyshabour, Iran, Time: **4:47:55** a.m.
Universal Time: **12:52:35** GMT
Neyshabour Coordinates: 36n12, 58e50
When required horoscope conditions where as follows:
Gemini Ascendant
Ascendant on the degree **18° 59″**
Sun at 18° 9′ **54″** of Gemini
Mercury at 18° 15′ of Gemini (in retrograde motion)
Sun-Mercury Distance was exactly 8 minutes (within 16 minutes range, fulfilling the Samimi or Cazimi requirement of the horoscope)
Sun-Mercury Cazimi is on the degree of the Ascendant 18° (at sunrise)
Jupiter at 11° 4′ of Libra
Jupiter-Sun/Mercury Distance about 113 degrees and five houses away (within 111-129 range, fulfilling the Taslees/Trine requirement of the horoscope)

> Important: Jupiter is not in the visible sky, but behind/below the Earth, "observing" or aspecting along the shorter arc, right-handedly (clockwise), the motions of the Sun-Mercury Cazimi from behind. This also fulfills the Nazer [observation] requirement of the horoscope.

In closing this chapter, it may be helpful to pause and reflect on the significance of this discovery. At no time in the past nearly thousand years anyone except for Khayyam, his parents, or perhaps those very intimate to him, had known the exact birth date and chart of Khayyam as provided masterfully with incredible precision in his reported horoscope.

We suddenly find ourselves in a situation where we know more about Khayyam's birth chart than anyone, even of his contemporaries and others since then. This leap of knowledge about Khayyam's birth date, unexpected and unpredictable in advance, was made possible by exploring a birth chart made necessary for astrological purposes prevalent in the culture during the times in which Khayyam lived. We discovered it by exploring our subject matter in a transdisciplinary and transcultural way, that is, beyond rigid disciplinary and cultural boundaries.

One of the most interesting aspect of the discovery made, in my own view and experience, has been the astonishing precision of the reported horoscope for Khayyam. I will return to this topic later, but the skills required to confirm a Samimi (Cazimi) conjunction depending on as few as 16 minutes must be the same skill that allowed Khayyam to help the establishment of a new solar calendar in Iran which surpasses the precision of Western calendar used today.

Another important point to reflect on is the timing of this discovery.

I am of course proud of having discovered the date in my lifetime. However, still, it seems even odd and strange that the possibility of this discovery came about for me in the larger scheme of historical timeline just before Omar Khayyam's birth millennium. I can claim, to some extent, that this was a result of my efforts; I did make changes in my life in recent years, realizing where my research was heading; I can even claim and will show that this result was made possible due to my respect for what I learned to be the Khayyami method, some of which will be explained later.

However, in the context of a longer historical timeline, I am both surprised and amused to consider that this discovery was made just short of Khayyam's birth date millennium, allowing me enough time for researching and publishing this report for it. I will be curious about this aspect of the present research and its questions as well, as the Khayyami studies in this series unfolds, given the hermeneutic method I have framed and I am applying in this series.

In any case, a significantly new door has opened for Khayyami studies now for understanding the life and works of Omar Khayyam. In my view, this discovery is bound to change everything we have read and known about Khayyam over the past millennium since his birth, discovering new things about him, and about what truths he wished to convey, secretly or not, to humanity through his synoptic writings. We have now entered a completely new, unchartered territory in Khayyami studies.

Being equipped with the wonderful knowledge of his true date of birth, let us now turn our attention in the next chapter to solving the longstanding problem of determining Omar Khayyam's definitive date of passing.

Abstract

This essay, titled "In Search of the Correct Gemini Degree: The Story of How Omar Khayyam's True Date of Birth Was Discovered Shortly Before Its Imminent Millennium," is the second chapter of the second book of the twelve-book series *Omar Khayyam's Secret: Hermeneutics of the Robaiyat in Quantum Sociological Imagination,* authored by Mohammad H. Tamdgidi. The second book is subtitled *Khayyami Millennium: Reporting the Discovery and the Reconfirmation of the True Dates of Birth and Passing of Omar Khayyam (AD 1021-1123).*

Tamdgidi devotes this chapter to a search for Khayyam's true date of birth. Although Swāmī Govinda Tīrtha deserves credit for bringing scholarly attention to Omar Khayyam's horoscope as reported in Zahireddin Abolhasan Beyhaqi's *Tatemmat Sewan el-Ḥekmat (Supplement to the Chest of Wisdom)* as a pathway toward solving the problem of Khayyam's birth date, he erred in the effort, causing more confusion. Something in the way Tīrtha handled the information implied in Khayyam's reported horoscope prevented him from truly solving his birth date puzzle. So, what did go wrong in Tīrtha's efforts?

To answer this question, the author adopt the procedure of step by step peeling away one or another false lead toward a core solution. The reason for this procedure is to eliminate any other possibilities that may, one way or another, exist and thus cast doubt on the definitive solution we hope to reach for the puzzles at hand. After all, if there is more than one solution that may plausibly compete with, let alone nullify, the solution the author offer, we cannot claim for sure that a definitive solution has been found.

Finding that Khayyam's birth date considerations on the basis of either the 3rd or the 8th degree for the Gemini to be incompatible with the requirements of Khayyam's reported horoscope, and encountering a wide range of manuscript source variations as reported in the chapter, Tamdgidi takes an alternative route by *directly* consulting and reporting the ephemeris data for the entire years during AD 1018-1055.

His procedure for compiling his data was follows. He first consulted the Swiss Ephemeris data that is not Neyshabour location specific, and the dates are given for day intervals only and not for the variations during the day. If the data came close to fulfilling the Gemini ascendance and Samimi (Cazimi) requirements, he reported it, cross-checking with the search engine for the more exact Neyshabour location and time variations, to the extent that it was necessary to rule out a date or regarding all the requirements of the horoscope, including the Taslees (Trine) requirement. He annotated each date sufficiently to explain why that date can be ruled out, or that it fulfilled a given requirement.

He discovered that there *was one, and only one, date* between years AD 1018 and AD 1055 that *definitively* fulfilled *all* the requirements of Khayyam's reported horoscope, including the degree of the Ascendant, when considering a degree of the Gemini in which the horoscope's Cazimi/Ascendant conjunction must fall. This date was, in the Gregorian calendar, June 10, AD 1021, at sunrise, Neyshabour's time. It was nearly a four minute period from 4:43:56 to 4:47:55 a.m. exactly at sunrise. During this short interval of time, the Gemini was Ascendant, the Sun and the Mercury were Cazimi on the same degree of the Ascendant 18° of Gemini (being in the Samimi distance of 8 minutes from each other), and Jupiter was positioned on the 11th degree of Libra, within a Taslees/Triangulation/Trine-fulfilling distance of about 113 degrees from both the Sun and Mercury.

Following his discovery, Tamdgidi tried further to understand how the Gemini degree 18 on which the date fell provides any hints about how the ambiguities surrounding the Gemini degree given across the various extant manuscript copies of Khayyam's reported horoscope can be reconciled with one another. While explaining the various variations, he discovers that through the process of successive recopying by various scribes, the letter ی became gradually corrupted, the letter being misread as the word فی such that later scribes assumed that the word was not a part of a degree given in abjad for ی but the word فی in the normal part of the sentence. He also offers explanations for why and how Soviet Russian scholars and astronomers failed in catching Tīrtha's mistakes regarding Omar Khayyam's date of birth, as well as, in part, his date of passing.

Based on the findings, the renderings of the horoscope of Omar Khayyam as reported by Beyhaqi in his *Tatemmat Sewan el-Hekmat (Supplement to the Chest of Wisdom)* should be corrected to the following in its Arabic, Persian, and English expressions:

«طالعه الجوزا و الشمس و عطارد على درجه الطالع ی ح من الجوزا و عطارد صمیمی و المشتری من التثلیث ناظر الیهما».

«طالعش جوزا بود و آفتاب و عطارد بر درجهٔ طالع ی ح از جوزا و عطارد صمیمی و مشتری از تثلیث ناظر بر آن دو».

"His ascendant was the Gemini, and the Sun and the Mercury were on the degree of the ascendent 18 of Gemini, and the Mercury was Samimi [Cazimi], and the Jupiter from Taslees [Trine aspectation] observing them both."

CHAPTER III—In Search of Omar Khayyam's True Date of Passing: Superposing the Birth Date Findings With Beyhaqi's "Tatemmat Sewan el-Hekmat" And Khazeni's "Mizan ol-Hekmat"

My main goal in this and the following two chapters will be to determine as definitively as possible the date of passing of Omar Khayyam on the basis of our new finding about his true date of birth as reported in the preceding chapter. My secondary purpose will be to trace how our new finding allows us to reimagine Khayyam's interactions with others during his lifetime from the vantage of his true age during such interactions.

I have chosen to split my search for Khayyam's definitive date of passing into three chapters for the reader's convenience, starting with this chapter; however, they should be seen as parts of the same, ongoing, search, their findings often superposing and overlapping with one another considerably.

The uneasy consensus date circulating today for Khayyam's passing is 526 LH, often associated with the year AD 1131 in the Christian calendar. This date has become plausible because of an ambiguity noted in copies of an account by Nezami Arouzi, a Khayyam contemporary who in his *Chahar Maqaleh (Four Discourses)* while tributing Khayyam as a teacher writes that he arrived in Neyshabour in the year 530 LH (around AD 1135-1136), learning that "some" years before Khayyam had died, leading him to inquire about the whereabouts of his grave and to visit the site, finding that the grave was covered with blossoms as Khayyam had previously told to him back in a meeting in 506 LH (about AD 1112-1113).

The word "some" used by Nezami Arouzi in those manuscript copies has been found to be either illegible or differently rendered across various manuscript copies, such that scholars have noted that it could be read as "four" (in Persian "chahar") or "fourteen" (in Persian "chahardah") or simply "some" (in Persian "chand"). This has in turn led to the speculation that he may have meant "four," which would then imply that the date of Khayyam's demise must have been four years later, around 526 LH. Had the ambiguous word been read as "fourteen," however, it would have implied that Khayyam's date of passing was around 516 LH (around AD 1122-1123), which is the date that appeared on Khayyam's gravestone in its one-before-last incarnation in mid 20th century (at the time when Swāmī Govinda Tīrtha published his *The Nectar of Grace* in 1941, leading him to argue that it is the correct date of Khayyam's demise). Later on, when the current mausoleum of Omar Khayyam was built, the date on his gravestone was changed to 517 LH (around AD 1123-1124), which is a lunar date often found in old historical records for Khayyam's passing.

In the above, I provided a range of double-year AD equivalents for the above lunar dates because, as I noted in this book's introduction, short of knowing the month, if not day, of Khayyam's passing, we could not for sure say in which year of the Christian calendar his death fell.

A reason why some scholars have been inclined to choose the later date of demise in 526 LH (AD 1131-1132) is that based on the currently held date of birth of Khayyam in the year AD 1048 (now proven in this book to be incorrect), corresponding to the year 439 LH, Khayyam's age at the time of death would resolve to that of about 87 lunar years (about 84 solar years), more befitting an old Khayyam, than the lower 77 lunar years (about 74 solar years) counting to the year 516 LH as a possible date of demise of a younger Khayyam. As I had noted before, Khayyam's current gravestone offers the year 517 LH as his date of passing, adding that he lived "seventy plus years."

Since we have now definitively discovered that Khayyam's birth took place on June 10 (Gregorian), AD 1021, this proves highly unlikely that Khayyam could have lived to the age of 110-111 solar (or 114-115 lunar) years, if his death is still regarded as having occurred on LH 526 (AD 1131-1132). Beyhaqi's account of the last day of Khayyam's passing portrays him as someone still with a sound mind and physical strength (and perhaps teeth, by the way, given the reported use of his golden toothpick), still able to read a complex philosophical book by Avicenna, to invite others for offering his last will on his own, and to perform his last fasting rites and prayers in sound mind, while being able to speak or recite his last words praying to God in prostration. Besides, such an extreme old age would not have escaped the attention of both those around Khayyam and of the chroniclers such as Beyhaqi reporting about him.

Given that no other dates have been reported, claimed, or speculated about between the years 517-526 LH as a possible date for Khayyam's passing, it seems most likely that Khayyam's date of demise took place sometime around 516-517 LH (AD 1122-1124). In other words, one of the significant outcomes of our discovery in this series of Khayyam's definitive birth date in AD 1021 (almost 27 years earlier than the date AD 1048 currently in fashion) is that it is now rather much more plausible for us to assume that a Khayyam born in AD 1021 could not have lived as late as AD 1131-1132 with the solar age of 110-111 (and still more in lunar years), and that most likely he died a centenarian at the age of around 101-102 solar (or about 104-105 lunar) years. Regarding the precise date, including month and day, and age of Khayyam's demise, however, the following details are worth noting.

As I shared earlier, Tīrtha himself, being unconvinced regarding the year 526 LH as a date for Khayyam's passing, tended to agree with the date etched on Khayyam's tomb at the time, that is, the year 516 LH. He borrowed from another manuscript, that of *Tarabkhaneh (House of Joy)*, by Yar Ahmad Rashidi Tabrizi, where Tīrtha (wrongly) reads Tabrizi giving the day and month of Khayyam's *death* as Thursday, 12th of Muharram (Tīrtha 1941:LXXVIII).

Such a month and day not having been claimed or corroborated by any other extant source and not even reconciling with the year Tīrtha himself claims was being offered by Tabrizi for Khayyam's passing, however, ended up being used by those wishing to give a full, including month and day, date for Khayyam's currently held consensus year of death (526 LH, around AD 1131-1132), so that it could be claimed that Khayyam's death occurred on Muharram 12th, 526 LH, corresponding to December 4th (Julian, equivalent to Dec. 11th, Gregorian, counting a seven day difference since the date falls in the twelfth century), AD 1131. Noted that it is the (false) adoption of Muharram 12th for the day and month of Khayyam's passing that has allowed some to choose AD 1131 as the year of Khayyam's demise; otherwise, technically it could have also happened in AD 1132, since 526 LH stretches from some months in AD 1131 into the year AD 1132. Also, note that the currently held uneasy consensus month and day, Dec. 4th, is actually in error even in the above (wrong) calculations, since Dec. 4 is a Julian date, that corresponds to and should be designated as Dec. 11, in the Gregorian calendar used today in the West and around the world. In other words, even the Dec. 4, AD 1131 regarded today as Khayyam's date of passing should be corrected to Dec. 11th, given Gregorian calendar is one in use today.

Rahim Rezazadeh Malek—the compiler of *Daneshnameh-ye Khayyami* (*The Khayyami Encyclopedia*) which gathers various manuscripts or extracts thereof attributed to Omar Khayyam and on which I drew on in the last chapter regarding Khayyam's horoscope—writes in his overview of the extant accounts of Khayyam's date of demise that Khayyam's student, Abdorrahman Khazeni (or a scribe copying his manuscript on the topic of a balance/scale mechanism which included a section authored by Omar Khayyam) had referred to him using the expression "may God rest his soul" in a book originally authored in the year 515 LH. Rezazadeh Malek wondered if this expression of mercy for Khayyam was in the original text authored by Khazeni (which would imply that Khayyam had passed away already in the year 515 LH or earlier), or was added by one or another scribe of his manuscript at any date later than Khayyam's passing.

If we regard either of the years 516 or 517 LH as Khayyam's date of demise, then it would be more plausible to assume that the mercy reference was added at a later date. But it is also possible to consider that if Khayyam died in 516 LH, he could have died soon after when that work by Khazeni was completed and signed as authored. In any case, this information about Khazeni may or may not offer clues toward resolving the puzzle of Khayyam's date of demise, and therefore invites further scrutiny.

Although my finding of Khayyam's date of birth in AD 1021 as reported in the previous chapter has effectively narrowed down the possible choices of dates for Khayyam's passing, it is clear from the above general introduction that we are still far from undisputably ascertaining, based on the limited amount of reliable extant manuscript available, the more exact dates of year, month, and day, of Khayyam's death.

My main purpose in this chapter and the two that follow, therefore, will be to revisit all the available texts and versions thereof more carefully, in an effort to find a way of convincingly interpreting the various texts and reconciling their differences to such an extent that we can arrive at an undisputable consensus regarding Khayyam's date of demise.

1. The Most Relevant Manuscripts to Be Studied for the Determination of Khayyam's Date of Passing

There are basically four manuscripts on which most have focused to determine the date of passing of Omar Khayyam. I have already referred to these texts in the preceding chapters and book of the series, but will list them again here.

The first manuscript is the biographical information offered for Khayyam in *Tatemmat Sewan el-Hekmat (Supplement to the Chest of Wisdom)* by Zahireddin Abolhasan Beyhaqi (AD 1097?-1169/490 LH?-565 LH). Also referred to as Ibn Fondoq, he was a young contemporary of Khayyam and reports meeting him as a child/youth in the presence of his father in 507 LH (AD 1113-1114). We know for sure now that Khayyam (b. AD 1021/412 LH) was at the time of that meeting about 92 solar or 95 lunar years old. If Beyhaqi met Khayyam as a child in 507 LH, he must have been somewhere between 7-17 years old. Given the nature of questions Khayyam asked the child about geometry and Arabic poetry, Beyhaqi must have been toward the upper end of that range, so he may have been born at the earliest around 490 LH (AD 1097). The book mentioned, *Tatemmat Sewan el-Hekmat*, was likely composed by Beyhaqi in mid 500s LH, when he was in his sixties.

The second source is *Mizan ol-Hekmat (Balance of Wisdom)*, by Abdorrahman Khazeni, also a grown-up contemporary of Khayyam and reportedly also one of his pupils in astronomy and scientific matters, implying that he must have also met him in person. His birth and death dates are not known but his career, as a freed slave of Greek/Byzantine origin who become himself an astronomer, flourished between the years AD 1115-1130 when he also served as an astronomer for Soltan Sanjar, a son of Soltan Malekshah, of the Seljuk dynasty. He included a contribution from Khayyam as a section in his book called *Mizan ol-Hekmat* (*Balance of Wisdom*, definitively completed sometime in the year 515 LH), on the topic of scale balance instruments used to determine the amount of precious materials in jewelry without having to disassemble them.

The third source is *Chahar Maqaleh (Four Discourses)* by Nezami Arouzi, a Khayyam contemporary who offered his respects to him as a teacher (whether actually or in reverence it is not known). His dates of birth or passing are not certainly known, but he reportedly flourished between AD 1110-1160. He must have been a grown-up when he reportedly met Khayyam in 506 LH (AD 1112-1113), although according to another account of his manuscript as reported by Yar Ahmad Rashidi Tabrizi in his *Tarabkhaneh*

(House of Joy), that or another meeting took place in 512 LH (AD 1118-1119), to which I shall return later. So, depending on the date, Khayyam was either 91 solar /94 lunar years old, or 97 solar/100 lunar years old at the time. Nezami Arouzi reports hearing from Khayyam about his future grave in that meeting, one that he visited after Khayyam's passing.

The fourth manuscript is one written and compiled by Yar Ahmad Rashidi Tabrizi, which has come to be known under the title *Tarabkhaneh (House of Joy)*. He uses the abjad numbers expressed in the title of his work *Tarabkhaneh* to convey the date of completion of writing his manuscript, 867 LH (Ṫ=9, R=200, B=2, Kh=600, A=1, N=50, H=5, adding up to 867, c. AD 1462). He was not a contemporary of Khayyam, of course, but his compilation of hundreds of Khayyami Robaiyat along with biographical anecdotes and information about his life, including some information relevant to his birth and passing dates drawing partly on an old copy he reports having personally read of the *Chahar Maqaleh (Four Discourses)* in Nezami Arouzi's own handwriting, has been drawn on extensively in an effort to determine Khayyam's dates of birth and death.

There are other older manuscripts that have been studied as sources for determining Khayyam's birth and passing dates, but most of these postdate, revise, embellish, and generally draw on the above four main sources in an attempt to report on Khayyam's life and his birth and passing dates.

I will produce both the Arabic or Persian originals of the texts studied while offering my English translations of them, when necessary. Please note again that in this and the next two chapters my focus is specifically on the question of Khayyam's date of passing. So, only those aspects of the texts and passages that directly pertain to this inquiry will be explored. Occasionally I may briefly highlight one or another substantive issues raised in the texts about Khayyam's life or works, but even then I will do so mainly in terms of the relevance of the materials for determining Khayyam's date of passing.

Another important point to keep in mind, one that we learned from the study of Khayyam's reported horoscope in the preceding chapter, is that studying a particular manuscript by any of our authors cannot take place out of the context of the *specific copy* of the manuscript from which the text is drawn. In other words, we now know that unless we have a clean and legible copy of the exact original manuscript *written by an author himself* at hand, we should assume that one or more versions of the manuscript as copied by one or more scribes along the same or different copying chain(s) may be subjected to variations that may miscommunicate, in one way or another, advertently or not, the original text or meaning intended by the author.

Whether or not we can judge such miscommunications themselves is a subject that can only be explored in context, and no universal presumption should be made as to whether we can in fact know about any error in communication in advance, and if so, what the correction may be. Besides, having only one copy of an extant manuscript is not necessarily better than having multiple versions, since the latter can in fact point us to aspects of the text that are unanimously accepted and other aspects that may invite further scrutiny because they happen to differ across multiple manuscript copies of the same work.

Finally, it is important to note that while a particular biographical information about a third person may not give direct information about Khayyam's date of passing, we are interested in finding out whether or not there can be found any corroborating evidence about when Khayyam could have interacted or associated with them. So, lack of information may be as important as its existence. For example, can we find *any* evidence for *any* events or interactions that could locate Khayyam in the years past 517 LH and before 526 LH? Have there been any reported interaction or association Khayyam may have had with anyone that are supportive or rejective of what we have found to be his definitive birth date, or corroborative for any hypothesis regarding any dates for his passing?

For the sake of simplicity and given the historical context, I will explore the dates in the following chapters in the lunar Hejri calendar, and only when necessary will I convert them to the Christian calendar for comparison.

In terms of discussion of the age of Khayyam or those of others, we should always keep in mind the distinction between lunar and solar time spans, especially when it comes to long-lived lives. Since I will be mainly using lunar dates in this exploration, the references to person's ages will be lunar years, unless I specifically qualify the lunar and/or solar year counts.

Before I begin combing the contents of the four manuscripts regarding clues about Omar Khayyam's date of passing, however, let me first comment on a famous topic in light of my discovery of his true date of birth.

2. Could Omar Khayyam Have Been Childhood Friends with Nezam ol-Molk and Hasan Sabbah?

The two prominent figures associated with Khayyam have been, of course, the famous Nezam ol-Molk, and Hasan Sabbah.

The "three friends story" has been something along the lines that they were schoolmates in childhood, close enough to swear to each others' blood that if any one of them grew up to hold high office or wealth, he would help the other two in meeting their goals. So, the story goes, it was Nezam ol-Molk who first gained high office as a vizier of a soltan, so the other two approached him for the promises made in childhood. Nezam ol-Molk asked what they wished for, willing to offer Khayyam rulership of some land. But Khayyam said ordering folks around was not in his nature, so to speak, and he was interested more in science, so asked for an annual allotment so he could pursue science; it was granted to him by Nezam ol-Molk. Hasan Sabbah asked for high office, and was granted, but then turned his back on his benefactor, and we know the story of what happened later on.

My point here is not to dwell on the truthfulness of the story's details itself, but simply to ask whether it would have been possible for these three, simply in terms of their ages and dates of birth, to be childhood friends.

Readers have perhaps noticed by now that my finding of Khayyam's true date of birth in 412 LH (AD 1021) has significantly reopened the *possibility* (not necessarily the truthfulness of) that famous story of the triadic friendship between Khayyam, Nezam ol-Molk, and Hasan Sabbah, suggesting that it may have been in fact possible.

The main reason the story began to fade away as a possibility, and relegated to the realm of fables, was the impossibility or implausibility of reconciling a Nezam ol-Molk born definitively in 408 LH (AD 1018) being a childhood friend with a Khayyam thought later to have been born in 439 LH (AD 1048), based on the (now proven wrong) date of birth for Khayyam "discovered" and reported by Swāmi Govinda Tīrtha in 1941. What further complicated and seemingly discredited the story was the later consensus arrived at regarding Khayyam's passing at a later date (526 LH, or AD 1131) than the one considered customarily for him (517 LH, or AD 1123). The truthfulness of that story, therefore, became dependent on the near impossibility of Khayyam having been born around Nezam ol-Molk's birth date 408 LH or AD 1018 (to be childhood friends with him) and yet having live long enough to die in the year 526 LH, or AD 1131, at the age of 110-11 solar (and even more lunar) years.

Now that we know the latter was erroneous, and that Khayyam (b. AD 1021/412 LH) was in fact only three or four years Nezam ol-Molk's (b. AD 1018/408 LH) junior, depending on how we count the years nominally, we can again entertain the possibility that Nezam ol-Molk, and even Hasan Sabbah, and Omar Khayyam were childhood friends and that there may have been some grains of truth to the story reported by others, after all.

Sabbah's date of birth is not known, but he reportedly died in 518 LH, a year after the commonly reported date of passing of Khayyam (517 LH, as etched also on his grave); Sabbah has also been reported to have lived to his hundred and died a centenarian.

If Sabbah was the same age or some years younger than the other two, but still close enough, it is possible to consider their childhood friendship to have been a possibility. In fact, Nezam ol-Molk being the senior of the three fits well with the possibility that he could have been the one to "go places" first, so to speak, to be then able to offer scientific allotments (in the case of a Khayyam being more interested in science and not in ordering others around) or political powers (in the case of a Sabbah seeking high office, and ending up in an Shia Ismaili resistance movement against the colonizing rulers of the regions at the time).

Nezam ol-Molk himself reports in his attributed *Vasaya* (or will) his having been a childhood friend with Khayyam (and Sabbah) and having shared with them instructions of a common early teacher, Imam Movaffaq.

3. Examining Beyhaqi's Biographical Entry on Omar Khayyam in "Tatemmat Sewan el-Hekmat"

Let us now begin with what we can find relevant to our inquiry in Beyhaqi's account for Khayyam himself in *Tatemmat Sewan el-Hekmat (Supplement to the Chest of Wisdom).*

The source of the information about the persons noted in the exploration below, unless I qualify otherwise, are the main text along with the extensive footnotes given in Mohammad Shafi's concise edition of the Arabic and the old Persian translation versions of *Tatemmat Sewan el-Hekmat.*[1] The entry numbers starting with A refer to the Arabic list, and with P refer to the old Persian translation list. I have also consulted and compared the above with an English/Arabic edition by Fuat Sezgin.[2] The biographical entry numbers in the English translation by Sezgin follow the Arabic entry numbers.

---

1. Al-Imam Zahireddin Abolhasan Ali Ibn al-Qasem al-Beyhaqi. 1351 LH (1932) (565 LH). *Tatemmat Sewan el-Hekmat.* Edited by Muhammad Shafi. Includes the Arabic and old Persian translations with extensive footnote commentaries. India: Lahore.

2. *Ali Ibn Zaid Al-Baihaqi Tatimma Siwan al-Hikma: Texts and Studies* (collected and reprinted by Fuat Sezgin in Collaboration with Carl Ehrig-Eggert, Eckhard Neuybauer), Institute for the History of Arabic-Islamic Science at the Johann Wolfgang Goethe University, Frankfurt am Main, 2005.

In his biographical entry for Khayyam, Beyhaqi mentions several persons by name with whom Omar Khayyam met, including himself.

Since identifying the historical and biographical timing of the ages or activities of these persons, to the extent known, can be helpful in situating Khayyam's age in context, I will flag these persons by name and briefly comment on what their involvements in the narrated stories tell us about Khayyam's living (or not) status at a particular time. My purpose at this point is *not* to go into any other aspects or details of Khayyam's biographical information given in Beyhaqi's dedicated entry or in any other sections of his compilation, unless specifically warranted and considered helpful.

I will of course explore these other aspects in future books of this series, as needed; here, my focus is strictly on the question of finding a way or any clues for definitive determination of Khayyam's date of passing.

(1) Shahab ul-Islam and al-Ghazzal (in Khayyam's entry no. A66/P64)

The first person mentioned in the entry on Khayyam is شهاب الاسلام الوزير عبدالرّزاق بن الفقيه الاجلّ ابی القاسم عبدالله بن علی or Shahab ul-Islam al-Vazir Abdol-Razzaq Ibn al-Faqih al-Ajal Abi al-Qasem Abdollah Ibn Ali. A nephew of the famous minister of Soltan Malekshah, Nezam ol-Molk (408-485 LH), Shahab ul-Islam served as a minister from 511-515 LH under the Seljuk Soltan Sanjar (who himself lived from 479-552 LH and reigned in Khorasan from 490 LH to 511 LH and as the soltan of the empire from 511 LH until 552 LH).

Shahab ul-Islam was reportedly born in 459 LH, and died on Muharram 19th, 515 LH; so, during his ministry's office, he must have been between 52 and 56 years of age. During this time, Soltan Sanjar was 32 to 36 lunar years of age. Given Shahab ul-Islam is referred to as a minister in the text, we should then assume Khayyam was still definitely living at least in the year 511 LH, and possibly at least until the first month of 515 LH, since the meeting noted in the biographical entry where Khayyam was present must have taken place sometime between 511-515 LH.

Present in the meeting was also امام القُراء ابو الحسن الغزّال or Imam ul-Qorra Abol-Hossein al-Ghazzal, whose death according to the book *Boghyat ul-Vo'at*[3] (بغية الوعاة), vol. II, p. 149, took place in 516 LH. He is not to be confused with the famous theologian turned Sufi Muhammad al-Ghazali, about whom there is also another reference in Khayyam's entry to which I will refer below.

Since we know Khayyam's true date of birth now, during the office of

3. See https://ia802902.us.archive.org/13/items/FP12042/02_12043.pdf.

Shahab ul-Islam as a minister (511-515 LH), and when that meeting took place, Khayyam was about 99 to 103 *lunar* years of age, or about 96-100 *solar* years of age. In the meeting, Khayyam was reportedly asked a theological question about the Quran, and he answered it so well and exhaustively that al-Ghazzal, a theologian himself, was surprised that anyone, especially a "philosopher" such as Khayyam, could be so well versed in theological questions—praising him accordingly and even calling himself his follower.

So, the above clearly shows Khayyam was alive in 511 LH at least. It also shows Khayyam still retained his intellectual powers in old age, given this meeting took place during 511-515 LH, when he was about 96-100 solar years old.

(2) Muhammad al-Ghazali (in Khayyam's entry no. A66/P64)

A second reported meeting in which Khayyam was present involved الامام حجّة الاسلام محمّد بن محمّد الغزالی or Imam Hojjat ul-Islam Muhammad Ibn Muhammad al-Ghazali.

He is the famed Islamic theologian of Persian descent who was born in 450 LH and died in 505 LH, living until the age of about 55 lunar years. He was an orthodox theologian by upbringing and a severe critic of philosophy who turned Sufi in the later stage of his life. Given that he died in 505 LH, just a year before the child Beyhaqi met Khayyam, this meeting could not have taken place anytime after 505 LH, when Khayyam was definitively living. Now, having discovered his true date of birth, we should note that Khayyam (b. 412 LH) was clearly 38 lunar years more senior than Ghazali (b. 450 LH), and 93 lunar years old (about 89 solar years old) when Ghazali died at the lunar age of 55 in 505 LH.

In the meeting as reported by Beyhaqi, Ghazali apparently asks Khayyam a sarcastic question that what in my view had a double meaning, regarding how one can determine a star or point in the sky as being a "pole," when there are many like it. Even though the subject was one discussed at the time as an astronomical or astrological question, Khayyam must have realized the double-meaning implied in Ghazali's questioning; that is, why Khayyam must be regarded as a "pole" when supposedly there are many like him, such as presumably Ghazali himself. So, the clever Khayyam does not take Ghazali's bait, so to speak, and engages in such a lengthy and distracting discourse that hours pass, Ghazali becomes exhausted and hearing the call for prayers rises to leave, saying, apparently as a chastisement for his much more senior Khayyam, "the truth [of the prayer call came] and falsehood left."

This story is telling of the unfriendly valuation that Ghazali had for Khayyam, and the animosity Khayyam must have felt on Ghazali's part as an upstart critic of his views and stature. It indicates the asymmetry of the ages between the two, where Ghazali, despite his animosity toward Khayyam, had to reckon with the seniority and stature of a Khayyam 38 years older than himself.

(3) Soltan Sanjar (in Khayyam's entry no. A66/P64)

Another meeting reported in Beyhaqi's entry for Khayyam took place when the still young future Soltan Sanjar (479-552 LH) was ill with smallpox and Khayyam was called in for medical diagnosis and treatment. Khayyam found the state of the child prince grave, saying so to the minister who had invited him, and an overhearing servant reported it to the young Sanjar, who from then on held a grudge against Khayyam.

Involved in the story was the minister Mojir ul-Dowleh (مجیرالدوله), who held office from 490-497 LH, during which Sanjar must have been somewhere about 11-18 years old; he was then still governing Khorasan, and not yet the entire Seljuk empire. Sanjar was born in 479 LH, so this event must have taken place around 490 LH, just when the minister had began his post. Khayyam (b. 412) was 78 lunar (or 75 solar) years old then. This story corroborates the previous one regarding when Khayyam lived, though does not add any more to the definitive year of 511 LH when we know Khayyam was still alive.

(4) Soltan Malekshah (in Khayyam's entry no. A66/P64)

Another meeting is reported between Khayyam with Soltan Malekshah, whose story was relayed by Beyhaqi's father to his son who later included it in the biographical entry.

The talk between the soltan and Khayyam was regarding the manners of a very young child greeting the soltan and Khayyam at the meeting, in a way that exceeded his age. Malekshah explains to the puzzled Khayyam with an anecdote regarding difference in birds, one knowing by rote from the beginning what to do, another knowing it by learning, which takes more time but could lead to the bird becoming so skilled as to deliver messages across lands.

Malekshah lived to the lunar age of 40 from 445 to 485 LH, his reign lasting about twenty years from early 465 to late 485 LH (AD 1072-1092). We now know (having discovered Khayyam's true date of birth in 412 LH) that Soltan Malekshah was 20 lunar years old and Khayyam was 53 lunar years in age when Malekshah began his reign in 465 LH. And when Soltan Malekshah died in 485 LH, he was 40 and Khayyam 73 lunar years old this clearly fits the status of a more senior advisor for Soltan Malekshah, to the extent that he was.

Note here that if we had abided by Khayyam's mistaken 439 LH (AD 1048) birth date per Swāmi Govinda Tīrtha, Khayyam would have been just six lunar years older than Malekshah when his reign began (465-439=26), or when Khayyam was (1072-1048=) 24 solar years old. Counting from Khayyam's true birth date (AD 1021), he was 51 *solar* year old when Soltan Malekshah began his reign.

(5) Beyhaqi the Author Himself (in Khayyam's entry no. A66/P64)

Beyhaqi also reports that as a child/youth and in the presence of his father he himself met Khayyam in the year 507 LH, when Khayyam greeted him warmly, testing him about his knowledge of poetry and geometry and praising him in the presence of his father.

At this time, Beyhaqi (who himself reportedly lived from 490 to 565 LH, some reporting his birth date to be later, in 499 LH) must have been somewhere between 8 to 17 lunar years of age. Khayyam (b. 412 LH) in 507 LH would have been about 95 lunar, or 92 solar, years old. Beyhaqi's father was obviously alive at that time, given Beyhaqi's acknowledging his presence during the meeting.

The questions Khayyam asks the young Beyhaqi are interesting in their range from seemingly simple (kinds of curves or arcs in geometry), to more involved: how to interpret a poem drawn from an epic collection of Arab poetry. To these I shall return in due course.

(6) Muhammad al-Baghdadi (in Khayyam's entry no. A66/P64)

Regarding the last day of Khayyam's life, another famous account as reported by Beyhaqi in his entry for Khayyam in *Tatemmat Sewan el-Hekmat (Supplement to the Chest of Wisdom)* is the following.

Al-Imam Muhammad al-Baghdadi (الامام محمّد البغدادی) is introduced as a relative of Khayyam using a word that could be interpreted as either a son-in-law, or a brother-in-law. Since Khayyam has been reported as having not married or had a child, and no one has authentically and formally claimed him as a parent or direct descendent, it has been assumed that Baghdadi must have been a brother-in-law, which means Khayyam likely had at least one sister.

Based on al-Baghdadi's account, Beyhaqi reports Khayyam's last day alive as follows (in Arabic, with my Persian and English translation provided; notes in the brackets are mine):

> و حکی لی خَتَنُهُ الامام محمد البغدادیّ انه کان یتخلّل بخلالٍ مِن ذَهَبٍ، وکان یتأمّل الالهیات من الشفاء، فلما وصل الی فصل الواحد والکثیر، وضع الخلال بین الورقتین وقال: أدع الأزکیاء حتی أوَصّي، فوصّی، فقام وصلّی، و لم یأکل ولم یشرب فلما صلّی العشاء الأخیرة سجد وکان یقول في سجوده: «اللهم تعلم أني عرفتك علی مبلغ امکانی، فاغفر لی، فإنّ معرفتی إیاك وسیلتي إلیك». و مات.

> برادرزاده اش امام محمّد بغدادی به من گفت: "با خلالی از طلا خلال می کرد و در حال مطالعه ی الهیات الشفاء بود. چون به فصل "واحد و کثیر" رسید، خلال را در میان دو ورق گذاشت و گفت: "صالحان را دعوت کن تا وصیّت کنم." پس وصیّت کرد، برخاست و نماز گزارد، و نه خورد و نه آشامید تا آخرین نماز شب. آنگاه سُجده کرد و در حین سُجده گفت: «خدای من، می دانی که تو را بنا بر توانم شناخته ام؛ مرا ببخش، چون شناختِ من از تو تنها راهم بسوی توست. و درگذشت."

> His brother-in-law Imam Muhammad al-Baghdadi told me: "He was using a golden toothpick while reading the Elahiyyat [theological section] of [the book] al-Shafa [of Avicenna]. When he reached the chapter on "The One and the Many," he inserted the toothpick between the two pages and said: "Invite the righteous so that I offer my will." He offered his will, then rose to praying and withdrew from any eating or drinking until he fulfilled the last evening prayer and prostrated. While prostrating he said: "My God, Thou Know that I have understood Thee to the best of my ability; forgive me, since my knowledge of Thee is my only path to Thee." And died.

Shafi footnotes (p. 116, Persian section) that Muhammad al-Baghdadi is one who has a (short) essay as listed in Hadaeq ul-Sahar fi Daqaeq ul-Sher (حدائق السحر فی دقائق الشعر) (Gardens of Dawn in Moments of Poetry, p. 28, no. 11 in the list) and included in his Majmouat ul-Rasael[4] (مجموعة الرسائل) by Rashideddin al-Vatvat (رشیدالدّین وطواط) (d. 573 LH). In the list, al-Baghdadi is again identified as a relative of Khayyam.[5] I could trace this text and can confirm it exists.

This Muhammad al-Baghdadi was most likely the famed medieval mathematician known as Machometus Bagdedinus, also known as Muhammad ibn abd al-Baqi Qadi al-Maristan (1050-1141), who authored a treatise on Euclid.[6] His book was widely known in Europe, translated into Latin many times. If this is the same person, which most likely it is, at the likely time of Khayyam's passing (517 LH, AD 1123) he must have been 73

4. See here: https://www.jamaa.net/books.library/?i=104692#main.

5. See here: http://arablib.com/harf?view=book&lid=2&rand1=RFcwSG45ZEBzMyVB&rand2=SjlYU1lEQyRvS2sx

6. See here: https://en.wikipedia.org/wiki/Muhammad_al-Baghdadi

solar years old, himself to die 18 solar years following Khayyam's death. His age would fit that of a brother-in-law of Khayyam, the latter being 39 solar years his senior. As we know Khayyam himself authored a major treatise as an appreciative critique of Euclid, so the two must have been conversant on the topic.

Note that Beyhaqi, interestingly, despite reporting what happened on Khayyam's last day, does not give a specific date for Khayyam's birth or passing, but provides us with the most important horoscope at the beginning of his text which has led us to finding Khayyam's definitive birth date.

So, based on the Beyhaqi entry on Khayyam in *Tatemmat Sewan el-Hekmat (Supplement to the Chest of Wisdom)*, as considered above, we can safely assume that Khayyam was still definitely living by the year 511 LH (AD 1117-1118) at least. The accounts above would not contradict the possibility that he could have lived at least until 515 LH (AD 1121-1122), given Shahab ul-Islam mentioned in the biographical entry lived until that year.

There is nothing in the specific biographical entry for Khayyam in *Tatemmat Sewan el-Hekmat (Supplement to the Chest of Wisdom)* that refers to any event or information suggesting that Khayyam was living anytime *after* 517 LH. All the meetings reported in the entry happened *before* that time. Given that the period between 517 LH to 526 LH (allegedly considered as a date for his passing), nine years, is a relatively long period of time, one would expect that at least some information or event during that time would report Khayyam to be still living then, but no such references can be found in Beyhaqi's entry for him in his biographical entry.

Now, I will further explore passages in which Khayyam's name is mentioned in *Tatemmat Sewan el-Hekmat (Supplement to the Chest of Wisdom)*, to see if they support the point I just made above.

4. Examining Other Entries by Beyhaqi in "Tatemmat Sewan el-Hekmat" Where Khayyam Is Mentioned

Besides the specific entry for Khayyam in Beyhaqi's *Tatemmat Sewan el-Hekmat (Supplement to the Chest of Wisdom)*, he is mentioned and referred to in several other biographical entries of the book. Since the associations made to other contemporaries in the book may offer helpful clues regarding when Khayyam lived, what he did at what age, and when he died, I will briefly survey these cases as well here. Note that while some of the considerations below may seem less directly relevant, they are still important to review, since it is important to see if there is any evidence that Khayyam could have lived beyond the date of 517 LH.

(7) Abol-Hasan al-Anbari (A53/P51)

One often overlooked person Beyhaqi associates with Khayyam is "Abol-Hasan al-Anbiri." In the Arabic edition, his name is expressed as follows: ابوالحسن الانبيرىّ الحكيم . In the old Persian translation it is expressed as ابوالحسن الانبارى الحكيم . The name starts with an alef with hamzeh such as أ and transliterated variously rendered as "al-ʾAnbari," or "al-ʾAnbāri," or "al-ʾAnbiri."

Beyhaqi refers to him as a philosopher inclined toward the science of geometry, from whom Khayyam benefited. "It was he who explained to him the *Almagest*" (in reference to Ptolemy's work) (p. 164, English edition of *Tatemmat Sewan el-Hekmat*[7]). While the above seems like a short, brief, sentence, the implications are significant. In other words, this person was one of the most important teachers of Khayyam especially on the subject of astronomy.

No dates of birth or death are given by Beyhaqi or separately known for this person. He apparently belongs to a set of associations Khayyam had made earlier in his life with those more senior than him, so added knowledge is not of direct use for us in regards to determining the exact date of Khayyam's *passing*.

Although it may appear as if we are going on a tangent from our purpose of searching for Khayyam's date of passing, it may be helpful trying to learn more of the little we know about this (neglected) teacher of Khayyam. After all, topics that may seem separate billiard balls, may not be so once we have concluded our journey.

Even though not much is known about this person, based on the little that has been reported of him in *Tatemmat Sewan el-Hekmat*, his sayings in both the Arabic and (additions, per Shafi's footnote comment, p. 70, Persian section) the old Persian translation echo important elements of what Khayyam learned and how he conducted his life.

Beyhaqi offers the following sayings or thoughts associated with the persons he surveyed in his book for al-Anbari.

Once a theologian asked him what he was teaching. Al-Anbari replied that he was interpreting the Quran. He was asked, "which verse?" Al-Anbari

7. *Ali Ibn Zaid Al-Baihaqi Tatimma Siwan al-Hikma: Texts and Studies* (collected and reprinted by Fuat Sezgin in Collaboration with Carl Ehrig-Eggert, Eckhard Neuybauer), Institute for the History of Arabic-Islamic Science at the Johann Wolfgang Goethe University, Frankfurt am Main, 2005.

replied, "the verse where God Says, 'Have they not seen the sky above them, how I Edified it?!' Al-Anbari then adds, 'I teach them *how* He Edified it.'

This of course also supports Beyhaqi's comment that Al-Anbari was an expert in Ptolemy's *Almagest*, and it was he who taught Khayyam the book. As it will be seen when examining Khayyam's writings, the notion of "succession order" of the intellect-soul-spheres Khayyam writes about, having discussed the same with Avicenna as a young student, may have originated in, or echoes, what Khayyam learned while reading Ptolemy's *Almagest* with al-Anbari.

In another saying reported by Beyhaqi, al-Anbari is quoted as having said, "the exposer of secrets is a traitor, no matter how eloquent his prose." He is also quoted as having said, "you must always be alert and awake and master your true enemies, which are anger and lust; and in all conditions follow truthfulness so as to have the right imagination so that your dreams are not disorderly and turbulent, and this will save your life, staying away from false unrests." These comments were not translated into English in Fuat Sezgin's English edition of *Tatemmat Sewan el-Hekmat* (2005, p. 164).

Who was this teacher who seems to have played a significant part in Khayyam's eduction regarding the geometry of the universe, so to speak, leading him to a lifelong search for the mathematical logic or geometry of how God edified the universe? Who is this man whose morality, and down-to-earth advice to always remain awake so as not to get involved in fake unrests, in keeping secrets, of confronting the challenges of being consumed by anger and lust may have guided Khayyam also to adopt a mode of living characterized by secretiveness, of controlling lust and anger as main enemies, of remaining awake, and trying to save his life from false unrests, and so on?

It is worth noting that it is possible the difficulty with finding any traces of this teacher of Khayyam has had in part to do with perceived asynchronicities of possible candidate lives with that of a Khayyam born in AD 1048. Now that we know Khayyam was born twenty seven solar years earlier than AD 1048, that is, in AD 1021, would we be able to find any traces of this important teacher who taught Khayyam the *Almagest*?

In a recently compiled edition (in 1384 SH, or 2005), in the Arabic original, of a partially survived manuscript about the history of Neyshabour, titled المختصر من كتاب السياق لتاريخ نيسابور or *al-Mokhtasar men Ketab ul-Siaq le-Tarikh Nisabour (A Summary of the Book "The Context of the History of Neyshabour")*, a book originally compiled by ابو الحسن الفارسي عبد الغافر بن اسماعيل or Abol-Hasan Abd ul-Ghafer Ibn Ismail Ibn Abd-Ghafer al-Farsi (451-

519 LH), one which was rather recently compiled and published in Iran by Mohammad Kazem al-Mahmoudi, we find someone named Abol-Hasan al-Anbari whose date of passing falls within the last part of the fifth century (around 460-500 LH) based on a classification system devised by the original compiler. Fortunately, in the edition compiled from only a partially surviving list of names in the manuscript, the section that would include the name "ʾAbol-Ḥasan" has survived and the man's approximate time of death would make his life's timeline more or less compatible with having been a senior contemporary to Khayyam, serving him as a teacher.

Another fortunate matter for us is that another paragraph of information for this person is given in this edition, whereas in another edition of the book compiled two centuries later, having a more inclusive list of names but lacking in detail (from which the name of this person is actually missing for some reason), such details have been eliminated for the sake of list inclusiveness.

One of the paragraph in Arabic is as follows, which can be roughly translated into English and Persian as I have done so further below (the name list number and the brackets are in the Arabic edition):

-2120-

[أبو الحسن الأنباري]

و منهم علي بن محمد الأنباري أبو الحسن الإمام من أفاضل عصره في الأصول و التذكير و العلوم الدقيقة، داق اللسان فصيح اللهجة، حسن الخاطر كيّس الطبع، طاف البلاد، و لقي الصدور، و وجد القبول.

[ʾAból-Ḥasan ál-ʾAnbāri]

And of them was Ali Ibn Muhammad al-Anbari Abu al-Hasan, the Imam [or leader/teacher] of the best scholars of his time in (both) religious principles and wise sayings as well as exact mathematical sciences, with piercing tongue, clear language, beautiful mind, graceful nature, well traveled, well connected (to the high status), accepted in hearts.

[ابوالحسن الانباری]

و از ایشان یکی علی بن محمد الانباری ابوالحسن بود، امام بهترین افاضل زمان خود، با اصول دین و سخنان حاکمانه و علوم دقیق، زبانی بُرّنده، کلماتی روشن، بینشی زیبا، سفر کرده در بلاد، و مرتبط با مردم، و مقبول در دلها.

This teacher is in the right place (Neyshabour), and right time and age context (the fifth century, passing away by its last quarter), with expertise in both the spiritual/philosophical and the mathematical exact sciences.

Note that this probability becoming a possibility of finding additional corroborative evidence for the teacher was itself made possible by our finding the true birth of Omar Khayyam in AD 1021 in this book, since the date AD 1048 would not reconcile at all with the age of our candidate for this teacher found in the person of the above ʾAból-Ḥasan ál-ʾAnbāri.

Although our knowledge of the date of birth and death of this teacher is still limited, the brief inquiry about the possibility of such a person being one of the teachers of Khayyam corroborates does not contradict either his discovered date of birth or his date of passing after 511 LH.

(8) Abol-Hasan Ali an-Nasawi (A64/P62)

A second person that Beyhaqi introduces but is not associated with Khayyam and yet is worth noting here is ابوالحسن علی النسوی or Abol-Hasan Ali an-Nasawi (p. 170, English edition). He is known for his authorship of astronomical writings (ibid.), and for being a philosopher as well as a mathematician.

It is important to note that this is *not* the Nasawi in response to whose request Khayyam wrote his important treatise on the created world and the obligation to worship, *al-Resalat fi al-Kown wa al-Taklif (Treatise on Universe and Obligation, or Treatise on the Created World and the Duty to Worship)*. To the latter I will return later in this series.

Beyhaqi interestingly reports the mentioned Nasawi as having lived to a hundred years (not specified whether lunar or solar), adding, "... his powers remained sound, except that weakness prevented him from walking in the markets and confined him to his house" (ibid.). Technically, we could say exactly the same condition may have also been applicable for Khayyam, who may have been even in better shape, given he was a physician as well.

In other words, while unrelated to Khayyam, this observation is important for us, since it shows that it was not too rare and uncommon to find scholars living to hundred years at that time, still with a sound mind.

Why Beyhaqi would not mention the same for Khayyam, if he knew his age for certain, is of course interesting and worth considering, given that for Khayyam he offers at least a horoscope (though not a birth date).

This may indicate that Beyhaqi must not have known that Khayyam lived to a hundred years, and had only met him as a child and not more recently. Apparently, his knowing Khayyam's horoscope had not been accompanied with a knowledge of the year in which Khayyam was born.

For us, having found (so far in this chapter) that Khayyam also at least lived until 511 LH (if not more), while realizing that on his last day he still had a sound mind, provides some information that persons such as him or Nasawi could have lived long ages and still retained their mental powers.

(9) Ali Ibn Muhammad al-Hejazi Qaeni (A83/P83)

Related to the issue of aging, another noted personality in Beyhaqi's work that also lived to an old age was actually a student of Khayyam, that is, على بن محمّد الحجازى القاينى or Ali Ibn Muhammad al-Hejazi Qaeni (numbered the same in Beyhaqi's list in both the Arabic and Persian editions) who lived to ninety years. Beyhaqi introduces him as one who was born in Qaen and lived in Beyhaq (today's city of Sabzevar) in Iran's Khorasan.

According to Beyhaqi, he was a physician, philosophically inclined, of moral behavior and beautiful character, who "lived ninety years and died in the year 546/1151" (p. 184, English edition). At the time when it came to giving age, usually solar years were meant, but if we say that his age given here is in lunar years, the latter information would place Hejazi's birth date around the year 456 LH, when Khayyam was about 44 lunar years old, which is compatible with the possibility that Khayyam was his teacher. Hejazi became associated with Soltan Sanjar, writing a book in his name on Turkish culture and another book in science celebrating a Kharazmshahian king, Atsiz Ibn Muhammad.

The English edition's note on the number of years Hejazi lived is based on Shafi's research in the main body of his text. However, in his own footnote (in the Arabic/Persian edition, p. 134, footnote (1)) Shafi in fact reports, based on another important book of history written by the same author Beyhaqi, that Hejazi's age "reached to an age of 100 *solar* years" (ibid.), that is about 103-4 lunar years. If so, this would bring his birth date back ten or more lunar years to about the year 442 LH (counting 104 lunar year of age).

This would mean for a young 20-25 years old Hejazi moving to Neyshabour after the destruction of his hometown (according to Beyhaqi in his other book of history of his times, as relayed by Shafi in the same footnote) and meetings there with Khayyam as a teacher, Khayyam must have been engaged in teaching before being invited by Soltan Malekshah to reform the calendar and build his observatory during the 465 to 472 LH period.

If Hejazi was around during, let us say hypothetically, 517 LH date of demise for Khayyam, he would have been about 75 lunar years old. As a doctor, and a pupil of Khayyam, we may consider it possible that he was one of the "righteous" and trusted folks invited by Khayyam by way of al-

Baghdadi to his death bed to hear his last will. And if his last will had anything to do with his Robaiyat, then Hejazi may have known about it.

(10) Alaoddowleh Faramarz Ibn Ali Ibn Faramarz (A65/P63)

Another person Beyhaqi introduces in association with Khayyam was a prince of Yazd, an ancient major city/region by the same name in today's Iran. He is introduced as "the learned and just prince, the Right Arm of the World and the Religion," علاءالدوله فرامرز بن علی بن فرامرز or Alaoddowleh Faramarz Ibn Ali Ibn Faramarz.

Given my focus now, short of a general overview below, I will not enter into the details of the story narrated by Beyhaqi about a meeting between the two, nor offer my own sense of why or how Beyhaqi is reporting it. In his footnote to the Arabic text written in Persian in the Persian edition of the book (p. 110, footnote 1), Shafi writes that the father of this prince was from the Kakouyeh dynasty and close to Soltan Malekshah. The prince's father died in battle in the year 488 LH.

Beyhaqi reports the story of a *previous* conversation between this prince and Khayyam, relayed to Beyhaqi by the prince during a meeting Beyhaqi had with the prince in the year 516 LH (AD 1122-1123), where Beyhaqi says his own father was also present. During the meeting, the prince reportedly showed[8] Beyhaqi's father a book he had written (مهجة التوحيد), in which, Beyhaqi says, the prince had defended the views of ابی البرکات or Abi al-Barakat, a Baghdadi physician (to whom I will return). In the course of their conversation on this topic, the prince tells Beyhaqi the following.

The prince says that once (he does not say when) he asked Khayyam for his opinion of the physician from Baghdad, Abi al-Barakat, who had expressed views critical of Avicenna. Khayyam replied by saying that the physician did not have the capacity to understand Avicenna, let alone be in a position to criticize him. The prince then asked Khayyam if it is possible for one to be intellectually stronger than Avicenna. Khayyam confirmed that to be in principle possible. The prince then said that what opinion Khayyam originally offered lowered him to the level of the prince's slave, since his slave could have said the same thing and outdone him in that. The prince's

---

8. Beyhaqi's father had reportedly gone completely blind in the year 503 LH (see Shafi, 1932, p. 588), so the reference to "showing" (عَرَضَ) must be figurative, rather than actual. This may explain why in these reported meetings, his father is present, not just in terms of the son being caring for his blind father, but also perhaps his father, despite ailment, meeting famed people in his "network" to introduce his son for his education and future career. The father must have tried this in his last years, since, according to Shafi, he died in 517 LH.

point was that to counter another person's limitations, it is best to do so with reason and argument rather than through polemic and slander. According to Beyhaqi, Khayyam "rose up in silence" (Shafi, p. 609).

I shall return to the substantive issues raised by this story in due course.

The meeting between Beyhaqi and the prince reportedly took place in 516 LH, in the presence of Beyhaqi's father. Shafi himself notes in his article on *Tatemmat Sewan el-Hekmat (Supplement to the Chest of Wisdom)* that Beyhaqi's father died in 517 LH (p. 591). There is nothing mentioned in Beyhaqi's relaying of the story regarding Khayyam having passed away by then, and no customary mercy wishing accompanies either the prince's nor Beyhaqi's references to Khayyam. This does not of course offer a definitive clue regarding Khayyam's date of passing, but it is noteworthy.

Given that the conversation Beyhaqi was having with the prince was in 516 LH, and Khayyam was specifically *the* topic of conversation between them, it would have been odd not to reference Khayyam as a deceased person and express the usual wishing of God's mercy for him, if Khayyam indeed had died by then. In other words, given the lack of references in the reported conversation to a Khayyam that had passed away, this story strongly favors the view that Khayyam had not yet died sometime in the year 516 LH.

(11) Abol-Maali Abdollah Ibn Muhammad al-Mianeji (Ein ol-Qozzat-e Hamedani) (A67/P65)

Another person introduced by Beyhaqi in association with Khayyam is ابوالمعالی عبدالله بن محمّد المیانجی or Abol-Maali Abdollah Ibn Muhammad al-Mianeji (meaning, from the town of Mianeh). Reportedly, Mianeji was a joint pupil of Khayyam as well as of Ahmad al-Ghazali, the Sufi brother of the famed Muhammad Ghazali (not the latter himself) whose conversation about the poles in the sky Beyhaqi reported in Khayyam's own biography (which I briefly addressed before).

Mianeji is reported to have been interested in integrating the mystical knowledge with that of the philosophers, authoring a book titled *Zobdat ol Haqaeq* (زبدة الحقائق or "The Cream of the Truths") reportedly in 525 LH (AD 1131-1132) (English edition, p. 175). Mianeji was reportedly imprisoned in Baghdad, and executed in Hamedan in 525 LH (AD 1131-1132) by horrible crucifixion due to an enmity between him and the vizier Abi al-Qaem al-Nasabadi (ابی القاسم الانسابادی).

In the old Persian edition of *Tatemmat Sewan el-Hekmat (Supplement to the Chest of Wisdom)*, it is noted that in his above-mentioned book, Mianeji sought to integrate Sufi and Greek truths, which is perhaps an interpretation/elaboration of what Beyhaqi meant by mixing philosophy and mysticism. The old Persian edition elaborates that the book is a rare jewel of the heart of the mystical-hearted.

Of his sayings, the edition mentions one suggesting that whoever succeeds in linking to the existence of the Necessary Being (God), is flooded with emotions that cannot be expressed in words and becomes more joyfully determined to seek the Perfect (p. 86, Persian edition).

Mianeji is also known, more famously in Iran today, as the Ein ol-Qozzat-e Hamedani (عین القضّات همدانی). He is known to have been born in the year 490 LH (AD 1097-1098). So, he must have been a late pupil of Khayyam, and would have been about 27 lunar years old, if and when Khayyam (for now, we say hypothetically) passed away in the year 517 LH. It would not be too remote to consider that he could have been among the "righteous" (trusted) invited to Khayyam's death bed and present when he died, and thus perhaps even informed of Khayyam's poetry and work on his Robaiyat.

What Mianeji (Ein ol-Qozzat-e Hamedani) learned from Khayyam, then, would have been inspired from the most mature years of Khayyam's intellectual life. Mianeji's (or Ein ol-Qozzat's) writing of the book *Zobdat ol Haqaeq* ("The Cream of the Truths") has been placed in the year 516 LH, a year before our considered day of Khayyam's passing, so Khayyam may have been aware of it. As we know from the reports of his last day reading Avicenna's *Shafa*, Khayyam could have as well been reading other material.

In due course, we will need to explore more the biography and background of this important pupil of Khayyam. Beyhaqi or others have accused of Khayyam of being miserly in teaching, yet, he himself is listing those who were Khayyam's students, we may note in passing.

For now, given our focus, it is important to note that if Khayyam's date of passing had occurred on the year 526 LH, which has become the uneasy consensus date in recent decades, it would have roughly coincided with or even shortly followed the definitively known year of execution of this pupil of Khayyam. We know that based on the confirmed date of Khayyam's birth as discovered for the first time in this book (412 LH/AD 1021), it is quite unlikely that his date of passing would have been that late implying an age of more than 110 solar or 114 lunar years.

Beyhaqi's account of Mianeji, despite the association he explicitly makes between him and his teacher Khayyam, does not offer any indication that their deaths both could have happened in the same year or close to one another. Again, of course this does not offer any conclusive evidence for our purpose of finding the definitive date or year of Khayyam's passing. All it does is to offer another missed opportunity for someone making a claim that Khayyam could have died in the year some have announced to be his date of passing.

Note that we have yet to find even a single report in Beyhaqi about a Khayyam living past the year 517 LH, other than the (separate) claimed report of Nezami Arouzi visiting his grave in 530 LH and saying, ambiguously, that he had died "four," "fourteen," or "some" years before.

Beyhaqi does not offer an age or date of birth for Mianeji in his account. In his footnotes to the English article edition, Shafi offers a slightly different information regarding Mianeji's execution date, and a further reference source for pursuing further research on this important pupil of Khayyam (p. 609, footnote (3)).

(12) Abu Hatam al-Mozaffar al-Asfezari (A68/P67)

Another person Beyhaqi introduces who had close associations with Khayyam is the philosopher, Abu Hatam al-Mozaffar al-Asfezari (ابو حاتم المظفّر الاسفزاری).

He is reported to have interacted greatly with Khayyam and was a close colleague and friend, perhaps even a confidant, being inclined to mathematics and mechanics. He is known to have made his own invention of a balance or water-scale to measure the amount of precious metals in jewelry without disassembling them. The king's (Soltan Sanjar's) treasurer reportedly became alarmed for being exposed for his cheating as a result of the use of such a balance; so, he destroyed it. Asfezari became so distraught that passed away from grief.

Al-Khazeni who wrote a book on the topic of such balances and included in it a contribution from Khayyam, included as well a section on Asfezari's contribution. I will elaborate more on this when I specifically explore al-Khazeni's book later in this chapter. It suffices here to say that al-Khazeni wrote in his book that he accomplished writing it in the months of the year 515 LH.

In his book, relating the passing of Asfezari from sorrow as noted also by Beyhaqi, Khazeni wishes God's Mercy on him. So, it is very much possible that Asfezari had passed away in the year 515 LH or before. The interesting point is that in the same text, in reference to Khayyam, no such mercy-wishing is offered in *some* manuscripts, implying that Khayyam must not have yet passed away by the time al-Khazeni's book was completed in the year 515 LH. Others have used the appearance of such a mercy-wishing statement in a manuscript copy of Khazeni's book as evidence for Khayyam's passing in that year. To an important evidence to the contrary, however, I shall return later.

Asfezari also wrote on topics such as astronomy and geometry. It is also important to note that Asfezari was among those invited along with Khayyam by Soltan Malekshah and his minister Nezam ol-Molk to build an observatory in Isfahan and reform the Persian calendar. Beyhaqi, while noting the expertise of Asfezari in matters astronomical and mathematical, does acknowledge Khayyam's expertise to be superior to that of Asfezari.

However, Beyhaqi also makes a point of contrasting Asfezari's friendly attitude toward those seeking his instruction with that of Khayyam whom he regards as having been miserly in teaching and writing, and manifesting a strong or harsh temper. The reader may have already noticed by now that for some reason Beyhaqi used every opportunity in the book to remind his reader of what *he claimed* to be the negative side of Khayyam's temper or character. To this issue I will return in due course later in this series.

In their introduction to their collection of Khayyam's treatises (1962), Rozenfeld and Iushkevich mistakenly note that the above al-Asfezari was a son of allegedly another al-Asfezari that collaborated with Khayyam in a team of astronomers tasked with reforming the Persian solar calendar. However, this is in fact the same al-Asfezari.

The reason the Russian scholars must have thought this must be a son of al-Asfezari may have something to do with what they presumed to be Khayyam's age, given their reliance on Tīrtha's (mistaken) finding that Khayyam was born in the year AD 1048. If that was the case, he would be a rather young astronomer involved in the calendar reform (which took place around 468-70 LH or about AD 1076-1078). So, the assumption was that others (including al-Asfezari) must have been more senior to him. Our discovery of Khayyam's true date of birth in AD 1021 confirms that around the time of calendar reform efforts, Khayyam himself was senior in age (about 54-56 solar years old, 1076-1021=55) befitting a leader of the astronomical team.

We also should note that it was this same al-Asfezari with whom Khayyam was having a gathering in Balkh in 506 LH (around AD 1112-1113), according to Nezami Arouzi. Another manuscript copy of Arouzi's book offers another date, 512 LH, for that gathering, as we will explore later in another chapter in this book. We find Khayyam still actually quite active around that time, despite his age; in 507 LH he meets the young Beyhaqi, and in 508 LH, he is consulted for a good time and date for Seljuk Soltan Muhammad to go hunting.

(13) Abol-Abbas al-Lowkari (A69/P77) and Other Direct or Mediated Pupils of Avicenna

Introduced by Beyhaqi but not, in his text, as someone associated with Khayyam is the philosopher and man of letters Abol-Abbas al-Lowkari (ابوالعبّاس اللوكرى). Lowkari is introduced as a student of Bahmanyar, who was in turn a student of Avicenna. Beyhaqi notes that Lowkari became blind in old age, without specifying how long he lived.

The reason I include Lowkari here and as noteworthy for the purpose of this chapter is that Lowkari has been separately associated with Khayyam, being among a group (that also included al-Asfezari, as introduced above) invited by Soltan Malekshah and his minister Nezam ol-Molk to reform the Persian solar calendar.

The association will become also significant when we consider the nature of Khayyam's and Lowkari's common associations with Avicenna. Here, of course, Beyhaqi associates Lowkari with Bahmanyar, a pupil of Avicenna, and not directly with Avicenna himself. What has been debated is whether Khayyam also had, or could have, any direct personal interactions with Avicenna, since there are not only many events indicating his interest in Avicenna's thought and belonging to his legacy, but also because Khayyam himself states in writing (in one of his philosophical writings) that he had discussions with Avicenna in person.

Before we explore these latter issues, however, it would be helpful for us to situate Lowkari in time more specifically, since Beyhaqi does not offer any indications in this regard in his text in *Tatemmat Sewan el-Hekmat (Supplement to the Chest of Wisdom)*.

In order to gain a sense of whether Lowkari had the same seniority as Khayyam or was instead his junior, we may consider the following.

Lowkari is mentioned to have been a pupil of Bahmanyar (بهمن يار , as spelled out in Beyhaqi, Arabic edition). Bahmanyar, also introduced by Beyhaqi in his book (A49/P47)), is known to have lived in the first half of the eleventh century, having died in the year AD 1056, or around 448 LH.

Other students of Avicenna introduced in *Tatemmat Sewan el-Hekmat* are: 1) Abu Mansur al-Hossein b. Taher b. Zayla (ابو منصور الحسين بن طاهر بن زيله) (A50/P48), known to have been a close pupil of Avicenna, having died in the year 440 LH (1048/1049 LH) or ten years later (1058/1059); 2) Abu Ubayd Abd al-Wahid al-Juzajani (ابو عُبيد عبدالواحد الجوزجانی) (A51/P49), the closest pupil of Avicenna who transmitted his autobiography and some of his writings, considered to have died in the year AD 1047, or around 438 LH; and 3) Abu Abdollah al-Masoumi (ابو عبدالله المعصومی) (A52/P50), another close and direct disciple of Avicenna, also introduced by Beyhaqi, known to have died in the year AD 1038, or around 430 LH.

Avicenna or Ibn Sina (شرف الملك ابو علی الحسین بن عبدالله بن سینا البخاری) (A27/P25) is of course himself introduced by Beyhaqi, in the longest biographical sketch of the collection, his dates of birth and passing being definitively known (22 August, AD 980 or Safar 2nd, 370 LH - June 21, AD 1037 or 27 Shaban 428 LH).

Now, for Lowkari himself, Beyhaqi introduces several pupils in *Tatemmat Sewan el-Hekmat*. One is Qotab al-Zaman Mohammad b. Abi Taher al-Tabasi al-Marwazi (قطب الزمان محمد بن ابی طاهر الطبسی المروزی) (A70/P78), who died in the Shawwal of 539 LH (April, AD 1145) after three years of being afflicted with plegia (paralysis or stroke). Another pupil of Lowkari was Ain al-Zaman al-Hasan al-Qattan of Marv (عین الزمان الحسن القطّان المروزی) (A98/P93), who was born in the year 465 LH (AD 1072) and died in 548 LH (AD 1153) according to outside sources. Another Lowkari pupil was Majd al-Afazel Abd al-Razzaq at-Turki (مجد الافاضل عبدالرزّاق الترکی) (A72/P66), no dates of birth or passing being known about him. Another Lowkari pupil introduced by Beyhaqi is Asad al-Mayhani (اسعد المیهنی) (A85/P85), having died in 527 LH (AD 1133).

So, let us put the above dates in chronological order.

Avicenna died in 428 LH as detailed above. His disciples died in 430 LH (Masoumi), 438 LH (Juzajani), 440 LH (Abu Mansur), and 458 LH (Bahmanyar). Lowkari is introduced as being a student of Bahmanyar, while Lowkari's own students died around the years 529, 539, and 548 LH, all after Khayyam's passing (regardless of what so-far presumed date of passing we may consider for Khayyam). Lowkari's date of passing is not exactly known but it is believed to have taken place in the first half the sixth lunar Hejri century (500s LH). As told by Beyhaqi, he went blind in old age before passing away.

Now that we know Khayyam's definitive date of birth (June 10 AD 1021, or Safar 19, 412 LH), we can specifically note the following.

Khayyam (b. 412 LH/AD 1021) was about sixteen and a half years old when Avicenna died in 428 LH (AD 1037). Therefore, Khayyam definitively had the chance of being contemporary not only with Avicenna, but also with

Avicenna's pupils for two (Masoumi), ten (Juzajani), twelve (Abu Mansur), and thirty (Bahmanyar) *more* years.

When Bahmanyar died in 458 LH, Khayyam was 46 lunar years old. So, it is entirely possible for a bright young, almost sixteen years old Khayyam to have been not only in educational conversations with Avicenna himself around his lunar ages 15-16 plus, but to have continued interacting with Avicenna's pupils for many more years, more so with Bahmanyar, the longest living direct senior pupil of Avicenna.

Khayyam could have therefore been a relatively more senior contemporary of Lowkari in matters of science (though not as a popularizing of philosophy as was Lowkari at least publicly), from whose associations their joint invitation (among others including Asfezari) to reform the Persian calendar may have been drawn.

Note here that we are able, thanks to our prior discovery of Khayyam's exact birth date, to transcend a binary logic whereby Khayyam has to be considered to have been *either* an Avicenna disciple *or* that of Avicenna's another disciple, namely, Bahmanyar.

We have a probability here that Khayyam could have been *both*, and more, that is, Khayyam could have been considered to be, after Bahmanyar in age, the youngest surviving disciple of Avicenna in his times. After all, Beyhaqi himself introduces Khayyam, *and only Khayyam*, among all those in his "chest of wisdom," to have been *the* "Avicenna of his time."

The difference with Lowkari may have been this. Lowkari was only a disciple of Bahmanyar, and too young to have had any overlap of years under the tutelage of Avicenna himself. But Khayyam is one who did have that opportunity, and this may explain the numerous occasions in which he himself, along with others, reminded us of his association with Avicenna.

So, as we shall see, this may also explain why in the year 472 LH (that is, around AD 1079, a definitely known date given in the manuscript itself), we find Khayyam (and *not Lowkari* or anyone else) being invited to translate into Persian Avicenna's "Splendid Sermon" in Isfahan when he also offered his own commentaries on it.

In that year, Khayyam is sixty lunar years old, Bahmanyar, the last surviving direct disciple of Avicenna having passed away about 14 lunar years prior, and Khayyam, the last surviving direct disciple of Avicenna with whom he had direct conversations in person, is a senior to Lowkari's junior status, to be invited to offer the master teacher's sermon in Persian translation, with his own commentaries.

(14) Muhammad b. Ahmad al-Mamouri al-Beyhaqi (A104/P101)

A rather saddening case of a person associated with Khayyam reported by Beyhaqi in *Tatemmat Sewan el-Hekmat* is that of the philosopher Muhammad b. Ahmad al-Mamouri al-Beyhaqi (محمّد بن احمد المعموری البیهقی). Our author Beyhaqi writes that al-Mamouri was a major mathematician, writing on conics, and acknowledged by Khayyam regarding his strength in the field.

Mamouri apparently accompanied the group of astronomers and experts invited by Soltan Malekshah (which included Khayyam, Lowkari, and Asfezari) for the construction of an observatory in Isfahan, and remained there until the time of Malekshah's son, Muhammad.

The sad story Beyhaqi relates regarding his last days is as follows.

During the time when the Ismailis (or Batenis) were being pursued, captured, and burned, Mamouri at some point found his own horoscope predictions astrologically ominous and decided to give up the protective condition of his life in the royal palace and go into hiding, thinking that he would then be spared the ominous fate he had foreseen in his horoscope.

It happens that one day, a Bateni (Ismaili) had been arrested and was being carried in the streets where Mamouri was hiding (in a safe house). Amid the uproar and people on the roofs watching the events, a woman called out that a "Qarmati" (regarded as heretics by the orthodox religious establishment) was in the house were Mamouri was staying, apparently thinking he was a Bateni. So, people entered and dragged him out and killed him. By the time the royal guards arrived and realized Mamouri had been mistakenly taken and killed, it was already too late. Khayyam, a close friend, must have been quite saddened by this event.

This event, apparently took place in the year 485 LH or in AD 1092, when Khayyam was about 73 lunar (or 71 solar) years old. That year was the same year Nezam ol-Molk was killed, followed by Soltan Malekshah's death a month later, and in fact the events noted above may have been related to the minister's assassination.

(15) Alaoddoleh Faramarz Ibn Ali Ibn Faramarz (A65/P63) and Abu al-Barakat (A93/P81)

Another person indirectly associated with Khayyam through the story narrated by the prince of Yazd, Alaoddoleh Faramarz Ibn Ali Ibn Faramarz (علاءالدولة فرامرز بن علی بن فرامرز), whom I related before, is the philosopher and physician, Owhad az-Zaman Abu al-Barakat ibn Maleka al-Tabib (اوحد الزّمان ابو البرکات بن ملکا الطبیب). Both persons are introduced by Beyhaqi.

Abu al-Barakat was the same person whose criticism of Avicenna had drawn the sympathy of the prince and, per his questioning, the prince's criticism in turn of Khayyam who found al-Barakat not qualified to criticize Avicenna since he did not have the capacity, in his view, to understand him.

Outside sources give al-Barakat's dates of birth and death as 480-560 LH (or about AD 1087-1165[9]). Beyhaqi himself offers (new Persian edition, pp. 91-92) a rather precise way of determining his birth date in his biographical entry for him when he offers the story of how al-Barakat died. Basically, according to Beyhaqi, Barakat lived ninety solar years. He died from fear of not having been able to cure Soltan Masoud (son of Mahmoud and grandson of Soltan Malekshah), shortly before Soltan Masoud died. The latter's date of death is known to have occurred in the year in AD 1152 (547 LH). Ninety solar years before then would be around the year AD 1062. So, Beyhaqi puts his lifetime a bit earlier than others have reported (compare these with the dates AD 1087-1165 given above).

Considering Beyhaqi's story of prince Faramarz telling Beyhaqi in 516 LH regarding seeking Khayyam's opinion on Barakat's critique of Avicenna, we may now realize that Barakat was about either (1062-1021=) 41, or (1087-1021=) 66 solar years junior to Khayyam. Even in the year 516 LH (about AD 1122), Barakat was somewhere between (1122-1087=) 35 and (1122-1062=) 60 years old (to Khayyam's having past 100). So, if the said conversation the prince had with Khayyam took place several years earlier, Barakat would be even younger.

So, now we can realize that the prince was chastising a senior philosopher and "the Avicenna of his time" for having expressed a rather blunt opinion about junior upstart philosopher, so to speak, as a prelude for more elaborations perhaps, if the prince himself had the patience to inquire more as to why Khayyam was asserting such an opinion.

The prince had already written a book (or was writing a book) sympathetic to Barakat (per Beyhaqi's reporting), so he already had predisposed himself for being biased and for taking Khayyam's bluntly expressed view with a grain of salt (or being insulted by Khayyam); after all, Khayyam was bluntly critiquing someone the prince had already stated (in writing) to be sympathetic toward.

Beyhaqi's biographical entry for al-Barakat shows his own bias in favor of him. His stories of al-Barakat mainly reports his having been a failing physician, being imprisoned for it, and dying in fear from his failure as a

9. https://ar.wikipedia.org/wiki/ابن_ملكا_البغدادي

doctor. Yet, Beyhaqi offers a high praise of him, elevating him by claiming that others called him the Aristotle of his time (new Persian edition, p. 91). Yet, all Beyhaqi says about Khayyam's being a physician, is his having expressed an opinion about an apparently sick child, Sanjar, who was in fact cured by Khayyam, apparently.

Whether al-Barakat acquired such a high name and status later in life per Beyhaqi's estimation (after Khayyam died) is beside the point that Khayyam was at the time of offering his opinion relating to a young al-Barakat ambitiously seeing himself above Avicenna. And yet, the "just" prince chose to chastise Khayyam, who was a nearly hundred years old "Avicenna of his time" per Beyhaqi's own words.

It is no wonder that Khayyam, much more senior even to the prince, "rose in silence." What else could he do, in shock of being asked an opinion and being summarily accused of not being allegedly as good as the prince's servant. That he remained silent is itself telling of Khayyam's character, reminding me of what al-Anbari had mentioned about controlling one's temper at the moment.

Biased in favor of his own opinion of al-Barakat as expressed in his book, the prince could have simply asked Khayyam further to expand upon what he offered as an initial opinion. Instead, he summarily judged and insulted Khayyam by demoting his status to that of his servant.

Is this story one of the "evidences" on which Beyhaqi has based his (mis) judgment of Khayyam character as being bitter or miserly with others?

(16) Bahmanyar (A49/P47) and Avicenna (A27/P25)

Given the foregoing implicit, indirect, or reported, associations of Abol-Hassan Bahmanyar, the disciple of Avicenna, with Khayyam, we should also consider Bahmanyar further.

Beyhaqi notes that Bahmanyar was of Zoroastrian communal origin, not speaking Arabic as much as others associated with Avicenna, and from the Azerbaijan region in the northwest of the present Iran. He wrote on topics such as education, logic, happiness, and music. Beyhaqi actually gives a date for his passing in 458 LH, adding that he died thirty years after the death of Avicenna (p. 92, Arabic edition). So, we can regard Bahmanyar's date of passing to be reliable.

For the same reason as above, we should also consider Avicenna himself, who was given the longest entry by Beyhaqi in his compendium. It is interesting to note that Beyhaqi not only provides a horoscope for Avicenna's birth date, but also provides his date of birth alongside it (p. 34, Persian). It is noteworthy that in his horoscope, to give a degree "29" the combination of the abjad letters (Kā) and (Ṫā) was used which represent the numbers 20 and 9 respectively. This again indicates how it would be necessary to use two abjad letters to represent the degrees beyond 10 in a horoscope (other than 20), as I noted in the previous chapter amid the discovery of the true date of birth of Omar Khayyam.

Having been born in the year 370 LH, Avicenna died at the lunar age of 58 in the year 428 LH. Beyhaqi notes, amid a long narrative drawing mostly on the details of Avicenna's life as reported by his closest pupil Juzajani, that he had learned all the knowledge available in his time on various subjects by the age eighteen, many by the time he was twelve (p. 27-38, Persian).

Given the example of Avicenna having learned all the sciences of his time by the age of eighteen, we should not be too surprised that Omar Khayyam, whom Beyhaqi himself acknowledges as having been regarded as the Avicenna of his own time, accomplished the same level of learning by the even earlier age of seventeen, as reported by Yar Ahmad Rashidi Tabrizi in his *Tarabkhaneh (House of Joy)*. In fact, the age of 17 for Khayyam (b. AD 1021) marks the date of Avicenna's passing (AD 1038), prior to which he must have benefited from direct conversations from his teacher Avicenna, himself, who resided his last few years in relative peace in Isfahan.

When we look back in time, sometime we may forget that a student beginning his lessons from a teacher cannot foresee that the teacher may die soon. Khayyam may have begun a longer-planned course of learning from Avicenna, not knowing that he would soon pass away in a matter of a couple of years.

Also, Avicenna's more senior students may not have survived long enough to comment on a bright young student who achieves his own fame later in life.

So, that may also explain why we do not find explicit mentions of Khayyam in the writings or oral reports of the more senior pupils of Avicenna. It is however reported rather authentically that Khayyam (also) read Avicenna's books with Bahmanyar.

Having considered various persons listed in *Tatemmat Sewan el-Hekmat (Supplement to the Chest of Wisdom)* by Beyhaqi in relation to Khayyam, we need to turn our attention to al-Abdorrahman Khazeni, who is also introduced in Beyhaqi's compendium.

5. What Can We Learn from Khazeni's Manuscript "Mizan ol-Hekmat" About Khayyam's Date of Passing?

Another person introduced by Beyhaqi (A103), to whom I have previously referred, is Abul-Fath Abdorrahman al-Khazin, or Khazeni (ابوالفتح عبدالرحمن الخازن). Since Khazeni has provided one of the four major manuscripts on which scholars have drawn in order to determine Khayyam's date of passing, I will dwell more carefully on his association, superposing it with what Beyhaqi also mentioned about him in *Tatemmat Sewan el-Hekmat (Supplement to the Chest of Wisdom).*

Abdorrahman Khazeni was the emancipated Greek slave of Ali al-Khazin al-Marwazi, and was educated in mathematical sciences, geometry, and astronomy, responsible for astronomical tables (ephemeris data) named after Soltan Sanjar. According to Beyhaqi's entry for him, his astronomical data needed further research but his data for Mercury, especially in retrograde, were precise and verified in observation (p. 196 of English edition of *Tatemmat Sewan el-Hekmat*).

It is interesting to note that in my study reported in the last chapter, Khayyam's birth date horoscope revealed that the Mercury was in retrograde during the morning hours and especially four minutes on June 10, AD 1021, from the vantage point of Neyshabour, fulfilling the conditions of his horoscope. It is possible that Abdorrahman Khazeni's expertise on the movements of Mercury had something to do with his training under the guidance of Khayyam who had a particular, personal, interest in measuring Mercury's motions, given his reported horoscope.

Khazeni has been regarded by some as a pupil of Khayyam, one who collaborated with him as part of a group of astronomers and philosophers who were joined at the invitation of Soltan Malekshah and his minister Nezam ol-Molk to build an observatory in Isfahan and to reform the Persian calendar. It appears that he must have joined the team as an able and skilled junior member, guided under the leadership of Khayyam in the team.

Let us then turn our attention to a closer look at the book by Khazeni. His book *Mizan ol-Hekmat* (*Balance of Wisdom)*, which includes a chapter from Omar Khayyam, was completed "in the months of the year 515," as stated by the author in the book itself.

As I have noted previously, Rahim Rezazadeh Malek, the compiler of *Daneshnameh-ye Khayyami (The Khayyami Encyclopedia)*, asked (p. 35) whether the appearance of the phrase "May God rest his soul" after Khayyam's name in the book in one of the manuscript copies of the book should be regarded as indicating that Khayyam had died by the time the book was completed. In his detailed background to the discovery and publication of various copies or editions of this book by Khazeni appearing in the pages 291-292 of his *Khayyami Encyclopedia*, however, Rezazadeh Malek did not offer even a single lead to *any* manuscript copies of Khazeni's collection where the said mercy-wishing statement appears in the text. His report in fact leaves room for the consideration that it was only in one of the manuscript copies of that work that such a mercy statement had been found, and not necessarily in all.

I have examined various editions of the manuscript copies of this book, and have yet to find any copy in which such a mercy related statement following the name of Khayyam appears. This includes a copy of the manuscript in the 1962 Moscow edition on Khayyam edited by B. A. Rozenfeld and A. P. Youschkevitch, where Khayyam's name is mentioned on page 62 of the handwritten manuscript section, or the Persian translation/edition of the book by Modarres Razavi, published in the month of Aban of 1346 SH (Oct. 1967), where, as translated from Arabic into Persian, Khazeni states "Then, Imam Abu Hafs Omar Khayyam Neyshabouri also reflected and thought about the construction of this balance, and offered geometrical and mathematical reasonings for the soundness of its function" (p. "J" in the introduction). There is *no* mention of mercy wishing. According to Mohammad Qazvini, the name "Ábu Ḥafṣ" used for Khayyam is not in error, as it was common then to use it for those with first name Omar.

What makes the issue of wishing God's mercy for Khayyam significant is that in the paragraph where Khazeni is offering a historical background for the various designs and construction of the balance, following the comment on Khayyam, he immediately offers a commentary on al-Imam Abu Hatam al-Mozaffar Ibn Ismail-e Asfezari, who, as I mentioned before, was also a person related to Khayyam (having collaborated with him, and with Khazeni on the task of reforming the Persian calendar). There, Khazeni relates how al-Asfezari could not finish his writing on the balance and died before it could be completed. In this case, Khazeni *does offer* a wish for God resting his soul (pp. 19-20). The lack of the same wish offered for Khayyam amid such an immediate textual context is, in my view, a convincing indication that Khayyam must have still been living in 515 LH, or any part of that year, when Khazeni's book was completed.

A detailed summary and translation with commentaries of Khazeni's book was published by N. Khanikoff in AD 1857 (writing completed on Oct.

23, 1856), whose English translation is readily available online in JSTOR.[10] It is titled, "Analysis and Text of كتاب ميزان الحكمة Book of the Balance of Wisdom, An Arabic Work on the Water-Balance, Written by 'Al-Khâzenî in the Twelfth Century" (transliterations are those offered in the original).

The article includes, in typed format, both original excerpts in the Arabic original, and the translation in English of his readings of and commentaries of the book, using a handwritten manuscript which was accessible to him. As translated by Khanikoff, Khazeni writes (emphasis in italics and notes in brackets are mine) in reference to his benefactor in compiling his book:

> I sought assistance from his beams of light irradiating all quarters of the world, and was thereby guided to the extent of my power of accomplishment in this work, and composed a book on the balance of wisdom, for his high treasury, *during the months of the year 515 of the Hijrah* [Khanikoff himself footnotes this as being the equivalent of AD 1121-22] of our Elect Prophet Muhammad—may the benedictions of God rest upon him and his family, and may he have peace! (p. 16)

In a footnote used to offer further biographical data regarding the various scientists and thinkers on whom Khazeni draws and some of whose works includes in his book, Khanikoff writes:

> Although our author has taken pains to define by synchronisms the periods of most of the philosophers whom he refers to in his introduction and table of contents, I think it proper to add, here, some more exact intimations of the dates which concern them.
>
> ...
>
> Ábû-Ḥafṣ `Umar ál-Khaiyâmi, author of an algebraic treatise lately translated by Woepcke, was born, according to a learned notice by this savant in Journ. Asiat. for Oct.-Nov. 1854, ... Séries, iv. 348, at Nîsâpûr, and died in that same city AD 1123.
>
> Being limited to the resources of my own library, I am unable to assign more definite dates to the other philosophers mentioned in this treatise. (Khanikoff 1857:25; I have retained the transliterations as appearing in the original)

I quote the above in order to show that before Tīrtha and back in the nineteenth century in Europe, as in older manuscripts in Iran, it was regarded as common knowledge that Khayyam had died in the year 517 LH, which usually was converted to the year AD 1123 (which could also mean the latter

10. See: https://www.jstor.org/stable/592172?seq=1#metadata_info_tab_contents.

part of 516 LH, since 517 LH could stretch from AD 1123 to 1124).

The key point here is to note that Khanikoff must have also found no reason (based on an alleged reference of mercy wishing for Khayyam in the Khazeni manuscript copy he was using) to believe that Khayyam had died in AD 1122 (515 LH), when the book was completed. So, he offers AD 1123 as Khayyam's date of passing.

On the pages 13-14 of his article, Khanikoff translates Khazeni as saying,

> Still later, under the victorious dynasty now reigning—may the Supreme God establish it!—the water-balance was taken up by the eminent teacher Ábû-Ḥafṣ 'Umar ál-Khaiyâmi, who verified what was said of it, and demonstrated the accuracy of observation upon it, and the perfection of operation with it—supposing a particular sort of water to be used—without having a marked balance. The eminent teacher Ábû-Ḥâtim á-Muẓaffar Bin 'Isma'il of 'Isfazâri, a contemporary of the last named, also handled the subject, for some length of time, in the best manner possible, giving attention to the mechanism, and applying his mind to the scope of the instrument, with an endeavor to facilitate the use of it to those who might wish to employ it. ... But he failed to note the distances of specific gravities from the axis, by parts divided off and numbers; nor did he show any of the operations performed with them, except as the shape of the balance implied them. It was he, too, who named it "the balance of wisdom." He passed away, to meet the mercy of the Supreme God, before perfecting it and reducing all his views on the subject to writing. (Khanikoff 1857:13-14; I have retained the transliterations as appearing in the original)

The above translation offered by Khanikoff again corroborates with the view that Khayyam must have been alive in 515 LH when Khazeni draws on him in his book. In the very passage where Khazeni is commenting on both Khayyam and al-Asfezari, he acknowledges the latter for having passed away, while not stating anything of the sort for Khayyam. The lack of such a mercy statement for Khayyam's passing is a clear indication that we can safely regard Khayyam as having been alive by 515 LH, or at least by the time the book was completed in that year. Khazeni himself says his book was completed during the months of 515 LH, without specifying the month.

In my view, it would be implausible that any scribe copying the manuscript would delete any mercy wishing statement for Khayyam if it was in the copy he was copying, indicating that the chain of copying including him must have remained true to the original copy of it in the twelfth century AD lacking any mercy wishing for Khayyam at the time of original drafting of the manuscript. If it happened that in one of the manuscript copies cited by Rezazadeh Malek a mercy wishing statement appeared following the mentioning of Khayyam in the book, we can safely assume that it must have been added by that scribe or another scribe before, not having necessarily appeared in the original manuscript, since apparently there were other copying-chains whose results do not include that statement.

We can therefore definitively regard Khayyam as having been alive in the year 515 LH.

Before moving on to the next chapter to explore Nezami Arouzi's *Chahar Maqaleh (Four Discourses)*, we can offer the tentative conclusion that in Beyhqi's *Tatemmat Sewan el-Hekmat (Supplement to the Chest of Wisdom)* there is simply no information that supports that Khayyam was alive anytime after 517 LH. We can also conclude that he was definitively alive sometime in 515 LH at least, and some information given may even imply that he was alive in the year 516 LH, since Beyhaqi related a conversation he had with the prince Faramarz in that year, where Khayyam is specifically mentioned as the topic of that conversation but no mercy wishing or other information is provided suggesting that Khayyam had passed away by then.

So, we can safely conclude, based on our reading of Beyhaqi's *Tatemmat Sewan el-Hekmat (Supplement to the Chest of Wisdom)* and also that of Abdorrahman Khazeni's *Mizan ol-Hekmat (Balance of Wisdom)*, that Khayyam was still alive in 516 LH at least, and that there were no other informating supporting the view that he was still living after the year 517 LH.

Abstract

This essay, titled "In Search of Omar Khayyam's True Date of Passing: Superposing the Birth Date Findings With Beyhaqi's 'Tatemmat Sewan el-Hekmat' And Khazeni's 'Mizan ol-Hekmat,'" is the third chapter of the second book of the twelve-book series *Omar Khayyam's Secret: Hermeneutics of the Robaiyat in Quantum Sociological Imagination,* authored by Mohammad H. Tamdgidi. The second book is subtitled *Khayyami Millennium: Reporting the Discovery and the Reconfirmation of the True Dates of Birth and Passing of Omar Khayyam (AD 1021-1123).*

Tamdgidi's main goal in this (and the following two chapters) is to determine as definitively as possible the date of passing of Omar Khayyam on the basis of the new finding about his true date of birth as reported in the preceding chapter. His secondary purpose is to trace how the new finding allows for reimagining Khayyam's interactions with others during his lifetime from the vantage of his true age during such interactions. He chose to split his search for Khayyam's definitive date of passing into three chapters for the reader's convenience, starting with this chapter; however, they should be seen as parts of the same, ongoing, search, their findings often superposing and overlapping with one another considerably.

Tamdgidi states that his purpose in this chapter and the two that follow is to revisit all the available texts and versions thereof more carefully, in an effort to find a way of convincingly interpreting the various texts and reconciling their differences to such an extent that one can arrive at an undisputable consensus regarding Khayyam's date of demise.

According to the author, there are basically four manuscripts on which most have focused to determine the date of passing of Omar Khayyam. The first manuscript is the biographical information offered for Khayyam in *Tatemmat Sewan el-Hekmat (Supplement to the Chest of Wisdom)* by Zahireddin Abolhasan Beyhaqi. The second source is *Mizan ol-Hekmat (Balance of Wisdom)*, by Abdorrahman Khazeni, also a grown-up contemporary of Khayyam and reportedly also one of his pupils in astronomy and scientific matters, implying that he must have also met him in person. The third source is *Chahar Maqaleh (Four Discourses)* by Nezami Arouzi, a Khayyam contemporary who offered his respects to him as a teacher (whether actually or in reverence it is not known). And the fourth manuscript is one written and compiled by Yar Ahmad Rashidi Tabrizi, which has come to be known under the title *Tarabkhaneh (House of Joy)*. This chapter covers the exploration of the first two of the above four main sources.

Tamdgidi states, based on the discovery of the true date of birth of Khayyam as reported in the earlier chapter of this book, that we can again entertain the possibility (not necessarily the certainty) that Nezam ol-Molk, and even Hasan Sabbah, and Omar Khayyam were childhood friends and that there may have been some grains of truth to the story reported by others. The research as reported in this chapter also highlights the significance of Abol-Hasan al-Anbari as a significant teacher of Khayyam in astronomy. It also notes that based on the findings about Khayyam's true birth date, it is certainly possible that he could have been a young student of Avicenna during the latter's last peaceful years of life living in Isfahan. The true date of birth sheds clear light on the senior status of Khayyam in relation to many of his contemporaries with whom he was interacting given his advancing age, strengthening the possibility that he may have as well served as the most senior and leading member of a team of astronomers invited by Soltan Malekshah and his minister Nezam ol-Molk to establish an observatory in Isfahan and reform the Persian solar calendar.

Following a careful rereading of the contents of the first two sources listed above, Tamdgidi offers the tentative conclusion that based on Beyhaqi's *Tatemmat Sewan el-Hekmat (Supplement to the Chest of Wisdom)* and Abdorrahman Khazeni's *Mizan ol-Hekmat (Balance of Wisdom)*, there is simply no information that supports that Khayyam was alive anytime after 517 LH. The information supports that definitively Khayyam was alive sometime in the year 515 LH, at least, and some information given may even imply that he was alive in the year 516 LH, at least, since Beyhaqi related a conversation he had with the prince Faramarz in that year, where Khayyam is specifically mentioned as the topic of that conversation but God's mercy wishing or other information is not provided suggesting that Khayyam had passed away by then.

CHAPTER IV—Searching More for Omar Khayyam's True Date of Passing: Superposing the Birth Date Findings With Present and Older Manuscript Copies of Nezami Arouzi's "Chahar Maqaleh"

In the absence of more explicit and undisputable textual evidence providing a date for Khayyam's passing, much of scholars' hopes in recent past have been pinned on specific passages in two other manuscripts, one being *Chahar Maqaleh (Four Discourses)* authored by Nezami Arouzi, and another *Tarabkhaneh*, authored and compiled by Yar Ahmad Rashidi Tabrizi.

What makes the above two sources unique for the purpose has been that the latter partly draws on an earlier manuscript copy of the former in providing further details about the last several years of Khayyam's passing. So, in a way, we need to ultimately consider these two important sources in a superposed way, overlapping with one another, even though we may focus on or another of them at a time.

A factor that has complicated the investigation for determining the date of Khayyam's passing, one that we already became familiar with when exploring the material in search of Khayyam's birth date, has been the fact that not the very original text by the author, but several manuscript *copies* produced by one or another scribe later on have survived the times and reached us, and it happens that they do not necessarily agree on some of the details, leading various contemporary scholars to argue in favor of one or another interpretation of the information given in the texts.

I begin in this chapter (to be continued in the next) by sharing and examining some relevant passages from the work of Nezami Arouzi, as given in his work *Chahar Maqaleh (Four Discourses)*. In the meantime I will further examine the other source, *Tarabkhaneh*, by Yar Ahmad Rashidi Tabrizi, to the extent that it draws on an old copy of the former. So, I encourage the reader to keep these two sources as being superposed and overlapping together as part of the broader sources we are exploring further in light of our finding in earlier chapters regarding the definitive date of birth of Omar Khayyam.

1. The Three References to Omar Khayyam in Nezami Arouzi's "Chahar Maqaleh"

Chahar Maqaleh (Four Discourses) is a book comprised of four long essays, each divided into various sections told as stories about significant persons or events of the times during which the author, Nezami Arouzi, lived.

A contemporary of Omar Khayyam, and claiming in his book that Khayyam to him held the status of a teacher (whether actually or in reverence we do not know for sure), Nezami Arouzi related in his book one or another of four categories of intellectuals whose respective skills or expertise were expected alone or in combination in the same person from those holding offices or positions close to kings or those in power: 1) secretary, 2) poet, 3) astronomer/astrologer, and 4) physician.

It turns out that, contrary to what we may expect today—namely that a writer close to Khayyam and claiming him as a teacher would include a few words at least, let alone a story, in the *poets'* section of the book about him—there is nothing of the sort *in the prevalent manuscript copies* of his book. However, there are three passages related to Khayyam in *Chahar Maqaleh (Four Discourses)*, all in the astronomy/astrology section.

When we say "astronomy" as a topic, however, we should keep in mind that in broad terms it includes astrology during those times. Whether or not he associates Khayyam with the latter is besides the point that the topic of one of the four parts or discourses of his book on the topic of astronomy/astrology was a single topic where he could then comment on whether this or another person, such as Khayyam, adhered to one or another belief or approach to the expertise or skills expected from kings in their royal courts.

Regarding the question whether Nezami Arouzi discusses Khayyam in relation to poetry in the book, also, we should keep in mind that when we make the above observation, we are doing so based on manuscript copies we today hold and regard as authentic. For example, as we shall see, regarding Khayyam's having been a poet, the absence of any reference in today's prevalent copies of the manuscript may not match exactly what others have reported from earlier copies of the same manuscript. I will note an example of this when I relate to *Tarabkhaneh (House of Joy)* by Yar Ahmad Rashidi Tabrizi who reports having seen and read another copy of the manuscript of *Chahar Maqaleh (Four Discourses)* in its author's (that is, Nezami Arouzi's) own handwriting.

In any case, in my view, what makes the three passages on astronomical matters in *Chahar Maqaleh (Four Discourses)* where Khayyam is discussed even more interesting and puzzling are that although Nezami Arouzi explicitly offers his opinion that Khayyam did not believe much in astrological matters, all what he narrates in the three stories of the astronomy section about him can in fact be more or less interpreted in favor of Khayyam's having had not just astronomical but also astrological insights and skills, and having been quite famed in doing so.

The way Nezami Arouzi narrates the stories, in other words, has astrological overtones accompanying his narration, leading him to feel puzzled at how Khayyam could have said this or done that, implying astrological skills, when according to Nezami Arouzi Khayyam was not inclined toward believing in astrological matters.

While my focus in this section will remain on finding a way to determine Khayyam's date of passing, I will try to provide at least some taste of the overall stories shared by Nezami Arouzi about Khayyam. When necessary, I will come back to the examination of these texts in the next chapter and later in the series when exploring other dimensions of Khayyam's works and life.

It is important to note that *Chahar Maqaleh (Four Discourses)* was written in Persian, and is itself considered to be one of the examples of fine prose in classical Persian. For that reason, and in order to examine the texts closely in the original Persian as well, I will provide the originals (as included in Rezazadeh Malek's *Daneshnameh-ye Khayyami*, and also as found in today's commonly prevalent manuscript of *Chahar Maqaleh* itself), and my English translations of them. I have added a few bracketed notes in the Persian and the English translations to inform the reader of any variations of the text.

The first widely considered anecdote Nezami Arouzi shares in his book that relates to Khayyam is as follows:

در سنهٔ ست و خمسایة بشهر بلخ در کوی برده فروشان در سرای امیر بو سعد جره خواجه امام عمر خیّامی و خواجه امام مظفّر اسفزاری نزول کرده بودند و من بدان خدمت پیوسته بودم در میان مجلس عشرت از حجة الحقّ عمر شنیدم که او گفت گور من در موضعی باشد که هر بهاری شمال بر من گل افشان میکند {یا، در سه نسخه: که هر سال دوبار بر من درختان گل افشان کنند} مرا این سخن مستحیل نمود و دانستم که چنوئی گزاف نگوید چون در سنهٔ ثلثین بنشابور رسیدم چهار {یا، در سه نسخه: و چند} سال بود تا آن بزرگ روی نقاب خاك کشیده بود و عالم سفلی ازو یتیم مانده و او را بر من حقّ استادی بود آدینه بزیارت او رفتم و یکی را با خود ببردم که خاك او بمن نماید مرا بگورستان حِیره بیرون آورد و بر دست چپ گشتم در پایین دیوار باغی خاك او دیدم نهاده و درختان امرود و زردآلو سر از آن باغ بیرون کرده و چندان برگ شکوفه بر خاك او ریخته بود که خاك او در زیر گل پنهان شده بود و مرا یاد آمد آن حکایت که بشهر بلخ ازو شنیده بودم گریه بر من افتاد که در بسیط عالم و اقطار ربع مسکون او را هیچ جای نظیری نمیدیدم ایزد تبارك و تعالی جای او در جنان کناد بمنّه و کرمه

[My translation:]

In the year 506 LH [AD 1112-1113] in the city of Balkh, in the alley of slave-traders and in the house of Amir Abu Sad Jarreh, Khwajeh Imam Omar Khayyami and Khwajeh Imam Mozaffar Asfezari had descended and I had joined them in service. Amid the happy gathering, I heard from the Hojjat ul-Haqq ["Argument of Truth"] Omar saying, "My grave will be in a position where each spring the northern breeze will shed flowers over me" [or, in three other manuscript copies: "... in a position where each year trees will spread flowers over me twice]. To me this statement seemed impossible and knew someone like him would not say something extravagant. When in the year 530 LH [AD 1135-1136] I reached Neyshabour, it was four [or, in three manuscripts: "and some"] years that such a great man had taken on the cover of the earth and this lower world had become orphaned from him, and he was rightly a teacher to me. One Friday I went to visit him and took someone with me to show me his grave. He took me out to the Heireh Cemetery and I turned left and on the base of a garden's wall I saw his grave. And the trees of pear and apricot had raised their heads from that garden, and so much blossom leaves had fallen on his grave that his grave was hidden under flowers. And I remembered the story I had heard from him in the city of Balkh. Crying befell upon me since in the entire world and regions of its inhabited quarter I did not see anyone, anywhere, like him. May God, Blessed and Exalted is He, place him in paradise in His Goodness and Benevolence.

The second anecdote by Nezami Arouzi relating to Khayyam is as follows:

اگر چه حکم حجّة الحقّ عُمَر بدیدم امّا ندیدم او را در احکام نجوم هیچ اعتقادی و از بزرگان هیچ کس ندیدم و نشنیدم که در احکام اعتقادی داشت در زمستان سنهٔ ثمان و خمسایة بشهر مرو سلطان کس فرستاد بخواجهٔ بزرگ صدرالدّین محمّد بن المظفّر رحمه الله که خواجه امام عمر را بگوی تا اختیاری کند که بشکار رویم که اندر آن چند روز برف و باران نیاید و خواجه امام عمر در صحبت خواجه بود و در سرای او فرود آمدی خواجه

کس فرستاد و او را بخواند و ماجرا با وی گفت برفت و دو روز در آن کرد و اختیاری نیکو کرد و خود برفت و با اختیار سلطان را برنشاند و چون سلطان برنشست و یك بانگ زمین برفت ابر در کشید و باد برخاست و برف و دمه در یستاد خنده ها کردند سلطان خواست که بازگردد خواجه امام گفت پادشاه دل فارغ دارد که همین ساعت ابر باز شود و درین پنج روز هیچ نم نباشد سلطان براند و ابر باز شد و در آن پنج روز هیچ نم نبود و کس ابر ندید احکام نجوم گر چه صنعتی معروف است اعتماد را نشاید و باید که منجّم در آن اعتمادِ دوری نکند و هر حکم که کند حواله با قضا کند

[My translation:]

Although I had seen the judgments of Hojjat ul-Haqq ["Argument of Truth"] Omar, I had not seen in him any astrological beliefs, and did not see and hear anyone among great men say that he had astrological beliefs. In the winter of 508 LH [can be narrowed to AD 1114 since season is given] the king sent someone to the Great Khwajeh Sadreddin Muhammad Ibn al-Mozaffar, May God have Mercy on him, to tell Khwajeh Imam Omar to make a judgment for our going hunting such that for several days no snow or rain would fall and Khwajeh Imam Omar was in the company of the Khwajeh and had arrived at his house. Khwajeh sent someone and called him and told him about what had happened. He left and for two days investigated and augured [note: the term used is اختیار which has astrological connotation] a good selection and himself went and based on his augured date [note: the word اختیار is again used] joined the king's mounting and when the king mounted and went for a distance it became cloudy, wind arose, and snow and fog befell. All laughed and the king wanted to return. Khwajeh Imam said the king must rest assured that in an hour the clouds will clear and for five days there will be no mist. The king rode on and clouds cleared and in those five days there was no mist and no one saw any clouds. Although making astrological judgments is a famous trade, they are not trustworthy and the astrologer must not trust far in them and when passing any judgments he must allow for the role of chance.

The third anecdote by Nezami Arouzi relating to Khayyam is as follows:

بر پادشاه واجب است که هر جا که رود ندیم و خدمتکار که دارد او را بیازماید اگر شرع را معتقد بود و بفرائض و سنن آن قیام کند و اقبال نماید او را قریب و عزیز گرداند و اعتماد کند و اگر بر خلاف این بود او را مهجور گرداند و حواشی مجلس خود را از سایهٔ او محفوظ دارد که هر که در دین عزّ و جلّ و شریعت محمّد مصطفی صلعم اعتقاد ندارد او را در هیچ کس اعتقاد نبود و شوم باشد بر خویشتن و بر مخدوم.

در اوائل ملك سلطان غیاث الدّنیا و الدّین محمّد بن ملکشاه قسیم امیر المؤمنین نورالله تربته ملك عرب صدقه عصیان آورد و گردن از ربقهٔ طاعت بکشید و با پنجاه هزار مرد عرب از حله روی ببغداد نهاد امیرالمؤمنین مستظهر بالله نامه در نامه و پیك در پیك روان کرده بود باصفهان و سلطان را همی خواند و سلطان از منجمان اختیار همی خواست هیچ اختیاری نبود و صاحب طالع سلطان راجع بود گفتند ای خداوند اختیاری نمی یابیم گفت بجوئید و تشدید کرد و دلتنگی نمود منجمان بگریختند .

غزنوی بود که در کوی گنبد دکّانی داشت و فال گوئی کردی و زنان بر او شدندی و تعویذ دوستی نوشتی علم او غوری نداشت بآشنائی غلامی از آن سلطان خویشتن را پیش سلطان انداخت و گفت که من اختیاری بکنم بدان اختیار برو و اگر مظفر نشوی مرا گردن بزن حالی سلطان خوش دل گشت و باختیار او برنشست و دویست دینار نشابوری بوی داد و برفت و با صدقه مصاف کرد و لشکر را بشکست و صدقه را بگرفت و بکشت و چون مظفر و منصور باصفهان باز آمد فال گوی را بنواخت و تشریف گران داد و قریب گردانید و منجمان را بخواند و گفت شما اختیار نکردید این غزنوی اختیاری کرد و برفتیم و خدای عزوجل راست آورد چرا چنین کردید همانا صدقه شما را رشوتی فرستاده بود که اختیاری نکنید همه در خاك افتادند و بناليدند و گفتند بدان اختیار هیچ منجم راضی نبود و اگر خواهد بنویسند و بخراسان فرستند تا خواجه امام عمر خیامی چه گوید .

سلطان دانست که آن بیچارگان راست میگویند از ندماء خویش فاضلی را بخواند و گفت فردا بخانهٔ خویش شراب خور و منجم غزنوی را بخوان و او را شراب ده و در غایت مستی ازو بپرس که این اختیار که تو کردی نیکو نبود و منجمان آنرا عیبها همی کنند سرّ این مرا بگوی آن ندیم چنین کرد و بمستی از وی بپرسید غزنوی گفت من دانستم که از دو بیرون نباشد یا آن لشکر شکسته شود یا این لشکر اگر آن لشکر شکسته شود تشریف یابم و اگر این لشکر شکسته شود که بمن پردازد.

پس دیگر روز ندیم با سلطان بگفت سلطان بفرمود تا کاهن غزنوی را اخراج کردند و گفت این چنین کس که او را در حق مسلمانان این اعتقاد باشد شوم باشد و منجمان خویش را بخواند و بر ایشان اعتماد کرد و گفت من خود آن کاهن را دشمن داشتم که یك نماز نکردی و هر که شرع را نشاید ما را هم نشاید.

[My translation:]

It is incumbent upon a king to test wherever he goes whatever counsel or servant he has regarding belief in religion and practice of its rites and traditions, so that if they bring luck to treat them as close and intimate and trust them, and if they bring the opposite [i.e., bad luck], to send them away so that his company's environs would be protected from their shading since he whoever does not believe in the religion of God (Great and Glorious is He) and the law of His chosen Muhammad, he would believe in no one and he would be ominous to himself and to his master.

In the beginning of the reign of the king Ghiyaseddin va al-Donya val-Din Muhammad Ibn Malekshah, Qasim Amir al-Momeneen, may God Illuminate his Grave, the prince of Arabs Sadaqeh rebelled and withdrew his neck from the rope of obeyance and with fifty thousand Arab men marched to Baghdad from Haleh. Amir al-Momeneen al-Mostazhar Bellah sent letter after letter and messenger after messenger to Isfahan and called for the king, and the king sought the astrologers' auguring [note: again the term اختیار is used, and used thereafter many times in the text, clearly pointing to the word's astrological connotations here as well] but nothing was augured since the star in the chart of the king was in retrograde and they said, "O master, we cannot find auguring possible." King said continue seeking, and asked them to intensify it, and became depressed about it. The astrologers fled.

There was a Ghaznavi [man] who had a shop in the dome alley and was a fortune-teller and women frequented him and he wrote friendship charms for them and his knowledge had little depth. Through acquaintance of a servant of the King, he prostrated in front of the king and said, "I will augur and on the basis of that auguring go. If you end up non-victorious, behead me." The king immediately felt better and set out based on his auguring and gave him two hundred Neyshabouri dinars. So, the king went and battled with Sadaqeh and broke his army, arrested Sadaqeh and killed him and after returning victorious and dominant to Isfahan he treated the fortune-teller well and gave him great honors and made him one of his intimates. And called his astrologers and told them, "You did not augur, but this Ghaznavi did augur and God made it come true; why did you do this?" They fell to the ground and cried and said, "No astrologer would have been satisfied with that auguring and if you wish send a letter to Khorasan to ask what Khwajeh Imam Omar Khayyami says."

The king knew that those helpless were telling the truth. He called a virtuous man among his counsels and said, "Tomorrow set up a wine drinking gathering in your house and call the Ghaznavi astrologer and give him wine and amid extreme drunkenness ask him, "since this auguring was not good and astrologers fault it a lot, so tell me, what was its secret?" The counsel did as told and in drunkenness asked him. The Ghaznavi said, "I knew that there could be only two outcomes, either the other army would break or this army. If that army broke, I would be honored. If this army broke, who'd be there to care about me?"

So the next day the counsel told the king, and they expelled the Ghaznavi astrologer and said, "A person such as this who would hold such a belief regarding Muslims is ominous." And he called his astrologers, and trusted them, and said, "I myself regarded that astrologer as an enemy, since he did not even pray and whosoever does not agree with the religious law, does not agree with us."

2. Examining the Three References to Omar Khayyam in the Prevalent Manuscript Copy of Nezami Arouzi's "Chahar Maqaleh"

Let us start with this last story related about Khayyami by Nezami Arouzi.

Besides the main point of the story being clear, for our purpose there are several clues implied regarding Khayyam that are helpful.

First, the timing of the event in terms of the reign of king Muhammad son of Malekshah and the rebellion by Sadaqeh provides us with a rather precise date about when the events told in the story took place. Ghiyaseddin va al-Donya val-Din Muhammad Ibn Malekshah (also referred to as Tapar, "he who finds," a son of the famous Soltan Malekshah) reigned thirteen years from 498-511 LH (about AD 1105-1118). The war with Sadaqeh took place in Rabi ol-Thani 501 LH (around December, AD 1107). Khayyam (b. 412 LH, AD 1021) would have been about 89 lunar years old (about 86 solar years) at that time.

Second, the story indicates the exemplary, referential, status Khayyam still held as a scientist astronomer at that time. However, given the context of the story regarding *astrological* readings, one can read the reverence he was held both as a source of authority in terms of the location of the stars and their retrograde motions (requiring astronomical skills) and *their astrological* significance and interpretation (requiring astrological beliefs).

Nezami Arouzi, of course, was stressing that in his view, and in the views of all the great men he knew, Khayyam did not hold any astrological beliefs. However, I think Khayyam's being referred in Nezami Arouzi's own story about him regarding his authority in an *astrological* context itself leaves some doubt as to the manner in which Khayyam may have considered the motions of stars as having, even metaphorically, some significance in the valuation one gives to human life events. If Khayyam did not hold any beliefs in astrology, why should he care what a star being retrograde or not implied astrologically, his advice influencing a king's decision to behead his astrologers or not?

I am especially mindful here of another story, told by the poet Khaqani, one I offered as an epigraph to this book, where Khayyam, feeling offended at a treasurer asking why he deserved to receive annual royalties from the king, offers a rather obviously astrological valuation, even as a metaphor, for the rarity of his skills and status. He reminds the treasurer that a thousand years must pass before the stars would align such that a seed like him is born.

I do not wish to belabor this point now as more than just a reflection on the ambiguity of the treatment Nezami Arouzi offers for Khayyam in his book, where on one hand he tells us Khayyam did not believe in astrology, and yet the stories he shares of him are actually told in astrological contexts, and inserted as stories in a section on astrology, being one of the skills expected of counselors to the kings.

The story, in other words, basically confirms that Khayyam was held not only as an authority in astronomy (to confirm for instance the retrograde motion of "stars" which we call now "planets"), but in terms of their motions' astrological valuation and significance for auguring, in this case of political and military events.

The second story quoted above is about Khayyam's ability to predict weather for a good hunting expedition by the king. Again, here the double significance of the skills being found in Khayyam is apparent.

Of course, one can regard Khayyam's ability in predicting weather as a sign of his skills in meteorology, which he has been considered to possess, and he is known to have written a book on topography and natural conditions, which has not reached us (yet).

However, the manner and context in which Nezami Arouzi is relating the story leaves the reader again with a sense that he found skills in Khayyam that are seemingly surprising to him. He is not mentioning anything about Khayyam having been an expert meteorologist as such, after all.

Even the language Nezami Arouzi uses for the nature of assistance sought from Khayyam is astrological (the term augur or اختیار is used). The king asking Khayyam to augur ("ekhtiar") a good time for hunting is clearly an indication that Khayyam was being consulted in his capacity as an astrologer, while we may also recognize that Khayyam could have also more terrestrial knowledge and skills to draw on to make his weather forecast.

Even Nezami Arouzi ends the story with a remark about *astrological* predictions, reminding his readers that in matters astrological, any decision or suggestion made better be qualified in terms of possibility and chance, rather than assumed to be telling of a definitively occurring event. This tells us that Nezami Arouzi himself had the astrological significance (or lack thereof) of the story in mind about Khayyam as he tells and ends his story.

In any case, the story about weather determination for hunting expedition takes place in the winter of 508 LH (about AD 1114), as stated in the story itself. This is also the same king mentioned in the other story above (Muhammad Ibn Malekshah) who reigned from 498-511 LH (about AD 1105-1118). At the time of this hunting event, Khayyam (b. 412 LH) was 96 lunar (about 93 solar) years old. While the age is high, we should recall that around this year and prior Khayyam is reported in many sources to be having meetings and participating in gatherings, and he must have been enjoying relatively good health in old age.

Moving backward further in examining the three stories, let us now turn to the first story.

The first story above narrated by Nezami Arouzi is one most relevant for our purpose in this chapter and the next, having caused as much confusion as hope in the search for the exact date of passing of Khayyam.

In both the Persian and in my English translation, I have inserted the variations in two places. There are other variations regarding other passages across the manuscripts, but I have only included the two places that are most relevant for our inquiry in this section. Other variations of the text include further events that happened in the story which is usually omitted, given the specific manuscript copy of the book, *Chahar Maqaleh (Four Discourses)*, surviving and prevalently read today.

Among the two inserts of variations I have made, one is related to the length of time Nezami Arouzi said it had passed since Khayyam's passing when he visited Neyshabour in the year 530 LH. One manuscript says "four" years, and others say or can be interpreted to mean "some" years. The second insert relates to what Khayyam reportedly "foretold" to Nezami Arouzi about his grave, the main difference being whether it was a matter of flowers being cast from trees on his grave in general or whether such falling of blossoms happened *twice* each year.

In his English translation of *Chahar Maqala* (1921), Edward Browne (p. 71, footnote 4), when translating this passage, footnotes by noting that he prefers the "each year twice" reading, for (in his opinion) what would explain Nezami Arouzi's expression of surprise following this, when he says that he found such a statement from Khayyam as sounding impossible, but knew that a person such as he would not utter nonsense. Browne suggests that trees shedding flowers over a grave is not anything impossible. What would seem impossible is that they would do so twice each year. So, he opts for translating the passage in its "twice each year" rendering.[1]

I think Browne has a point here, and it (partly at least) explains the expression of wonder by Nezami Arouzi regarding Khayyam's statement, and it is in fact such an expression of puzzlement on the part of Nezami Arouzi that provides, again, another instance where he attributes certain abilities to Khayyam that borders on astrological foretelling talents—or at least it could be interpreted as such in our reading of his narrative.

Of course, we can interpret Nezami Arouzi's puzzlement in terms of Khayyam's prediction of his own passing soon, but even that implies astrological connotations. But then why would it be puzzling to Nezami Arouzi if he supposedly "returns" to Neyshabour twenty four years later (from 506 LH to 530 LH) to find Khayyam had died a "few" years before?

1. Here are Browne's own words: "The editor of the text has adopted the reading of the Constantinople M.S., 'every spring-tide the north wind will scatter blossoms on me,' but the reading here adopted seems to me preferable, for there would be nothing remarkable in the grave being covered with fallen blossoms *once a year*; what was remarkable was that it should happen *twice*." (Edward G. Browne, 1921, *Chahar Maqala - Nizami I Arudi of Samarqand*, p. 71, footnote 4)

In any case, it is this passage from Nezami Arouzi that has been the basis of the current uneasy consensus year for the passing of Khayyam, that is AD 1131 (or 526 LH).

I have already written on how the Julian calendar month and day, Dec. 4, that is equivalent to the Gregorian Dec. 11, of that year came into play and I will return to it in due course again, and in more detail later in the next chapter. However, at this point, I wish to address again the determination of the consensus year AD 1131 on the basis of Nezami Arouzi's passage, and how such an interpretation from his text can be effectively rejected as a plausible alternative.

First, until the present and the publication of my report of discovery in this book, we had assumed that Khayyam had been born in the year AD 1048. This allowed for the possibility that he could have lived long enough to pass away in the year AD 1131, at the age of about 83 solar years.

However, now, equipped with the definitive knowledge of Khayyam's birth date in AD 1021 (412 LH), we can consider the date AD 1131 to be practically implausible, if not entirely impossible. According to such a scenario, Khayyam would be about 110-111 solar years (or about 114-115 lunar years) old at the time of his passing. Not only such an unusually advanced age would not have escaped the attention of his contemporaries, but the account of his last day as related by Beyhaqi also does not readily corroborate with the information we have about the physical and mental conditions of a man 110 or more solar years (even more lunar years) old.

Another plausible factor that cannot be ruled out as an evidence against Khayyam having lived past the year 517 LH (around AD 1123) is that there is absolutely no account, event, or evidence reported by *any* chronicler of his time and thereafter, that Khayyam was alive past the year 517 LH and during the 517-526 LH period. We simply do not have it, except for this ambiguously dated account by Nezami Arouzi. The ten-year period is still a long time, and the fact that we do not have *any* reports about him during those years cannot be readily dismissed as being irrelevant to our inquiry.

In his conventional account, as found in manuscript copies prevalently read today, Nezami Arouzi offers two dates. One is when he met Khayyam in the company of others in the year 506 LH, when Khayyam shared with him foretelling his dying and of his grave's condition. Then, there is a date that he visited Neyshabour in the year 530 LH. These two dates have been accepted as given so far as this specific passage from prevalent copies of this specific manuscript of *Chahar Maqaleh* is concerned. However, as we shall see, other accounts of what Nezami Arouzi said in his book have also been offered, as reported by others such as the one read by Yar Ahmad Rashidi Tabrizi as reported in his *Tarabkhaneh* in Nezami Arouzi's "own handwriting."

What has been disputed is the reading of the date of "four" or "some" years before the visiting year 530 LH, when Nezami Arouzi says Khayyam had died. Those who follow one manuscript that clearly states "four" conclude that the year of Khayyam's date must have been 526 LH. Those who disagree with that reading, and regard the wording ambiguous, regard the year of Khayyam's death not to be readily determinable based on the reading of the word as "some." "Some" could be anywhere between one and 24 years (going back to from 530 LH to the year 506 LH, as reported in the same passage).

As I had related before, Tīrtha was among those not convinced about the reading of the word as "four," considering instead that perhaps the word was "fourteen," which would place Khayyam's passing around the year 516 LH, which is the date Tīrtha himself agreed with, and found the same date on Khayyam's tomb at the time of his writing to be supportive of that claim.

But even then, Tīrtha was not convinced that the account itself was sound, considering such an interpretation. In his view, for a student of Khayyam who sounds so much in reverence of him, it seems rather odd that he would wait four years, let alone fourteen years (if Khayyam died in 516 LH), before going and visiting his grave, or even that he would not even know Khayyam had died for four, let alone fourteen, years when he visited Neyshabour in 530 LH.

For further explanation, Tīrtha then turned to another copy of Nezami Arouzi's manuscript of *Chahar Maqaleh* as reported in a manuscript later written centuries after, called *Tarabkhaneh* by Yar Ahmad Rashidi Tabrizi. To this manuscript I will turn soon in the next chapter. For now, I wish to continue focusing on Nezami Arouzi's presently prevalent account to understand why such an ambiguity could have arisen regarding his rendering of Khayyam's date of passing in the first place.

3. The Problem of Gross Historiographical Inaccuracies In Nezami Arouzi's "Chahar Maqaleh" As Unanimously Acknowledged By Scholars

Nezami Arouzi reportedly wrote *Chahar Maqaleh (Four Discourses)*, or finalized it, around the year 550 LH. His own date of birth is not known, but it is universally accepted that he must have been born before the year 500 LH, of course, since he himself reports having met Khayyam, presumably as an adult and his student, in the year 506 LH.

If we say he may have been at least 20, 25, or 30 lunar years old when he met Khayyam in Balkh, we can then safely assume that he must have been respectively around 65, 70, 75 lunar years old when writing *Chahar Maqaleh.*

Encyclopedia Iranica (under the topic "Chahār Maqāla") places the writing of this book around the years 550-552 LH (AD 1155-1157), adding "when the author was already at an advanced age." The same source places his undetermined birth date in the last quarter of the fifth LH or eleventh AD centuries.

Was Nezami Arouzi of a sound mind, as far as memory is concerned, or at least as far as judging from the presently prevalent manuscript copy of his book is concerned?

The reason we have reasons to raise that question is as follows.

As related in *Encyclopedia Iranica* and also as shared in an expert's introduction written by the late Iranian distinguished scholar Mohammad Qazvini for the publication of *Chahar Maqaleh*, Nezami Arouzi himself offers in his book information that sheds light on the chronology of his travels, including to Neyshabour, during his lifetime. They are as follows:

1) In 504 LH (AD 1110-1111) he was in his hometown Samarqand, collecting information on the poet Rudaki;

2) In 506 LH (AD 1112-1113) he was in Balkh, where he visited Khayyam and Asfezari on a happy occasion when he heard Khayyam foretell his death and his future grave's condition;

3) In 509 LH (AD 1115-1116) he was in Herat;

4) The next year, in 510 LH (AD 1116-1117) he accompanied Soltan Sanjar in Tus, meeting the poet Amir Moezzi, and visiting the tomb of the poet Ferdowsi, and going to Neyshabour in the meantime;

5) In 512 LH (AD 1118-1119) he went to Neyshabour;

6) In 514 LH (AD 1120-1121) he was again in Neyshabour, meeting Amir Moezzi again and being told a story about Ferdowsi. It is believed that he was around Neyshabour for 4-5 years around that time.

7) Then, he visited Neyshabour again in the year 530 LH (AD 1135-1136), when he reportedly heard of Khayyam's death and visited his grave, finding it in the same condition that Khayyam had foretold in 506 LH; and

8) In the year 547 LH (AD 1152-1153) he was in Herat and lived there in hiding for a while.

The author of the entry on Nezami Arouzi in the *Encyclopedia Iranica*, Gholam-Hossein Yusofi, echoing the opinion provided by Mohammad Qazvini in his classic introduction to the manuscript regarding the historical accuracies (or lack there) of the stories shared in the book, while still praising the literary merits of the book as a fine example of Persian literature, writes:

> The historical information found in Čahārmaqāla, however, is seriously marred by repeated errors (confusion of names, dates, etc.), even in the case of events in the author's lifetime (he confuses the Saljuq sultans Sanjar and Masʿūd, ...) (note: transliterations are those offered in the source)

In his apt editorial introduction to the book *Chahar Maqaleh*, having praised the book otherwise as a literary work, Mohammad Qazvini also details a number of historical errors as follows (in my translation).

We do not have to be familiar with the details given to sense the basic drift of his argument:

> From the research and investigation undertaken in *Chahar Maqaleh* it becomes known that Nezami Arouzi, despite the height of status in virtuosity, and his forerunning superiority in literary matters, manifests weakness in the techniques of historiography, and historical errors such as mixing up of the names of famous personalities with one another, chronological antedating or postdating of dates, and imprecision in recording of events and ways of doing these have been committed numerously. In footnotes to the text we have dealt with these and explained the errors depending on space allowed, and for example here we provide a summary of them:
>
> ... Even in two stories relating to Eskafi, the literary counsel of Samanids, he has committed so many major errors that would not be forgivable for anyone especially by example of an author primarily:
>
> First, he has presumed Eskafi to be the literary counsel of Nouh ibn Mansour ibn Nasr ibn Samani, whereas he was the literary counsel of his grandfather, Nouh ibn Nasr, who had died nearly twenty years before his (grandson's) time and has basically missed his times;
>
> Second, he has regarded Aleptakin, the founder of Ghaznavid government, to be a contemporary of the mentioned Nouh ibn Mansour, when he had died a long time before his seating, and has thus completely misunderstood his reign;
>
> Third, he has assumed that Saboktakin sent an army to Khorasan in the company of Simjourian and waged war with Aleptakin, when Aleptakin had died more than thirty years before this event, and moreover, Saboktakin's army expedition was itself to wage war with Simjourian, not in their accompaniment, and this is one of the famous historical events;
>
> Fourth, he has regarded the famous general Abu Ali Ahmad ibn Mohtaj Chaqani (besides the abbreviation he has introduced to his name and

> birthplace and position, regarding him as Abol-Hasan Ali ibn Mohtaj al-Kashani Hajeb ul-Bab) as a contemporary of Nouh ibn Samani, when the general had passed away twenty two years before his reign and has not understood his reign;
>
> Fifth, he has regarded the mentioned Abu Ali Mohtaj as contemporaneous with the war expedition of Saboktakin to Khorasan, when he had died thirty nine years before this event;
>
> Sixth, he has regarded Makan ibn Kaki as a contemporary of Nouh ibn Nasr ibn Nouh ibn Nasr ibn Ahmad Samani, when he was a contemporary of his father, Nasr ibn Ahmad, having died thirty nine years before his reign's start and has not understood his reign;
>
> Seventh, he has regarded Tash Sepahsalar as the general of the Samani army that waged war against Makan ibn Kaki, when historians unanimously agree that the general in that war was Abu Ali ibn Mohtaj Chaqani, and major mistakes and ridiculous mix-ups of the author in these two stories cannot be resembled to anything but that musing which Zamakhshari brings in Rabi al-Abrar [here follows a saying of obvious errors or contradictions]

He is referring to the "musing" in order to show how a mixture of completely nonsensical "facts" or issues appear in a single text at once. The musing Qazvini is humorously referring to has been translated as follows.

> "Salma al-Muwaswis testified against a certain man before Jaʿfar b. Sulayman, saying: 'God save thee! [He is] a Sunni Shiʿite and a fatalist adherent of the doctrine of Free Will, who cursed al-Hajjaj b. az-Zubayr, who destroyed the Kaʿba in despite of 'Ali the son of Abu Sufyan.' Said Jaʿfar: 'I know not whether I should envy thee more for thy knowledge of history or thy knowledge of genealogies!' 'God save the Amir', he replied, 'I learned all this where I left school!'"

You may notice that on its face-value, the above is full of obviously contradictory statements. Let me myself add here an equivalent of the above humorous musing in Persian, often used as a proverb in Iran, for utterances that are completely nonsensical and contradictory. It is as follows:

> "Khasan and Khosein were, all three, daughters of Moqavieh, and were killed in Medina by a wolf."

Well, it is not Khasan, but Hasan; not Khosein but Hosein. They were two, not three. They were sons, not daughters, of Ali, not Moqavieh. It is not Moqavieh, but Moʿavieh. They were not killed by wolves. Hasan was poisoned by his wife, and Imam Hosein (or, Hussain) was martyred by Shemr in the Karbala desert. And the one said to be killed by wolf was not them but prophet Yousef, and he was not actually killed by wolf but his brothers lied that such a thing happened, because they had thrown him into a well, not in Madineh, but on their way from Kanʿan to Egypt!

The point of all this is that according to Qazvini, Nezami Arouzi has made so many gross errors that, aside from his fine Persian prose, the chronologies and historiographies of his stories have become rendered in complete nonsense as far as many dates and names are concerned.

Qazvini continues to list many more errors of historical record in *Chahar Maqaleh* in his introduction, which are not necessary to relay here for our purpose at hand, since what I have relayed above should be sufficient to get my main point across. Just to add another instance, as relayed by Qazvini, Nezami Arouzi regards Nezam ol-Molk's assassination as having taken place in Baghdad, even though all historians agree it happened in Nahavand. He regards the famous medical scientist Mohammad ibn Zakaria-ye Razi as a contemporary of Mansour ebn-e Samani, when he died at least thirty years before his reign; and Qazvini adds, "… on the basis of such a false and shaky grounds he has made up a long-winded, fabricated, story."

For one reason or another, our presently used manuscript copy of the book *Chahar Maqaleh* offers a fine example of ancient Persian writing but quite a faulty historical record, any details of which must be carefully examined for error. Either Nezami Arouzi himself, or those who copied his book at some point down copying chains—even when rendered in "perfectly clean copies"—mixed up people, dates, reigns, kings, personalities, and places.

The point of the above is to suggest that it is entirely possible that even the matters of date or chronology of events shared in Nezami Arouzi's story about Khayyam foretelling his grave's condition may have also been subjected to such gross clumsiness and inexactitude, either in authorship, or at the hands of a careless copier somewhere down the line of a copying chain.

Qazvini does not dispute the substance of the story about Khayyam, but for us, reading his evaluation of the historiographical accuracy of *Chahar Maqaleh*, it is important to consider the error-proneness of his *dates* as part of the overall clumsiness in which the stories were reported in time and place.

It happens that Qazvini has caught Nezami Arouzi's errors on historical events and personalities about whom we have accurate information independently. Why should we assume that the dates he offers, or his manuscript copiers have offered, in his book regarding Khayyam are any less error-prone, especially when we have nothing else to judge them with? But then, actually and fortunately, later on we may find something to compare them with when we study *Tarabkhaneh (House of Joy)*, but for now let us continue this part of the inquiry.

4. What Explains the Differences Between the Prevalent and Older Manuscript Copies of Arouzi's "Chahar Maqaleh"?

As I have already noted, given our discovery of Khayyam's date of birth in 412 LH, and given the absolute absence of *any* stories or reports by *anyone* about Khayyam past the date 517 LH, presumably until the current consensus date 526 LH (AD 1131) for him, we can legitimately switch our curiosities about the question of the accuracy of the date 526 LH ambiguously given in the text, to the question of *what could explain* such obvious and repeated errors of historical record.

Here, I wish now to draw the readers' attention again to the point I was raising in the previous chapter and the first book of this series about the difference between the very original manuscript written by an author and the numerous copies produced by scribes down various copying chains.

The more famous a book or manuscript becomes, the more we expect it to be copied, and thus there arise more chances that the original text could morph into copies that appear to be old and authentic, even found to be "mint condition," so to speak, but otherwise contain inaccuracies that may or may not be correctable down the historical time. Minor errors, misreadings, or misinterpretations of numbers could thereby prevent our understanding of a horoscope, and, in this case of a date. And *Chahar Maqaleh* has been certainly an important, famous text, numerously copied in time.

But here, we even have a case of various manuscripts themselves not agreeing with one another regarding a particular word "four," or "some." While this may seem unfortunate to some, in my view, it is actually quite fortunate, and may even be a cause for celebration, that we find mismatches across copies of significant words such as the above, since it helps us further magnify our doubts regarding the points concerned.

This is especially important, when we confront a book that despite its merits as a fine example of Persian prose and literature, includes obvious matters of historical and chronological inaccuracy, ones that are widely acknowledged to be characterizing it. But, to dismiss everything, and throw the baby with the bathwater, so to speak, would be wrong also. For, it is entirely possible that some of the errors and problems that are relevant to us are results of miscopying of the manuscripts down the various copying chains, and we should seek to find a way of understanding the text in a way that can offer fruitful ways of understanding our subject matter without taking for granted everything in it as a matter of indubitable fact.

I think given the significant implausibility of reading the word as "four" for the number of years before the year 530 LH when Nezami Arouzi visited Neyshabour, for two main reasons mentioned (our discovery of Khayyam's accurate date of birth, and the absolute lack of any report of Khayyam having lived past the year 517 LH), it is more plausible to consider that the reading of the word "some" (or "chand" or چند in Persian) is the accurate reading, or part of an actual expression. This would offer an opportunity of reading either "fourteen" (sending us back to the year 516 LH or its whereabouts) or just simply "many" years back in time, to when we could more realistically expect Khayyam to have died.

In any case, I tend to agree with Swāmi Govinda Tīrtha on his point regarding the implausibility of Nezami Arouzi having waited fourteen years to visit Khayyam's grave, unless specific reasons or events prevented one or another option.

There is also a possibility that various elements in the notes of Nezami were somehow patched up in a "final" edition in mid 500s LH, where the stories of the same event had been written in different versions, and when patched together, they ended up conveying something not originally intended.

For example, Nezami Arouzi himself reports visiting Neyshabour on several occasions. Let us go over these once again, having our question in mind in terms of other probabilities.

He could have met Khayyam in 506 LH in Balkh, but again in Neyshabour in 512 LH, and again trying to visit him or his grave in 530 LH. He may have visited his grave many times, actually, but highlighted the first time, by placing it at the wrong time.

For example, in the passage I translated previously, he says he arrived at Neyshabour in 530 LH. Then he says, on "a Friday," I went to see his grave. It is possible that this "Friday" is not the one in 530 LH, but a Friday in one of his earlier visits, but since the passages are patched up, it appears as if he is associating the visiting of Khayyam's grave in 530 LH, when in fact, he had visited it first before, say, in 517 LH. We have other versions of his story, actually, to consider that patch ups such as the above could have taken place.

I would like to draw attention here to this brief report in an old Latin manuscript in which, the Persian source is actually also quoted in Persian, to which Rezazadeh Malek, the compiler of the *Daneshnameh-ye Khayyami (Khayyami Encyclopedia)* had drawn our attention.

He wrote (in my translation):

In *Mojmal-e Faseehi* [مجمل الفصیحی] and also in *Majma ol-Fosaha* [مجمع الفصحاء], the date of demise of Khayyam has been noted as 517 Lunar Hejri. Thomas Hyde in his book on the history of the Parthian Iranians and Ancient Medes (Veterum Persarum et Parthorum et Medorum Religionis Historia) published in Oxford on AD 1700, has quoted Khayyami's date of passing from a Persian source (which he has not identified) as follows:

> "The demise of the Prince of the Wise[2], the King of the Scientists[3], and the Role Model of the Virtuous[4], the Master Scholar Omar Khayyam was on the date five hundred seventeen in Neyshabour." (p. 35)

Consulting Hyde's own manuscript, dated AD 1700, I found the following, copied in Persian actually, from his source (given as "In Libro Perfico D. Bunclei, Num. 44, de Morte Celeberrimi *Astronomi Omar Cheiyām, fequente modo legitur*, page 529-530):

مذکور و مسطور است که وفات ملك الحکما سلطان العلما قدوة الفضلاء علام خواجه عمر خیام در سنه سبع عشر و خمس مایه بوده است در نیشابور و در تمام علوم و حکمیات یگانه و اعلم زمانه بود، خواجه نظامی عروضی سمرقندی که اعلم وقت خود بود و یکی از شاگردان خواجه عمر بوده و حکایت موت خواجه عمر میکند که مرا در بلخ با خواجه عمر اتفاق ملاقات افتاد و مجلس میداشتم در اثناء سخن گفت که قبر من در موضعی باشد که هر بهار باد شمال بروی گل افشان بود، مرا از ان تعجب آمد با خود گفتم که این مرد گزاف نگوید تا بعد از موت او چون مرا چندگاه به نیشابور گذر افتاد قبر او دریافتم دیدم که قبر او قریب دیوار باغی بود که درختان میوه دار گلنار سر از دیوار بیرون آورده چندان شکوفه بر سر او ریخته بود که در آن میان قبر او نمی نمود تعجب از گفتار خواجه عمر آرزوی خانه او کردم و چون بخانهٔ او رفتم بعد از پرسش او گفتم که خواست او چنین بود و از حال او آگاهی دادم مادرش گفت من نیز بعد از موت او عجبی دیدم و آن اینست که شبی عمر را از خدای بآمرزش میخواستم و ضرع و ابتهال می نمودم همدرین بخواب رفتم عمر را بخواب دیدم که رباعی بر من میخواند چون بیدار شدم رباعی بر خاطر من یاد نماند و او را رباعی بسیار است بحکمت آمیخته و در شرع سخنان او بعضی ممنوع است اما یك رباعی نوشته شد که بعد از وفات او مادر او را بخواب دید پرسید که ای فرزند حق تعالی با تو چه کرد این رباعی بر مادر خواند مادر خیام از خواب بیدار شد این رباعی یاد داشت بعد از آن مشهور شد و رباعی که در خواب خوانده شد اینست

ای سوختهٔ سوختهٔ سوختنی
وی آتش دوزخ از تو افروختنی
تا کی گوئی که بر عمر رحمت کن
حق را تو که ای برحمت آموختنی

[My Translation, including of the poem; I have broken the passage into

2. "Malek ol-Hokama" [ملك الحکماء].

3. "Soltan ol-Olama" [سلطان العلماء].

4. "Qodvat ol-Fozala" [قدوة الفضلاء].

paragraphs to indicate where something is being quoted, at times as a quote within a quote:]

It has been reported and written that the demise of the Prince of the Wise, the King of the Scientists, and the Role Model of the Virtuous, the Master Scholar Omar Khayyam was on the date five hundred seventeen in Neyshabour and he was in all sciences and philosophies unique and an intellect of his time[.]

Khwajeh Nezami Arouzi Samarqandi who was an intellect of his period and was a student of Khwajeh Omar tells the story of his passing as such:

> "It happened that in Balkh I met Khwajeh Omar in a gathering; amid conversation he said my grave will be in a position where each spring the northern wind will shed flowers on it. I was surprised by that and told myself this man would not speak extravagantly, and after his death when I happen to pass by Neyshabour some times, I sought his grave, and saw that his grave was near the wall of a garden where fruitful trees bearing vividly red flowers [or, of pomegranates] rose above the garden's wall and blossoms were shed on his grave such that his grave was not visible[.] Surprised by Khwajeh Omar's saying, I desired to seek his house and when I went to his house and after asking spoke of his saying and shared what happened and his mother said,
>
> > "I also saw strange things after his death and that is, one night I asked for God's Forgiveness of him, and cried and grieved and in this state went asleep and saw Omar in a dream reading a robai [quatrain] for me. When I woke the robai remained in my memory[.]"
>
> And he has many robai mixed with wisdom and in religion many of his such sayings are forbidden. But one robai was written after his passing and his mother saw him in dream asked "O child, what did God the Most High Do to you." He read this robai to his mother and his mother woke and noted down the robai which became famous after that and the robai that was read in the dream was as follows:
>
> > *O the burned out, burn worthy, and burnable one!*
> > *O the one from whom hell's fire must have begun!*
> > *Until when do you ask God's Mercy for Omar?*
> > *Who are* you *to teach how God's Mercy should be run?"*

I will return to the amusing matter of Khayyam's "mother story" shortly, but my purpose here is to show that in fact, in another manuscript of *Chahar Maqaleh (Four Discourses)* being reported by Hyde, we have Nezami Arouzi not giving *any* specific dates whatever (amid what appears to be saying in the first person singular), and instead explicitly refers to the fact that Nezami Arouzi visited Neyshabour چند گاه "some times"—which could be read, less plausibly, as he visited Neyshabour "after sometime," but in fact may mean *more plausibly* in terms of having visited his grave "*many times*," in one of which he found the grave covered in this story with flowers from trees, proceeding then to visit Khayyam's house, and so on. Note that the mentioned "pomegranate" or گلنار can be used for any vividly red flower. So, this could be just the narrator's own version of what he was reading in Nezami Arouzi's text copy.

The word "some" or "chand" (or چند) is here used in a completely different way coming before گاه , not in terms of a number of years before a certain date of Khayyam's passing before Nezami Arouzi's visiting Neyshabour, but in terms of many times (چندگاه) that he visited Neyshabour, which confirms and coincides with the *number of times* he himself reports in *Chahar Maqaleh* to have visited Neyshabour on various occasions.

In other words, when Nezami Arouzi says he had visited Khayyam's grave "some times" ago, he may not have meant some years (which would lead to the question of how many years back we should go), but to so *many times* before, in one of which, his reported visiting of Khayyam's grave took place. If interpreted this way, much of the ambiguity and confusion caused by the word "chand" (many) can be resolved in favor of "many times" rather than "many years" before, and this would also clarify why what he says would be acceptable to Tīrtha as well—that is, Nezami Arouzi visits Neyshabour many times. In one, he meets Khayyam in person, who tells him about his future grave. In the next, he visits, finding Khayyam had just died, continuing to visit his grave. Then, he also visits Neyshabour in 530 LH, reflecting back on a past time, on a Friday, when he visited Khayyam's grave, and so on.

In any case, in the very sketch Hyde draws of Khayyam it is clearly stated that Khayyam's date of death was 517 LH, so there is no question that in the text he was reading to report on Khayyam, he found nothing that contradicted that date as a generally accepted time for Khayyam's passing.

Note again how the above point is *very important*. In other words, in the source manuscript Hyde was consulting, there must not have been any account of a year 530 LH visit by Nezami Arouzi to Neyshabour, which would then be followed by mentioning, say, "four" years prior for Khayyam's date of demise.

Now, coming back to the amusing story of Khayyam's "mother," I intentionally continued with the quote to offer an example of what could happen when an originally reasonable story becomes mythologized in subsequent telling and retelling *in one of the manuscript copies* and not necessarily in all.

Actually, as odd as the story may seem, it is not that far removed from how Iranians even today try to make sense of their dear ones having died. They usually report having seen dreams of them, having entered (or not) paradise, sometimes telling dreamers some tasks needing to be done and completed (such as paying debt to someone, asking for someone's forgiveness, and so on), before the entry to paradise is allowed.

So, what is happening then at the time of grieving for Khayyam, and conversations others have about him and who dreamed what about him, do not surprise me at all to be something rare and implausible. In fact, it is very close to how things happen in common culture in Iran even to this day, and it shows things have not changed even since then.

I am not of course judging the content of those sayings, but simply the kind of conversations Iranians have about a recently deceased. Here we have a case not of simply copying a passage by one or more scribes, but by the telling and embellishment of a story in the imagination of folks who have found Khayyam's life and story enigmatic to know and share with others.

There are many sides to what we can learn from even such an amusing story woven around a narrative originally stated by Nezami Arouzi.

First, any Western scholar who claims that Khayyam's fame is merely an invention of a nineteenth century Edward FitzGerald should pause to rethink such a claim, for the existence of these stories about his having written "many robais," that some were religiously forbidden but had wise contents, etc., tell of a tradition that is homegrown and goes back centuries to Khayyam's own time. Instead of an always Orientalist reading of how a FitzGerald made an "Omar" famous, we should always keep in mind that "Fitz" becoming famous himself had everything to do with the fame of an "Omar" about whom generations were making myths for centuries.

Even though FitzGerald played an important role in making Khayyam well-known globally (whether in a helpful way or not, or a mixture thereof, remaining to be judged in this series, as far as I am also concerned), the claim made by some that Khayyam was somehow not well-known in his own land *is itself an Orientalist myth* that can be readily dispelled by even such far-fetched stories as told about an alleged mother of Khayyam seeing him in a dream and hearing and noting down a certain robai that can indeed be found in many surviving manuscript collections of his quatrains.

These are issues that I will explore in future books of this series, but it may suffice here to say that often what happens is that a certain folk mythology or story is woven around a definite robai attributed to Khayyam. The story itself may sound odd or far-fetched, but this does not mean that the robai around which it is woven is itself inauthentic and not attributable to an historical Khayyam. They read an interesting quatrain and in trying to interpret why he wrote it, they make a story that may or not have anything to do with why Khayyam wrote the quatrain. But this does not mean we should doubt the attributability of the quatrain itself to Khayyam.

Besides, the very notion that Khayyam is recalled by Nezami Arouzi as having composed "many robais," that they include kernels of wisdom but are forbidden according to some folks' religious interpretations prevalent at a time, tell of a tradition that has endured to our present—and in fact phenomena such as the FitzGeraldian attraction to and mesmerization by Khayyam, his own building of his own brand of British myth around him, serving well, advertently or not, colonial interests, and the broader way in which the West came to build myths of also quite amusing, far-fetched, even cultish, images of him in the Western folk culture—are themselves not "factual" sources, but further manifestations and consequences of the same interests that in other contexts produced stories such as Khayyam's mother dreaming about him in grief. Such myths of course imply a lack of knowledge by those making or conveying them of the true date of Khayyam's passing or his age at death.

As far as my purpose in this chapter regarding the search for Khayyam's date of passing is concerned, it is clear that for a centenarian whose passing at the age of 110 solar years is obviously in doubt, survival of his mother would be impossible. However, where this element in the story itself came from, may be worth keeping in mind and exploring further.

What is noteworthy is that in the two other sources Rezazadeh Malek cites, we also find the year 517 LH given as the date of Khayyam's passing, one which also again draws on a contemporary source citing Nezami Arouzi; this time, however, we find absolutely no traces of a "mother" grieving after his death. The story is completely stripped of such fantastical elements and is told in a different way, yet still drawing on Nezami Arouzi.

For instance, in *Mojmal-e Faseehi* we find the following in the events of the year 517 LH. Just to note, authored by Faseeh Khavafi (c. 777-845 LH /AD 1375-1441), this book offers important events for each year basically organized chronologically. For the year 517 LH we read:

وفات حکیم عمر الخیام

وفات الامام ملك الحکماء خواجه عمر بنیشابور و او در حکمت یگانه و اعلم زمان خود بود و خواجه عروضی نظامی سمرقندی که یکی از تلامذه اوست حکایت میکند که در بلخ با خواجه امام الحکما عمر اتفاق ملاقاتی افتاد در اثناء سخن میگفت که قبر من در موضعی باشد که هر بهار باد شمال برو گلفشان کند مرا از آن سخن تعجب آمد و دانستم که او سخن گزاف نگوید تا بعد از آن بچندگاه در بهار بنیشابور بسر قبر او رفتم و آن در کنار دیوار باغی افتاده بود و درختان میوه سر از دیوار باغ بیرون آورده چندان شکوفه بر قبر او ریخته بود که قبر او در آن میان نمینمود و او را رباعی بسیارست بحکمت و مذهب حکیم آمیخته و در شرع سخنان او (خواندن) ممنوع است اما يك رباعی او نوشتم که شاید که حق عزّ شأنه او را بدین رباعی آمرزیده باشد

ای سوختهٔ سوختهٔ سوختنی
وی آتش دوزخ از تو افروختنی
تا کی گوئی که بر عمر رحمت کن
حق را تو که ای برحمت آموختنی

[My translation:]

Death of the Philosopher Omar Khayyam

Death of the Leader, the Prince of Philosophers, Khwajeh Omar in Neyshabour[,] and he was unique in philosophy and was the intellect of his time and Khwajeh Nezami Arouzi Samarqandi who is one of his students narrates that in Balkh he happened to meet Khwajeh Omar and amid conversation he said, "My grave will be in a position where each spring the northern wind sheds flowers on it." "And this statement came as a surprise to me and knew that he would not speak extravagantly. And after that in some time [or many times] in the spring I went to his grave in Neyshabour, and it was by the side of a garden wall, and fruit trees rose their head from the garden's wall and so many blossoms had fallen on his grave that the grave was not visible in their midst. And he has many robais mixing philosophy and religion, and under religious law his sayings (or reading them) is forbidden but I wrote one robai so that perhaps God Almighty would Forgive him with this robai:

O the burned out, burn worthy, and burnable one!
O the one from whom hell's fire must have begun!
Until when do you ask God's Mercy for Omar?
Who are you *to teach how God's Mercy should be run?*

As is evident, in the above story, lacking any references to any mother or dream or such story, the same basic story from Nezami Arouzi is relayed, giving the date 517 LH as Khayyam's assumed date of passing, with clear references to his "many" robaiyat, their basic nature of mixing wisdom with religion, being perceived as not following and instead questioning religious orthodoxy, and still famously being narrated down the historical time, with a sample quatrain attributed to him directly.

In the next chapter, I will highlight how in some manuscripts, the person identified at Khayyam's grave is simply rendered as a "white-haired elderly" (پیر زال) suggesting that it was misreading of others, not knowing Khayyam's age at birth, that led them to regard the person as a "mother" and not, say, a "sister," or even an elderly man or male relative.

It is also noteworthy that in another of the sources cited by Rezazadeh Malek, that is, in *Majma ol-Fosaha*, authored in more recent times in 1284 LH (c. AD 1867) by Reza Qolikhan Hedayat, the date given for Khayyam's passing is, again, 517 LH (c. AD 1123).

Besides those cited above, it is the case that before twentieth century, most assumed, per historical record or precedent presumption, that Khayyam's passing took place in the year 517 LH. Among those more well-known for having explored Khayyam or his attributed Robaiyat in one or another capacity, are also E. H. Whinfield (1893: p. 11) and A. V. Williams Jackson (a traveller who visited Khayyam's tomb back in 1911, whose images actually appear in his book *From Constantinople to the Home of Omar Khayyam,* according to whom, citing Edward Browne, his death occurred in the year 1123 AD, p. 254), coinciding with 517 LH.

5. An Important Discovery Just Made Regarding Khayyam's Authorship of Robaiyat As Reported By His Living Contemporary Nezami Arouzi

Having reached the end of this chapter, we should note something important.

In comparatively examining various manuscripts of Nezami Arouzi's *Chahar Maqaleh (Four Discourses)*, something very significant has been revealed, aside from the question of Khayyam's date of death.

We have found indications that indeed Nezami Arouzi did, quite clearly, refer to Khayyam's having composed Robaiyat after all, and that he wrote many of them, and that they (or at least some) became known during his lifetime to such an extent that *some* were considered critical of religion (at least by some believers), and thus regarded as forbidden.

So, the notion that Nezami Arouzi does not refer to Khayyam as a poet in his *Chahar Maqaleh (Four Discourses)* is simply not true, because it is only in *some copies* of the manuscript reaching us that we find the sections referring to his Robaiyat as having been, for one reason or another, omitted.

It appears that in fact there existed other manuscript copies in which Nezami Arouzi referred to Khayyam as a poet of Robaiyat, in some accounts being embellished with the story of an old woman (mother, or sister) seeing him in a dream responding to his adversaries also in a robai. Regarding whether it was a "mother," "sister," or simply an old white-haired person that sat by Khayyam's grave, I will have more to say in the next chapter.

The reason Nezami Arouzi does not include Khayyam in the poets' section of his *Chahar Maqaleh (Four Discourses)* is because he is discussing the role played by poets *in royal courts*, or professional poets who live on such a skill or fame, whether appreciated or not (such as Ferdowsi), poets who made a living, or are expected to serve royal courts, by way of poetry.

Khayyam's poetry is *of a completely different sort*, not fitting such a place in *Chahar Maqaleh* as such. Khayyam was not a public, royal poet of any sort as such, so there is simply no reason to include him in one of the four essays Nezami Arouzi dedicates to the intellectual capacities and skills of those needed to serve a royal court.

Besides, given that Khayyam's poetry was largely privately kept or intended to be secretive for one reason or another, or, as Nezami Arouzi puts it, was religiously forbidden, there are less stories to tell, and more secrets to be kept regarding them as well (which may also explain why Nezami Arouzi does not visibly narrate stories about them, but, still, they end up being mentioned in passing as part of the story of his having visited Khayyam's grave. In other words, Nezami Arouzi indeed ends up discussing Khayyam as a poet, as the author of the Robaiyat, and giving explicit information about their nature and character, but not in the section of the book on poets, but in the section on astronomy/astrology, as part of the story of his visitation of Khayyam's grave, as a personal dimension of Khayyam's life.

Since our purpose in this chapter has been to determine Khayyam's date of passing, we will not dwell on the above point that has become revealed regarding Khayyam's poetry and will pick up on this finding at a later point in the series. For now, we should consider it a highly significant findings, indicating that indeed Nezami Arouzi, a living contemporary of Khayyam, was aware of Khayyam's poetic work and reported it in his *Chahar Maqaleh*; the reason it has been missing in some copies of the manuscript accessible to us in more recent times is only a coincidence, since in older manuscripts of the same, Khayyam is clearly reported as being famed as the author of the Robaiyat.

In this chapter, what I have tried to establish is the plausibility of the serious doubts scholars have about the dates given by Nezami Arouzi about all events, including those related to Khayyam, and this itself is a necessary step in our efforts toward finding the true date of his passing. In that sense, rejecting prior held false narratives about Khayyam's date of passing is also a necessary and essential part of our inquiry into finding the definitively correct date of passing for him.

And it happens that in the process of this problematization of common tales about the alleged date 526 LH for Khayyam's passing amid miscopyings and misreadings of Nezami Arouzi's text, we have discovered precious new interpretive evidence that he as one of his close living contemporaries, one of his close pupils in fact or in reverence, knew that Khayyam wrote "many" quatrains, that they were "famous," *some* of which were considered, by *some*, religiously forbidden, which may have more to do with the religious beliefs of those "some" making such accusations than with what Khayyam himself meant by composing those quatrains.

Another consideration that can result from our study in this chapter is the following.

On one hand, in Khayyami scholarship, given the controversies held about the number of quatrains Khayyam wrote, which are authentic or not, and how seriously readers should take the 'tales' Yar Ahmad Rashidi Tabrizi narrates about some of the Khayyami quatrains in his *Tarabkhaneh (House of Joy)* collection, a list that also can include the questions his book raises about Khayyam's date of birth or death or horoscope, scholars have tended to not treat seriously his text as a worthwhile source for stories about Khayyam's life.

Moreover, on the other hand, scholars have had a mixed feeling, so to speak, about Nezami Arouzi's *Chahar Maqaleh (Four Discourses)* as a source for knowledge about Khayyam's life as far as dates given are concerned. He has of course provided the most important texts to draw on about his visit with Khayyam, the blossoms story, and so on. However, the date implied in his story for the visit has been so much in dispute and subjected to so many interpretive variations that, in the context of the overall inaccuracies and absurd historiographical errors evident in his overall text despite its Persian linguistic prose value, the date give has itself added more to the puzzles than solving them.

The historiographical and factual errors in his text, as found in the current, prevalently available, manuscript copy are so much that it may be worth considering how much of such errors were caused by an author regarding himself as a pupil of Khayyam, and how much they may instead be, at least in some or most part, a result of numerous copying done by scribes of this important text over the centuries across separate copying chains. Instead of blaming all the historiographical errors in *Chahar Maqaleh (Four Discourses)* on Nezami Arouzi, in other words, we may also entertain the possibility that at least parts of such evident errors are results of scribes' works down copying chains.

What I would like to propose as a consideration is that indeed, given what Yar Ahmad Rashidi Tabrizi reports regarding having read an originally author-written copy of the text that significantly and meaningfully differs from the one prevalently used today, we confront the errors made as not necessarily by Nezami Arouzi, but also in part by copiers of Nezami Arouzi's *Chahar Maqaleh (Four Discourses)* over the past centuries, copiers who have tried, because of their own biases of interpretations, advertent or not, to "clean up" Nezami Arouzi's text in favor of its Persian prose value, perhaps even truncating it regarding some of its "tales," at the cost of losing important facts and narratives that are important for those in particular engaged in Khayyami studies.

For example, a scribe, finding the part of the story by Nezami Arouzi about the "white-haired elderly" (or even "mother" as found in the original he was copying), may find the story not befitting the stature of Khayyam and decides just to cut that part out of his copy. Another scribe who finds blossoming "twice a year" so impossible that decides just to omit that notion out of the text. Another scribe who is afraid of being accused of propagating "forbidden religious poems" would find it safer to omit that part of the story.

When you try to edit or copy a text, you can do a lot by deleting away passages, or making errors in dates and names, if you are not versed in the detailed historical contexts or the substantive significance of what you are copying. So, that may explain, at least partly, some of the "errors or omissions" of dates and names or historiographical events scholars have found in Nezami Arouzi's text while appreciating its prose at the same time.

For our purpose, what we are finding is that the prevalently used copy of Nezami Arouzi's *Chahar Maqaleh (Four Discourses)* seems to be significantly different, both in terms of dates given and in terms of presence or absence of parts of the tales narrated about Khayyam. In the presently read manuscript copy, Nezami Arouzi's report of visit to Khayyam's grave ends with the blossoms story, more or less. But, in the older copies having been reportedly read by people such as Yar Ahmad Rashidi Tabrizi, or even some readers in recent centuries in the West, we find the story is longer, including references to an elderly by the grave, visiting Khayyam's house, and hearing references to Khayyam as a composer of the Robaiyat, about their nature, number, and so on.

Such details are *not* what Yar Ahmad Rashidi Tabrizi adding to the story as tales. They are part of the story being told by Nezami Arouzi, and in turn being reportedly read by Yar Ahmad Rashidi Tabrizi in his author-written copy of *Chahar Maqaleh (Four Discourses)*.

So, if we can set aside the customary doubts about Yar Ahmad Rashidi Tabrizi's own reliability of narration, and study his text anew to judge for ourselves whether what others say of his authorship is true or not, including regarding what information he offers about what he read in Nezami Arouzi about meetings with Khayyam in Balkh and the time of his death and burial, we may find new value that were previously neglected because of our own "observing" lenses about the worth and meanings of our sources.

In the next chapter, I will show that indeed by expanding our horizons of probabilities about the nature and content of our sources as found in Yar Ahmad Rashidi Tabrizi's *Tarabkhaneh (House of Joy)* and how it superposes with Nezami Arouzi's *Chahar Maqaleh (Four Discourses)* based on the older author-written copy to which he reports having had access, we may indeed find new ways of approaching and solving the puzzle of the date for Khayyam's passing.

What we do know, and conclude this chapter with, is that now the view that none of Khayyam's contemporaries refer to Khayyam as the author of the Robaiyat may actually be verifiably not true, and at least subject to serious doubt.

One of his close pupils with personal interaction with him, that is, Nezami Arouzi, in his own hand-written manuscript of *Chahar Maqaleh (Four Discourses)*, as reported by Yar Ahmad Rashidi Tabrizi in *Tarabkhaneh (House of Joy)*, had clearly referred to Khayyam as the author of many Robaiyat, that he was famous but religiously forbidden for some of them, and this may be a part of the story of why they remained "secretly" hidden from public view.

Abstract

This essay, titled "Searching More for Omar Khayyam's True Date of Passing: Superposing the Birth Date Findings With the Prevalent Manuscript Copy of Nezami Arouzi's 'Chahar Maqaleh,'" is the fourth chapter of the second book of the twelve-book series *Omar Khayyam's Secret: Hermeneutics of the Robaiyat in Quantum Sociological Imagination,* authored by Mohammad H. Tamdgidi. The second book is subtitled *Khayyami Millennium: Reporting the Discovery and the Reconfirmation of the True Dates of Birth and Passing of Omar Khayyam (AD 1021-1123).*

In this chapter, Tamdgidi reports on the plausibility of serious doubts that can be cast on the dates given by Nezami Arouzi about all events covered in his book, including those related to Khayyam. Nezami Arouzi's text is a fine prose of Persian writing, but definitively not one that accurately reports historical dates and details. In Tamdgidi's view, this questioning of Nezami Arouzi's prevalent manuscript copy for the accuracy of its dates is a necessary step in the efforts toward finding the true date of Khayyam's passing. Rejecting prior held false narratives about Khayyam's date of passing is a necessary and essential part of this inquiry.

It happens that in the process of problematizing conventional tales given about the alleged date 526 LH for Khayyam's passing amid miscopying and misreadings of Nezami Arouzi's text, Tamdgidi reports discovering new interpretive evidence that Nezami Arouzi as one of Khayyam's close living contemporaries, one of his pupils in fact or in reverence, indeed knew that Khayyam wrote "many" quatrains, that they were "famous," and that they were, by some, regarded as religiously forbidden, which may have more to do with the religious beliefs of those making such assessments than with the religious nature of Khayyam's quatrains themselves.

Tamdgidi also suggests that, if we can set aside the customary doubts about Yar Ahmad Rashidi Tabrizi's own reliability of narration, and study his text anew to judge for ourselves whether what others say of his authorship is true or not, including regarding what information he offers about what he read in Nezami Arouzi about meetings with Khayyam in Balkh and the time of his death and burial, we may find new value that were previously neglected because of our own "observing" lenses about the worth and meanings of our sources.

According to the author, what we do know is that now, as related in this chapter, the view that none of Khayyam's contemporaries refer to Khayyam as the author of the Robaiyat may actually be verifiably not true, and at least subject to serious doubt.

CHAPTER V—Omar Khayyam's True Date of Passing Discovered and Reconfirmed: Superposing the Birth Date Findings With All "Tarabkhaneh," "Chahar Maqaleh," And "Tatemmat Sewan el-Hekmat" Accounts

This brings us to the last and the most important and consequential source for our exploration in search of the definitive date of passing of Omar Khayyam: the book titled *Tarabkhaneh* (meaning the house of joy or happiness, also implying poetry and musicality) by Yar Ahmad Rashidi Tabrizi.

As we shall see, by moving on to this book we are not really moving away from Nezami Arouzi's *Chahar Maqaleh*, since Rashidi Tabrizi himself also draws on the latter, in fact an older, seemingly more authoritative copy of it, as part of his efforts at portraying Khayyam's life and final years.

Tarabkhaneh (House of Joy) has been studied variously by scholars and different commentaries have been written on it. Beside the fact that it reports a large collection of Robaiyat attributed to Omar Khayyam, it also has a narrative of various anecdotes of information about his life. Whether or not any such stories are factual or myths, similar to the Khayyam's mother story I discussed in the previous chapter, to which I will also return below, I think the passages concerning the information given about the events surrounding Khayyam's life and passing are significant and worthy of close examination on their own merits, offering a sense of how people were receiving his attributed poetry at the time. I will particularly intersect my revisiting passages from Rashidi Tabrizi's book with the commentaries made by various other scholars on it, including those offered by Swāmi Govinda Tīrtha on this source and its relevant passages.

1. Turning to Yar Ahmad Rashidi Tabrizi's "Tarabkhaneh" While Not Entirely Leaving Nezami Arouzi's "Chahar Maqaleh": Considering the Commentaries By Golpinarli and Homai

Below, I will share the most relevant passages from *Tarabkhaneh* which we need to study closely of our purpose in this chapter.

Note that in the Persian original and my English translations below the dates given are themselves in contention and only reflective of particular readings of the passages, information whose questioning is the very subject matter of our investigation in what follows.

تاریخ شریف حکمت مآبی یوم الخمیس ۱۲ محرم سنه ٤٥٥ بمقام دهك از توابع دهستان از نواحی فیروزغند از ملوکات استراباد مدت عمرش ۵۸ شمسی و در سن هفده سالگی تمام علوم حکمت را کسب کرده بود و اوّل کسب کمال پیش حضرت رئیس الحکما و المحققین شیخ الاسلام و المسلمین ناصرالدّین شیخ محمّد منصور نورالله مرقده که استاد حکیم سنائی اند و حکیم در حدیقه بتعریف ایشان میفرماید ... و در اوان شباب ببلخ بسر بردی و در اواخر عمر در نیشابور بودی و بتحقیق چنان معلوم شد که هرگز میل اتهال نکرده و ازو هیچ نتیجهٔ و فرزندی غیر ازین رباعیّات و دیگر تصانیف منشور در حکمت بعربی و فارسی نمانده و دیگر چنان مشهورست که در حالت نزع او جماعتی بر بالینش نشسته بودند و التماس وصیت کرده اند او بجواب این رباعی فرموده

چند از پی حرص و آز تن فرسوده
ای دوست روی گرد جهان گردیده
رفتند و رویم و دیگر آیند و روند
یکدم بمراد خویشتن نابوده[1]

دیگر موضح میدارد که این فقیر در سبزوار نسخهٔ بخطّ نظامی عروضی دید و بر ذیل نسخهٔ مکتوب انکه در اثنی عشر و خمسایه در بلخ در خدمت حضرت استادی حکمت مآبی رسیدم و رخصت کعبهٔ مکرمه طلبیدم در اثنای سخنان فرمود که بعد از عود قبر مرا در موضعی یابی که باد شمال بر او گل افشانی کند بعد از سه سال که مراجعت افتاد در خاطر خطور میکرد که که هرگز از ان مظهر سخنان گزاف و مکرّر استماع نیفتاده و چون باستراباد رسیدم استفسار احوال ایشان رفت چنان معلوم شد که به نیشابور تشریف آورده اند مشیا علی الرأس احرام ملازمت بسته بنیشابور راند گفتند که در همین ولا بجوار حق پیوسته اند بزیارت ایشان عزیمت نموده شد ملاحظهٔ رفت در کنار دیوار باغی ایشانرا دفن کرده بودند و درختان میوه دار که از دیوار باغ سر بیرون کرده و چندان شکوفه باد از دیوار باغ بیرون فشانده که قبر در میان شکوفه ناپیدا شده بود معلوم شد که ان سخن که حکیم فرموده بود بگزاف نبوده بعد از رقّت و استمداد بمسکن شریفش متوجّه گشتم پیر زالی دیدم نشسته محزون چون مرا دید آشنا یافت استفسار احوال کرد بعد از وظایف تعزیت و خاطرجوئی اخبار استاد شاگردی که

1. This robai has appeared, in my view more accurately, in other collections as follows:
چند از پی حرص در تن فرسوده\ای دوست روی گرد جهان بیهوده\رفتند و رویم و دیگر آیند و روند\یکدم بمراد خویشتن نابوده

ممّهد بود تاکید یافت و چون تفتیش حالات ماضیه رفت گفت بعد از وفات به نه روز او را در واقعه دیدم که بسیار خوش حال بود پرسیدم که با وجود ملاهی و مناهی خوش حالی از چیست با وجود انك لیلا و نهارا دعای من این بود که خدایا بر عمر رحمت کن ازین سخن که گفتم بسیار مکدّر گشت و بهم بر آمد و خشمگین شد و این رباعی گفت

ای سوختهٔ سوختهٔ سوختنی
وی آتش دوزخ از تو افروختنی
تا کی گوئی که بر عمر رحمت کن
حق را تو که ای برحمت آموختنی

چون بیدار شدم این رباعی بخاطر من مانده بود امّیدی که حق تعالی همگنانرا از خوان نعمت و رحمت خود بی نصیب نگرداند ...

[My translation, including those of the poems:]

The honorable date of the philosophical authority is Thursday, Muharram 12th, 455 [LH] in the location Dehak from the environs of Dehestan in the Firoozghand region of Ostarabad lands the length of his life being 58 solar years and in the age of seventeen he had acquired all the philosophical sciences and the beginning of his perfecting education was at the presence of the leader of philosophers and scholars Sheikh-ol-Islam val-Moslemeen Nasereddin Sheik Muhammad Mansour, may God Enlighten his shrine, who was the teacher of philosopher Sanai and Hakim [Sanai] in his *Hadigheh* praises him [that is, his teacher, not Khayyam] as follows [a poem follows here that does not pertain our inquiry here, so I omit ...] and in early youth he lived in Balkh and toward the end of his life in Neyshabour and per investigation it became known that he was never inclined to wed and no results or children remained except for these robaiyat and other writings in philosophy in Arabic and Persian and also it is famous that in deathbed a crowd had gathered around his bed and begged for a will and in response he recited this robai

You run around the world in worn body, my friend,

For a while after greediness until your end.

They left, we leave, and all who'll come again will go,

Not reaching once to what we did at first intend.

Further it is explained that [I] this humble man in Sabzevar saw a manuscript in Nezami Arouzi's handwriting and toward the bottom of the written copy was that: in 512 [LH] in Balkh I reached a meeting of the philosophical authority [Khayyam] and asked his blessing for my going to the honorable Kabeh and amid conversation he said after your return you will find my grave in a location where the northern wind sheds flowers on it. After

> three years when I returned I had in mind that from a presence such as his never extravagant and repetitive words came and when I reached Ostarabad I asked how he was doing and it became known that he had arrived at Neyshabour and I headed on foot determined to go in offering my respect in Neyshabour and they said he had just about then passed away toward God and I proceeded to visit him and saw he was buried beside a garden wall and fruitful trees rising from the garden and wind had shed so many blossoms from the garden over the wall that the grave was hidden below the blossoms and so it became clear that what the noble man had uttered was not extravagant and after much sadness and wishing well I sought after his honorable house and saw a white-haired elderly sitting in grief and when she [or he] saw me recognized me and asked how I was doing, and after performing mourning rites and remembrances the fact of our being teacher-student became emphasized and when the past events were recalled she [or he] said, "nine days after he died I saw him in dreams and found him very happy; I asked given the means of forbidden amusement what was your happiness for, since I have been day and night praying for God's Mercy for Omar. From these words I said, he became sad, agitated, and angry and recited this robai:
>
> O the burned out, burn worthy, and burnable one!
>
> O the one from whom hell's fire must have begun!
>
> Until when do you ask God's Mercy for Omar?
>
> Who are *you* to teach how God's Mercy should be run?
>
> When I woke up, this robai had remained in my memory, in the hope that God Most High does not deprive all equal human beings from the table of His blessings and mercy!"

As you may note, in the above Rashidi Tabrizi relays what appears to be a similar story about Nezami Arouzi's meeting Khayyam at some point and then visiting his grave. However, there are several important aspects of this narration that are different from all others, some of which directly pertain to our purpose in this chapter regarding discovering Khayyam's date of passing.

Aside from issues such as, strictly speaking, no "mother of Khayyam" is involved in the story, using a gender neutral expression "Peer-e Zal" (پیر زال) which literally means a "white-haired elderly," it could be interpreted to mean a range of persons, such as a man or women, mother or sister, and so on. So, if we consider the reports, as also noted in the account, that Khayyam never married, and therefore did not have a wife or offspring, and also consider our own findings that Khayyam must have died a centenarian and therefore could not have a mother still living and visiting his grave, while also considering that Beyhaqi does mention what appears to be Khayyam's brother-in-law present on his death bed, that is, Imam Muhammad al-Baghdadi (who we know, as I suggested earlier in previous chapters, was in his seventies), we may readily conclude that if there was such an elderly at Khayyam's grave and the person was a female, it may have been his elderly sister.

I do not wish to belabor this point here, other than noting that this shows there are so many different variations of the story told in such details that one should be careful in considering any manuscript copy or narration of what transpired as the only correct one. It is most likely that the reported elderly woman at Khayyam's grave (perhaps originating from Nezami Arouzi), was interpreted, in the absence of knowledge of Khayyam's centenarian age by the scribes later on reading the texts while copying his text, as his mother (and not sister), and the wrong story was later passed down through some copying chains perhaps even in "clear copies" of that manuscript to reach some readers.

In any case, there are several other aspects of this narration that are unique.

First is that Nezami Arouzi's meeting with Khayyam is reported to have taken place not in 506 LH but in 512 LH, and an element is added to the story regarding Nezami Arouzi intending to go for Hajj to Mecca, and Khayyam's foretelling about his grave's condition is somehow tied to Nezami Arouzi's returning from Hajj. So, a specific number of years (three) are noted by Nezami Arouzi as having transpired before he goes to see Khayyam, finding him having passed away in Neyshabour just around that time.

At its face value, one may conclude—as the compiler of the Rashidi Tabrizi manuscript, the Turkish scholar Abdol-Baqi Golpinarli (عبدالباقی گلپینارلی), also did (to which I shall return shortly)—that adding three years to 512 LH would offer the year 515 LH as the year in which Khayyam's death reportedly took place. But then the text could have also been read as meaning that the three years was to counted not after Nezami Arouzi's meeting with Khayyam in 512 LH, but three years after his return from Hajj. I will return to this matter later.

Second, is given what appears to be a date for Khayyam's birth, this time being offered by Rashidi Tabrizi himself, independently from what he reports about Nezami Arouzi.

Golpinarli read his Yar Ahmad Rashidi Tabrizi's manuscript *Tarabkhaneh*, of which I quoted the above, as offering Muharram 12th, 455 LH, as the date, followed by stating that Khayyam lived 58 solar years. This is then followed by some details about Khayyam's contemporary, the poet Sanai, that they shared the same teacher, and so on.

Sanai's dates of birth and passing are not exactly known but have been roughly estimated (as given in the *Encyclopedia Iranica* under the title of the poet "Sanai") as AD 1087-1130 (about 480-534 LH). The overlap implied with Khayyam presumably born in the year 455 LH (this would be about sixteen lunar years after Tīrtha's wrong 439 LH/AD 1048 birth date estimate) their sharing an early teacher seems implausible of course unless considered to have not taken place at the same time. This would mean that at a time Khayyam (in the company of others) is invited to translate Avicenna's "Splendid Sermon" in Isfahan, he would be about 17 years old, which is extremely implausible.

The trouble with all these issues of dates emanates from the troubles Golpinarli and many other scholars have had in reading the strange scripts used to offer the year and age as noted above in the copy of Rashidi Tabrizi's manuscript of *Tarabkhaneh (House of Joy)* they have examined.

Just to offer a taste for example of how Golpinarli has gone about, in his introduction (dated 21 Jumadi al-Awwal 1367 LH or April 1, 1948) to Rashidi Tabrizi *Tarabkhaneh*, justifying how he has read his copy, consider below (in my translation):

> In the part of *Tarabkhaneh* that concerns Khayyam's life, other than the date of his birth, it seems truthful that Yar Ahmad [Rashidi Tabrizi] registers Khayyam's death in 515 [LH] which is confirmed by the author of *Mizan ol-Hekmat*[2]. Yar Ahmad Rashidi, at the end of his writing which is the 10th part of *Tarabkhaneh* says "this humble man in Sabzevar saw a manuscript in Nezami Arouzi's handwriting and toward the bottom of the written copy was that: in 512 [LH] in Balkh I reached a meeting of the philosophical authority [Khayyam] and asked his blessing for my going to the honorable Kabeh and amid conversation he said after your return you will find my grave in a location where the northern wind sheds flowers on it. After three years (that is in the year 515 [LH] [the year added by Golpinarli as emphasis]) when I returned I had in mind that from a presence such as his never extravagant and repetitive words came and when I reached Ostarabad I asked how he was doing and it became known that he had arrived at Neyshabour and I headed on foot determined to go in

2. Note that here Golpinarli has assumed that the mercy wishing for Khayyam in Khazeni's book is universally common among all manuscripts and it proves Khayyam's birth date to have definitely taken place in 515 LH. I have already rejected this view based on reliable evidence in Chapter III.

> offering my respect to Neyshabour and they said he had just about then passed away toward God ..." This story is in the third essay of Nezami Arouzi's *Chahar Maqaleh* mentioned, but there Nezami meets Khayyam in the year 506 and in the year 530 returns to Neyshabour when Khayyam had passed away four (or according to other copies, "some") years before. Since *Tarabkhaneh* explains that Khayyam died in the year 515 LH, and this is confirmed in *Mizan ol-Hekmat*, it is apparent that *Tarabkhaneh* corrects *Chahar Maqaleh* and without any doubt the dates 506 and 530 written in *Chahar Maqaleh* are handwriting errors. (pp. 39-40)

And regarding the given date of birth for Khayyam, Golpinarli adds (my translation):

> The author of *Tarabkhaneh* registers the date of birth of Khayyam as Thursday, Muharram 12th, 455 [LH]. Even in the manuscript read by Mr. Jalaleddin Homai it is noted that his horoscope was Taurus and his star is Venus, and at his birth his star was in Sharaf constellation. But Yar Ahmad [Rashidi Tabrizi] who notes Khayyam's birth date to be 455 and his death in 515 says that his age was 52 solar years [here, Golpinarli himself apparently makes an error of his own, as he corrects himself by offering the calculated age to be 58, which I translated above]. The manuscript of *Tarabkhaneh* that has no. 1370 in the Persian manuscripts of the library of Istanbul University, has the same error. It is clear that this error has been caused by the way the digit "eight" is written. Yar Ahmad [Rashidi Tabrizi] has written "fifty eight" like this ... [see the image below in Figure V.1 of how Golpinarli tries to copy the digits as given in his copy]. This number can also be read as 52. Someone who has been born in 455 and has died in 515 calculating in lunar years would have lived 60 years which in solar year calculation would be about 58 years. After the correction of this error we say that Khayyam's date of passing corresponds to truth but his date of birth [as given in *Tarabkhaneh*] is an absolute error since our Hakim at the beginning of his descriptive translation of Avicenna's treatise on Existence says [in Arabic, "was invited by brethren in Isfahan in the year 472 to translate the sermon of Sheikh Abu Ali Ibn Sina ..." if we accept his birth date to be, as Yar Ahmad [Rashidi Tabrizi] says 455, he must have translated and described that treatise when seventeen years old and this seems impossible, and he himself says in the robai 344: "The cup of my life reached seventy." Of course, when translating and explaining such a treatise thirty or forty years had passed in his life, so his birth date is between 432-442 [LH]. Yar Ahmad [Rashidi Tabrizi] regards Abu Said Abu al-Khayr and Ghazali and Naser Khosrow and Sanai as contemporaries of Khayyam and this is correct. (pp. 40-41; notes in brackets are mine)

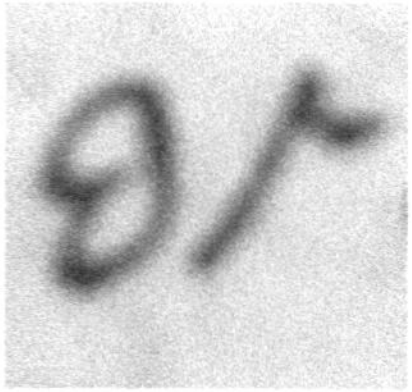

Figure V.1

Golpinarli's (p. 40) Image of the Number for the Age of Khayyam as Given in His Copy of "Tarabkhaneh"

This brings me to sharing also the views and investigations of the late Iranian scholar, among others, of Khayyam, Jalaleddin Homai (جلال الدّین همایی), who wrote an introduction and extensive footnotes while introducing a copy (or copies) of Rashidi Tabrizi's (d. ca. 867 LH/AD 1462) *Tarabkhaneh* published in Shahrivar 1342 SH (1963) in Tehran.

It is noteworthy that while Golpinarli himself draws (as he notes elsewhere in his introduction) on Homai in his introduction, as translated above and published in 1949, he was drawing on earlier commentaries of Homai's notes on *Tarabkhaneh* since obviously Homai's edition used for my considerations below was published after Golpinarli's edition, and in fact therein Homai draws on the work and errors committed by Golpinarli himself.

Since Homai's commentaries on *Tarabkhaneh*, a collection of quatrains and life anecdotes about Khayyam published in 867 LH (about AD 1462), have provided one of the several sources of discourses on Khayyam's dates of birth and passing, I will share his views in detail below while translating his words in the edition of the book published originally in 1963.

My point at this point is to offer the reader a sense or taste of what information, arguments, puzzles, or questions have been offered when reading *Tarabkhaneh* so that I can then both appreciatively and critically draw on their arguments in search of a definitive date of passing for Khayyam. These conversations show to what extent, short of having any other evidence, the passages from Nezami Arouzi and *Tarabkhaneh* have become scrutinized and studied, and why I have to also engage with these passages and conversations around them in order to arrive at a definitive determination of Khayyam's date of passing.

In what follows, I will not enter into the long discussion Homai enters in his edition regarding the authenticity, or not, of any Robaiyat found in *Tarabkhaneh*. This will have to await other books of this series. At this point, as noted before, my purpose is to focus on the question of Khayyam's date of passing.

Homai draws on three different copies of *Tarabkhaneh*, one dated 1002 LH (about AD 1594) that he himself owns, inherited from his uncle (he uses the letter "S" for this copy). Then there is a second copy he draws on, dated from the tenth century lunar Hejri (about 16th century AD), shared with him by Mojtaba Minovi (1903-1977) (مجتبی مینوی), a major scholar of Khayyam; Homai uses the abbreviation "Mi" for this second copy. The third copy, abbreviated as "Kh," which is a text summarizing *Tarabkhaneh*, again owned by Homai himself, dated around 970-980 LH (about AD 1560s-1570s). He also draws on and compares the Golpinarli edition (using abbreviation "Gol"), which he says is dated 1332 SH (AD 1954) (pp. 67-69). Homai himself dates his own introduction to the book—where, in footnotes and endnotes he shares his commentaries about Khayyam's date of passing (and birth)—signed on Farvardin 14th, 1342 SH (April 3, 1963).

Since I have already offered in Persian and English translation the basic texts of the stories in *Tarabkhaneh* relating to the dates of birth, and the final years and passing of Khayyam above (with the variations to be detailed below withstanding), I will not repeat those texts here and will focus on translating the detailed commentaries by Homai on various aspects of Rashidi Tabrizi's texts in *Tarabkhaneh*. These commentaries are variously offered in footnotes by Homai across the pages 147-152 of the book.

In the main text, when offering his interpretation of the dates offered in *Tarabkhaneh* for Khayyam's birth, Homai also offers the date Muharram 12th, 455 LH, and Khayyam's age at death as 52 solar years.

Here, Homai corrects (in footnote 7) Golpinarli's seeming error of having offered Khayyam's age (presumed being reported in *Tarabkhaneh*) as "58" since, Homai adds, Golpinarli himself offers the age as "52" elsewhere in the text. In my reading, Golpinarli is not fully decided as to which is correct, since he does make a point of saying that the digit "2" could be read as "8" given how it is written in a slanted way.

For English readers not familiar with Arabic/Persian digits as commonly known today, the letter 2 is written as ۲ , and the letter 8 is written as ۸ . If you imagine the letter eight in Persian is somewhat rotated counterclockwise, in handwriting, and the right wing of it is somewhat shorter than the left wing of the letter, so to speak, it may resemble the letter 2 in Persian. Again, in Figure V.1 above, I have copied Golpinarli's rendering, to see how the digit on the right can be supposedly read, in his view, as either ۲ or ۸ (in Persian).

Homai continues to elaborate in the long footnote (7, continuation; I have omitted extra notes with dotted lines that are not immediately relevant for our purpose here):

> To explain, this date of birth and age for Khayyam is undoubtedly wrong since Khayyam, as written by Ibn Asir [ابن اثیر] and a set of historians and astronomers in the year 467 LH was among a group of scientists who had gathered in Isfahan in the court of the Malekshah Seljuki for observing stars and for reforming the Jalali calendar ... and it is customarily impossible that an immature child of twelve-thirteen years old becomes involved with master philosophers and mathematical sciences such as Abol-Mozaffar Asfezari, Meimoun ibn Najeeb Vasati, and Abol-Abbas Lowkari in such an important scientific work. And also we know that the translation of Avicenna's "Splendid Sermon" was written in the year 473 LH, and before then, in the year 472 LH in his trip to Shiraz he had written his treatise in reply to some scientific problems for the supreme judge of Fars, and it is remotely possible, nearly impossible, that a youth of 17-18 years old could accommodate such a writing or status that scientists or major figures of the time would inquire from him about problems of scientific nature.
>
> So, the birth of Khayyam in the year 455 LH, as written by the author of *Tarabkhaneh* is not correct; and what has become almost certain for myself, humbly, is that his birth has happened in the year 439 LH[3] and the length of his life has amounted to about 70-80 years. However, it is not impossible that the month and the day of his birth are those same Muharram 12th as written in *Tarabkhaneh*.
>
> Incidentally, this writer myself determined from the principles and exact technical calculations that in the year 439 LH its first of Muharram was a Sunday so that its 12th of its Muharram would have exactly corresponded to a Thursday; and near to that year, we also had other years such as the years 436 LH and 444 LH in which the 12th of Muharram coincided with a Thursday. But, if it becomes certain that the birth of the Hakim was on a Thursday, Muharram 12th, the more it happened in earlier than the year 440 LH, the more it would be acceptably near to the year offered in other

3. Readers should recognize that this date and age is roughly the same as the one Tīrtha had advocated (439 LH is about AD 1048), and since Homai leans on Khayyam's death having occurred around 515 LH, the same age estimate as that of Tīrtha is offered. The difference here is that Tīrtha takes the year offered in association with Muharram 12th to be that of Khayyam's *death* (presumably in 555 LH, which Tīrtha himself rejects). In other words, Tīrtha, having determined (now we know wrongly) that Khayyam's birth date had occurred on May 18, AD 1048 (Julian), he used the opportunity of 12th Muharram to associate it with Khayyam's date of passing (which he placed in the year 516 LH). I will return to Tīrtha on these issues later in this chapter.

sources.

But in the year 440 LH itself, its first of Muharram is Thursday, and its twelfth, even considering the approximation of calculations and sighting of the Moon, which does not exceed a day, does not correspond to a Thursday.

To explain, in these comparative calculations, based on the viewing of the Moon crescent, which indicates the first of the actual month, a day or so of difference arrived at and moreover, it rarely may happen, strange as it may appear, that in the year 455 LH, as written in *Tarabkhaneh*, it would be possible that within a difference margin of one day its 12th of Muharram would coincide with a Thursday, since the first of Muharram of that year falls on a Saturday, which, per calculation, its 12th of Muharram would fall on a Wednesday and it is possible that incidentally, per viewing of the crescent, the 12th of Muharram in that year could have corresponded to a Thursday.

It should not remain unmentioned that these kinds of calculations may be affected by estimations, signs, and certainties, and there is no definitive reason to conclude that since a birth has fallen on a given day it must have fallen on that year also since the correspondence of the number of month's day with days of the week is not limited to one or two years but it could happen in many days that such correspondence may occur, as exemplified by the years mentioned above. So, this reasoning, as the scientists say, is just a claim. But to reject and deny it one can resort to such calculations.

And, again, I add that in the other manuscript copy of *Tarabkhaneh*, per what we promised in prior commentaries and will report it exactly later on, it has more material than other copies regarding the date of birth, including the birth horoscope which is written as "his ascendant was in Taurus, whose ruler, Venus, is in Sharaf [exalted] location"; incidentally, Abol-Hassan Ali ibn Zeyd Beyhaqi, author of *Tatemmat Sewan el-Hekmat*, who himself was a contemporary of Khayyam and in the year 505 [*sic*[4]] LH has met him [Khayyam] and recognized his presence, has offered his horoscope differently and in more detail as: "His ascendant was the Gemini and the Sun and the Mercury were on the degree of the ascendant in the degree "Ḥ"[5] [ح] of the Gemini and the Mercury was Samimi and the Jupiter was in Taslees observing both."

If someone is familiar with the principles of astronomical extractions and calculations, he can from these estimations and signs derive historical points. For example, he can make known how this condition that has been

4. Actually, Homai mistakes this date, as the date given by Beyhaqi therein is 507 LH.

5. Note that Homai here again offers the customary reading of the horoscope, with the letter of the degree indicated as ح.

told about Khayyam's horoscope could have occurred in what month of year; or, for example, if all the specifics of month, day, year or hour of birth, they could research how it is possible whether these positions of stars could have happened, or not? And in such and such an hour, of such and such a day of the ascendant was the Gemini or the Taurus. Research and discovery of these matters for someone[6] specializing in these techniques is not difficult, but since the purpose here is not to describe Khayyam's biography, I do not elaborate more on these matters.

As the writer of these lines, upon consideration of these matters in the margins of the book *Mesbah ol-Hadayeh*, page 4, in an occasion I quoted from *Tarabkhaneh*, and since it was not then room for further elaboration and research, in an implied way I said: "It is obvious that in this manuscript copy or its original source there is an error; however, the recording of the day, month, and year and birth horoscope of and determination of the approximate length of Khayyam's life cannot be ignored." My intention was not to affirm the writings of *Tarabkhaneh* but from the signs that it gives us we can discover the correctness or errors in the material, like how I offered examples in the above lines. Otherwise, I have never believed that Khayyam's birth took place in the year 455 LH(!) [exclamation mark, *sic*]. However, one of the contemporary thinkers, wishing God's Mercy for him, from greediness of catching points or from kindness that he had on the people of science, regarded my point immaturely to mean that I was completely accepting the words of Yar Ahmad [Rashidi Tabrizi] the author of *Tarabkhaneh* who, in his view was "an illiterate man or the charlatan brick layers (journal *Yadegar*, vol. 3, no. 4)" and had been fooled by this "lying man"; whereas I had not affirmed his statements and said anything that meant affirming all his sayings.

And my intention was not anything other than this, that it is possible that a scholarly person may even find a way that even from these disorderly writings one cannot just easily pass them by and ignore any material as if unheard or unseen. For example, why would it be impossible to consider that even if he was mistaken in the number of the year, he could be correct in giving the right month or day. Moreover, the digit of the year of the birth date and age of Omar Khayyam in the majority of copies of *Tarabkhaneh* has been given in Indian or geometry digits so the errors of the scribe in them are plenty. Then, perhaps his writings in the original had an authoritative source that has become corrupted in the hands of the scribe. Therefore, certainly one cannot say that the author of a book

6. I am happy to note here that as one of those "someones" I have succeeded (as reported in an earlier chapter in this volume) in doing what the late Homai predicted as being possible back in 1963.

> has intentionally committed falsehood, forgery, or deception, even though his superficiality and poorness of scientific acumen is apparent all over his writing, but historical errors are not unique to him. Which book is there whose author can be exempted from errors and inadvertent mistakes? I don't even mention the books and articles of our contemporaries. The very book itself of *Chahar Maqaleh* of Nezami Arouzi which is among important ancient Persian writing is full of errors and historical mistakes and at times in a single story has many glaring mistakes; and even I do not claim innocence ...[7] (pp. 147-149)

Elsewhere, in a follow-up on his footnotes, Homai draws on the standard versions of the story as given in Nezami Arouzi's *Chahar Maqaleh* and reflects on the extent to which it can offer leads to Khayyam's date of passing, especially regarding the date 530 LH and the "four" or "some" years before it (for Khayyam's date of demise):

> ... Let's not leave unmentioned that the statement related to Nezami's entry into Neyshabour from which one can possibly derive the date of passing of Khayyam, even in approximation, in the usual manuscript copies of *Chahar Maqaleh* is definitely not trustworthy since even the slightest misstatement that may have entered in this regard could have a significant impact on what is claimed, for example this difference between "some" and "four" that has been recorded in the Leiden edition, or the possibility of misstatement of the word "Salaseen" [for "thirty,"or ثلاثین, in reference to the date 530 LH] or "four" for "fourteen" and so on.

The essence of what Homai argues for, regardless of the tentative dates he proposes for Khayyam's dates of birth and passing, is that simply because we have old manuscript copies that include stories or anecdotes that do not sound right or authors that are far from being perfectly scholarly in relaying information about their subject, should not prevent us from scrutinizing them in order to find reasonable clues, if any, in favor of learning about one

7. Homai displays here a thoughtful and mature attitude about how delicate matters such as the exploration of inherited manuscripts should be approached. Although my findings in this chapter will differ from his in its results, in terms of approach, he offers, in my view, an open-minded way of going about studying ancient texts. Just because we have little at our disposal for resolving longstanding puzzles such as those about Khayyam's life and works, this does not mean that we should pass by what we have as if they do not exist or cannot be seen. Precious new insights can in fact be found in these texts, and I am happy that in this chapter also I will succeed in reliably discovering the date of Khayyam's passing on the basis of such very texts, when studied carefully. In fact, I think judgments about Yar Ahmad Rashidi Tabrizi's *Tarabkhaneh (House of Joy)* may have been somehow premature in certain respects, which I will hopefully try to rectify in the course of this series.

or another aspects of Khayyam's life and works. His rejection of simplistic taken-for-grantedness of what is offered in these texts, however, has also another side—that, in exploring those clues, we should be careful not to be satisfied with ready-made answers, and question the value of any piece of information given in a reasonable and critical fashion.

Unfortunately, we are not offered any images of the actual manuscript copies used by either Homai or Golpinarli in order to explore the nature of the dates given for the birth date or the age of Khayyam in *Tarabkhaneh*. The most we have from Golpinarli is his rendition of the two digit number which he interprets as representing either the number 52 or 58 for the solar age of Khayyam (see Figure V.1 above). They, however, both seem to agree that in their reading of their respective manuscripts, the year given for Khayyam's date of birth (as erroneous as they themselves both agree it to be) is Muharram 12th, 455 LH.

They are both inclined to agree that Rashidi Tabrizi's story of Nezami Arouzi's meeting with Khayyam in 512 LH plus three years added for his return visit to meet Khayyam (finding him passed away) leads to a tentative date of 515 LH for Khayyam's passing. The date given by Rashidi Tabrizi for Khayyam's birth (455 LH) is definitely wrong, in their view, but the month and day given for the *birth* day, if correct, would lead to the possibility, for Homai, of supposing that Khayyam could have been born in the year 439 LH (AD 1048), but for him it could be the years 436 or 444 also, since Muharram 12th falls on a Thursday on those dates as well.

Before proceeding to bring in Tīrtha's contribution into this discussion, I should point out again that Homai and Golpinarli's assumption that Khazeni's book *Mizan ol-Hekmat* gives us a certain 515 LH date for Khayyam's date is by no means convincing. Their basic argument is that since Khazeni says in his book that it was completed in the year 515 LH, and that in the copies available to Homai and/or Golpinarli, there is a mercy-wishing statement after Khayyam's name, then we can reliably assume that Khayyam's death occurred in that year.

First, even if we take their argument at its face value—that such a mercy-wishing statement is given for Khayyam by Khazeni, the author himself, as he completed the book—this can by no means lead us to conclude that the death could have taken place that year; for, it could have happened earlier than 515 LH.

Second, there can be other manuscripts, as I have referenced one of them existing actually, where the mercy-wishing *for Khayyam* appears nowhere at all in the text. Since it is very unlikely that a scribe would delete such a statement from his or her original manuscript copy at a later date, especially when the same statement is preserved for al-Asfezari, it is safe to assume that down at least some of the copying chains, the mercy-wishing statement did not exist in the text, and that if it existed in one or other copies in other chains, it must have been added by a scribe recopying the manuscript at a time when Khayyam had definitely been known to have died.

So, it is safe to assume, in fact, that Khayyam had not died in the year 515 LH or part thereof, or that no conclusions can be reached from examining Khazeni's book regarding Khayyam having died that year.

The reader may ask whether the additional information given by Rashidi Tabrizi regarding Nezami Arouzi's visit to Balkh in 512 LH, three years after which he reports Khayyam to have died, is sufficient corroborating evidence to conclude that Khayyam died in the year 515 LH. I shall return to this shortly, arguing that the answer to the question does not have to be necessarily in the affirmative.

2. Superposing With the Manuscript Copy of Yar Ahmad Rashidi Tabrizi's "Tarabkhaneh" Shared by Swāmi Govinda Tīrtha in His "The Nectar of Grace"

What I wish to add to these considerations now is the interesting material Tīrtha inadvertently contributed in his *The Nectar of Grace* (1941)[8], which, when examined carefully, can in fact lead us to a solution to the problem of determining not only the year, but even the season and month of Khayyam's passing, a beautiful solution worthy of our wonderful Omar Khayyam.

Tīrtha, in his efforts at relaying various old texts referring to Khayyam and while seeking to find the date of Khayyam's demise, actually shared with us images of three pages in *his copy* of Rashidi Tabrizi's *Tarabkhaneh* which he had used for the purposes at hand.

I share the first of these page images from his book in Figure V.2. This first page image which Tīrtha shared in his book is basically the passage in Nezami Arouzi's *Chahar Maqaleh* as relayed by Rashidi Tabrizi where Khayyam's date of *birth* (which Tīrtha mistakenly attributes to a dating by Rashidi Tabrizi of Khayyam's death) and his age are given. The other two pages include Nezami Arouzi's story of how he met Khayyam in Balkh in

8. Swāmī Govinda Tīrtha's book, *The Nectar of Grace: Omar Khayyam's Life and Works* (1941), is freely accessible and downloadable/searchable online as a pdf document at this address: https://archive.org/details/nectarofgrace031160mbp/page/n10.

512 LH and revisiting his grave three years afterward (which could be after that meeting or after his return from a Hajj pilgrimage he undertook after that meeting). I will later reproduce the third page also for another reason further below.

I have already shared the basic text in both its original Persian and in translation previously. My point in sharing the image of the actual handwritten manuscript copy of the first page in Figure V.2 page is to direct the reader's attention to the digit symbols used in Tīrtha's source copy of *Tarabkhaneh.*

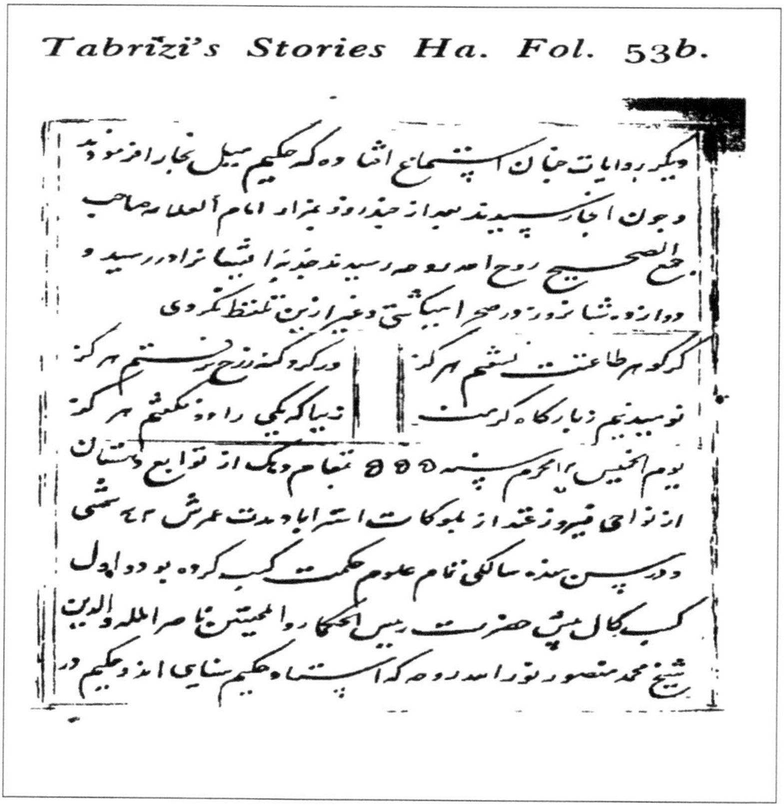
Tabrīzi's Stories Ha. Fol. 53b.

Figure V.2

Tīrtha's First Page Image of the Page of Tabrizi's Relaying of the Passage from Nezami Arouzi's "Chahar Maqaleh" Offering the Date of Birth and Age of Khayyam

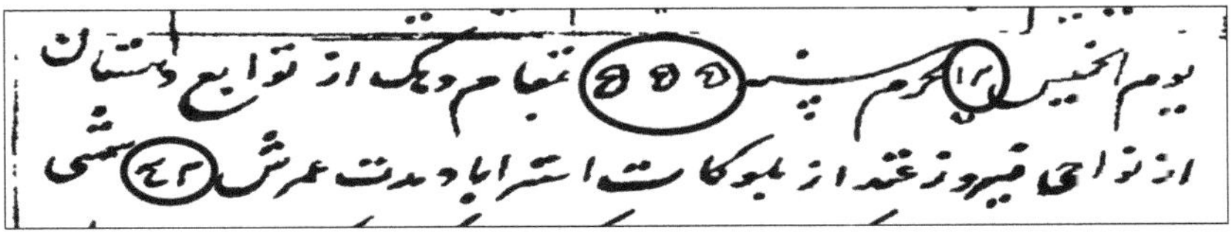

Figure V.3

Circled from Left to Right Are the Age, the Year of Birth, and the Day of Birth of Khayyam as Given in Tīrtha's First Page Image of the Page of Tabrizi's "Tarabkhaneh," Relaying the Passage from Nezami Arouzi's "Chahar Maqaleh" Offering the Date of Birth and Age of Khayyam

In Figure V.3, I have magnified the lines in the passage where the age, the year of birth, and the day of month is given (circled respectively from left to right, regardless of the lines, for Khayyam).

Since it is important to share how Tīrtha has translated and interpreted these passages, I will quote below relevant passages from him where he draws on, paraphrases, or translates parts of the passages from Rashidi Tabrizi offering his own and then Nezami Arouzi's account of visiting Khayyam and his grave. Note how for Tīrtha the age given is "72," and the year given is "555," and the day of birth given in Muharram is (as agreed by others) 12.

Tīrtha writes (I have edited out using dots parts of the passage not relevant to my purpose here; also to note, Tīrtha usually assumes he is referring to lunar Hejri dates, unless otherwise noted; I maintain his transliterations):

> (a) "Thursday 12 Muharram 555, at Dahak a village of Dehistān in the province off Ustarābād."
>
> (b) "The duration of his life 72 solar years." ...
>
> Note: —(a) The hiatus in the beginning of this story has created confusion in the three copies of Tabrizī compilation, *viz.*, Ha., Sc. and Sd. Persian Tadhkiras[9] usually give the dates of demise of authors. If we add the word *Wafātash*[10] in the beginning of the narrative the whole reads as follows. "He

---

9. This term تذکره is used for old texts offering biographical entries for famed personalities.

10. This word وفاتش in Persian means "his death." Tīrtha is basically trying to argue (unconvincingly) that the Muharram date given in Rashidi Tabrizi is associated with Khayyam's *death*, not birth, because he asserts (wrongly) that the old biographical entries gave only dates for death, and not, at times, also of birth. So, he is imagining adding the word "his death" (in Persian, *Wafātash*) here.

demised on Thursday 12 Muharram 555 at Dahak a village, etc."[11]

The year 555 is obviously a clerical error according to the subsequent story, and also because 12 Muharram 555 H. is not on Thursday.

—(b) The age is 72 (or 74) years in Ha. and has been obviously miscopied in Sc. and Sd. ...

... Tabrīzī states: "I saw in Sabzawār a manuscript in the handwriting of Niẓāmi Urūdī with the following endorsement: —

'In the year 512 I went to Balkh to present my respects to my teacher the source of Philosophy. I requested permission to proceed on pilgrimage to Mecca. In the course of conversation he said:

'On return you will find my grave in a place where the northern winds will shower flowers.'

'It took over three years till I could return. My mind was perturbed because I had never heard from that great person any untrue or contradictory words. When I reached Ustarābaad I enquired after his welfare. I was informed that only recently he had reached the proximity of the Lord. I proceeded to Nīshāpūr to visit his grave, and saw that he was buried by the side of a Garden. The fruit trees of the garden extended outside, and the wind had showered blossoms so profusely on the grave that it was hidden thereunder.'

Note: —The same story is found in *Chahār Maqālā* ... which states the year of meeting 506 H. instead of 512 H. and Niẓāmi Urūdī's return in thirty instead of after three years.

The readings of the MSS. of Chahār Maqālā' [sic] are evidently incorrect. We know from the MS. of ʿOmar Khayyam's Algebra ... that in 527 H. when the MS. was copied the numerals were written in contracted Arabic words. It is quite possible that Niẓāmi Urūdī wrote 512 in this peculiar notation which was misread by later scribes.[12]

---

11. These source abbreviations correspond in Tīrtha's bibliography to the following manuscripts respectively: "Ha." scribed in AD 1462 in Hyderabad Dn., first owner Bahrām banda-i-Shāh-i-Wilāyat 897 LH; "Sc." scribed in AD 1485, dated 890 LH; and "Sd". copy held in library Nūr-i-Osmāniā. (Tīrtha, pages XIII and XVIII). The image in Figure V.2 which Tīrtha has shared is as noted on top from his source Ha.

12. This observation by Tīrtha may be worth considering as a source of errors for dates given in Nezami Arouzi and old texts. There is a type of handwriting called Siaq, which was often used in trade to record transactions, taxes, quantities, prices, etc. Only those specifically educated in using them, often as part of practical training in the trades, could write and read them. In the past, such a handwriting was more commonplace, and scribes were familiar with it, and used them in scribing and copying books. Misreading of these numbers could explain

> On the whole, the version given by Tabrīzī from the MS. he actually saw may be accepted as correct. Niẓāmi Urūdī met 'Omar Khayyam in the later part of 512 H., and returned after more than three years, i.e., in the early 516 H. to find that his master had demised recently. We may reasonably accept Thursday 12 Muharram 516 H. as the date of ʿOmar's demise which Tabrīzī meant to give. The date inscribed on ʿOmar's tomb at Nīshāpūr is 516 H.[13] (Tīrtha, pp. LXIX-LXXI)

It is clear from the above that Tīrtha was inclined to associate the date given by Rashidi Tabrizi involving the month of Muharram to Khayyam's demise, rather than his birth. I have already shown how this is entirely arbitrary and unconvincing for several reasons.

First, it is not true that the old biographical accounts gave only dates of demise. Even in his own sharing of the accounts from Beyhaqi, there is a horoscope for birth, and Beyhaqi offers the date of birth for highly significant figures such as Avicenna in *Tatemmat Sewan el-Hekmat (Supplement to the Chest of Wisdom)*, as another example.

Second, Tīrtha cannot explain why a place such as Dehak is given for the presumed death of Khayyam (since the place given after the date of presumed death should logically be treated as giving a place of death), when the account he shares and copies from Rashidi Tabrizi clearly states he died and was buried in Neyshabour.

While it is possible to regard Khayyam as having died in the same house he was born in, located in Ostarabad, in a general region near Neyshabour, clearly, as agreed upon by all scholars, Rashidi Tabrizi is giving the time and place of *birth* of Khayyam in that passage.

Third, Tīrtha does not offer any explanation for why even the date 555 LH is given, beyond simply saying it is in error, obviously, since a few passages down Rashidi Tabrizi himself tells us that Khayyam died about three years after Nezami Arouzi visited him in Balkh in 512 LH (or, after his return from Hajj). In other words, why would Tīrtha even think it possible that 555 was referring to a date of passing, when he knows and acknowledges that a few paragraphs later Rashidi Tabrizi himself relays Nezami Arouzi's story of how Khayyam died three or so years after 512 LH?

Of course, Tīrtha has another (self-serving, we may add) reason to ignore

at least some of the misdating and misreading of old texts as far as digits are concerned.

13. As I have noted before in this book, this tomb referred to by Tīrtha in his book published in 1941 is the one that used to stand before Khayyam's remains later on were moved to his present resting place. It still exists but as part of a square in Neyshabour named after Khayyam.

or deny the date given as being related to Khayyam's birth, since a few pages before he had himself declared that Khayyam's birth had been discovered by him to have occurred on May 18, AD 1048 (which he failed to note it is in Julian calendar, by the way), or May 24 (Gregorian) which would fall on a Saturday actually, not a Thursday (more than 24 hours away, so no possibility of errors being plausible here, as Homai had advised).

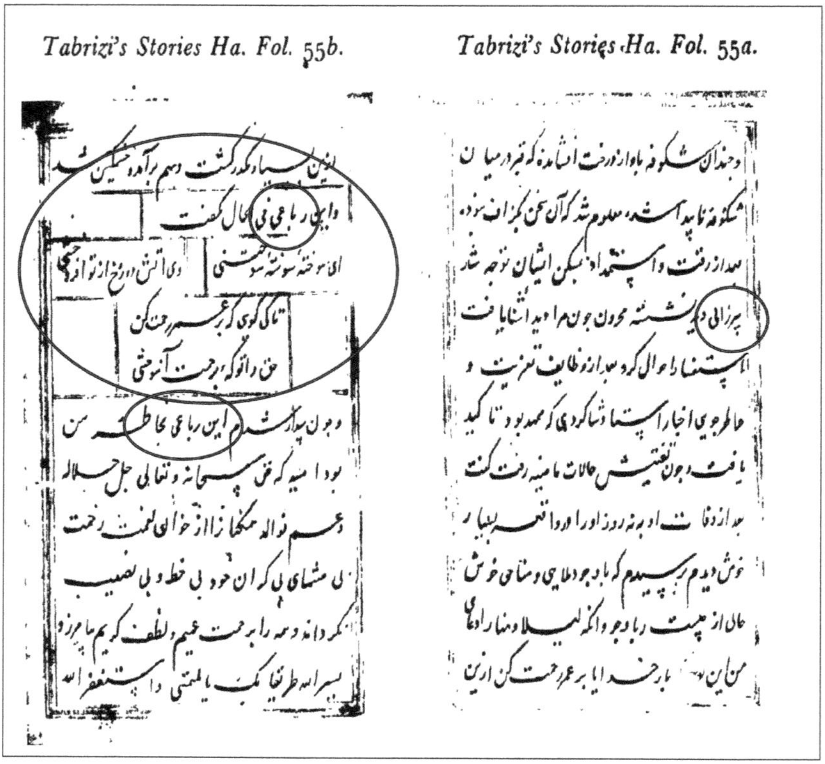

Figure V.4

Tīrtha's Third Page Image of the Page of Tabrizi's Relaying of the Passage from Nezami Arouzi's "Chahar Maqaleh" Referring to "White-Haired Elderly" and to Omar Khayyam's Composition of Robais

However, I will show below that by offering us an image of the page of Rashidi Tabrizi's manuscript, as shared earlier in Figures V.2 and V.3, Tīrtha has inadvertently offered us very interesting and helpful clues from an unexamined manuscript of *Tarabkhaneh*, so that we can proceed to investigate this matter in such a way that can provide a definitive answer to our central question in this chapter, volume, and series, for Khayyam's date of passing.

Before moving further, let me just add that in other images of the passages of *Tarabkhaneh (House of Joy)* shared in his book, one I reproduce in Figure V.4 above, Tīrtha has also inadvertently given us an example for the part of the story where Nezami Arouzi refers to a "white-haired elderly" (پیر زال) and also references are made to Khayyam having written a Robai, one which we have widely found in his collections. The word "zāl" (زال) is gender-neutral, and even the white-haired (implying also "old") father of Rostam, the famous hero of Shahnameh (by Ferdowsi), was named "Zāl." So, a "white-haired elderly" does not have to imply a female, let alone a "mother."

So, this is clearly an evidence that by no means was there any reference to a "mother" in copies of the text itself, and that Nezami Arouzi, a living contemporary of Omar Khayyam, close enough to him to regard him as a teacher, who new his house, and visited it, actually has left an undisputable record about Khayyam having composed robais, or quatrains, since the point about his Robaiyat appears as part of *Nezami Arouzi's* story of visiting Khayyam's grave and house and speaking to a "white-haired elderly." By the way, the latter being not a "mother" of Khayyam actually makes more sense given how, in the story, Khayyam becomes supposedly so angry at the person that swears at and wishes hell for the person—not something one would do and wish for one's elderly mother!

3. Why the Year Given in "Tarabkhaneh" for Khayyam Is Intended to Be, And Can Only Be, For 444 LH

In Tīrtha's shared image of the page of Rashidi Tabrizi's manuscript copy, one that I also provided earlier in Figure V.2 and magnified in Figure V.3, it can be clearly seen that, in this particular copy of the manuscript, the three digits for the year are the *same* digits. Noticing this is *very* important.

We are not in a position of directly judging how the digits are rendered in other manuscript copies of Tīrtha, nor in those studied by Homai or Golpinarli (as far as the year is concerned), since they have not shared actual images of them with their readers. However, in Golpinarli's (not his actual manuscript source's) rendition of the age for Khayyam in the manuscript he used as his source, he identified the age as either 58 or 52.

You can see in the image of Figure V.1 that I provided earlier of

Golpinarli's handwritten rendition of what he was seeing in his manuscript copy source, the digit for five is exactly the same as the three digits offered for the year in Tīrtha's Ha. manuscript as found in Figure V.2 and magnified in Figure V.3. Tīrtha himself reads the same-digited year in his source as 555. Homai also agrees with Golpinarli (in one of the places he mentions it) that the age given in his source is 52, so in his sources he must have also seen the same digit used for 5 as far as the age is concerned.

Homai, additionally, points out that these digits used were drawn from "Indian or Geometric" digit system used by scribes at the time (which was a correct guess, actually). Both Homai and Golpinarli must have seen the same digit used for X55 as two digits of the year given in their manuscripts, since they have an agreement that the year given in their source manuscript is the year 455.

Figure V.5

Old Indian Digits Corresponding Also to Abjad Alphabets, Indicating the Numerical Values of Single Digits (Top Rows), Double Digits (Middle Rows), and Triple Digits (Bottom Rows). (Source: http://www.jasoncolavito.com/ancient-alphabets-explained.html, Itself Drawing on the Book "Kitab Shawq al-Mustaham" (AD 863) by Ibn Wahshiyya)

In Tīrtha's source manuscript, however, the digit for the *decades* of the *age* given is markedly different from the digit 5 (which can be clearly seen in Tīrtha's source image as offered in Figures III.2 and III.3), which has obviously led Tīrtha to read the digits used for the age of Khayyam as 72, not 52. From the above, it is obvious that Tīrtha's manuscript copy is *very* different from the sources used by Homai and Golpinarli. In other words, we are facing a source that had not been seen or examined by Homai or Golpinarli and may be from a *completely different copying chain.*

In Figure V.5 I provide the image of an old Indian digit system that offers various signs for the single (first double-row, from right to left, 1, 2, 3, ..., 9), double (second double-row, from right to left, 10, 20, 30, ..., 90), and triple (third double-row, from right to left, 100, 200, 300, ..., 900, 1000) digit numbers. As is evident, the symbol used to represent the digit 5 (abjad letter ه , which is also written as ﮬ perhaps explaining its shape for the letter having the abjad numerical value of 5), is the same as the digit used in Tīrtha's source manuscript to represent the year 555 and in Golpinarli and Homai sources the first, decades, digit of the age (52). So, the judgments by Tīrtha, Homai, and Golpinarli, that the noted digit symbol represents the number 5 agree with this independent source listing the digit symbols in one (among three) old Indian digit systems.

You can see that in the Arabic, and in the old Indian, and many Persian style renderings of the digit four (even practiced to this day), we find a style that with a slight modification of "closing the loop," so to speak, of the digit four, it could be made into resembling the old Indian digit 5.

My reason for focusing on the shape of digits in the old Indian/Arabic/Persian language as shown in preceding figures is to draw the reader's attention not only to digit five, but also to digit 4, as can also be seen in Figure V.6.

	0	1	2	3	4	5	6	7	8	9
Arabic	٠	١	٢	٣	٤	٥	٦	٧	٨	٩
Persian	۰	۱	۲	۳	۴	۵	۶	۷	۸	۹

Figure V.6

Numbers from Zero to Nine (Left to Right Above) Rendered From Top to Bottom in English, Arabic, and Persian Language

In Figure V.7 I provide a comparative image of digits in Hindi (used in Arabic), Farsi (Persian), and Urdu digits (from 1 on the left to 2, 3, ..., to 9, and zero, moving to the right). Here you can see how even in the Hindi version, the digit four, if its loop is closed, could resemble the digit five in the old Indian style. The Persian 4 can resemble usually any of the three, depending on individual handwriting.

Hindi digits (used in Arabic):	١	٢	٣	٤	٥	٦	٧	٨	٩	٠
Farsi digits:	۱	۲	۳	۴	۵	۶	۷	۸	۹	۰
Urdu digits:	۱	۲	۳	۴	۵	۶	۷	۸	۹	۰

Figure V.7

Numbers From One to Zero (Left to Right) Rendered Above From Top to Bottom in Hindi/Arabic, Farsi, and Urdu Languages (Source: http://pubs.opengroup.org/onlinepubs/9638399/overview.htm)

In Figure V.8 I try to show how this "closing of the loop," so to speak, can happen. In handwriting, the variations of how rounded the letter 4 could be rendered can be wide. It may happen even that the two ends of letter four round out to come so close that it may readily resemble the closed loop, old-style digit 5 altogether. At times it may not be easy to decide which is which, so we end up with a manuscript scribe reading them as 555, and another as 445, because the first one was not closed-loop enough. This may in fact explain why some scribes read the date given as 555, and others as 455, when the actual intended date could have been 444, actually.

While we are considering the way the digits look, I draw the reader's attention to the digit seven also in Figure V.7 (i.e., the seventh digit from the left in either row, which can be also compared to the digit 7 column in Figure V.6). In Urdu, the digit seven looks like the digit seven turned clockwise 90 degrees. It is, so to speak, sideways, such that instead of the digit v in Arabic/Farsi, we have a sideways digit as shown for Urdu. Also, notice that the digit 2 is consistently rendered similarly across all the systems shared in the preceding figures.

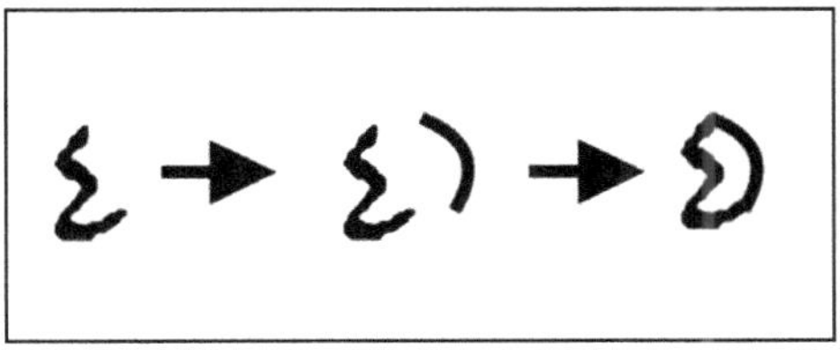

Figure V.8

How by Closing the Loop of Four, the Digit Can Be Made to Look Like Five In the Old Indian Style

My purpose in sharing the above at this point is to alert the reader to the possibilities of how, in the hands of scribes not paying too much attention to the subject matter of what they are scribing, since their job is just copying the manuscript and earn their livelihood, and for letters that have no inherent meaning (so that they cannot be ascertained at their face value to be rendered correctly or not) a digit four may appear like a five in the old Hindi/Urdu style.

I am not claiming *yet* that these speculations, in and of themselves, lead us to any conclusive determination of what the year of presumed "birth" as given in Rashidi Tabrizi's *Tarabkhaneh* is; I am just offering all the "probabilities" we need to consider in the quantum spirit of our research's method.

Let us now return to the date of birth given in *Tarabkhaneh.*

Homai, Golpinarli, and Tīrtha, all agree that the day and month given is Muharram 12th. I also agree that is what the text suggests (as I have circled on the right side of Figure V.3). Tīrtha thinks it is referring to a date of passing, others (and I) believe it is in reference to a birth date. But for now, let us set aside that difference.

We also all agree that the day of week is a Thursday, as it is obviously written in Arabic words. So, we must all agree that the year given should be one in which its Muharram 12th is a Thursday. Since the date is given in Arabic words, using a month in Arabic calendar, and the year (سنه) also precedes the year given, we all must also agree that the year given is based on the lunar Arabic calendar.

We all agree that the year 555 LH given by Rashidi Tabrizi cannot be so for a *death* date for Khayyam, let alone his birth. It is just impossible for either events. A few passages later, actually, Rashidi Tabrizi himself explicitly quotes the author (Nezami Arouzi, whose book is in his own handwriting reportedly for Tabrizi) as saying that he met Khayyam in Balkh in 512 LH, and three years later (or three years after a Hajj pilgrimage), upon visiting the area, found Khayyam had died. There has never been any claims or evidence that Khayyam could have died as late at 555 LH. Yar Ahmad Rashidi Tabrizi himself is not claiming it either. So, without having to draw conclusions as to the exact timing of when the "three years" end, we can safely conclude that it would be rather impossible that Nezami Arouzi could agree or be saying that Khayyam died in the year 555 LH.

Besides, Nezami Arouzi is quoted as saying that he found Khayyam had died and was buried in Neyshabour. So, the place name "Dehak" in Ostarabad that Rashidi Tabrizi offers in association with the date of Muharram 12th is not in reference to Khayyam's place of death, but must be intended also as indicating Khayyam's place of birth.

For a similar reason as above, it is impossible to consider that Rashidi Tabrizi would give a date of 555 LH as a date of *birth* for Khayyam. How could he, when he himself soon after quotes Nezami Arouzi as saying that Khayyam died three years or so after 512 LH, when he met him in Balkh?

So, without any doubts whatever, we are confronting an error on the part of the scribe(s) copying what source they had in front of them when copying the manuscript at some point down their chains.

Homai and Golpinarli read in their sources the digits for the year as 455 LH; it is even possible (as I think it does exist) that in another manuscript we find a scribe writing *in words* the year as "four hundred fifty five," spelled out (in Arabic, of course). Such a copy would not necessarily render any definitive proof that the intended year must have been 455. The scribe in *that* copy may have simply been writing in words the same date that he thought he was reading and appeared in digits in his source.

In Tīrtha's manuscript, which seems to be different from all other sources read by Homai and Golpinarli, the year is given in three *same* digits. Since we know it cannot be 555, nor 333, nor 666, nor any other digit that would fall in the same era during which Khayyam lived, and since it is moreover clear that he is intending to give a birth date for Khayyam, so it must fall in the fifth lunar century (400s), and for that there is only one possibility.

The year being given in Tīrtha's copy *must* have *undoubtedly* been, in the original source, 444 LH.

Indeed, online calendar conversion tools today indicate that Muharram 12th, 444 LH, was a Thursday. Homai had considered that year as a possibility for the year, when he said in that year Muharram 12th falls on a

Thursday. But according to his source, as in Golpinarli, the year given was not that indicated by three same digits, but by 455; so he did not entertain that possibility.

No one has claimed that the year given in any copy of the Rashidi Tabrizi manuscript is rendered in any digits other than 4 or 5. So, we have several, but limited, possibilities to consider, our criteria being in which of those years Muharram 12th fell on a Thursday.

In Table V.1, I provide a list of all such possibilities for the years—that is, 444, 445, 454, 455, 544, 545, 554, 555—using readily accessible online calendar conversion tools indicating on which day of the week Muharram 12th fell.

Table V.1

Various Combinations of Years in Lunar 400s and 500s With Digits 5 and/or 4, Indicating on Which Day of the Week Muharram 12th Fell

Year (LH)	Month	Day	Day of Week	Possibility
444	**Muharram**	**12**	**Thursday**	**The only exactly matching day**
445	Muharram	12	Tuesday	Ruled out
454	Muharram	12	Saturday	Ruled out
455	Muharram	12	Wednesday	One day from Thursday
544	Muharram	12	Sunday	Birth date in 500s ruled out
545	Muharram	12	Thursday	Birth date in 500s ruled out
554	Muharram	12	Tuesday	Birth date in 500s ruled out
555	Muharram	12	Saturday	Birth date in 500s ruled out

As can be seen in Table 6.1, the *only year* in lunar 400s with digits 4 and/or 5 in which Muharram 12th fell on a Thursday, was the year 444 LH. There is a possibility in the year 545 LH for the same, but all the years in lunar 500s can be absolutely ruled out as candidates for Khayyam's *birth* day, and no one ever has claimed that late year to be a year of death for Khayyam any ways.

Homai points out that it may be remotely possible that depending on when the Moon crescent is sighted, a day of difference before or after a Thursday may be introduced as a possibility. It is for this reason that he and Golpinarli regarded 455 LH as a possibility even though they knew Muharram 12th did not fall exactly on Thursday in that year, and in any case, they ruled out such a year as an error since it would make Khayyam to be too young to have undertaken a mature scholar's tasks in lunar 470s while still allegedly in his teens.

But then there is another obvious reason we could rule out 455 LH as a presumably intended date.

For Homai there is no question that the age given in Rashidi Tabrizi is 52. 52 plus 455 adds to the year 507 LH. Even if we say 52 is in solar years, it would add to 509 or 510 LH. Whether the age is considered lunar or solar it would *never* lead to a 512+3=515 date allegedly being given (at its face value) by Nezami Arouzi for Khayyam's date of passing.

This is where we can understand, though not necessarily accept, why Golpinarli finds himself reluctantly (while making his own typographical error as well) entertaining the possibility that the age given in Rashidi Tabrizi may be 58 (rather than 52) solar years, since this would mean 455 plus 58 solar years (that is, in his view, about 60 years) would add up to 515 LH.

In any case, both Homai and Golpinarli both agree that even the year 455 LH is too late a date for Khayyam's birth date. However, since in their manuscript copy sources they were not finding the year being given in three similar digits, they were not seriously entertaining the possibility of the year 444 LH as being Rashidi Tabrizi's originally intended date for Khayyam's birth date.

Tīrtha's manuscript copy source, however, is very different. The same three digits in the year does allow for the possibility, but, they are rendered in the digit for 5 not 4. This even confused Tīrtha, since it led him to readily dismiss the year as being about Khayyam's birth and considered that it could have been intended for giving Khayyam's date of demise, which he rejected as a possibility any ways.

But, Tīrtha's different copy inadvertently has offered us a completely different opportunity here.

Since we know that it is simply impossible to find any year with three same digits in lunar 400s other than 444 in which Muharram 12th falls on a Thursday—since this is literally *the only possible choice*, if we consider the same-three-digit version for the year apparent in Tīrtha's source copy—we are *necessarily* led to conclude that the scribes had difficulty in accurately reading the digits given in the sources they had available, so they were led to conclude that at least two or all three digits of 4 they were reading in their copy sources resembled what they were reading in their own time to be similar to the digit 5.

Recall that, for instance, Tīrtha's Ha. edition of *Tarabkhaneh* is copied and/or owned in Hyderabad in the lunar 890s (not too long after Rashidi Tabrizi himself wrote his work in 867 LH). The scribes were copying for an audience for which Hindi/Arabic/Persian digits (as I have shared in various figures previously) were natively used. Having difficulty in deciphering their originals, and, as scribes, not perfectly following what they were copying, they were led to believe that variously one or another digits of the year were five, and not four. In one copy, they wrote it down as 455, and in another they wrote it down as 555, when the author-intended year was, and *could only be*, 444 LH, were Muharram 12th to fall on a Thursday in it. But they did not have, like us today fortunately, an online calendar handy to check their choices right away so as to render their copy correctly.

Now, turning to the age given in the manuscript copy, Tīrtha, being Indian himself and native to the language in which these digits were used, has no doubt that the age given in his source manuscript of Rashidi Tabrizi for Khayyam is 72. The digit 2 is clearly that, and it matches the same digit in Muharram's date of 12th given in the same manuscript.

For the digit 7, various interpretations can be entertained.

In Figure V.3, inside the circle on the left, the age digit given for 7 can be considered (the lower part) to be a small sideways tilted 7 as found in the Urdu alphabet given in Figure V.7. The whole digit there can also be read as an "'Ein" (ع) which in the abjad alphabet would have the value of 70, as can be seen in the middle row of Hindi double-digits in Figure V.5.

It is also possible to consider that, since in the system in Figure V.5 the double-digitness of 7 (i.e., 70) is indicated by adding a superdot on top of the single digit, and if the scribe was Urdu script inclined to write the digit 7 as a sideways Arabic/Persian ۷ then one can see that a sideways 7 with a line on top could have been meant to suggest *seventy*, rather than seven, years (plus the two added next to it as two or ۲). It is certainly the case that the age given in Tīrtha's source is not a 52, nor a 58, because in his source the first digit does not resemble the digit 5 at all. So, what Tīrtha suggests is 72 for the age being attributed to Khayyam in his source, and I am in agreement with him on this.

Now, what is interesting is that, in Tīrtha's reading of the age as being 72, without his having made any claims or speculations of the year as being 444 LH—recall that he in fact clearly decided that the year given, mistakenly by the scribe, is 555 LH—leads us to come up with the nearly correct date for Nezami Arouzi's story of Khayyam having died three years or so after his meeting him in Balkh in 512. That is, the year 444 plus 72 years adds to 516. But note that the age Yar Ahmad Rashidi Tabrizi is stating is clearly qualified to be in *solar* years, and in the text itself Nezami Arouzi specifically says "solar" (شمسی); so, the age is meant to be *more than* 72 *lunar* years.

So, we have to now be more precise in our calculations.

If Tīrtha had noticed this, it would have certainly made him happy, since it would have offered support for his claim that Khayyam died in the year 516 LH or a year after, and not in 526 LH. But, Tīrtha's lack of such enthusiasm indicates that he did not even entertain the idea that Rashidi Tabrizi was giving the year 444 LH as Khayyam's date of birth. This is so, because Tīrtha, of course, had already claimed to have "discovered" Khayyam's birth date to have fallen in the year 439 LH (AD 1048), so he was not predisposed to entertain Tabrizi giving a birth date for Khayyam that would be at odds with Tīrtha's own claimed discovery of the birth date in the year 439 LH.

Tīrtha was so certain of his discovery that he did not even entertain the fact that Muharram 12th in the year 439 would actually fall on a Thursday, which would have certainly made him at the same time happy, and not so happy, since his own "discovered" date of May 18 (Julian) AD 1048 actually does not fall on Muharram 12th, nor a Thursday, but on the 1st of Dhul-Hajjeh, a Wednesday.

In any case, none of these really mattered since Tīrtha had already decided on what Khayyam's birth date is, and used the opportunity of mistaken attribution of Rashidi Tabrizi's date to Khayyam's demise as a way of finding some use for Muharram 12, which he then arbitrarily applied to his 516 LH date for Khayyam's death, leading all subsequent scholars astray such that now, quite unreasonably and laughably, and not really befitting a genius mathematician and astronomer and calendar reformer that was Khayyam, the consensus date of Khayyam's death has become Muharram 12th, applied also erroneously by others to the year 526 LH, resulting on a further erroneous date of passing for Khayyam as Dec. 11 (Gregorian) or Dec. 4 (Julian), AD 1131, in *winter*. *Winter* is usually long past the season of fruit-tree blossoms falling.

4. Solving the Puzzle of Omar Khayyam's Year, Season, and Month of Passing By Way of Superposing All the Accounts: The Difference the Apricot and Pear Blossoms Make

In what follows, I will share how I discovered a reliable, definitive solution to the puzzle of Omar Khayyam's date of passing, not only for its year, season, and month, but even to its day (narrowable even to the part of day), as far as the most reliable past accounts are concerned.

My discovery is textually reliable and evidence-based and integrates all the seemingly disparate accounts surrounding Khayyam's date of passing into a coherent solution, one that is certainly more defensible than the definitively inaccurate uneasy consensus date of passing currently considered for him.

To explain the method in its broadest terms, I accomplished this by way of "superposing" ("intersecting" or "overlapping") the many seemingly separate stories about his passing. The reason I prefer the quantum term "superposition" (as explained in the first book of this series) to the other two above is that the latter two imply an inherent separation to begin with. However, since the various stories are actually of the *same* event, such separations are regarded as not inherent in the event itself, but of how the stories became over time told by a variety of sources, at times corrupted by scribes, losing their integrity in the historical chatter, so to speak. The solution is possible because the superposition of the various stories, cleared of their fragmentations, allows us to narrow down the date of Khayyam's passing to the remarkably specific margin of a specific day, even to its part.

Before I proceed, I wish to remind readers again why the currently held uneasy consensus date for Khayyam's passing is itself a completely unreliable myth that is certainly not sound textual basis. So, if you wish to be skeptical about what I am about to offer as a solution, it makes sense to first become so regarding the uneasy consensus date held today for Khayyam's passing.

The currently held date of Khayyam's passing, that is, Muharram 12th, 516 LH (per Tīrtha, convertible into the Christian Gregorian calendar date March 30, AD 1122) or 526 LH (convertible into the Christian Gregorian calendar date Dec. 11, AD 1131, which is mistakenly considered as Dec. 4 Gregorian these days) were completely nonsensical and arbitrarily made as far as its month and day are concerned. "Muharram 12th" simply resulted from a misreading by Tīrtha of a birth date given by a source (*Tarabkhaneh*) for Khayyam as his date of passing. So, while the years of the date being given (555 LH) was obviously wrong to begin with for either Khayyam's birth or passing, Tīrtha (and later others) basically said, "well, why not use the month and day for Khayyam's passing, any way." And they did so, leading us to be now stuck with that wrong date for Khayyam's passing.

I have already explained this matter before, so do not wish to take more space and your time for it. But the point here is to remind the reader that what is now widely announced and reported online or even in scholarly literature about the month and day beside the year of Khayyam's passing (Dec. 4, AD 1131, which should actually be Dec. 11 Gregorian) is itself an arbitrary construction based on that tagged along "Muharram 12" and not even based on any reasonable textual evidence.

In contrast, what I will offer as a solution will be entirely based on the superposition of a variety of most reliable manuscript evidence reporting the events surrounding Khayyam's passing, and the result is in fact remarkably narrowable while being textually reliable. We do not have any other source to rely on regarding Khayyam's date of passing other than such sources, and my effort will offer the most defensible solution to date that integratively coheres the various fragments of the stories shared by all observers (oddly, as we shall see, including Khayyam's himself, by the way, on the day he died).

As I did before regarding the discovery of Khayyam's date of birth, I will first try to arrive at a solution based on available textual clues. I will then try to reconsider various points of view hitherto surveyed in order to synthesize a new consensus perspective that not only agrees with the solution found, but also explains the diversity of viewpoints that have one way or another been expressed over the centuries regarding Khayyam's date of passing.

Let us then turn to our main second purpose in this book, that is, finding the date of passing of Omar Khayyam as exactly as possible based on currently available sources at hand.

We know of course that Rashidi Tabrizi's offered date, Thursday, Muharram 12th, year 444 LH, for Khayyam's birth is not accurate in and of itself, since we know ourselves independently that it is not correct—given our own discovery earlier in this book of Khayyam's true date of Birth on Safar 19, 412 LH, or, June 10, AD 1021 Gregorian, or Khordad 20, 502 SH.

The horoscope for Muharram 12, 444 LH (that is May 20, AD 1052 Gregorian, which is the same for May 14 that year in the Julian calendar) does not at all satisfy Khayyam's horoscope conditions as given in Beyhaqi—there are simply no times[14] in May of that year where the Sun and the Mercury are

---

14. See the ephemeris data for that date and entire month here: http://www.astro.com/swisseph/ae50/ae__50_1050.pdf.

anywhere close to 16 minutes Samimi (Cazimi) with one another. Besides, Jupiter is near Mercury in the next house, and not five houses away.

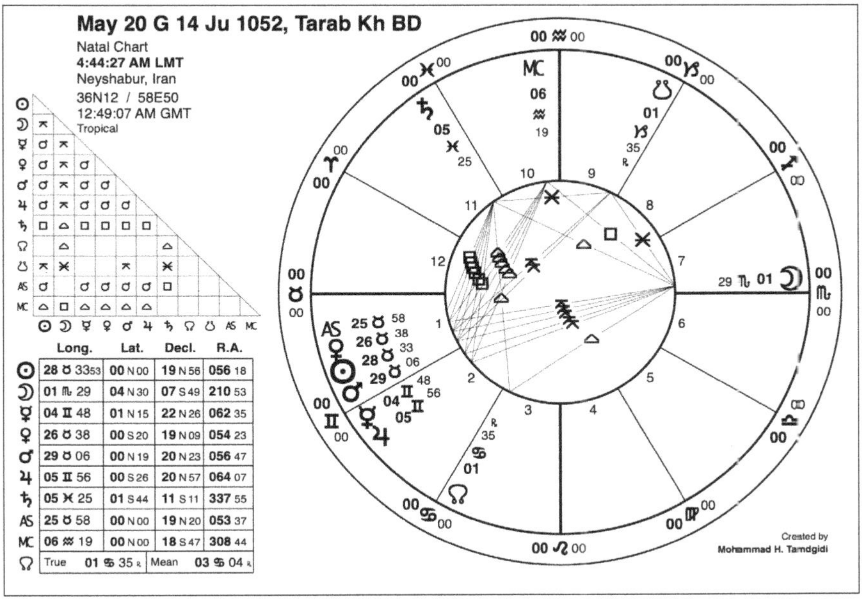

Figure V.9

The Birth Chart for the Erroneous Birth Date Given for Khayyam in Tabrizi's *Tarabkhaneh (House of Joy)*, Provided for Muharram 12, 444 LH (May 20 Gregorian, or May 14 Julian, AD 1052)

I am providing a birth chart or horoscope for that date in Figure V.9, set arbitrarily for the early morning sunrise time. While the chart clearly shows it does not fulfill *at all* the requirements of Khayyam's true horoscope as provided by Beyhaqi, the chart is actually quite interesting and significant in another way. It shows a date that is Taurus ascendent, with Venus being in Taurus, which is a Sharaf (Exalted) constellation for it.

This chart provides clear and further evidence not only for the fact that Yar Ahmad Rashidi Tabrizi meant Muharram 12, 444 LH, to be a birth date for Khayyam (erroneously, of course), but actually explains why he offered Taurus as Khayyam's ascendant and why in his account for Khayyam's horoscope Venus is an exalted location in Taurus.

Therefore, we have not only verified what date of birth Tabrizi was, erroneously, offering for Khayyam, but also learned why he was giving a Taurus ascendant for Khayyam, in the sense that he came up with that horoscope by simply consulting an astrologer to see what Khayyam's chart would look like for that date. Interestingly, he finds that Venus is exalted and finds it significant to report, because Venus in astrology represents joy and happiness, music, and poetry, which is what Yar Ahmad Rashidi Tabrizi's *Tarabkhaneh (House of Joy)* is about in reporting Khayyam's life and poetry. The (wrong) horoscope further confirmed for him that somehow poetry and music and happiness had a prominent astrological significance for Khayyam.

While he was wrong in terms of the birth date and chart given for Khayyam, however, as we shall see, and as we can even see in prior true birth charts provided for Khayyam (see Figure II.5 in this book's previous Chapter II), Venus is *indeed even there* in an exalted, Sharaf, location in Taurus. So, the coincidence is telling of how we may ourselves, hermeneutically, know more about how Khayyam *himself* may have interpreted his own chart based on the standard medieval astrological system prevalent at the time, in which he himself, as a believer or not, was certainly an expert.

We may even ask ourselves how did Yar Ahmad Rashidi Tabrizi himself come up with his proposed (erroneous) date for Khayyam's birth date, 444 LH, related to which he then also suggested a horoscope including Taurus ascendance and Venus exaltation?

My answer to the above is that given there is no mention or even apparent knowledge by Yar Ahmad Rashidi Tabrizi of Khayyam's Beyhaqi-reported horoscope in Gemini, with the date not being even explicated there, he must have been perhaps trying to speculate on his own regarding the date and its horoscope, possibly working the timeline "backward," so to speak, from a date widely and matter-of-factly known to be Khayyam's year of passing, that is, 517 LH. The age of 72 years may have even be drawn speculatively from some of the quatrains he lists for Khayyam in the book, in one of which the composer says he has reached his seventy, and making it solar, it would be about seventy-two.

It may be speculative for us to wonder, beyond the above, about where Yar Ahmad Rashidi Tabrizi obtained his version of Khayyam's date of birth and its supposed horoscope, but interesting for us are certain assumptions in his account that are telling of when he assumed Khayyam *must have died*. What follows will also shed some light on why I suggest the above.

Let us go back to our task at hand, then, of discovering for ourselves when more exactly Khayyam passed away.

Why is the information given in Rashidi Tabrizi important for our purpose of finding Khayyam's date of passing, even though we know the date of birth given in his text is actually wrong, as is also the same his given age?

The significance of the whole matter is this.

Rashidi Tabrizi does not himself straightforwardly give a date for Khayyam's death. But it is possible to assume that he knew the exact year, at least, based on a combination of what Nezami Arouzi was offering in his story, and his own view of what his date of birth and age at death were.

What makes this rather an interesting lead to follow is Rashidi Tabrizi's being very explicit and specific in mentioning the age given as being 72 *solar* years; he makes sure to included the word *shamsi* (i.e., solar, that is شمسی) in the text.

Why would he qualify it as such, other than due to trying implicitly in his own mental calculations to be accurate with his dates as far as the intersection of his own proposed birth date and Nezami Arouzi's projected death date for Khayyam was concerned?

Lunar 444 plus 72 *lunar* years gives you the lunar year 516. But Lunar 444 plus 72 *solar* years gives you a *later* date, since the solar year is longer than a lunar year. He wanted to make sure his reader does not conclude from his writing that Khayyam died in the year 516 LH, but *after*.

In other words, Rashidi Tabrizi, by emphasizing in passing the "solar" counting of the age, must have been trying to direct his readers not to make an off-hand error in assuming that Khayyam died either in 515 or in 516. For him, as it should be for us (as we find the year date 517 LH on Khayyam's tombstone even today, for instance, and as we find in most old historical records), the date of Khayyam's date falling in the year 517 LH was undisputed and may have been so obvious and taken for granted that Tabrizi did not even feel the need for mentioning it directly. So, in his mind, by adding "shamsi" (that is, "solar") he just wanted to make sure his readers add the numbers being given (444 LH plus 72) correctly, with 72 being considered in *solar* values, to lead them to what he presumed all knew, the year 517 LH, *not* 515 LH, *nor* 516 LH, to be Khayyam's year of passing.

Remember that Khayyam's birth was being reported by him in the twelfth day of the first month of the lunar calendar (Muharram), so almost all of that year counts as a year in counting the age. So, Rashidi Tabrizi's text offers us, whether he intended it as such or not, a very interesting puzzle to solve in order to arrive at a solution that meets the requirements of both *his* (wrong) birth date for Khayyam and Nezami Arouzi's story, along with those of other accounts.

Let us first consider the implications of the above, for ourselves, in solar calendar. Of course Yar Ahmad Rashidi Tabrizi must have been considering this within a lunar calendar environment, while being aware of the Persian solar year time-span of Khayyam's (erroneous) age being given. But we will consider the lunar Islamic calendar as well, as needed.

If we consider the above in solar calendar, we can proceed as follows.

If Khayyam is (supposedly of course) considered to have been born on Muharram 12, 444 LH per *Tarabkhaneh*, that would correspond to May 20, AD 1052 (Gregorian). This means that 72 *solar* years from then would *end*, that is, would be completed nominally, on May 20, AD 1124.

When we say Khayyam aged 72 *solar* years, what does this exactly mean? When does that "72" begin and when does it end (since obviously being 72 in age is not just a day, or a month, but extends for a year)?

It means we have a year's *entire margin*, not just a single day or month, to consider for his being 72, for having reached 72, and for when he could have died.

When you turn sixty one, you turn sixty one the day after the end of your sixtieth year, and you remain sixty one, technically speaking, until the last day of your sixty first year. A baby born on a certain date, remains for one year in his or her *first* year and the day following his or her first birth day, enter his or her *second* year. So, someone who turns 72, remains 72 for a year from its first day to its last day, 72 ending on that last day, when he turns into his 73rd year of age.

So, even just supposing the above (erroneous) birth date, Khayyam completed being 1 solar year old on May 20, AD 1053, completed being 2 solar years old on May 20, AD 1054, and so on, completing being 72 solar years on May 19, AD 1124. The day after that (on May 20, AD 1124), he would have entered his 73rd year of age.

So, Khayyam being 72 solar years means he was so, nominally, from May 20, AD 1123 to May 19, AD 1124 during which he could claim to be more or less 72 years old. Since we are speaking of nominal years rather than including strict leap days, we can just consider the above time span to be the year during which Khayyam was nominally 72 solar years old.

To avoid detailed calculations of conversions from the two solar and the one lunar calendars to one another including the leap years involved, and so on, I will just note the lunar and Persian solar equivalents of the above 72

Christian solar year old range in Set A below.

Set A:

Solar Christian Gregorian: May 20, 1123 - May 19, 1124

Lunar Islamic: Rabi ol-Awwal 15, 517 - Rabi ol-Awwal 25, 518

Solar Persian Islamic: Ordibehesht 29, 502 - Ordibehesht 29, 503

So, first of all, we have now, from the point of view of Rashidi Tabrizi, definitively ruled out the possibility that Khayyam's passing could have happened either in 515 LH or 516 LH. This is itself a significant finding. There is no doubt now that Yar Ahmad Rashidi Tabrizi could not have meant either the years 515 LH or 516 LH to be Khayyam's year of passing.

Note that Tabrizi could have easily revised his date for Khayyam's birth or age given to match that of Nezami Arouzi, by saying Khayyam lived 72 *lunar* years. If so, Muharram 12th, 444 LH, plus 72 lunar years could have given us Muharram 12th, 516 LH, which would have been the end point of Khayyam's 72nd year of age, meaning that, given Muharram is the first month of the lunar year, we had nearly the whole of previous year, 515 LH, to consider as having been the year of Khayyam's passing, and this easily could have been patched up with Nezami Arouzi's 512 plus 3 years (following return from Hajj) to give us 515 as Khayyam' date of birth.

But Rashidi Tabrizi for good reasons did not do so and for this he must be credited, I think, despite any other shortcomings his book on Khayyam may have had (which can be considered in the same way regarding any other of our old sources, by the way). Since Tabrizi must have had the year 517 LH in mind all along without explicating it, intended or not, he made it a bit more interesting and complicated for us, though, by noting only that the age must be considered in solar and not in lunar years.

Tabrizi was giving us a strong hint not to make an error of considering either 515 or 516 LH as Khayyam's date of death. In his view, in other words, also, as all older information about Khayyam's date of passing handed down in historical timeline, there was no question that Khayyam died after 516 LH. It was simply a matter of common knowledge that Khayyam had died in 517 LH, as even today can be found on his grave, so he wanted to make sure that by inserting the word "solar" for the age, we would end up with that year for our Khayyam. It is true that the 72 solar year calculation leaves open the possibility of the year 518 LH for Khayyam's passing, but we will find other textually reliable ways of ruling that out also.

So, again, this is a significant discovery as far as the implications of

Rashidi Tabrizi's account and view regarding Khayyam's date of passing is concerned. I want to reiterate again that his account basically rules out the years 515 LH and 516 LH as possible years of passing for Omar Khayyam, bringing him into the circle of all sources that can validate 517 LH as the year of Khayyam's passing as traditionally considered in old times.

Just a side note to add here, even if we consider 517 LH to be the year, we cannot say yet it is AD 1123 or 1124, since the lunar calendar year falls partly on both Christian solar years. We know of course the local population were not giving birth or death dates in Western Christian calendars. So, it is possible to consider that when trying to offer a Western calendar equivalent, Western scholars reading in old texts that Khayyam died in the year 517 LH, they simply assumed that it fell in AD 1123, and not AD 1124 also, giving the former as Khayyam's date of passing, instead of the latter. While such a possibility is worth keeping in mind, if we were to follow the locally specific 517 LH as Khayyam's year of passing, we would have the following range in Set B to superpose various accounts with (note that the lunar calendar is few days shorter, so converted solar year periods are shorter):

Set B:

Solar Christian Gregorian: March 8, AD 1123 - February 25, AD 1124

Lunar Islamic: Muharram 1, 517 - Dhu al-Hijjah 30, 517 LH

Solar Persian Islamic: Esfand 16, 501 - Esfand 5, 502 SH

If we compare the above two sets A and B of three calendar dates, given the year 517 LH time-span narrows down further the first set of dates during which Khayyam could have been in his supposed 72nd year of age, we will have the slightly shorter ranges in Set C below (eliminating the part of lunar year in 518 LH, basically).

Set C:

Lunar Islamic: Rabi ol-Awwal 15, 517 - Dhu al-Hijjah 30, 517

Solar Christian Gregorian: May 20, 1123 - February 25, 1124

Solar Persian Islamic: Ordibehesht 29, 502 - Esfand 5, 502

Although we have, in my view, perfectly legitimate justification to consider historical tradition of considering only 517 LH for Khayyam's year of passing (after all, Khayyam's tombstone even sets the date in the year 517 LH, as most reliable old historical records do), let us just leave the above Set C for now, and turn to Nezami Arouzi's story, for there I will show that there is another textually-reliable way, a second route, to narrow down Khayyam's year of passing to only the year 517 LH, independently confirming that the year 517 is indeed the year of Khayyam's passing.

Let me show how that can indeed be done.

First, we should not take lightly and keep in mind that Rashidi Tabrizi explicitly notes that he himself had read a manuscript of *Chahar Maqaleh* in Nezami Arouzi's *own* handwriting.

This is highly significant since it is telling us how far we should hold the 512 LH account of Khayyam's meeting with Nezami Arouzi (in the presence of al-Asfezari) as the most reliable compared to the 506 LH meeting time reported in other popularized versions of his story. Tīrtha has noted that the error from 506 LH to 516 LH may have resulted from using contracted Arabic, or Siaq, symbols for the dates given, so scribes may have simply mistaken one date for another.

But, Nezami Arouzi may have even met Khayyam in 506 LH also. But the same source also places Nezami Arouzi in Neyshabour in 512 LH, and that is significant, and the hand-written Nezami Arouzi manuscript Tabrizi is quoting from in his *Tarabkhaneh (House of Joy)* clearly and elaborately reports significant events for the meeting held on 512 LH and its thereafter.

In other words, we are specifically being told by an author, Yar Ahmad Rashidi Tabrizi, that he had seen and was relaying the original author written text, avoiding the mediation of copying scribes. We must again be grateful for Yar Ahmad Rashidi Tabrizi making that clear for us. He did not have to, but he did, in effect trying to tell us something like, "trust me, I saw it in Nezami Arouzi's *own handwriting.*"

According to Nezami Arouzi as found in Rashidi Tabrizi (one that is also shared in Tīrtha's manuscript copy), Nezami says he visited Khayyam in 512 LH, in the presence of his old friend al-Asfezari and others, in a happy and joyful gathering, in order to ask for his permission/blessing to go to Mecca for Hajj. Nezami says that amid the conversation Khayyam oddly tells him that upon Nezami Arouzi's return from Hajj he would find Khayyam passed away, buried in a grave that is covered with blossoms shed, reportedly according to some manuscripts, twice a year.

Tīrtha had made good sense in noting that it would be odd for someone like Nezami Arouzi, so revering of Khayyam, to be uninformed of Khayyam's death for four years, let alone fourteen years. According to Yar Ahmad Rashidi Tabrizi, Nezami Arouzi had wondered about Khayyam's "prediction" of his death after returning from his pilgrimage, but did not actually know that he had died. He came to visit him "three years later," finding out that Khayyam had just passed away, perhaps 9-10 days earlier, given the conversation with the "white-haired elderly." So, this story as related by Yar Ahmad Rashidi Tabrizi makes much more sense.

Now, let us pause at something very important here, which may also provide another hint at the 512 LH meeting version of the account as being more authentic than other accounts.

Although I mentioned this previously, let us ask this question.

What was the happy and joyful (مجلس عشرت) gathering about in 512 LH? Why was Khayyam talking about death and his grave in that gathering, and in what month or on what (even) day, roughly may we wonder that meeting in 512 LH was taking place?

If we follow Tīrtha's (and current consensus's erroneous) date for Khayyam's birth as having taken place on May 18 (Julian) or 24 (Gregorian), AD 1048, which corresponds to Wednesday, Dhu al-Hijjah 1st, 439 LH, Khayyam would be about 73 lunar years old in the year 512 LH (and even less in solar years). "Not a big deal, really," we may say. Why would Khayyam be thinking and talking about death on a happy occasion, at such a still relatively young advanced age, especially for someone so treasuring life, a physician generally still in good health? Well, the reason is as follows.

In 512 LH, more exactly on Safar 19th of that year, Khayyam became, in the *lunar* calendar, 100 years old—both a sweet and a bitter occasion. Sweet, because he made it to his lunar 100th year; bitter or sad, because he was nearer to his demise, he must have thought, for which he must have been preparing and about whose grave's location he may have been speculating. We may even consider astrological speculations he may have made about his date of demise, but I will explore that question in the next book of the series.

The meeting in Balkh may have *actually happened* on that anniversary day, that is, on Safar 19th, 512 LH. Why celebrate it on any other day of that year? Nezami Arouzi's account actually is telling of a joyful gathering (مجلس عشرت). Why would one celebrate an anniversary on any day other than the anniversary day, especially if it marks one's hundredth (lunar) birth date?

As a reformer of the Persian solar calendar, Khayyam would of course be happier if he had become 100 *solar* years old, but he was not there yet (being at the time about 97 solar years old); so he was still a few, about three years, short. And could not for sure know, of course, whether he was going to make it or not to his solar 100th, so was speculating about a possibly impending death in the following few years, and preparing for it.

But still, this was a turning point and marker of age for him, and certainly a cause for celebration, with an old friend (al-Asfezari) and younger one, Nezami Arouzi, who respected Khayyam as a teacher, and was there for another reason most likely, that of seeking blessings for his pilgrimage to Mecca, and may not have even known Khayyam reached 100 lunar years old, given Khayyam was inclined to keep such personal things to himself. At least Khayyam (along with his old friend al-Asfezari, perhaps one of his oldest surviving confidants) knew the turning point year had arrived, in lunar terms at least.

Having been born on Safar 19, 412 LH, which falls amid the second month of the lunar calendar, plenty of time remains in the 512 lunar year for a centenarian to celebrate his lunar anniversary, so if the gathering was taking place then for that occasion, it could have been held anytime that year. However, I think it is quite plausible to consider that the meeting was in fact taking place on Safar 19, 512 LH in Balkh, as I noted earlier.

So, let us proceed further with the story.

Nezami Arouzi tells us that he was visiting Khayyam to receive his permission/blessing to go to Mecca for the Hajj pilgrimage. We of course do not know exactly when in 512 LH he was visiting Khayyam, and are just considering the above most plausible anniversary day.

Nor do we know if Nezami Arouzi's planned pilgrimage to Mecca was to take place in that same year (512 LH) or, if this meeting was taking place in the last month or so of 512. We may assume that he was planning his pilgrimage not for the end of 512 LH, but for the end of 513 LH (though most likely not later than that, of course, as Nezami Arouzi seemed to be already planning the trip), given that Hajj takes place in the last month of lunar calendar.

Nezami Arouzi says he was asking Khayyam for permission, which is perhaps a polite way of asking for his blessing, or spiritual or even material support for the journey ahead at that time. So, he may not have yet actually planned the trip, but was looking forward to planning it in a near future.

Iranian scholar Qazvini, in his introduction to *Chahar Maqaleh*, says that based on his reading of the text, despite all the errors involved, he could set up a chronology of where Nezami Arouzi was at different times. He says Nezami saw Khayyam in 506 LH in Balkh (based on the conventional manuscripts of *Chahar Maqaleh*, of course), and then he was in Neyshabour in 512 LH, and was around that area for a few years. There is no stories in the book about Nezami Arouzi going for Hajj, but this does not mean it did not happen; nor does this mean he did not visit Balkh again in 512 LH. The book does not intend to offer a chronology of all the events in Nezami Arouzi's own life. Besides, we should also recognize here that Qazvini was not basing his chronology on Rashidi Tabrizi's account of *Chahar Maqaleh* but on what he was reading in the conventional more recently made available text of *Chahar Maqaleh*.

So, it is possible that following his meeting with Khayyam in 512 LH in Balkh, Nezami Arouzi was still around Neyshabour planning his Mecca pilgrimage for a while, then heading to Mecca. Upon return, he did not go to visit Khayyam immediately, but returned three years after, which could mean either three years after the meeting in 512 LH or three years after his return from Mecca.

From what I have gathered about traveling time for Hajj, on foot with caravans, in those times, it could take at least 2 months, if not more, to reach Mecca, and the same time span to return. We simply do not know how long it could have taken for Nezami Arouzi to plan and conduct the journey, and exactly when. It certainly was a major undertaking, some pilgrims even perishing in the course of travel given the hazards, which is perhaps one reason why Nezami Arouzi was seeking Khayyam's blessings before his planned trip.

Pilgrimage happens in the last month of the lunar month (Dhu al-Hijjah). So, if Nezami Arouzi was heading to Mecca that year in 512 LH, the original meeting with Khayyam could have taken place sometime early or mid year in 512 LH, either before or after Ramadan, and likely not in Ramadan.

From the end of Ramadan, there is about two month interval to embark on the difficult 2 month journey to Mecca. There being no mention of any month or specifically Ramadan in Nezami Arouzi's story of 512 LH, it is possible that the meeting with Khayyam took place sometime before the Ramadan of that year, but most likely not in the month of Ramadan itself. But all this could be considered for the year 513 also, that is, if Nezami Arouzi's pilgrimage took place in the last month of 513 LH.

Given the active blessing or support Nezami Arouzi was seeking from Khayyam in 512 LH, it is highly unlikely to consider his pilgrimage to have been planned for anytime later than at most the following year (late 513 LH), if not in that same year (late 512 LH).

In any case, when Khayyam tells Nezami Arouzi that upon return he would find him passed away, it is clear that such a return from Mecca would not be in the year 512 LH (even if undertaken in late 512 LH), nor in the year 513 if undertaken in late 513 LH, but in the year following each of those years respectively—in 513 LH or 514 LH. If we allow at least 2 months for the return journey after the Hajj season, we should be considering the third month (Rabi ul-awwal) of either 513 LH or 514 LH as being the earliest month Nezami Arouzi would give Khayyam a visit again upon return.

However, Nezami tells us that he could not return immediately but only three years later. So, we can plausibly consider the three years he speaks of as beginning not from when he met Khayyam in 512 LH, but from when he was supposed to return in 513 LH or 514 LH after his Meccan pilgrimage. So, the earliest date he would be back from Mecca (not necessarily in terms of his visit to Neyshabour) in 513 LH or 514 LH would be in the third month of one of those years.

When Nezami Arouzi said he returned in three years from when he (and Khayyam) presumed he was originally going to return, we are speaking of a period starting from Rabi ol-Awwal of 513 LH or Rabi ol-Awwal of 514 LH (depending on when Nezami Arouzi undertook the pilgrimage in the same year of his meeting with Khayyam, or the following year).

Three years from either date, depending on when we consider the Hajj travel to have taken place, would fall around the third month of either 516 LH (if he returned in early 513 LH) or 517 LH (if he returned in early 514 LH). Given the roughly "three year" interval and 512 LH meeting time Nezami Arouzi offers in his story as reported in *Tarabkhaneh*, it is nearly impossible to assume that he could have taken the pilgrimage in late 514 LH, returning in early 515 LH, when counting his three years from then would fall in the year 518 LH.

Let us consider various possibilities of the three years, for now ignoring the lunar or solar time span of those three years (for three years, a month's length difference can be considered).

1. Dhu al-Hijjah 30, 512 LH (if considered from the time of meeting with Khayyam any time by the end of 512 LH) + 3 years = Dhu al-Hijjah 30, 515 LH

2. Rabi ol-Awwal 30, 513 LH (if considered from the time of return from Hajj undertaken in late 512 LH) + 3 years = Rabi ol-Awwal 30, 516 LH

3. Rabi ol-Awwal 30, 514 LH (if considered from the time of return from Hajj undertaken in late 513 LH) + 3 years = Rabi ol-Awwal 30, 517 LH

4. Rabi ol-Awwal 30, 515 LH (if considered from the time of return from Hajj undertaken in late 514 LH) + 3 years = Rabi ol-Awwal 30, 518 LH

5. Dhu al-Hijjah 30, 515 LH (if considered from the time of return from Hajj undertaken in late 514 LH) + 3 years = Dhu al-Hijjah 30, 518 LH

In the above options, we can observe the following.

Option 1 can now be ruled out, since the time of return does not fall in a period fulfilling Khayyam's 72 solar year age requirement. So, Nezami Arouzi's saying that he returned "three years after" to find Khayyam having just (recently) died, as evident in his report, *could not have been meant* in terms of its having taken place three years after his *meeting* with Khayyam, even if that meeting took place on the very last day of the year 512 LH.

Yar Ahmad Rashidi Tabrizi was quoting and reading Nezami Arouzi, so he must have been also assuming that what he himself was offering in terms of timeline was not in conflict with what Nezami Arouzi was reporting. Tabrizi could not make the "solar" 72 year qualification, in other words, while reporting (by way of Nezami Arouzi) that three years after a meeting (anytime) in 512 LH, Nezami Arouzi found Khayyam had died, since that meant he returned in the years 515 LH, and this would violate Yar Ahmad Rashidi Tabrizi's own 72 solar years age rule for Khayyam.

Options 2 can also be ruled out, since Nezami Arouzi's return from Mecca and visiting Khayyam would have ended up at a time (during 516 LH) Khayyam's age would fall outside the range of 517-518 LH range I calculated earlier, during which Khayyam would be considered in his 72nd year of solar age.

Option 5 can also be ruled out. If Nezami Arouzi took his trip as late as the ending Hajj month of 514 LH, meaning he returned anytime after the third month of 518 LH to visit Khayyam finding him passed away, this would mean Khayyam had died past his 72 solar years age, that is, when he had entered the age of 73.

So, from the above we can tentatively conclude that after his meeting with Khayyam in 512 LH, which could have taken place any time that year (though, in my view it happened most likely on Safar 19, on Khayyam's 100th lunar birthday anniversary), Nezami Arouzi did *not* embark on pilgrimage that year in late 512 LH, but did so at the end of the following lunar year, that is in late 513 LH. That is also why, as Qazvini observed in his chronology, he was around Neyshabour for a while.

So, Nezami returned sometime around the third month of 514 LH (assuming it took him two months to return from Hajj in late 513 LH). Three years after 514 LH around that month, he says, he went to visit Khayyam, finding him just passed away.

So the range of possibilities could be any time from Rabi ol-Awwal 517 LH (option 3) to Rabi ol-Awwal 518 LH (option 4).

The above range coincides with the range I previously calculated for the time Khayyam could claim to be during his 72 solar years age. I provide the ranges again across the calendars (Set A):

Set A:

Solar Christian Gregorian: May 20, 1123 - May 19, 1124

Lunar Islamic: Rabi ol-Awwal 15, 517 - Rabi ol-Awwal 25, 518

Solar Persian Islamic: Ordibehesht 29, 502 - Ordibehesht 29, 503

The question for us to answer now is the following.

Did Khayyam, according to Rashidi Tabrizi, and the story he reported from Nezami Arouzi's own handwritten manuscript, die toward the beginning, mid way, or toward the end of that period's margin when he could be technically said to be still in his 72nd solar year of age?

To find a textually reliable answer for this, rather than simply assuming (based on historical tradition that report Khayyam having died in the year 517 LH), let us turn to another important aspect of Nezami Arouzi's account, one that has become famous and widely entertained and celebrated.

The reader has probably heard the blossoms on Khayyam's grave story so many times, including in this book, that by now he or she must be getting tired of it. Well, I am sorry to say that I will have to return to it again for another wonderful reason that has never been considered before, one that perhaps Khayyam wished, for one reason or another, Nezami Arouzi and now us, to keep in mind. Otherwise, why, as Nezami Arouzi, someone of his stature would make such an odd "prediction"?

In his story of returning to visit Khayyam after three years, Nezami Arouzi wrote that he returned, while keeping in mind what Khayyam had told him in 512 LH, that he would find Khayyam passed away and buried as described. He was hoping that Khayyam's saying had not come true. But, it must have been on his mind, since he had thought it odd for someone like Khayyam to offer such a "prediction."

Nezami writes he arrived in Ostarabad to visit Khayyam's house (which he seems to imply), but heard that he had left for Neyshabour. Going to Neyshabour right away, he sadly learned that Khayyam had passed away just about that time, using an expression (همین ولا) that indicates the passing and burial had very recently just taken place, perhaps within ten days or so (given the tale he hears from a "white-haired elderly), and was buried in his previously described grave. In Islam burial immediately follows passing, so there is no reason to doubt that Khayyam having just been buried meant he had also just passed a day or so earlier.

If Nezami Arouzi was returning three year after when he returned from Mecca, it would have been around the third month of the lunar year 517 LH (falling in the month of May that year, AD 1123, around the second month of solar Persian calendar, Ordibehesht) or later. Being in that month or soon later can make a difference for us. So, let us pay closer attention here.

Nezami Arouzi must have visited Khayyam's grave sometime into late Spring and early Summer, local season's time, in other words, finding that it was covered with *already shed* blossoms/flowers on the ground from trees already fruitful. Blossoms being shed, fruit trees full, tells us that Khayyam must have *died and been buried in late Spring or early summer of that year.*

Being poetic as he was (at least in regard to the grave, let us say for now), of course Khayyam must have chosen a site which would be befitting him, covered with shed blossoms. So, why not choose a site which would be covered with blossoms even more, say, twice a year?

How? By being adjacent to trees of pears *and* apricots, as told by Nezami Arouzi. In other words, whether or not we consider the manuscript accounts which tell of the blossoms covering Khayyam's grave once or twice a year, Nezami Arouzi's classic account speaks of *two kinds* of blossoms.

Apricot trees tend to shed their blossoms the earliest, pear trees doing so later. In Iran, the time for harvesting apricot is from late Khordad (around June 10) to mid Mordad (August 10), and for pear, the dates are from mid Tir (July 10) to as late Aban (early November).[15] Note that these are *harvest* times, so the times for shedding of blossom and beginning of fruit-bearing are earlier. Apricot trees begin blooming late March with the beginning of Spring; pear trees begin blooming later. However, as is reported in Iran, it often happens that blooming happens in different, earlier and later times. Even in contemporary times we find online news from Iran report when trees have reportedly bloomed in the Fall, at times even in exceptionally warm winters. The point is, we should abide by a usual schedule of blossoms shedding here, late Spring, early Summer, for apricot blossoms at least.

Khayyam must have known his topography and climate conditions in his hometown and region. But, by having different fruit trees around, he was surely going to have blossoms at least twice a year, each year.

The point is that Nezami Arouzi's timeline for his return visit to find

15. See http://www.shahdiran.ir/about-us/the-harvest-season

Khayyam having passed away does seasonally correspond to the late Spring, early Summer of 517 LH. If he had visited Khayyam's grave that much into late Spring, into the month of June or later, in the year 518 LH, it would *fall outside the required 72 solar years* of age range we have considered above.

So, we have good reason now to rule out the possibility that Nezami Arouzi visited Khayyam's grave in 518 LH, since within the range of timeline possibility to fulfill the 72 solar years age requirement, the blossom had not yet been in the falling season yet in 518 LH.

So, Khayyam's blossom's shedding story has now helped us determine more definitively that the year in which Nezami Arouzi visited Khayyam's grave, about ten days earlier of which Khayyam had died, was in fact in the year 517 LH, which is the year historically and traditionally on record for Khayyam's passing. And, moreover, since it happened in the late Spring and early Summer months of that year, it clearly falls in the Western Gregorian year AD 1123. Besides, having independently arrived from a different "blossoms" route to the year 517 LH, we can then safely superpose also the findings with the nearly unanimous old records of Khayyam having passed away in the lunar year 517 LH.

We can now confidently confirm, then, that Khayyam passed away in the blossoms shedding season of the calendar years 517 LH, AD 1123, and 502 SH. We arrived at this finding independently from the old historically and traditionally established year of passing for Khayyam, that is, 517 LH. But the latter, of course, when superposed, further confirms our finding.

Now, it is time to turn our attention to a strange aspect of the report of Khayyam's last day as reported by Beyhaqi in *Tatemmat Sewan el-Hekmat (Supplement to the Chest of Wisdom)*, itself based on what Beyhaqi heard, most authentically, from Khayyam's close relative, himself an accomplished mathematician, and a brother-in-law of Khayyam.

5. Narrowing the Passing Date Further to Its Day: The Odd Intentionalities Implied in Reliable Accounts About Khayyam's Own Intended Efforts in Determining the Place and Time of His Passing

In what follows, I will show that Rashidi Tabrizi's (erroneous) date for Khayyam's birth and a solar age of 72 for Khayyam in combination with his follow-up reading from Nezami Arouzi's own handwritten text, entirely giving a different date for meeting Khayyam (512 LH rather than 506 LH), plus a return to Beyhaqi's account of the last day of Khayyam before passing as told by his relative Muhammad al-Baghdadi, can offer us a very interesting opportunity to narrow down on the possibilities to even the day of when more exactly Khayyam died.

I believe we have every good reason to consider that Khayyam, an astronomer who was also a master calendar reformer to be highly conscious of the timing, and not just the location, of his own passing.

Of course when we read old accounts, we may find aspects of it amusing or hard to believe, and attribute the matter to the "just tales" aspect of the events. Even Nezami Arouzi found it odd that Khayyam would be making such "prediction."

In other words, Nezami Arouzi himself reports having been surprised to hear from Khayyam regarding the condition of his grave. There seemed to be something intentional, something planned ahead, with how Khayyam was speaking of his forthcoming demise, as far as his burial location was concerned.

As noted earlier, some accounts speak of blossoms shedding on the grave generally, of one or another tree, and others reportedly of shedding twice. Nezami Arouzi himself speaks of pear and apricot trees both, which imply the possibility of twice shedding of blossoms. This latter may be a reason for his being somewhat surprised regarding the nature of the "twice" shedding of blossoms.

But Nezami Arouzi may have also been surprised by another aspect of what Khayyam reportedly told him: the rather blunt prediction, even in years, of Khayyam's passing following Nezami Arouzi's return from Hajj. So, there seemed to be some "prediction" on the part of Khayyam involved in terms of the *timing* of his passing, not just his burial *location*.

Khayyam of course had not specified a particular year apparently, and it happens Nezami Arouzi returned three years after his return from Mecca. Of course, one can speculate that an old man, Khayyam himself included, may have thought that he is bound to die soon, so he made that prediction while finding himself celebrating his 100th lunar birth day, not knowing exactly how much longer he had be alive. And it turns out he made it to his 100th *solar* anniversary as well and passed it even by two more years.

However, the oddness of the stories being reported from Khayyam does not end with Nezami Arouzi's story, we must realize. Al-Baghdadi's report to Beyhaqi regarding Khayyam's last day has similar odd overtones, if we pay closer attention to the textually reliable story, since there are aspects to it that may not catch our attention at first in terms of the extent of its oddity.

The strangest aspect of the story, in my view, was not that of his putting a golden tooth-pick on the first page of the chapter in Avicenna's book, *Shafa*, titled "On the One and the Many." That was of course odd also, and to that also I will return.

The strangest part of the story, I think, was how Khayyam clearly anticipated his imminent passing that very day, and all that followed resulted from that aspect of the event.

According to the story, Khayyam laid his golden toothpick in the book on that page, called for a gathering of his "trusted" friends to express deliver his last will, then *stopped eating and drinking,* interpreted as if he was fasting for the last time, and following his last, evening prayer, prostrated offering his last words of pray to God, and dies.

So, he actually died following an awareness of its impending happening, fasting (not drinking food or drink, explicitly stated as such) as if not only preparing for it, but perhaps even precipitating it, as if he wished to choose his own time to die by making it happen, now that he felt it was imminent. The account certainly does not show a man fearful of his impending death. He was, instead, quite in control, so to speak, seeking to shape even its timing as he perhaps also "predicted." For him, death was a passage toward his God, so, his acts on that day were in every way a fearless way of embracing that eventuality, now that it seemed to be happening at last.

We may associate such events as simply incidental. But here, we have a report indicating that Khayyam was, for whatever reasons, given he was also a physician, knowing his age, and perhaps other reasons we may discover in our further studies in the series, expected and knew his time had come, and took actions that indicated he knew his death was to happen imminently. Clearly stopping eating and drinking does not indicate fearing or resisting death, but one of conscious choice and acceptance, and a willingness to make its timing intentionally so.

Now, going back to the prior findings of Khayyam's year, season, and likely month(s), of passing in 517 LH, I wish to add the following.

First, we know that Khayyam must have definitively known his own birth date to have occurred on Safar 19, 412 LH. So, the number "19" was not something out of his considerations.

It is highly plausible to consider that Khayyam died sometime in the month of June of that year, in late Spring, which in solar Persian Islamic calendar he himself helped reform at the time, would fall in the month Khordad. June was in late Spring time-frame, when we would end up finding blossoms shed on any grave he would have prepared for himself.

The definitive birth day we have discovered in this book of the series for Khayyam falls on June 10 (AD 1021), or Khordad 20 (502 SH). The lunar day of his birth was Safar 19 (in 412 LH), which of course we would not expect to be the same month of day in 517 LH, given the shorter and changing lunar calendar compared to solar ones.

It would be hard to believe that Khayyam would have died in the month of June without himself realizing how close it was to his 102nd birth day in the solar calendar, that is, Khordad 20, 502 SH, or its eve on Khordad 19.

Here is where the golden toothpick aspect of the story may inspire us to think that he may have been pointing to something regarding the timing, the day, of his anticipated death.

We will explore Khayyam's writings in-depth, but what is clear from his writings is that he was strongly inclined toward the Pythagorean view of existence in mathematical terms, in terms of numbers. "All is number," is clearly a view of existence we can also attribute to Omar Khayyam, as we shall see in later books of this series.

So, when he points to the chapter on "One and the Many" which has of course a world of philosophical and spiritual meanings for him, as it had for Avicenna, implying the grand enigma of how from a One a created world of multiplicity of existence may follow, the notion and the gesture he makes also implies a pointing to numbers. There is much significance in Khayyam's last gesture of pointing to that chapter, which deserve our continuing attention in later books of the series. But for now, let us consider the following.

The word One (واحد) in Arabic and Persian has the abjad value of 19 (for the letters و ا ح د). This is not a coincidence but something that has a long tradition in numeral studies of the Quran and the sacred texts, the number 19 being associated with God and the Quran's abjad scriptural architecture.

I think it would be interesting to entertain the idea that Khayyam was pointing to that chapter, that title, and that last act of his anticipated union with his God through his last fasting and prayers, as also coinciding with his anticipated timing of his death, which could coincide with the closing of the looping circle of his existence by dying on the eve of the same day he was born.

He had been born on Safar 19th, for sure. Here, it was a chance to also die on the 19th of Khordad, in the solar Islamic calendar he himself helped reform in his life, on the eve of his birth day, and perhaps dying late at midnight, on the cusp of his birth day, on Khordad 20th, 502 SH.

Khordad 19th, 502 SH, the eve of his 102nd birth day, fulfills the year season, and the month conditions of the accounts shared by others about Khayyam's date of passing. It actually falls on June 10, AD 1123 (Gregorian) for that year, given their different leap year calculations in prior years.

In other words, Khayyam may have poetically considered the timing of his imminent passing on June 19th (to parallel Safar 19th for his birth), on the eve of his solar birth day (Khordad 20th) as meaningful in terms of the closing loop of his own life's "circle of coming and going."

We do not have to absurdly borrow a "Muharram 12th" trick from a mistaken date of passing clearly intended as (also a mistaken) date of birth in Rashidi Tabrizi's *Tarabkhaneh* to set an exact date of passing for an astronomer and calendar reformer genius that was Omar Khayyam. He deserves better.

Our findings can provide us with an opportunity for establishing a textually-reliable date of passing on his birth date, one that closes the "circle of coming and going" of his life.

The dates of his passing would be as follows:

- June 10, AD 1123 (Gregorian)

- Khordad 20, 502 SH (Persian solar) (which can be commemorated in terms of his last day on Khordad 19 reaching its midnight cusp passing to his birth day on Khordad the 20th, according to the Persian solar calendar whose reform, and in fact survival, as we shall see, he himself made possible)

- Rabi ol-Thani 6, 517 LH

Short of having any other reported date for Khayyam's passing, let us set his birth month and day of his birth (June 10th, in Iran falling on Khordad 20th usually), as also his month and day of passing, for an astronomer-poet whose circle of coming and going closed its loop on the same month's day.

6. The Two-Year Celebration Window: From the Millennium of Omar Khayyam's Birth on June 10, 2021 to the Ninth Centennial of His Passing on June 10, 2023

By superposing the various accounts from Zahireddin Abolhasan Beyhaqi, Nezami Arouzi, Abdorrahman Khazeni, and Yar Ahmad Rashidi Tabrizi, we have now firmly established that Khayyam's passing must have taken place in 517 LH. It could *not* have taken place in 516 LH, because it would not satisfy the 72 solar years age requirement of Rashidi Tabrizi. It could not have taken place in 518 LH, since it would not satisfy (with any further stretch of plausibility) the three-year past pilgrimage trip as well as the blossoms-shedding story of Nezami Arouzi when visiting Khayyam's grave.

We have therefore *conclusively and firmly* established and now reliably reconfirmed that Khayyam's year of passing was AD 1123 (517 LH), and not the erroneously one considered today, AD 1131. All indications are that Rashidi Tabrizi intended to reaffirm, in his own way, by stressing Khayyam's *solar* age of 72, that his passing took place neither in 515 LH, nor in 516 LH, but in the historically and traditionally unanimous date year, 517 LH.

Besides, given our earlier discovery in this book of Khayyam's definitive birth date in the year AD 1021, we had already concluded that a late, AD 1113, date for his passing would be nearly impossible and implausible, so it can now be safely ruled out altogether.

Those in the West who use one Christian calendar, or in the Arab world only a lunar Hejri calendar, are not confronted with the superposing double-calendar complications Iranians face trying to juggle both a solar and lunar calendar (not to mention now the Christian calendar, which is solar). In Iran today when trying to mark religious dates, and in the past also to mark events of birth and passing, lunar calendar is (was) used. But to calculate the year-*length*, as in age *time-span*, they usually use *solar* calendar lengths. So, it was not uncommon for Yar Ahmad Rashidi Tabrizi to give a date of birth on a lunar calendar, and an age in solar calendar lengths, as this is how Iranians (broadly speaking) are used to counting their age. They do not think of their age in lunar years, but *always* in solar years, even though the religious events are (and in the past, dates of birth and passing were) considered in the lunar calendar, their equivalents in the solar calendar always recalculated.

Having been born on June 10 (Greg.), AD 1021, and having died in on June 10 (Greg.), AD 1123, Khayyam completed his 102nd *solar* year of life, closing the circle of his "coming and going" also poetically. What we do know now is that the reformer of Iran's solar calendar died a solar centenarian as well.

In 512 LH Khayyam, in his *lunar* centennial year, must have thought he was not going to live much longer into his *solar* centennial, so was arranging his grave and talking about it, most likely on Safar 19 of that year in a happy gathering with his old friend al-Asfezari, on the 100th lunar (97th solar) anniversary of his birth. He must have thought that hopefully after "3 years" he could make it to his solar centennial itself. But, as fortune may have it, he made it to his solar centennial and past it for another two years.

The way Rashidi Tabrizi's *Tarabkhaneh* communicated to us the information about Khayyam, both in terms of the large volume of the Khayyami Robaiyat he collected and passed on as pollens for memorializing

Khayyam, as well as the more or less fanciful myths he was reporting surrounding actual information about his life and about some of the quatrains, may now be considered more significant than scholars have considered in the past.

Khayyam died in 517 LH, corresponding to AD 1123, and 502 SH. At the time of his passing, he was a 102 *solar* years (or a 105 *lunar* years) old centenarian. Actually, his passing in the lunar month Rabi ol-Thani happened just two months after his birth month Safar, so he had just started his 105th lunar years in age, so technically, we can regard him as having aged 104 *lunar* years.

We have two years from June 10, 2021 to June 10, 2023 to celebrate the first millennium of Omar Khayyam's birth and the ninth centennial of his passing. Khayyam was born on Khordad 20, 400 SH, and died on Khordad 20, 502 SH. So, the period to celebrate corresponds to the two year in Persian calendar starting from Khordad 20, 1400 SH to Khordad 20, 1402 SH. I suggest that Khordad 20 in the Iranian calendar and June 10 in the Western calendar be designated and commemorated as the Omar Khayyam's solar calendar days of "coming and going" at home and abroad.

This twelve-book series titled *Omar Khayyam's Secret*, whose publication commences on June 10, 2021 to conclude by June 10, 2023, hopefully, is and will be my own gift to the people Iran and the world in celebration of the life, works, and legacy of an enigmatic Omar Khayyam whose story has just begun to truly unfold, strangely on the exact millennium of his birth date for us today, as the world is still trying to find a way toward happiness from the griefs now of a devastating global pandemic.

Abstract

This essay, titled "Omar Khayyam's True Date of Passing Discovered and Reconfirmed: Superposing the Birth Date Findings With All "Tarabkhaneh," "Chahar Maqaleh," And "Tatemmat Sewan el-Hekmat" Accounts,'" is the fifth chapter of the second book of the twelve-book series *Omar Khayyam's Secret: Hermeneutics of the Robaiyat in Quantum Sociological Imagination,* authored by Mohammad H. Tamdgidi. The second book is subtitled *Khayyami Millennium: Reporting the Discovery and the Reconfirmation of the True Dates of Birth and Passing of Omar Khayyam (AD 1021-1123).*

In this last chapter of the book, Tamdgidi explores the most important and consequential source in search of the definitive date of passing of Omar Khayyam: the book titled *Tarabkhaneh* (meaning the house of joy or happiness, also implying poetry and musicality) by Yar Ahmad Rashidi Tabrizi. He notes, however, that by moving on to *Tarabkhaneh* we are not really moving away from Nezami Arouzi's *Chahar Maqaleh*, since Rashidi Tabrizi himself also draws on the latter, in fact an older, seemingly more authoritative copy of it, as part of his efforts at portraying Khayyam's life and final years. In fact, in this chapter, the author explore the above also in their superposition with the account provided by Zahireddin Abolhasan Beyhaqi in his *Tatemmat Sewan el-Hekmat (Supplement to the Chest of Wisdom)* regarding the last day of Khayyam as reported by his brother-in-law, Muhammad al-Baghdadi.

Tamdgidi then shares in the rest of the chapter how he discovered a reliable, definitive solution to the puzzle of Omar Khayyam's date of passing, not only for its year, season, and month, but even to its day (narrowable even to the part of day), as far as the most reliable past accounts are concerned. His discovery is textually reliable and evidence-based and integrates all the seemingly disparate accounts surrounding Khayyam's date of passing into a coherent solution, one that is certainly more defensible than the definitively inaccurate uneasy consensus date of passing currently considered for him. To explain the method in its broadest terms, Tamdgidi accomplished this by way of "superposing" ("intersecting" or "overlapping") the many seemingly separate stories about his passing. The solution is possible because the superposition of the various stories, cleared of their fragmentations, allows us to narrow down the date of Khayyam's passing to the remarkably specific margin of a specific day, even to its part.

Tamdgidi also reminds his readers that the currently held date of Khayyam's passing, that is, Muharram 12th, 516 LH (per Tīrtha, convertible into the Christian Gregorian calendar date March 30, AD 1122) or 526 LH (convertible into the Christian Gregorian calendar date Dec. 11, AD 1131, which is mistakenly considered as Dec. 4 Gregorian these days) were completely nonsensical and arbitrarily made as far as its month and day are concerned. "Muharram 12th" simply resulted from a misreading by Tīrtha of a birth date given by a source (*Tarabkhaneh*) for Khayyam as his date of passing. So, while the years of the date being given (555 LH) was obviously wrong to begin with for either Khayyam's birth or passing, Tīrtha (and later others) basically said, "well, why not use the month and day for Khayyam's passing, any way." And they did so, leading us to be now stuck with that wrong date for Khayyam's passing.

We do not have to absurdly borrow a "Muharram 12th" trick from a mistaken date of passing clearly intended as (also a mistaken) date of birth in Rashidi Tabrizi's *Tarabkhaneh* to set an exact date of passing for an astronomer and calendar reformer genius that was Omar Khayyam. He deserves better. The author's findings can provide us with an opportunity for establishing a textually-reliable date of passing on his birth date, one that closes the "circle of coming and going" of Khayyam's life. His dates of passing would be as follows:

- June 10, AD 1123 (Gregorian)
- Khordad 20, 502 SH (Persian solar) (which can be commemorated in terms of his last day on Khordad 19 reaching its midnight cusp passing to his birth day on Khordad the 20th, according to the Persian solar calendar whose reform, and in fact survival, as we shall see, he himself made possible)
- Rabi ol-Thani 6, 517 LH

Khayyam died in 517 LH, corresponding to AD 1123, and 502 SH. At the time of his passing, he was a 102 s*olar* years (or a 105 l*unar* years) old centenarian. Actually, his passing in the lunar month Rabi ol-Thani happened just two months after his birth month Safar, so he had just started his 105th lunar years in age, so technically, we can regard him as having aged 104 *lunar* years.

Conclusion to Book 2: Summary of Findings

In the essay titled "Book 2 Preface: Recap From Prior Books of the Series," an opening to this second book of the twelve-book series *Omar Khayyam's Secret: Hermeneutics of the Robaiyat in Quantum Sociological Imagination*, subtitled *Khayyami Millennium: Reporting the Discovery and the Reconfirmation of the True Dates of Birth and Passing of Omar Khayyam (AD 1021-1123)*, I offered a summary of the first book of the series. The purpose of the preface was to provide the readers of this second book of the series a brief background about the major findings of the prior book(s) of the series.

In the overall series I share the results of my decades-long research on Omar Khayyam, the enigmatic 11th/12th centuries Persian Muslim sage, philosopher, astronomer, mathematician, physician, writer, and poet from Neyshabour, Iran, whose life and works still remain behind a veil of deep mystery. The purpose of my research has been to find definitive answers to the many puzzles still surrounding Khayyam, especially regarding the existence, nature, and purpose of the Robaiyat in his life and works. To explore the questions posed in the series, I advance a new hermeneutic method of textual analysis, informed by what he calls the quantum sociological imagination, to gather and study all the attributed philosophical, religious, scientific, and literary writings of Khayyam.

In the first book of the series, subtitled *New Khayyami Studies: Quantumizing the Newtonian Structures of C. Wright Mills's Sociclogical Imagination for A New Hermeneutic Method*, following a common preface and introduction to the series, I had developed the quantum sociological imagination method framing his hermeneutic study in the series as a whole. In its prefatory note I shared the origins of my study and how the study is itself a moment in the trajectory of a broader research project. In its introduction, I described how centuries of Khayyami studies, especially during the last two, have reached an impasse in shedding light on his enigmatic life and works, especially his attributed Robaiyat.

The four chapters of the first book were then dedicated to developing the quantum sociological imagination as a new hermeneutic method framing the Khayyami studies in the series. The method builds, in an applied way, on the results of my recent work in the sociology of scientific knowledge, *Liberating Sociology: From Newtonian Toward Quantum Imagination: Volume 1: Unriddling the Quantum Enigma* (2020), where I explored extensively, in greater depth, and in the context of understanding the so-called "quantum enigma," the Newtonian and quantum ways of imagining reality.

In the first book, I shared the findings of that research in summary amid new applied insights developed in relation to Khayyami studies. In the first chapter, I raised a set of eight questions about the structure of C. Wright Mills's sociological imagination as a potential framework for Khayyami studies. In its second chapter, I showed how the questions are symptomatic of Newtonian structures that still continue to frame Mills's sociological imagination. In the third chapter, I explored how the sociological imagination can be reinvented to be more in tune with the findings of quantum science. In the last chapter, the implications of the quantum sociological imagination for devising a hermeneutic method for new Khayyami studies were outlined. In conclusion, the findings of the first book of the *Omar Khayyam's Secret* series were summarized.

This second book of the *Omar Khayyam's Secret* series, subtitled *Khayyami Millennium: Reporting the Discovery and the Reconfirmation of the True Dates of Birth and Passing of Omar Khayyam (AD 1021-1123,* was dedicated to exploring in depth the hitherto findings and controversies surrounding the dates of birth and passing of Omar Khayyam.

In the essay, titled "Introduction to Book 2: The Dilemma and Significance of Omar Khayyam's Dates of Birth and Passing," I explained how in recent decades, an uneasy consensus has generally emerged in Khayyami studies and public media regarding the dates of birth and passing of Omar Khayyam. Nowadays, one can readily find various online, bibliographic, encyclopedic, academic, or other published sources stating that Khayyam was born on Thursday, May 18, AD 1048, and died on Friday, December 4th, AD 1131. Such dates are then celebrated or commemorated according to the solar Gregorian Christian calendar used today in the West.

Obviously, the determination of the exact dates for Omar Khayyam's birth and passing, which would then identify the exact historical period during which he lived (marked by rapidly changing events, rulers, and personalities), is vital for any adequate and realistic research on his life and works amid the broader context of his times.

Studying the interplay between personal troubles and broader public issues involving Khayyam's life in a quantum sociological imagination framework (as introduced in the preceding, first book of this series) requires such a careful determination of the outer boundaries of the chronology of his life and works in relation to those of his contemporaries amid local, regional, and broader world-history contexts. An accurate determination of the dates of Khayyam's birth and passing can provide significant information about more exact intersections of various periods of his biography with those of others amid the tumultuous times during which one or another of his writings, including his poetry, if any, may have been composed.

However, the uneasy consensus on Khayyam's dates of birth and passing as noted above is not a universally settled matter. The uneasy consensus today regarding Khayyam's birth date, if not exactly his date of passing, is rooted in a specific piece of biographical information passed on from his contemporaries to the present: his birth horoscope, or natal chart. In this regard, the study by the Indian scholar Swāmī Govinda Tīrtha is of singular importance.

Amid his major study of Omar Khayyam's life and writings in his *The Nectar of Grace: Omar Khayyām's Life and Works* (1941), one that included studies and translations of several excerpts of the philosophical (not scientific) writings and (his own) free verse translations of quatrains attributed to Khayyam, Tīrtha proposed a way of calculating Khayyam's birth date based on the horoscope of his birth handed down in a manuscript of biographical entries by the scholar of medieval Islamic period and Khayyam contemporary (as a young child) Zahireddin Abolhasan Beyhaqi, titled *Tatemmat Sewan el-Hekmat (Supplement to the Chest of Wisdom).*

We owe to Swāmī Govinda Tīrtha the wonderful idea of determining the date of birth of Khayyam through a study of his birth horoscope, and his efforts at determining Khayyam's date of passing also offer ideas that can shed helpful lights toward solving that question as well. However, we should keep in mind that the *soundness* of the way he went about determining those dates *based on the way he interpreted and analyzed the horoscope* and other sources using the specific manuscript copies he had at hand is a completely *different* matter, worthy of critical revisitation.

In my introduction to this second book, some preliminary information about the nature of the Islamic lunar and Iranian Islamic solar calendars as well as Gregorian and Julian Western calendars were provided, while an overview of Khayyam's tombstones and their inscriptions were also shared. I then stated my purpose in this second book of the *Omar Khayyam's Secret* series to be as follows: (1) to carefully and critically revisit Swāmī Govinda Tīrtha's study of Khayyam's horoscope which lies at the very source of the prevailing uneasy consensus today regarding the dates of birth and death of Omar Khayyam; and, if Tīrtha's findings are verifiably proven to be wrong, (2) to offer an alternative solution to the determination of the true dates of birth (and by implication and further investigation, passing) of Omar Khayyam by way of careful reexamination of that horoscope.

In the first chapter titled "Contributions, Inconsistencies, and Inaccuracies of Swāmī Govinda Tīrtha's Findings Regarding Omar Khayyam's Dates of Birth and Passing," I began by noting how, as a part of his book *The Nectar of Grace: Omar Khayyām's Life and Works,* published in 1941, the Indian scholar Swāmī Govinda Tīrtha tried to resolve longstanding doubts about Omar Khayyam's dates of birth and passing, his approach and findings subsequently contributing in a significant way to the uneasy consensus held today in the world regarding those dates.

In his work, Tīrtha basically proposed that the solution to the problem of determining the date of birth of Omar Khayyam can be found in following up on the clues given in a horoscope for Khayyam's birth that had been reported long ago in Zahireddin Abolhasan Beyhaqi's *Tatemmat Sewan el-Hekmat (Supplement to the Chest of Wisdom)*, a passage of which Tīrtha noted several scholars before him had taken notice but had not realized its significance for the purpose at hand (Tīrtha, p. XXXII). Based on Tīrtha's calculations and considerations, Omar Khayyam's dates of birth and death were "discovered" by him to be as follows: Birth date: 4:48 a.m., Wednesday, May 18, AD 1048. Date of demise: Thursday, Muharram 12th, 516 LH (in the years AD 1122/1123).

In the first section of the chapter, I offered an overview of how Tīrtha went about determining Omar Khayyam's dates of birth and passing. My purpose therein was not yet to critique Tīrtha's efforts. In the second section, however, I explored both the internal consistencies and the factual accuracies of Swāmī Govinda Tīrtha's solutions to the problems of determining Omar Khayyam's dates of birth and passing. It is one thing to invalidate a claim based on external facts, and another to show that it is internally flawed, that is, it does not even fulfill the conditions it has itself set for its claim.

In offering my critique in that chapter, I first assumed that Tīrtha's reading of Beyhaqi's reported horoscope is correct. In other words, I specifically took for granted that Tīrtha's reading that at the time of Khayyam's birth the Sun and Mercury were on the Ascendant on the *third* degree of the Gemini for Neyshabour's eastern horizon was correct. I then evaluated whether Tīrtha followed his own definitional requirements and procedural guidelines when using Khayyam's reported horoscope for the purpose of determining Khayyam's dates of birth and passing, and whether the data he himself provides support his conclusions. I also evaluated Tīrtha's findings in terms of their external accuracy. By external accuracy I meant to evaluate whether what Tīrtha claimed to be the astronomical data or calendrical uses supporting his findings were actually correct. I then showed that Swāmī Govinda Tīrtha's findings have been for the most part both internally inconsistent as well as factually inaccurate.

I demonstrated in the chapter that there is absolutely no defensible grounds for considering Wednesday, May 18, AD 1048 to be Omar Khayyam's birth date. For all practical purposes, Iran and the world are celebrating Khayyam's date of birth on the *wrong* date. Tīrtha's otherwise worthwhile effort passes neither the test of internal consistency nor that of external, factual accuracy of his *own* premises and procedures. Nor can we be sure that the exact year, let alone the month and day, of Khayyam's passing as proposed by Tīrtha as prevalently accepted today are accurate.

In a following chapter, I planned on relaxing the assumption of correctness of Tīrtha's reading of the *third* degree of the Gemini in Khayyam's reported horoscope, and further evaluating Tīrtha's solutions for Khayyam's dates of birth and passing.

I devoted the second chapter titled "In Search of the Correct Gemini Degree: The Story of How Omar Khayyam's True Date of Birth Was Discovered Shortly Before Its Imminent Millennium," to a search for Khayyam's true date of birth.

Although Swāmī Govinda Tīrtha deserves credit for bringing scholarly attention to Omar Khayyam's horoscope as reported in Zahireddin Abolhasan Beyhaqi's *Tatemmat Sewan el-Hekmat (Supplement to the Chest of Wisdom)* as a pathway toward solving the problem of Khayyam's birth date, he erred in the effort, causing more confusion. Something in the way Tīrtha handled the information implied in Khayyam's reported horoscope prevented him from truly solving his birth date puzzle. So, I asked, what did go wrong in Tīrtha's efforts?

To answer this question, I adopted the procedure of step by step peeling away one or another false lead toward a core solution. The reason for this procedure was to eliminate any other possibilities that may, one way or another, exist and thus cast doubt on the definitive solution we hope to reach for the puzzles at hand. After all, were there more than one solution that may plausibly compete with, let alone nullify, the solution I offered, we could not claim for sure that a definitive solution had been found.

Finding that Khayyam's birth date considerations on the basis of either the 3rd or the 8th degree for the Gemini to be incompatible with the requirements of Khayyam's reported horoscope, and encountering a wide range of manuscript source variations as reported in the chapter, I took an alternative route by *directly* consulting and reporting the ephemeris data for the entire years during AD 1018-1055.

My procedure for compiling the data was follows. I first consulted the Swiss Ephemeris data that is not Neyshabour location specific, and the dates are given for day intervals only and not for the variations during the day. If the data came close to fulfilling the Gemini ascendance and Samimi (Cazimi) requirements, I reported it, cross-checking with the search engine for the more exact Neyshabour location and time variations, to the extent that it was necessary to rule out a date or regarding all the requirements of the horoscope, including the Taslees (Trine) requirement. I annotated each date sufficiently to explain why that date can be ruled out, or that it fulfilled a given requirement.

I discovered that there *was one, and only one, date* between years AD 1018 and AD 1055 that *definitively* fulfilled *all* the requirements of Khayyam's reported horoscope, including the degree of the Ascendant, when considering a degree of the Gemini in which the horoscope's Cazimi/Ascendant conjunction must fall. This date was, in the Gregorian calendar, June 10, AD 1021, at sunrise, Neyshabour's time. It was nearly a four minute period from 4:43:56 a.m. to 4:47:55 a.m. exactly at sunrise. During this short interval of time, the Gemini was Ascendant, the Sun and the Mercury were Cazimi on the same degree of the Ascendant 18° of Gemini (being in the Samimi distance of 8 minutes from each other), and Jupiter was positioned on the 11th degree of Libra, within a Taslees/Triangulation/Trine-fulfilling distance of about 113 degrees from both the Sun and Mercury.

Following my discovery, I tried further to understand how the Gemini degree 18 on which the date fell provided any hints about how the ambiguities surrounding the Gemini degree given across the various extant manuscript copies of Khayyam's reported horoscope could be reconciled with one another. While explaining the various variations, I discovered that through the process of successive recopying by various scribes, the letter ی became gradually corrupted, the letter being misread as the word فی such that later scribes assumed that the word was not a part of a degree given in abjad for ی but the word فی in the normal part of the sentence. I also offered explanations for why and how Soviet Russian scholars and astronomers failed in catching Tīrtha's mistakes regarding Omar Khayyam's date of birth, as well as, in part, his date of passing.

I therefore stated that, based on the findings, the renderings of the horoscope of Omar Khayyam as reported by Beyhaqi in his *Tatemmat Sewan el-Hekmat (Supplement to the Chest of Wisdom)* should be corrected to the following in its Arabic, Persian, and English expressions:

> «طلعه الجوزا و الشمس و عطارد على درجه الطالع ى ح من الجوزا و عطارد صميمى و المشترى من التثليث ناظر اليهما».

> «طالعش جوزا بود و آفتاب و عطارد بر درجهٔ طالع ى ح از جوزا و عطارد صميمى و مشترى از تثليث ناظر بر آن دو».

> "His ascendant was the Gemini, and the Sun and the Mercury were on the degree of the ascendent 18 of Gemini, and the Mercury was Samimi [Cazimi], and the Jupiter from Taslees [Trine aspectation] observing them both."

In the third chapter titled "In Search of Omar Khayyam's True Date of Passing: Superposing the Birth Date Findings With Beyhaqi's 'Tatemmat Sewan el-Hekmat' And Khazeni's 'Mizan ol-Hekmat,'" and the two following it, my main goal was to determine as definitively as possible the date of passing of Omar Khayyam on the basis of the new finding about his true date of birth as reported in the preceding chapter. My secondary purpose was to trace how the new finding allowed for reimagining Khayyam's interactions with others during his lifetime from the vantage of his true age during such interactions.

I chose to split my search for Khayyam's definitive date of passing into three chapters (starting with the third chapter) for the reader's convenience; however, I noted that they should be seen as parts of the same, ongoing, search, their findings often superposing and overlapping with one another considerably.

I also stated that my purpose in the third chapter and the two that followed it was to revisit all the available texts and versions thereof more carefully, in an effort to find a way of convincingly interpreting the various texts and reconciling their differences to such an extent that one can arrive at an undisputable consensus regarding Khayyam's date of demise.

In my view, there are basically four manuscripts on which most have focused to determine the date of passing of Omar Khayyam.

The first manuscript is the biographical information offered for Khayyam in *Tatemmat Sewan el-Hekmat (Supplement to the Chest of Wisdom)* by Zahireddin Abolhasan Beyhaqi.

The second source is *Mizan ol-Hekmat (Balance of Wisdom)*, by Abdorrahman Khazeni, also a grown-up contemporary of Khayyam and reportedly also one of his pupils in astronomy and scientific matters, implying that he must have also met him in person.

The third source is *Chahar Maqaleh (Four Discourses)* by Nezami Arouzi, a Khayyam contemporary who offered his respects to him as a teacher (whether actually or in reverence it is not known).

And the fourth manuscript is one written and compiled by Yar Ahmad Rashidi Tabrizi, which has come to be known under the title *Tarabkhaneh (House of Joy)*.

The third chapter covered the exploration of the first two of the above four main sources.

I stated, based on the discovery of the true date of birth of Khayyam as reported in the earlier chapter of this book, that we can again entertain the possibility (not necessarily the certainty) that Nezam ol-Molk, and even Hasan Sabbah, and Omar Khayyam were childhood friends and that there may have been some grains of truth to the story reported by others. The research as reported in this chapter also highlighted the significance of Abol-Hasan al-Anbari as a significant teacher of Khayyam in astronomy. I also noted that based on the findings about Khayyam's true birth date, it is certainly possible that he could have been a young student of Avicenna during the latter's last peaceful years of life living in Isfahan.

The true date of birth sheds clear light on the senior status of Khayyam in relation to many of his contemporaries with whom he was interacting given his advancing age, strengthening the possibility that he may have as well served as the most senior and leading member of a team of astronomers invited by Soltan Malekshah and his minister Nezam ol-Molk to establish an observatory in Isfahan and reform the Persian solar calendar.

Following a careful rereading of the contents of the first two sources listed above, I offered the tentative conclusion that based on Beyhaqi's *Tatemmat Sewan el-Hekmat (Supplement to the Chest of Wisdom)* and Abdorrahman Khazeni's *Mizan ol-Hekmat (Balance of Wisdom)*, there is simply no information that supports that Khayyam was alive anytime after 517 LH. The information supports that definitively Khayyam was alive sometime in the year 515 LH, at least, and some information given (in the texts studied in the chapter) may even imply that he was alive in the year 516 LH, at least, since Beyhaqi related a conversation he had with the prince Faramarz in that year, where Khayyam is specifically mentioned as the topic of that conversation but God's mercy wishing or other information is not provided suggesting that Khayyam had passed away by then.

In the fourth chapter, titled "Searching More for Omar Khayyam's True Date of Passing: Superposing the Birth Date Findings With the Prevalent Manuscript Copy of Nezami Arouzi's 'Chahar Maqaleh,'" I reported on the plausibility of serious doubts that can be cast on the dates given by Nezami Arouzi about all events covered in his book, including those related to Khayyam.

Nezami Arouzi's text is a fine prose of Persian writing, but definitively not one that accurately reports historical dates and details. In my view, this questioning of Nezami Arouzi's prevalent manuscript copy for the accuracy of its dates is a necessary step in the efforts toward finding the true date of Khayyam's passing. Rejecting prior held false narratives about Khayyam's date of passing is a necessary and essential part of this inquiry.

It happens that in the process of problematizing conventional tales given about the alleged date 526 LH for Khayyam's passing amid miscopying and misreadings of Nezami Arouzi's text, we discover precious new interpretive evidence that Nezami Arouzi as one of Khayyam's close living contemporaries, one of his pupils in fact or in reverence, indeed knew that Khayyam wrote "many" quatrains, that they were "famous," and that they were, by some, regarded as religiously forbidden, which may have more to do with the religious beliefs of those making such assessments than with the religious nature of Khayyam's quatrains themselves.

I also suggested that, if we can set aside the customary doubts about Yar Ahmad Rashidi Tabrizi's own reliability of narration, and study his text anew to judge for ourselves whether what others say of his authorship is true or not, including what information he offers about what he read in Nezami Arouzi about meetings with Khayyam in Balkh and the time of his death and burial, we may find new value that were previously neglected because of our own "observing" lenses about the worth and meanings of our sources.

In my view, what we do know is that now, as related in the fourth chapter, the view that none of Khayyam's contemporaries refer to Khayyam as the author of the Robaiyat may actually be verifiably not true, and at least subject to serious doubt.

In the fifth and last chapter, titled "Omar Khayyam's True Date of Passing Discovered and Reconfirmed: Superposing the Birth Date Findings With All "Tarabkhaneh," "Chahar Maqaleh," And "Tatemmat Sewan el-Hekmat" Accounts,'" I explored the most important and consequential source in search of the definitive date of passing of Omar Khayyam: the book titled *Tarabkhaneh* (meaning the house of joy or happiness, also implying poetry and musicality) by Yar Ahmad Rashidi Tabrizi.

I noted, however, that by moving on to *Tarabkhaneh* we are not really moving away from Nezami Arouzi's *Chahar Maqaleh*, since Rashidi Tabrizi himself also draws on the latter, in fact an older, seemingly more authoritative copy of it, as part of his efforts at portraying Khayyam's life and final years. In fact, in the fifth chapter, I explored the above also in their superposition with the account provided by Zahireddin Abolhasan Beyhaqi in his *Tatemmat Sewan el-Hekmat (Supplement to the Chest of Wisdom)* regarding the last day of Khayyam as reported by his brother-in-law, Muhammad al-Baghdadi.

I then shared in the rest of the chapter how I discovered a reliable, definitive solution to the puzzle of Omar Khayyam's date of passing, not only for its year, season, and month, but even to its day (narrowable even to the part of day), as far as the most reliable past accounts are concerned.

My discovery is textually reliable and evidence-based and integrates all the seemingly disparate accounts surrounding Khayyam's date of passing into a coherent solution, one that is certainly more defensible than the definitively inaccurate uneasy consensus date of passing currently considered for him.

To explain the method in its broadest terms, I accomplished this by way of "superposing" ("intersecting" or "overlapping") the many seemingly separate stories about his passing. The solution was possible because the superposition of the various stories, cleared of their fragmentations, allowed us to narrow down the date of Khayyam's passing to the remarkably specific margin of a specific day, even to its part.

I also reminded readers that the currently held date of Khayyam's passing, that is, Muharram 12th, 516 LH (per Tīrtha, convertible into the Christian Gregorian calendar date March 30, AD 1122) or 526 LH (convertible into the Christian Gregorian calendar date Dec. 11, AD 1131, which is mistakenly considered as Dec. 4 Gregorian these days) were completely nonsensical and arbitrarily made as far as its month and day are concerned. "Muharram 12th" simply resulted from a misreading by Tīrtha of a birth date given by a source (*Tarabkhaneh*) for Khayyam as his date of passing. So, while the years of the date being given (555 LH) was obviously wrong to begin with for either Khayyam's birth or passing, Tīrtha (and later others) basically said, "well, why not use the month and day for Khayyam's passing, any way." And they did so, leading us to be now stuck with that wrong date for Khayyam's passing.

In my view, we do not have to absurdly borrow a "Muharram 12th" trick from a mistaken date of passing clearly intended as (also a mistaken) date of birth in Rashidi Tabrizi's *Tarabkhaneh* to set an exact date of passing for an astronomer and calendar reformer genius that was Omar Khayyam. He deserves better. My findings can provide us with an opportunity for establishing a textually-reliable date of passing on his birth date, one that closes the "circle of coming and going" of his life.

The dates of his passing would be as follows:

- June 10, AD 1123 (Gregorian)
- Khordad 20, 502 SH (Persian solar) (which can be commemorated in terms of his last day on Khordad 19 reaching its midnight cusp passing to his birth day on Khordad the 20th, according to the Persian solar calendar whose reform, and in fact survival, as we shall see, he himself made possible)
- Rabi ol-Thani 6, 517 LH

Khayyam died in 517 LH, corresponding to AD 1123, and 502 SH. At the time of his passing, he was a 102 *solar* years (or a 105 *lunar* years) old centenarian. Actually, his passing in the lunar month Rabi ol-Thani happened just two months after his birth month Safar, so he had just started his 105th lunar years in age, so technically, we can regard him as having aged 104 *lunar* years.

Abstract

This essay, titled "Conclusion to Book 2: Summary of Findings,'" offers a summary of the findings of the second book of the twelve-book series *Omar Khayyam's Secret: Hermeneutics of the Robaiyat in Quantum Sociological Imagination,* authored by Mohammad H. Tamdgidi. The second book is subtitled *Khayyami Millennium: Reporting the Discovery and the Reconfirmation of the True Dates of Birth and Passing of Omar Khayyam (AD 1021-1123).*

The essay "Book 2 Preface: Recap From Prior Books of the Series," served to provide the readers of this second book a brief background about the major findings of the prior boo of the series. In "Introduction to Book 2: The Dilemma and Significance of Omar Khayyam's Dates of Birth and Passing," he explained how in recent decades, an uneasy consensus has emerged in Khayyami studies and public media regarding the dates of birth and passing of Omar Khayyam: Thursday, May 18, AD 1048, and on Friday, December 4th, AD 1131.

In the first chapter titled "Contributions, Inconsistencies, and Inaccuracies of Swāmī Govinda Tīrtha's Findings Regarding Omar Khayyam's Dates of Birth and Passing," he began by noting how, as a part of his book *The Nectar of Grace: Omar Khayyām's Life and Works,* published in 1941, the Indian scholar Swāmī Govinda Tīrtha tried to resolve longstanding doubts about Omar Khayyam's dates of birth and passing, his approach and findings subsequently contributing in a significant way to the uneasy consensus held today in the world regarding those dates. He demonstrated in the chapter that there is absolutely no defensible grounds for considering Wednesday, May 18, AD 1048 to be Khayyam's birth date. For all practical purposes, Iran and the world are celebrating Khayyam's birth on the *wrong* date.

The author devoted the second chapter titled "In Search of the Correct Gemini Degree: The Story of How Omar Khayyam's True Date of Birth Was Discovered Shortly Before Its Imminent Millennium," to a search for Khayyam's true date of birth. He discovered that there *was one, and only one, date* between years AD 1018 and AD 1055 that *definitively* fulfilled *all* the requirements of Khayyam's reported horoscope, including the degree of the Ascendant, when considering a degree of the Gemini in which the horoscope's Cazimi/Ascendant conjunction must fall. This date was, in the Gregorian calendar, June 10, AD 1021, at sunrise, Neyshabour's time. He therefore stated that, based on the findings, the renderings of the horoscope of Omar Khayyam as reported by Beyhaqi in his *Tatemmat Sewan el-Hekmat (Supplement to the Chest of Wisdom)* should be corrected to accurately state the Gemini degree to be 18.

The third chapter was titled "In Search of Omar Khayyam's True Date of Passing: Superposing the Birth Date Findings With Beyhaqi's 'Tatemmat Sewan el-Hekmat' And Khazeni's 'Mizan ol-Hekmat,'" the fourth titled, "Searching More for Omar Khayyam's True Date of Passing: Superposing the Birth Date Findings With the Prevalent Manuscript Copy of Nezami Arouzi's 'Chahar Maqaleh,'" and the fifth and last chapter, titled "Omar Khayyam's True Date of Passing Discovered and Reconfirmed: Superposing the Birth Date Findings With All "Tarabkhaneh," "Chahar Maqaleh," And "Tatemmat Sewan el-Hekmat" Accounts.'" In the course of the explorations the author discovered that not only a living contemporary of Khayyam, a close pupil in reverence, had in his older copies of his manuscript *Chahar Maqaleh* acknowledged Khayyam as the author of the Robaiyat, but also that by way of a superposed study of all the above sources, we can verifiably confirm, based on the most reliable texts, that Khayyam died, on a mathematically and calendrically precise day of his birth, June 10, AD 1123, closing the circle of coming and going of his life as not only a lunar, but also a solar centenarian, completing his solar age, 102.

Appendix: Transliteration System and Book 2 Glossary

In the English edition of this series, as needed, I will offer transliterations of proper names originally expressed in Persian or Arabic. I will also offer transliterations, when intended, to accompany the Khayyami Robaiyat in Persian. Any included or quoted longer text originally written in Persian or Arabic will not be transliterated but will be rendered in its own original language. In the bibliography, instead of transliterations, I will include the bibliographic information in the original language in which it was published while providing the information in English translation; if it has been published in English translation, I will provide it instead of my own translation, unless additional notes are needed for correction or clarification.

As explained in the brief transliteration note in the front matter of this book, throughout this series, in order to simplify the rendering of Persian of Arabic texts free of unfamiliar (to the general English-speaking reader) expressions, I will not use diacritics (including those for ʿein ع or hamzeh ء) in the main body and its footnotes, except for where warranted for substantive research purposes, such as when intending to offer full transliterations alongside the Persian originals for the Khayyami Robaiyat. Instead, I invite interested and specialist readers to consult a separate cumulative transliteration glossary of words specific to each book (and earlier ones) that I have placed in this appendix following the transliteration system being introduced.

For instance, the names "Omar" or "Khayyam" are used throughout the series without diacritics, but in the transliteration table, its proper rendering as Omar or Khayyam (as well as its original in Persian/Arabic, i.e., "عمر" or "خیّام") will be given. For the word رباعیّات I will use "Robaiyat" (again, without diacritics) which is a more accurate phonetic expression for the word as pronounced in Persian, while providing in the transliteration table in this appendix the full transliteration of the word as expressed in Persian, that is "Robaʿiyāt." I will use the spelling "Rubaiyat" only when the specific Western tradition associated with the "free translations" of the Robaiyat by Edward FitzGerald or others similarly undertaken are referred to in the account.

In the case of authors' names or their work titles written in Arabic or Persian—again, in order to simplify the reading experience in English—I will use the simpler transliteration without diacritics, while providing the actual names and work titles in the original language in the bibliography. Regarding sources continually engaged with in the study, I will offer a simple transliteration of the titles followed by its English translation in the main text (or footnotes) while providing the full transliteration also in the cumulative transliteration glossary in the appendix of each respective book.

For instance, instead of using the title "*Tatemmaẗ Ṣewán él-Ḥekmaẗ*" for the original Arabic ("تتمة صوان الحكمة"), an important manuscript studied in this series, I will use its transliteration and its English translation as "*Tatemmat Sewan el-Hekmat (Supplement to the Chest of Wisdom)*" in order to convey a simpler and immediate sense of the nature of the source to the English-speaking reader. The full transliteration of the title along with the title in the original language is given in the transliteration glossary in the appendix. As another example, I will render the proper name "Zahireddin Abolhasan Beyhaqi" as such in the main text or footnote while providing its proper rendering in the transliteration table as "Żahireḽddin Abu al-Ḥasan Beyhaqi" and "ظهیرالدّین ابوالحسن بیهقی" in the transliteration glossary in the appendix.

In this English edition of this book and its series, words (with any diacritics) in languages originally using Latin alphabet are rendered as in the original. When quoting transliterated Persian and Arabic words, I will render them (including their diacritics) as found in the source, whatever transliteration system the source has used, which can vary from one source to another. However, my own transliterations of Persian and Arabic texts will follow their pronunciation in Persian. So, Arabic (or any other language) words internalized in Persian language will be transliterated according to their Persian pronunciation, except for the transliterations already in common use.

In the case of a quote in the original Arabic or Persian, I will offer the English translation (noting in parenthesis whether it is from a previously published source, or my own translation); however, whether or not I also offer the original text in Persian or Arabic in transliteration or original language will depend on the context—i.e., depending on the substantive significance of the original text for the purpose of research at hand.

In all of the above considerations, if there arises a substantive need to offer the transliteration in the main text, I will certainly do so. For instance, in offering an opportunity to read the Khayyami Robaiyat in their original Persian pronunciation, it will be necessary to offer a transliteration that is expressive of the Persian pronunciation of the words. Unfortunately, in this regard existing transliteration systems can be misleading since they often rely on Arabic pronunciations of the words, leading to mispronunciations that are not suitable for the proper reading, reciting, and understanding of the Persian poems.

In what follows, I will present my own suggested transliteration system that somewhat overlaps with, but is also significantly different from, other prevailing (mostly Arabic-language based) systems of transliteration. The reason for my offering a different system rather than borrowing from an existing one is two-fold.

First, the main purpose is to designate the transliteration letters and symbols such that the possibility of correct conversions back to the original written texts in Persian or Arabic is retained. For instance, transliterating تتمة as *Tatamat* does not necessarily lead to a correct spelling and writing of the word as it stands in the original Arabic (it would rather result in the rendering of the word as تتمت, which is not the same as found in the original), whereas using the transliteration *Tatemmaẗ* (as defined in the following system) for the word would offer the possibility of converting the word back to the correct spelling and writing in the original Arabic. This system would thus eliminate the need to offer the actual Arabic or Persian original texts in text (or its footnotes)—unless necessary for other reasons.

Second, the purpose is to offer a system of transliteration using which the original words in Persian (or Arabic words already internalized in the Persian lexicon) can be pronounced as they would be with a Persian accent (while still retaining the possibility of conversation back to the original word in writing, as noted above). Most transliteration systems tend to produce Arabic phonetics and accents; however, for the purpose of this research (especially when it comes, for instance, to the proper pronunciation of words in the Persian Robaiyat) it is important to convey and pass on to readers a transliteration system that more faithfully conveys Persian phonetics and accents for Persian words or even for Arabic words that have become internalized in Persian and are pronounced with a Persian accent.

The Persian alphabet includes the Arabic plus four additional letters (پ ژ چ گ) while some Arabic diacritics are not commonly used in Persian writing. Moreover, several different Arabic letters are pronounced the same in Persian (such as ذ ز ض ظ which are all pronounced the same way as 'z,' or ت ط which are pronounced the same as 't,' or س ص ث which are usually pronounced the same as 's'), differently from the Arabic, where the distinctions of phonetics associated with each letter are noticeably maintained. While the use of the different letters in writing is still necessary even in Persian since they construct different words carrying different meanings, in their pronunciation, especially when (for instance) poetry is concerned, using a Persian accent is indispensable.

For instance, it is more proper for the non-native Persian speaker to read a Persian poem, say a Khayyami quatrain, using a Persian accent rather than an Arabic accent resulting from other transliteration systems. Even the very manner in which the terms robai "رباعی" or its plural robaiyat "رباعیّات"—terms that are in fact Arabic but became a part of the Persian lexicon when the Arabic designation was used for the older Persian words "tarāneh" or "sorood"—have been transliterated as "rubai," or its plural "rubaiyat" reflects an Arabic pronunciation rather than ones as pronounced in Persian (which is robai and robaiyat, respectively).

As other examples: the word "Isfahan" is actually pronounced Eṣfahān in Persian; Iran is pronounced like "Earān" not "I ran"; Khayyam is pronounced as Khayyam—not like "kayam" or ending like "I am" but ending like "from." The "Kh" is pronounced in a guttural way and not as a "K," but such a sound is non-existent in English language, though learning it is a must for anyone seeking to practice correct Persian pronunciation and accent. This is unfortunate since "Kh" is used widely in Persian language, particularly in names, going back to ancient times. The Russian language has this letter, X, and thereby can offer a closer phonetic example (as can be listened to in google translation page for the word "Khayyām" in Russian, Хайям).

There are perfectly legitimate reasons to establish transliteration systems that differ from Arabic-based systems. It is of course true that there is no single "Persian" accent, as the Iranian population is itself comprised of different ethnic groups practicing their own dialectics and accents of Persian. However, still, one can distinguish a clearly Persian accent originating in the Fars (Fārs) or Khorasan (Khorāsān) regions since early times and now spread throughout Iran, including Tehran, and despite its regional accent variations it can be clearly contrasted with the Arabic. The main point here is to encourage non-Persian speaking readers to reproduce the Persian accent in reading Persian phrases and poems rather than practicing an Arabic accent that often results from using prevailing transliteration systems.

In proposing a Persian-friendly transliteration system in the following table, I have tried to construct each transliterated letter from a letter that is close to its expected sound. For instance, I construct the equivalent of the letter ذ using the letter z rather than 'd' (which is common in Arabic transliterations which use the combination 'dh' for ذ). So, I use the letter z to construct all the alphabetical variants from the Arabic that in Persian sound the same as 'z'—that is, for ز ذ ض ظ I suggest ż ẓ z̧ and z respectively. Similarly, I use "s" to built all the letters that in Arabic exist as س ص ث (which are transliterated respectively as ş, ṣ, and s). For ت and ط I respectively suggest t and ṫ respectively. Their distinctions in writing, however, are retained to allow for correct conversions back to the original spelling/writing in the Arabic or Persian.

The overall purpose is to use a transliteration system that results in Persian pronunciation such that even when the diacritics are removed, the sounds intended are closer to the Persian pronunciations than those in Arabic.

Contextual Persian/Arabic Alphabet with Beginning, Middle, or Ending Variations				Letters Used for Pronunciation and Transliteration		Examples	ABC Extended Mac Keyboard Keystroke(s)
آ				ã	Ã	*As in Qorãn or Ãb:* قرآن *or* آب*; pronounced as in wAter; alef has a "hat." (Notice, Qorãn is rendered here in its Persian pronunciation.)*	*option-n + a/A*
ا			ـا	ā	Ā	*As in bābā or bāzār:* بابا *or* بازار*; pronounced as in wAter; the "hat" of alef is dropped.*	*option-a + a/A*
أ				á	Á	*As in Áhmad:* احمد *or* أحمد*; pronounced as in bAg; the alef is written with or without a diacritic mark above.*	*option-e + a/A*

Contextual Persian/Arabic Alphabet with Beginning, Middle, or Ending Variations				Letters Used for Pronunciation and Transliteration		Examples	ABC Extended Mac Keyboard Keystroke(s)
ـَـ				a	A	*As in kalameh:* کَلَمه*; as in bAg, diacritic mark above letters, added or not.*	*regular a/A*
إ				é	É	*As in the first letter of éḥterām:* احترام *or* اِحترام*; pronounced as in bEd; the alef is written with or without a diacritic mark below.*	*option-e + e/E*
ـِـ				e	E	*As in the third letter of éḥterām:* اِحتِرام*; pronounced as in bEd, diacritic mark below letters, written or not.*	*regular e/E*
ِ				-e	-E	*As in Khayyām-e Neyshābouri:* خیّامِ نیشابوری *Diacritic mark below, written or not, linking a name/word to its following adjective (Khayyām from Neyshābur).*	*lowercase dash + regular e/E*
أ				ó	Ó	*As in ómeed:* اُمید*; pronounced as in Orchard; the alef is written with or without a diacritic mark above.*	*option-e + o/O*
ـُـ				o	O	*As in bozorg:* بُزُرگ*; pronounced as in Opium; diacritic mark above letters, written or not.*	*regular o/O*
اً إٍ اٌ				ȁ ȅ ȍ	Ȁ Ȅ Ȍ	*As in ettefāqȁ:* اتّفاقاً*; pronounced as 'an' at the end of a word. Although not common in Persian, in Arabic the same diacritic or its variation can appear below or above alef preceded by 'e' or 'o' vowels.*	*option/shift-y + a* *option/shift-y + e* *option/shift-y + o*
ا			ـا	â	Â	*As in kâin:* کاین *(an abbreviation of* که این*); pronounced as kin; the alef is written but not pronounced.*	*option-6 + a*

Contextual Persian/Arabic Alphabet with Beginning, Middle, or Ending Variations				Letters Used for Pronunciation and Transliteration		Examples	ABC Extended Mac Keyboard Keystroke(s)
				^	^	*As in raḥm^n:* رحمن*; the alef is not written, but is pronounced.*	*option-6 – space*
ب	ﺑ	ﺒ	ﺐ	b	B	*As in bozorg:* بزرگ*; pronounced as in Bell.*	*regular b/B*
پ	ﭘ	ﭙ	ﭗ	p	P	*As in pedar:* پدر*; pronounced as in Penguin. This letter exists in Persian alphabet, but not in Arabic. In Arabic, usually 'b' or 'f' is used for the 'p' pronunciation (that explains the origin of "Fārsi" which is Arabized "Pārsi").*	*regular p/P*
ت	ﺗ	ﺘ	ﺖ	t	T	*As in tamās:* تماس*; pronounced as in Tea.*	*regular t/T*
ث	ﺛ	ﺜ	ﺚ	ș	Ș	*As in șolș:* ثلث*; pronounced in Persian as 's', as in Sand; pronounced in Arabic as "th" as in faiTH. Notice here the 's' sound is prioritized rather than the 'th' sound in transliteration since the purpose here is to offer Persian transliteration of Persian and internalized Arabic words.* *Persian speakers do not pronounce this letter as 'th,' unless, of course, they are specifically reading Arabic texts with the intention of reproducing Arabic accents (as in reciting the Qorān, for example).*	*option-c + s/S*
ج	ﺟ	ﺠ	ﺞ	j	J	*As in Jamsheed:* جمشید*; pronounced as in Judy or July.*	*regular j/J*

Contextual Persian/Arabic Alphabet with Beginning, Middle, or Ending Variations				Letters Used for Pronunciation and Transliteration		Examples	ABC Extended Mac Keyboard Keystroke(s)
چ	چـ	ـچـ	ـچ	ch	Ch	*As in chashm or cheshm: چشم; as in CHurCH. This letter is present in Persian, but not in Arabic, alphabet. In Arabic, usually 'j' is used as a substitute for it.*	*regular ch or Ch*
ح	حـ	ـحـ	ـح	ḥ	Ḥ	*As in Ḥalab: حلب; pronounced as in Home. In Arabic, it has a deeper H sound.*	*option-x +h/H*
خ	خـ	ـخـ	ـخ	kh	Kh	*As in Khāk: خاک; this sound is not present in English; pronounced as the letter X in Russian. Khayyām or خیّام is pronounced using this letter.*	*regular kh/Kh*
د			ـد	d	D	*As in Del: دل; pronounced as in DaviD.*	*regular d/D*
ذ			ـذ	ẓ	Ẓ	*As in leẓẓat: لذّت; pronounced in Persian as in Zebra; pronounced in Arabic as a DH. Notice that the sound 'z' is used here to transliterate this letter, since is closer to how it is pronounced in Persian.*	*option-c + z/Z*
ر			ـر	r	R	*As in rāh: راه; pronounced as in Robert.*	*regular r/R*
ز			ـز	z	Z	*As in zanboor: زنبور; pronounced as in Zebra.*	
ژ			ـژ	zh	Zh	*As in Zhivāgō: ژیواگو; pronounced in Persian as in ZHivāgo; this letter is present in Persian, but not in Arabic, alphabet.*	*regular zh/Zh*
س	سـ	ـسـ	ـس	s	S	*As in Sāsān: ساسان; as in Sand.*	*regular s/S* *regular ss/SS*

Contextual Persian/Arabic Alphabet with Beginning, Middle, or Ending Variations				Letters Used for Pronunciation and Transliteration		Examples	ABC Extended Mac Keyboard Keystroke(s)
ش	شـ	ـشـ	ـش	sh	Sh	*As in Shivā: شیوا; as in Shoe.*	*regular sh/Sh*
ص	صـ	ـصـ	ـص	ṣ	Ṣ	*As in ṣolḥ: صُلح; as S in Persian, but as a deep S in Arabic.*	*option-x +s/S*
ض	ضـ	ـضـ	ـض	ẓ	Ẓ	*As in ẓamimeh: ضمیمه; as in Z in Persian, deep mix of Z and D in Arabic. Notice that the sound 'z' is used here to transliterate this letter, since this is closer to how it is pronounced in Persian.*	*option-x + z/Z*
ط	طـ	ـطـ	ـط	ṫ	Ṫ	*As in ṫās: طاس; pronounced as T in Persian, but as a deep T in Arabic.*	*option-w + t/T*
ظ	ظـ	ـظـ	ـظ	ż	Ż	*As in żolm: ظلم; pronounced as Z in Persian, but as a deep Z or D in Arabic. Notice that the sound 'z' is used to transliterate this letter, since this is closer to how it is pronounced in Persian.*	*option-w + z/Z*
ع	عـ	ـعـ	ـع	ʿ `	ʿ `	*Precedes a variety of other letters as stand alone (As in meʿmār: معمار) or to give the next element a prior accent, as in Robāʿiyāt, ʿOmar, ʿAli, ʿEmād. It can also appear at the end of word, robʿ.*	*American Diac: Keyboard option+l or ABC Extended keyboard: "grave accent" key next to number 1 on keyboard*
غ	غـ	ـغـ	ـغ	gh	Gh	*As in ghareeb: غریب; pronounced in Persian as a deep G, as in GHraib. This sound, in its Persian rendering, is not present in English, but is abundant in French for 'r,' for example.*	*regular gh/Gh*

Contextual Persian/Arabic Alphabet with Beginning, Middle, or Ending Variations				Letters Used for Pronunciation and Transliteration		Examples	ABC Extended Mac Keyboard Keystroke(s)
ف	فـ	ـفـ	ـف	f	F	*As in Fārsi:* فارسی*; pronounced as in Father.*	*regular f/F*
ق	قـ	ـقـ	ـق	q	Q	*As in Qorãn:* قرآن*; pronounced in Persian as a deep K. This sound, in its Persian rendering, is not present in English, but is abundant in French for 'r,' for example. Q and Gh sound the same in Persian.*	*regular q/Q*
ک ك	کـ كـ	ـکـ ـكـ	ـک ـك	k	K	*As in kāshef:* کاشف*; pronounced as in Kin. In Arabic, a hamzeh on top is used for this letter and the upper slant is omitted when used alone or at the end of the word.*	*regluar k/K*
گ	گـ	ـگـ	ـگ	g	G	*As in Galu:* گلو*; pronounced as in Gas. This letter is present in Persian, but not in Arabic, alphabet. Usually K is used instead in Arabic as a substitute for it.*	*regular g/G*
ل	لـ	ـلـ	ـل	l	L	*As in lāleh:* لاله*; pronounced as in Lady.*	*regular l/L*
	ل			ł		*As in youméłddin:* یوم الدّین*; the 'l' is written but is silent in pronunciation.*	*option-l + l*
م	مـ	ـمـ	ـم	m	M	*As in mellat:* ملّت*; pronounced as in Media.*	*regular m/M*
ن	نـ	ـنـ	ـن	n	N	*As in nāder:* نادر*; pronounced as in NaNcy.*	*regular n/N*
و			ـو	v	V	*As in vizheh:* ویژه*; pronounced as in Violin.*	*regular v/V*
و			ـو	w	W	*As in ówlād:* اولاد*; pronounced as in Wonderful.*	*regular w/W*

Contextual Persian/Arabic Alphabet with Beginning, Middle, or Ending Variations				Letters Used for Pronunciation and Transliteration		Examples	ABC Extended Mac Keyboard Keystroke(s)
و			ـو	ō	Ō	*As in mōz:* موز *; written vowel and pronounced as in bOwl.*	*option-a +o*
و			ـو	oo ou	OO OU	*As in mooyrag:* مویرگ*; written long vowel and pronounced as in rUde, or gOOd.* *Sometimes, in Persian, a double-o or 'ou' is used to convey the same sound, as in Behrooz.*	*regular oo* *regular ou* *regular ou*
و				va ō	VA Ō	*As in gorg va meesh, or gorg ō meesh:* گرگ و میش*; in Persian, pronounced as 'va', meaning 'and' connecting a word to the next word. It is less formally also pronounced as 'ō' also meaning 'and.'* *In these senses, it is used as a stand alone word, separated from preceding and following words.*	*regular v* *option-a + o*
و				ŵ	Ŵ	*As in khŵāst or khŵish:* خواست *or* خویش*; 'v' is written but is silent in pronunciation.*	*option-6 + w/W*
ه	هـ	ـهـ or ـﻬـ	ـه	h	H	*As in mehr:* مهر*; pronounced as in Home. When this letter is used at the end of the word, it is usually pronounced as an "e" or a softer almost inaudible 'H.'*	*regular h/H*
ی ي	یـ	ـیـ	ـی	i	I	*As in bishomār:* بیشمار or بی‌شمار *; pronounced as in kEY.*	*regular i/I*
یٰ				ă	Ă	*As in 'alĭ:* علیٰ*; written as 'i' but pronounced as 'ā.' Usually a small alef is used on top of* ی *to indicate the 'ā' sound.*	*option-u + a/A* *small alef unicode U+0670*

Contextual Persian/Arabic Alphabet with Beginning, Middle, or Ending Variations				Letters Used for Pronunciation and Transliteration		Examples	ABC Extended Mac Keyboard Keystroke(s)
	یـ	ـیـ		y	Y	*As in zāyandeh:* زاینده*; pronounced as in blInd.*	*regular y/Y*
ۀ ه ی			ـۀ ـه ی	-ye	-YE	*As in maghāleh-ye:* مقاله *or* مقاله ی*; a hamzeh over the 'h' or a* ی *after* ه *pronounced as in YEH. This is a variation of -e, the difference being due to its usage when the word ends with a 'h.'*	*regular dash/ ye/YE*
ی	یـ	ـیـ	ـی	ee	EE	*As in Jamsheed:* جمشید*; pronounced as in sEEn; a long 'i.'*	*regular ee/EE*
ء				ʾ ʼ	ʾ ʼ	*As in 'Alāʾéḻddin:* علاء الدّین*. This sign is called "hamzeh." In this case, it appears stand-alone.*	*American Diacs Keyboard: Option+j* *or ABC Extended Keyboard: option-e + space*
أ				ʾa ʻa	ʾA ʻA	*As in ʾabu:* أبو *pronounced as in Ask; alef with a hamzeh above, used in Arabic and not commonly used in Persian (where hamzeh is omitted).*	*a/A + option-e + space*
إ				ʾe ʻe	ʾE ʻE	*As in ʾenshāʾallāh:* إنشاء الله *pronounced as Entire; alef with a hamzeh below, used in Arabic and not commonly used in Persian (where hamzeh is usually omitted).*	*e/E + option-e + space*
ؤ				oʾ oʻ	Oʾ Oʻ	*As in mōʾaşşer:* مؤثّر*.*	*o + option-e + space*

Contextual Persian/Arabic Alphabet with Beginning, Middle, or Ending Variations				Letters Used for Pronunciation and Transliteration		Examples	ABC Extended Mac Keyboard Keystroke(s)
ئ	ـئ	ئـ	ئ	ʾ	ʾ	*A 'y' with hamzeh, or a hamzeh that has its own "tooth." Examples: As in mas'aleh:* مسئله*; masā'el:* مسائل*, shey':* شئ*. It is pronounced usually as a hamzeh, not as a 'y'. (Notice, shey' is spelled according to the Persian, not Arabic, pronunciation of the term.)*	*option-v + space (if needed)*
ة				ẗ		*As in resālaẗ:* رسالة*; pronounced in Arabic as 'ah' if not linked to next word, as in* رسالة في*, and as 'at' if linked to next word, as in* رسالة الغفران*.*	*option-u + h/H*
ّ						*As in KhaYYām:* خیّام*; letter is repeated; if the sign* ّ *appears above a letter in Persian or Arabic, it doubles the consonent in pronunciation (the sign is called 'tashdeed').*	*repeat the letter*

Book 2 Cumulative Glossary of Transliterations

In Text	Persian Transliteration	In Original Language
Amir Moezzi	*Amir Mo'ezzi*	امیر معزّی
Attar, Farideddin	*'Aṭṭār, Faridełddin*	عطّار، فریدالدّین
Azar	*Āẕar*	آذری
Azeri	*Āẕari*	آذری
Bargnaysi, Kazem	*Bargnaysi, Kāżem*	کاظم برگ نیسی
Chahar Maqaleh (Four Discourses)	*Chahār Maqāleh*	چهار مقاله
Darkhast-Nameh (Requested Letter)	*Darkhŵāst Nāmeh*	درخواست نامه
Dhu al-Hijjah	*Ẕol-Ḥajjeh*	ذوالحجّه
Dhu al-Qadah	*Ẕol-Qa'deh (or Dhu al-Qi'dah)*	ذوالقعده
Euclid or Oqlidos	*Oqlidos (also transliterated by others as Uqlidos)*	اقلیدس
Farabi, Abu Nasr	*Fārābi, Ábu Naṣr*	فارابی، ابو نصر
Farsi	*Fārsi (Pārsi)*	فارسی
Hafez Shirazi	*Hāfeż Shirāzi*	حافظ شیرازی
Heireh	*Ḥeireh*	حیره
Homai, Jalaleddin	*Homāyi, Jalālełddin*	همایی، جلال الدّین
Ibn Sina (or Avicenna)	*Ébn-e Sinā or Ábu 'Ali al-Ḥosein ebn-e 'Abdollāh ebn-e al-Ḥosan ebn-e 'Ali ebn-e Sinā*	ابن سینا - ابو علی الحسین بن عبدالله بن الحسن بن علی بن سینا
Ibrahim	*Ébrāhim*	ابراهیم
Ilkhani	*Ilkhāni*	ایلخانی
Imamzadeh Mahrouq	*Émāmzādeh Maḥrouq*	امامزاده محروق
Iran	*Earān*	ایران
Isfahan	*Esfahān*	اصفهان
Islam	*Eslām*	اسلام
Ismaili	*Esmā'ili (among others, also transliterated by others as Ismā'ili)*	اسماعیلی

In Text	Persian Transliteration	In Original Language
Jawab an Salasa Masael: Zarurat al-Tazadd fi al-Alam wa al-Jabr wa al-Baqa (Answer to Three Questions: The Necessity of Contradiction in the World, Fate, and Survival)	*Jawāb ʿan Ṣalāṣa Masāʾel: Ẓarurat ol-Taẓādd fi âl-ʿĀlam wa âl-Jabr wa âl-Baqāʾ*	جواب عن ثلاث مسائل: ضرورت التضادّ فی العالم و الجبر و البقاء
Jumada al-Awwal	*Jamādi ól-Awwal*	جمادی الاوّل
Jumada al-Thani	*Jamādi ól-Ṣāni*	جمادی الثانی
Khaqani Sharvani	*Khāqāni Sharvāni, Afẓalėłddin Badil ebn-e ʿAli ebn-e ʿOṣmān*	خاقانی شَروانی، افضل الدّین بدیل بن علی بن عثمان
Khayyam, Khayyami	*Khayyām, Khayyāmi*	خیّام، خیّامی
Khazeni, Abdorrahman	*Khāzeni, ʿAbdoł-Raḥmân (ʿAbdołrraḥmân al-Khāzeni or Ábu al-Fatḥ ʿAbd al-Raḥmān Manṣoor al-Khāzeni (other transliterations, al-Khāzini)*	خازنی ، عبدالرحمن - ابو الفتح عبدالرحمن منصور الخازنی
Khordad	*Khordād*	خرداد
Kurd	*Kord*	کُرد
Lur	*Lor*	لُر
Malekshah	*Malekshāh*	ملکشاه
Medina	*Madineh*	مدینه
Masjed Jame	*Masjed Jāmeʿ*	مسجد جامع
Mojmal-e Fasihi	*Mojmal-e Faṣiḥi*	مجمل فصیحی
Mosaddegh	*Moṣaddeq*	مصدّق
Muharram	*Moḥarram*	محرم
Majma ol-Fosaha	*Majmaʿ ól-Foṣaḥāʾ*	مجمع الفصحاء
Majma ol-Anvar (Sum of Lights) — This is another name for Chahar Maqaleh (Four Discourses)	*Majmaʿ ól-Ánvār*	مجمع الانوار
Malek ol-Shoara-ye Bahar	*Malek ól-Shoʿarā-ye Bahār*	ملك لشعرای بهار
Manteqotteir (Conference of the Birds)	*Manteq ół-ṫeir (among others, also transliterated by others as Mantiq-ut-Tayr)*	منطق الطّیر

In Text	Persian Transliteration	In Original Language
Masael Nojoomiyeh Azennaha men Kalam Omar al-Khayyami (Problems in Astrology: I think is from Omar Khayyam)	*Masā'el Nojoomiyeh: Ażennaha men Kalāmi 'Omar al-Khayyāmi*	مسائل نجوميّه اظنها من كلام عمر الخيامی
Mizan ol-Hekmat (Balance of Wisdom)	*Mizān ól-Ḥekmaẗ*	ميزان الحكمة
Molana Jalaleddin Rumi	*Molānā Jalālełddin Rumi*	مولانا جلال الدّين رومی
Mosaheb، Gholam-Hossein	*Moṣāḥeb، Gholām-Ḥosein*	مصاحب، غلامحسین
Nazer	*Nāżer*	ناظر
Neyshabour	*Neyshābour*	نیشابور
Nezami Arouzi	*Nežāmi 'Arouẓi (among others, also transliterated by others as Nizāmi 'Aruẓi)*	نظامی عروضی
Nezam ol-Molk	*Nežām ól-Molk or Ábu 'Ali Ḥasan ibn 'Ali Ṫusi (among others, also transliterated by others as Nizam al-Mulk)*	نظام الملك
Nezari (of Ismailis)	*Nezāri*	نزاری
Nowrooznameh (The Book on Nowrooz) or Nowrooznameh: Resaleh dar Kashf-e Haqiqat-e Nowrooz (The Book on Nowrooz: Treatise on Discovering the Truth of Nowrooz)	*Nowrooznāmeh: Resāleh dar Kashf-e Ḥaqiqat-e Nowrooz*	نوروزنامه: رساله در کشف حقیقت نوروز
Omar	*'Omar*	عمر
Omar Khayyam	*'Omar Khayyām or Ábu al-Fatḥ Qiyāşełddin 'Omar ebn Ebrāhim Khayyām Neyshābouri (among others, also transliterated by others as Ábu al-Fatḥ Qiyās al-Ddin 'Omar ibn Ibrāhim al-Khayyām al-Neyshābouri)*	عمر خیّام یا ابو الفتح غیاث الدّین عمر بن ابراهیم نیشابوری
Qajar	*Qājār*	قاجار

In Text	Persian Transliteration	In Original Language
al-Qowl ala Ajnas al-Lazi be al-Arbaat (Statement on the Four-Fold Types)	*al-Qowl 'ală Ajnās al-Lazi be al-Árba'aẗ*	القول على جناس الذى بالاربعة
Rabi ol-Awwal	*Rabi' ól-Awwal (also Rabi' al-Awwal)*	ربیع الاوّل
Rabi ol-Thani	*Rabi' ól-Ṣāni*	ربیع الثانی
Ramadan	*Rameẓān*	رمضان
Razi, Mohammad ibn Zakaria	*Rāzi, Moḥammad ebn-e Zakariā*	رازی، محمد بن زکریای
Resalat al-Zia ol-Aqli fi Mozoo el-Elm al-Kolli (Treatise on the Light of Intellect on the Subject of Universal Science)	*Resālaẗ al-Ẓiā' al-'Aqli fi Moẓoo' al-'Elm al-Kolli*	رسالة الضياء العقلى فى موضوع العلم الكلّى
Resalat fi al-Baraheen ala Masael al-Jabr wa al-Moqabeleh (Treatise on the Proofs of the Problems of Algebra and Equations)	*Resālaẗ fi al-Barāheen 'ală Masā'el al-Jabr wa al-Moqābeleh*	رسالة فى البراهين على مسائل الجبر و المقابله
Resalat fi al-Kown wa al-Taklif (Treatise on Universe and Obligation, which can also be expressed as Treatise on the Created World and the Duty to Worship)	*Resālaẗ fi âl-Kown wa âl-Taklif*	رسالة فى الكون والتكليف
Resalat fi al-Vojood (Treatise on Existence)	*Resālaẗ fi al-Vojood*	رسالة فى الوجود
Resalat fi Ehtial le-Marefat Maqadir al-Zahab wa al-Fezzah fi Jesme Morakkab Menhoma (Treatise on the Art of Defining Quantities of Gold and Silver in a Body Consisting of Them)	*Resālaẗ fi Eḥtiāl le-Ma'refat Maqādir al-Ẓahab wa al-Feẓẓah fi Jesme Morakkab Menhomā*	رسالة فى احتيال لمعرفت مقادير الذهب و الفضه فى جسم مركّب منهما
Resalat fi Lavazem ol-Amkaneh (Treatise on the Requirements of Locations)	*Resālaẗ fi Lavāzem ól-Amkaneh*	رسالة فى لوازم الامكنه

In Text	Persian Transliteration	In Original Language
Resalat fi Moshkelat ol-Hesab (Treatise on the Problems of Arithmetic)	*Resālaï fi Moshkelāt ol-Ḥesāb*	رسالة فی مشکلات الحساب
Resalat fi Qesmat Rob al-Dayereh (Treatise on the Division of a Circle Quadrant)	*Resālaï fi Qesmat Robʿ al-Dayerah*	رسالة فی قسمت الربع الدایره
Resalat fi Sharh ma Eshkala men Mosaderat Ketab Oqlidos (Treatise on the Explanation of Problems of Postulates in Euclid's Book)	*Resālaï fi Sharḥ ma Éshkala men Moṣāderāt Ketāb Oqlidos*	رسالة فی شرح من اشکل من مصادرات کتاب اقلیدس
Resalat Jawaban le-Solse Masael (Treatise on Response to Three Questions)	*Resālaï Javāb le-Ṣolṣ Masāʾel*	رسالة جواب لثلث مسائل
Resalat Mokhtasar fi al-Tabiiyyat (Brief Treatise on Nature)	*Resālaï Mokhtaṣar fi âl-Ṫabiʿiyyāt*	رسالة مختصر فی الطبیعیّات
Resaleh dar Elm-e Kolliyat-e Vojood (Treatise on the Science of the Universals of Existence)	*Resāleh dar ʿElm-e Kolliyāt-e Vojood (when expressed in Arabic, "Resālaï fi Kolliyyāt al-Vojood"*	رساله در علم کلیّات وجود (رسالة فی کلیّات الوجود)
Resaleh-ye Selselat ol-Tartib (Treatise on the Succession Order)	*Resāleh-ye Selselaï ól-Tarteeb*	رساله ی سلسلة الترتیب
Robaiyat (used in Persian pronunciation)	*Robāʿiyāt*	رباعیات
Rubaiyat (used in reference to Western pronunciation)	*Rubāʿiyāt*	رباعیات
Sadi	*Saʿdi*	سعدی
Safar	*Ṣafar*	صفر
Saghir	*Ṣaghir*	صغیر
Samimi (Cazimi)	*Ṣamimi (Cazimi)*	صمیمی
Seljuk	*Saljooq*	سلجوق
Sanai Ghaznavi	*Sanāʾi Ghaznavi*	سنائی غزنوی

In Text	Persian Transliteration	In Original Language
Sasanian	*Sāsāniān*	ساسانیان
Shaban	*Sha'bān*	شعبان
Shafa or al-Shafa or al-Shifa (Healing)	*ál-Shafā' or al-Shafā' or al-Shifā'*	الشفاء
Sharh al-Moshkel men Ketab al-Moosiqi (Explanation of Difficulty in the Book of Music)	*Sharḥ al-Moshkel men Ketāb al-Moosiqi*	شرح المشكل من كتاب الموسيقى
Shawwal	*Shawwāl*	شوّال
Shia	*Shi'ah (at times also transliterated as Shiite or Shi'ite)*	شیعه
Soltan	*Solṫān*	سلطان
Tarabkhaneh (House of Joy)	*Ṫarabkhāneh (House of Joy)*	طربخانه
Tarjomeh-ye Khotbeh-ye Qarra-ye Ebn-e Sina (Translation of the Splendid Sermon of Avicenna)	*Tarjomeh-ye Khoṫbeh-ye Qarrā-ye Ébn-e Sinā*	ترجمه ی خطبه ی قرّای ابن سینا
Taslees	*Taşleeş*	تثلیث
Tatemmat Sewan el-Hekmat (Supplement to the Chest of Wisdom)	*Tatemmaẗ Ṣewán él-Ḥekmaẗ*	تتمة صوان الحكمة
Tehran	*Tehrān*	تهران
Turk	*Tork*	تُرک
Turkoman	*Torkman*	تُرکمن
Yathrib	*Yaşreb*	یثرب
Yar Ahmad Rashidi Tabrizi	*Yār Áḥmad Rashidi Tabrizi*	یار احمد رشیدی تبریزی
Zahireddin Abolhasan Beyhaqi	*Żahirełddin Ábolḥasan Beyhaqi (or Żahir al-Din Abu al-Ḥasan 'Ali ibn Zayd Beyhaqi)*	ظهیرالدّین ابو الحسن علی بن زید بیهقی
zamaneh	*zamāneh*	زمانه
Zeej-e Malekshahi (Malekshahi Ephemeris)	*Zeej-e Malekshāhi*	زیج ملکشاهی

Book 2 References

Abol-Hasan Abd ul-Ghafer Ibn Ismail Ibn Abd-Ghafer al-Farsi. 1384 SH (2005). *Al-Mokhtasar men Ketab ul-Siaq le-Tarikh Nisabour (A Summary of the Book "The Context of the History of Neyshabour")*. Edited by Mohammad Kazem al-Mahmoudi. Tehran: Markaz-e Pazhooheshi-e Miras-e Maktoob (Research Center of Written Inheritence).
ابو الحسن الفارسي عبد الغافر بن اسماعيل. المختصر من كتاب السياق لتاريخ نيسابور. به اهتمام محمد كاظم المحمودى. ١٣٨٤. تهران: مركز پژوهشى ميراث مكتوب.

Al-Baihaqī, ʿAlī Ibn Zaid. 2005. *Tatimma Ṣiwān al-Ḥikma: Texts and Studies*. Collected and reprinted by Fuat Sezgin in Collaboration with Carl Ehrig-Eggert, Eckhard Neuybauer. Hisotoriography and Classification of Science in Islam, volume 8. Frankfurt am Main: Institute for the History of Arabic-Islamic Science at the Johann Wolfgang Goethe University.

Al-Beyhaqi. Al-Imam Zahireddin Abolhasan Ali Ibn al-Qasem. [565 LH] 1351 LH (1932). *Tatemmat Sewan el-Hekmat*. Edited by Muhammad Shafi. Includes the Arabic and old Persian translations with extensive footnote commentaries. India: Lahore.

[Arouzi, Nezami] Browne, Edward G. (trans.). 1899. *The Chahar Maqala ("Four Discourses") of Nidhámí-I ʿArúḍí-I Samarqandí*. Hertford: Stephen Austin and Sons.

Bargnaysi, Kazem. 1386 SH (2007). *Hakim Omar Khayyam va Robaiyat [Hakim Omar Khayyam and Robaiyat]. Tehran: Fekr-e Rooz.*
برگ نیسی، کاظم. ١٣٨٦. حکیم عمر خیام و رباعیات. تهران: فکر روز.

[Beyhaqi, Zahireddin Abolhasan] Owjabi, Ali (ed.). 1388 (2009). *Dorrat ul-Akhbar va Lomʿat ul-Anvar: Bargardan-e Farsi-e Tatemmat Sewan el-Hekmat* [Pearls of Reports and Glitter of Lights: Persian Translation of Supplement to the Chest of Wisdom]. Tehran: Hekmat Press.
اوجبی، علی. درّة الاخبار و لمعة الانوار: برگردان فارسی تتمه صوان الحکمة. تهران: نشر حکمت.

Fasihi Khavafi. 1385 SH (2007). Mojmal-e Fasihi. 2nd Volume. With Introduction,

Correction, and Research by Seyyed Mohsen Naji Nasrabadi. Tehran: Asatir.
فصیح خوافی. مجمل فصیحی، بخش دوم. مقدمه، تصحیح و تحقیق سیّد محسن ناجی نصرآبادی. تهران: اساطیر، ۱۳۸٦.

Hedayat, Reza Gholikhan. 1381 SH (2002). *Majma ol-Fosaha*. Edited by Mazaher Mosaffa. 1st part of first volume. Tehran: Entesharat-e Amir Kabir (Amir Kabir Publications).
هدایت، رضاقلیخان. ۱۳۸۱. مجمع الفصحاء. به کوشش مظاهر مصفًا. تهران: انتشارات امیر کبیر.

Hyde, Thomas. 1700. "Pag. 187. In Libro Perfico D. Bunclei, Num. 44, de Morte Celeberrimi Afronomi Omar Cbeiyam, fequente modo legitur." Pp. 529-530 in *Veterum Persarum et Parthorum et Medorum Religionis Historia*.

Jackson, A. V. Williams. 1911. *From Constantinople to the Home of Omar Khayyam: Travels in Transcaucasia and Northern Persia for Historic and Literary Research*. Norwood, MA: Norwood Press.

[Khazeni, Abdorrahman] Khanikoff, N. 1857. "Analysis and Text of كتاب ميزان الحكمة Book of the Balance of Wisdom, An Arabic Work on the Water-Balance, Written by 'Al-Khâzenî in the Twelfth Century" (Pdf available at https://www.jstor.org/stable/592172?seq=1#metadata_info_tab_contents).

Lambert, Jean and Alfred-Louis De. 1987. "Un récit nommé khayyām: La rivalité Gazāli-Khayyam selon al-Bayhaqi et la première notice biographique concernant le Maître de Nīshāpūr, *Arabica*, T. 34, Fasc. 2 (Jul.), pp. 197-220.

Mills, C. Wright. [1959] 2000. *The Sociological Imagination*. London: Oxford Univ. Press.

Nezami Arouzi, Ahmad ibn Omar ibn Ali. [550 LH] (1909) (1327 LH). *Chahar Maqaleh [Four Discourses]*. Based on the Manuscript Prepared and Edited by the late Mohammad Qazvini printed by Brill, Leiden (Holland), with Added Literary Terms, Phrases, and Explanatory Remarks.Tehran: Elm o Honar/Seda-ye Moaser.
نظامی عروضی سمرقندی، احمد بن عمر بن علی. [۵۵۰ هجری قمری] ۱۳۲۷ (هجری قمری). چهار مقاله. طبق نسخه‌ای که بسعی و اهتمام و تصحیح مرحوم محمد قزوینی بسال ۱۳۲۷ هجری قمری در چاپخانه‌ی بریل لیدن (هلاند) چاپ شده. با شرح لغات و عبارات و توضیح نکات ادبی. به کوشش دکتر محمد معین (استاد دانشگاه تهران). تهران: انتشارات ارمغان.

Nicolas, J.B. 1867. Les quatrains de Khèyam. Paris, L'Imprimerie Impériale.

[Rashidi Tabrizi, Yar Ahmad] Homai, Ostad Allameh Jalaleddin. 1367 SH (1988). *Robaiyat-e Khayyam (Tarabkhaneh)*. Tehran: Moassesseh-ye Nashr-e Homa.
همایی، استاد علامه جلال الدین. ۱۳٦۷. رباعیات خیام (طربخانه) یار احمد بن حسین رشیدی تبریزی. تهران: مؤسسه نشر هما.

Rashidi Tabrizi, Yar Ahmad. [867 LH (AD 1462)] Gölpinarli, Abdülbaki (ed./compl.). 1386 SH/2007. *Robaiyat-e Hakim Khayyam: Tarabkhaneh-ye Yar Ahmad Rashidi, va Resaleh-ye Selselat ol-Tartib, Khoṭtbeh-ye Tamjid-e Ibn Sina* [The Rabaiyyāt of Hakim Khayyam: *Tarabkhaneh* by Ahmad Rashidi, The Treatise on Succession Order (Treatise on the Universals of Existence), and the "Praise Sermon of Avicenna"]. Tehran: Khaneh-ye Ketab (Book House).
رشیدی تبریزی، یار احمد. [۸۷۹ هجری قمری برابر با ۱٤٦۲ میلادی] ۱۳۸٦ . رباعیات حکیم خیام: طربخانه‌ی یار احمد رشیدی، و رساله‌ی سلسله الترتیب و خطبه‌ی تمجید ابن سینا. تهران: خانه کتاب.

Rezazadeh Malek, Rahim (ed.). 1998/1377. *Danesh-nameh-ye Khayyami: Majmueh-ye Rasael-e Elmi, Falsafi va Adabi* [Khayyami Encyclopedia: A Collection of Scientific, Philosophical and Literary Writings]. Tehran: Elm o Honar/Seda-ye Moaser.
رضازاده ملك، رحیم. ۱۳۷۷. دانشنامه‌ی خیامی: مجموعه‌ی رسائل علمی، فلسفی، و ادبی. تهران: علم و هنر - صدای معاصر.

Rozenfeld, Boris Abramovich, and Adolf Pavlovich Iushkevich. 1961/1962. *Traktaty [Tracts or Treatises] of ʿOmar Khayyām* [Treatises of ʿOmar Khayyām - In Russian with reproductions of original sources on Khayyām]. Moscow: Izd. Vostochnoi Litery.

[Rozenfeld, B.A., and Yushkevich, A. P.] Mozaffarzadeh, Baqer (trans.). 1383 (2004). "Omar Khayyam: Life and Works" (Introduction to the 1962 Moscow edition of *The Treatises of Omar Khayyam*, by Boris Abramovich Rozenfeld and Adolf Pavlovich Yushkevich). Tehran: Sherkat-e Entesharat Elmi va Farhangi (Scientific and Cultural Publications Co.). Second printing 1391 SH (2012).

مظفرزاده، باقر (مترجم). عمر خیام: زندگی و آثار. نویسندگان: باریس آبراموویچ روزنفلد و آدولف پاولوویچ یوشکیویچ. تهران: شرکت انتشارات علمی و فرهنگی. ۱۳۸۳، چاپ دوم ۱۳۹۱.

Tamdgidi, Mohammad H. 2002. "Mysticism and Utopia: Towards the Sociology of Self-Knowledge and Human Architecture (A Study in Marx, Gurdjieff, and Mannheim)." Ph.D. diss., State University of New York at Binghamton.

Tamdgidi, Mohammad H. 2005. "Orientalist and Liberating Discourses of East-West Difference: Revisiting Edward Said and the *Rubaiyat* of Omar Khayyam," *Discourse of Sociological Practice,* 7(1&2):187-201.

Tamdgidi, Mohammad H. 2007. *Advancing Utopistics: The Three Component Parts and Errors of Marxism*. London and New York: Routledge/Paradigm.

Tamdgidi, Mohammad H. 2009. *Gurdjieff and Hypnosis: A Hermeneutic Study*. Foreword by J. Walter Driscoll. New York: Palgrave Macmillan.

Tamdgidi, Mohammad H. 2020. *Liberating Sociology: From Newtonian Toward Quantum Imaginations: Volume 1: Unriddling the Quantum Enigma*. Belmont, MA: Okcir Press.

Tamdgidi, Mohammad H. 2021. *Omar Khayyam's Secret: Hermeneutics of the Robaiyat in Quantum Sociological Imagination*: Book 1: *New Khayyami Studies: Quantumizing the Newtonian Structures of C. Wright Mills's Sociological Imagination for A New Hermeneutic Method.* Belmont, MA: Okcir Press.

Tīrtha, Swāmi Govinda. 1941. *The Nectar of Grace: Omar Khayyām*'s *Life and Works.* Allahabad: Kitabistan. (Pdf of the manuscript is freely available at: https://archive.org/details/nectarofgrace031160mbp/page/n10).

Whinfield, E. H. 1980 (1883). *The Quatrains of ʿOmar Khayyām: The Persian Text with an English Verse Translation.* London: The Octagon Press.

Yusofi, Gholam-Hossein. 1990. "Chahār Maqāla." *Encyclopedia Iranica*. Vol. IV, Fasc. 6, pp. 621-623. (https://iranicaonline.org/articles/cahar-maqala)

Internet Resources (these links were reachable at the time of publication of this book's first edition):

http://arablib.com/harf?view=book&lid=2&rand1=RFcwSG45ZEBzMyVE&rand2=SjlYU1lEQyRvS2sx

http://pubs.opengroup.org/onlinepubs/9638399/overview.htm

http://www.al-mostafa.info/data/arabic/depot/gap.php?file=001509-www.al-mostafa.com.pdf

http://www.astro.com

http://www.astro.com/swisseph/ae50/ae__50_1050.pdf

http://www.astro.com/swisseph/swepha_e.htm

http://www.iranchamber.com/calendar/converter/iranian_calendar_converter.php

http://www.jasoncolavito.com/ancient-alphabets-explained.html

http://www.shahdiran.ir/about-us/the-harvest-season

https://ar.wikipedia.org/wiki/ابن_ملكا_البغدادي

https://archive.org/details/nectarofgrace031160mbp/page/n10

https://commons.wikimedia.org/wiki/File:Tombstone_of_Omar_Khayyam.JPG

https://en.wikipedia.org/wiki/Astrolabe#/media/File:Iranian_Astrolabe_14.jpg

https://en.wikipedia.org/wiki/Muhammad_al-Baghdadi

https://ia802902.us.archive.org/13/items/FP12042/02_12043.pdf

https://iranicaonline.org/articles/cahar-maqala

https://lifeasahuman.com/2019/arts-culture/art/historical-marvels-the-journey-of-the-astrolabe/

https://www.medievalastrologyguide.com

https://namnak.com/تفسیر-حروف-ابجد-کبیر-و-صغیر.p38073

https://stevemorse.org/jcal/julian.html

https://www.amazon.com/Persarum-Parthorum-religionis-historia-secunda/dp/1171072988

https://www.jamaa.net/books.library/?i=104692#main

https://www.jstor.org/stable/592172?seq=1#metadata_info_tab_contents

Note: The referred page numbers given in the following index in the print edition of this book may be different from its ebook editions, also depending on the readers' ebook view customizations. However, the live links on the ebook editions correctly resolve to the proper passages with which the indexed words are associated.

Book 2 Index

Numbers

A

B

H

I

L

M

N

O

P

T

U

V

W

Z

CPSIA information can be obtained
at www.ICGtesting.com
Printed in the USA
LVHW050844100621
689815LV00015B/1312

9 781640 980075